Costa Blanca

The coast and the interior of Alicante

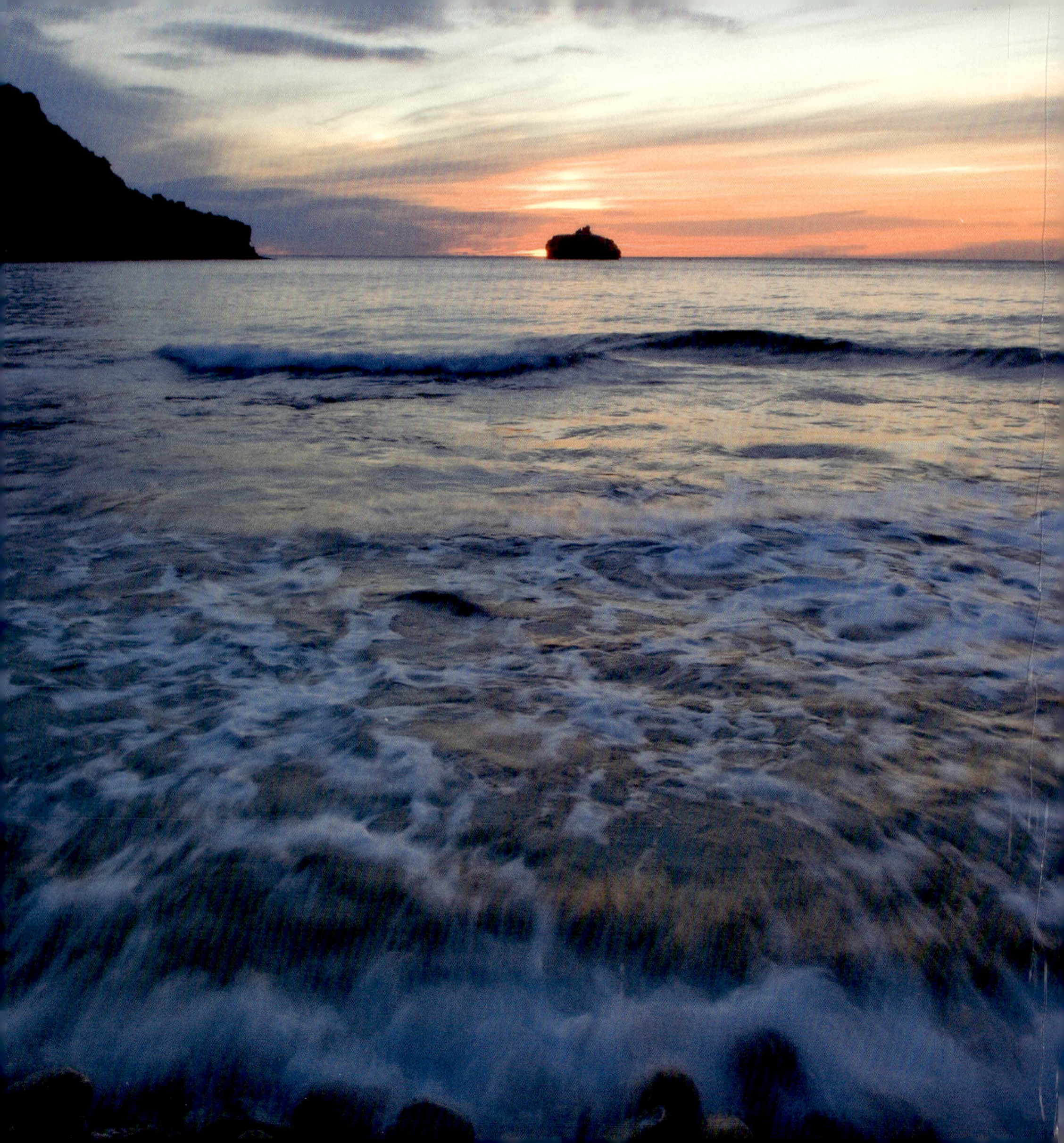

Costa Blanca

The coast and the interior of Alicante

Text and photos
RAFA PÉREZ

TRIANGLE BOOKS

Page Contents

Marina Alta

Marina Baixa

Alacantí

Vega Baja del Segura

Vinalopó

Alto Vinalopó

Vinalopó Medio

Bajo Vinalopó

Alcoià - Comptat

Alcoià

Comptat

Costa Blanca

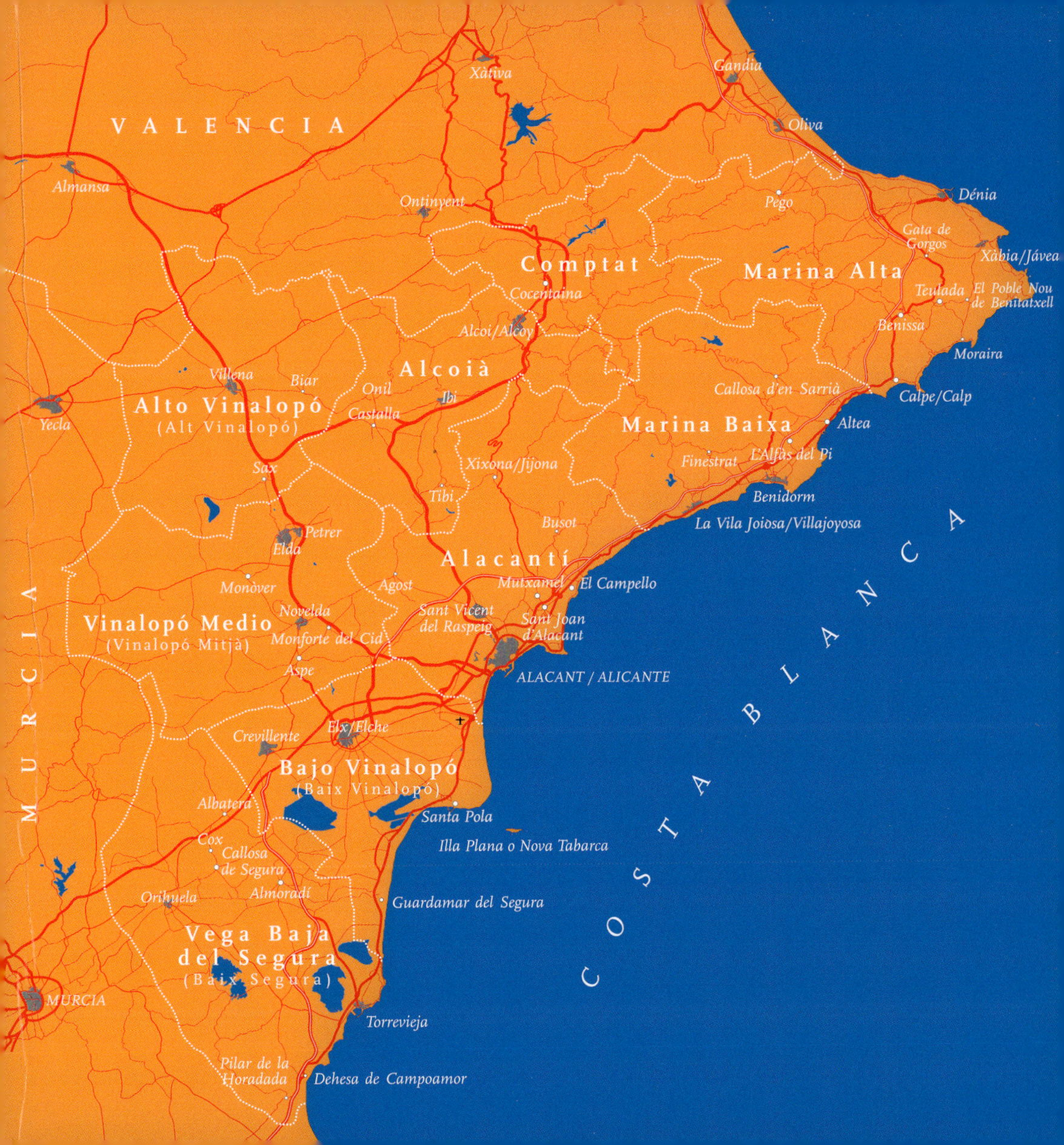
VALENCIA
MURCIA
COSTA BLANCA
Xàtiva
Gandia
Oliva
Almansa
Ontinyent
Pego
Dénia
Gata de Gorgos
Xàbia/Jávea
Comptat
Marina Alta
Cocentaina
Teulada
El Poble Nou de Benitatxell
Alcoi/Alcoy
Benissa
Moraira
Alcoià
Villena
Biar
Onil
Ibi
Alto Vinalopó
(Alt Vinalopó)
Castalla
Callosa d'en Sarrià
Calpe/Calp
Yecla
Marina Baixa
Altea
Sax
Xixona/Jijona
Finestrat
L'Alfàs del Pi
Tibi
Benidorm
Busot
La Vila Joiosa/Villajoyosa
Petrer
Elda
Alacantí
Monòver
Agost
Mutxamel
El Campello
Novelda
Sant Vicent del Raspeig
Sant Joan d'Alacant
Vinalopó Medio
(Vinalopó Mitjà)
Monforte del Cid
Aspe
ALACANT / ALICANTE
Crevillente
Elx/Elche
Bajo Vinalopó
(Baix Vinalopó)
Albatera
Santa Pola
Illa Plana o Nova Tabarca
Cox
Callosa de Segura
Almoradí
Orihuela
Guardamar del Segura
Vega Baja del Segura
(Baix Segura)
MURCIA
Torrevieja
Pilar de la Horadada
Dehesa de Campoamor

The 218 plus kilometres of coastline and the high number of hours of sunlight per year are the visiting card of a brand, Costa Blanca, which encompasses the whole province of Alicante. The quality of its beaches was already enjoyed by Iberians, Romans and Arabs. These beaches, together with the high inland area, which makes the province one of the most mountainous in Spain, and a scattering of perfumed orchards, shape a landscape that is pure Mediterranean essence.

From the counties of La Marina, where the mountains blend with the sea, the landscape drops gradually, between dizzying cliffs, coves of crystalline water and beaches of rounded pebbles, until reaching the Vega Baja del Segura and its beaches of fine golden sand. For many years, the towns of Benidorm, Torrevieja and Altea were ambassadors of the province's tourist promotion, but today the range of options is much broader. The average annual temperature is 18 degrees, the diversity of landscapes and routes of the Costa Blanca invite one to discover it all year round. The beaches are just the beginning: they have natural parks formed by salt flats, wetlands and palm groves, castles in Vinalopó, modernist architecture in Alcoy and Novelda, and the gastronomic excellence at the hand of chefs and oenologists who make full use of the land. We will find the footprint of the past in caves, excavations with prehistoric paintings and among its fabulous museums, feature the MAHE in Elche or the MARQ in Alicante, considered one of the best in Europe. The watchtowers of the coastline remind us that, throughout history, not everyone came with good intentions; the lighthouses of the coastline, such as that of L'Albir, warn the fishermen returning home from a sea that they today share with lovers of water sports. When spring comes, the inland mountains of the province

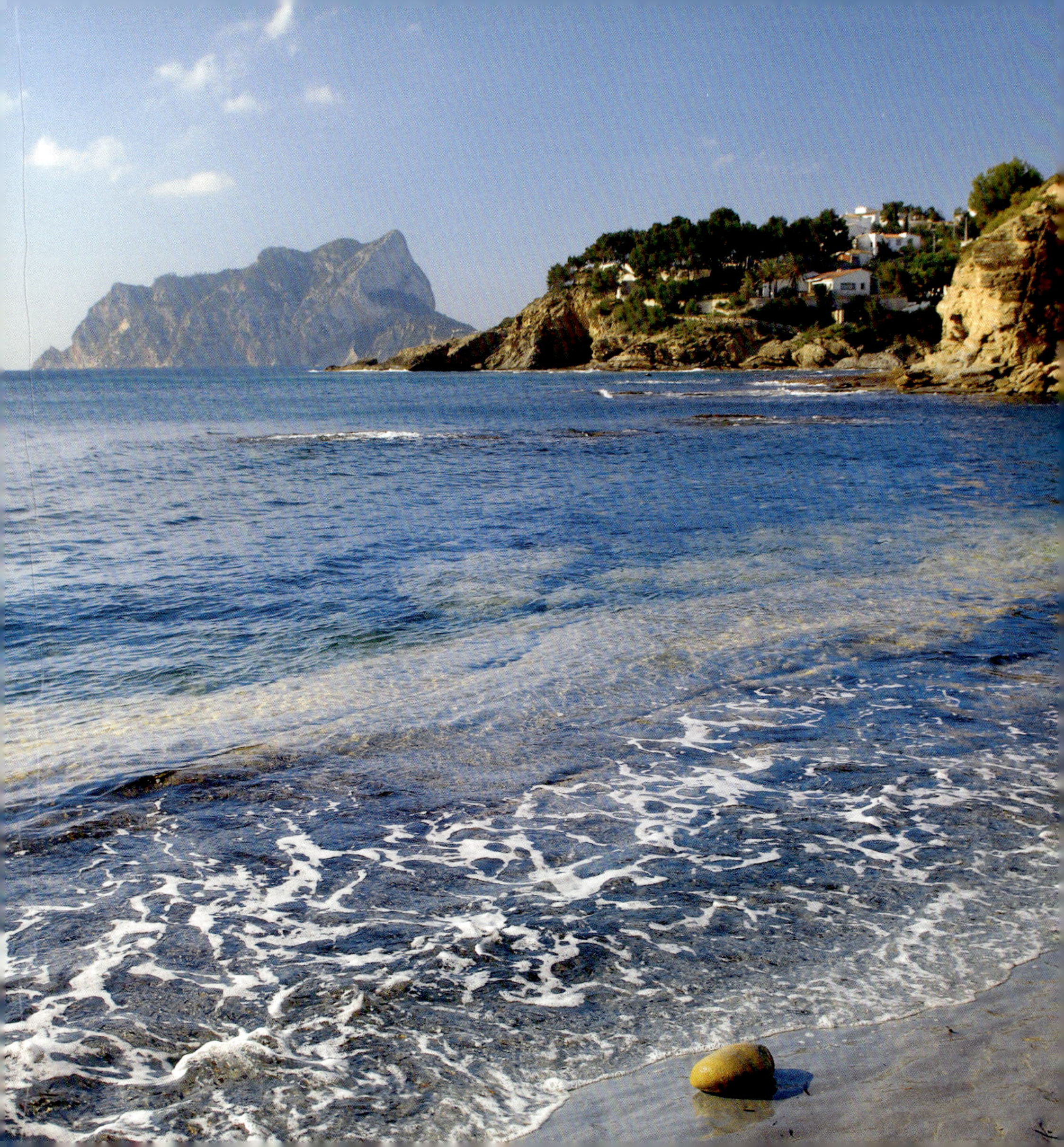

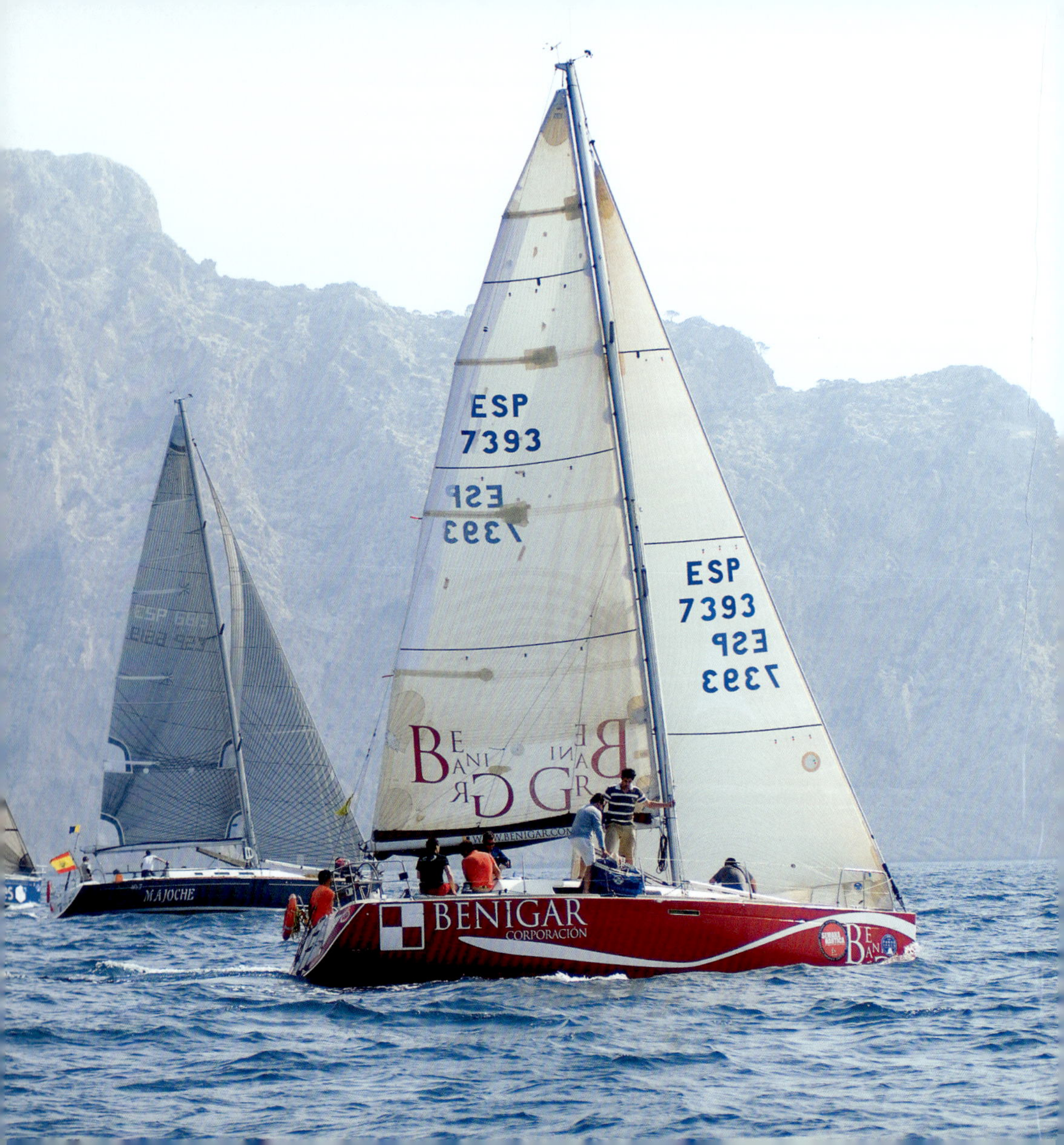
ESP
7393
BENIGAR
CORPORACIÓN
MAJOCHE

show their best aspect: it is the time of the blossoming of the cherry trees, almond trees, when walkers cross their paths and climb their walls.

The inhabitants of the Costa Blanca have an open and cheerful character, traits that they show in the many festivals they hold in the province throughout the year. From the Procession of the Three Wise Men of Alcoy, the oldest in Spain, to the Enfarinats of Tibi, along with the Easter celebrations, Bous a la Mar, the Hogueras and the Misteri de Elche, which is declared a Masterpiece of the Oral and Intangible Heritage of Humanity. Explosions of colour, the worship of fire and, as it could not be any other way, of the sea in the processions that take place every year on the day of the Virgin of the Carmen. The *filaes* of Moors and Christians, who parade throughout the Valencia Community, have a leading role in Alcoy and Villajoyosa. Several of their festivals have the recognition of International Interest.

The hotel infrastructures have also been able to meet the challenge of what the Costa Blanca offers to those who come to discover it: all the colours of the Mediterranean.

Marina Alta

Dénia

Xàbia / Jávea

El Poble Nou de Benitatxell

Teulada - Moraira

Benissa

Calp

The valleys of La Marina

Gata de Gorgos

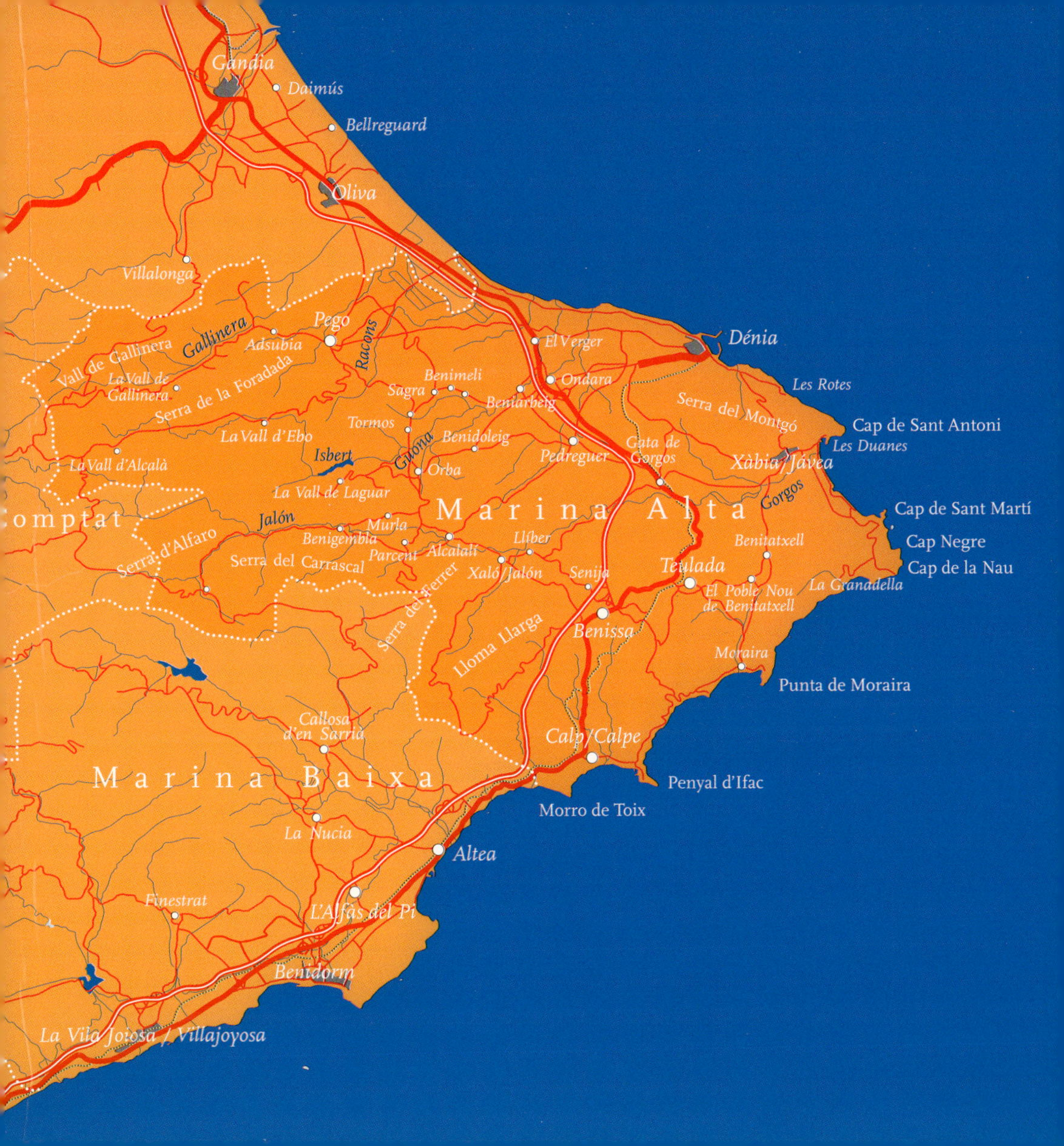

Gandia
Daimús
Bellreguard
Oliva
Villalonga
Pego
Adsubia
Gallinera
Racons
Vall de Gallinera
La Vall de Gallinera
Serra de la Foradada
El Verger
Dénia
Benimeli
Sagra
Ondara
Beniarbeig
Les Rotes
Serra del Montgó
Cap de Sant Antoni
Les Duanes
Tormos
La Vall d'Ebo
Benidoleig
Pedreguer
Gata de Gorgos
Xàbia/Jávea
La Vall d'Alcalà
Isbert
Gúona
Orba
La Vall de Laguar
Marina Alta
Gorgos
Cap de Sant Martí
omptat
Jalón
Murla
Benigembla
Llíber
Benitatxell
Cap Negre
Cap de la Nau
Serra d'Alfaro
Serra del Carrascal
Parcent
Alcalalí
Xaló/Jalón
Senija
Teulada
El Poble Nou de Benitatxell
La Granadella
Serra del Ferrer
Benissa
Lloma Llarga
Moraira
Punta de Moraira
Callosa d'en Sarrià
Calp/Calpe
Marina Baixa
Penyal d'Ifac
Morro de Toix
La Nucia
Altea
Finestrat
L'Alfàs del Pi
Benidorm
La Vila Joiosa / Villajoyosa

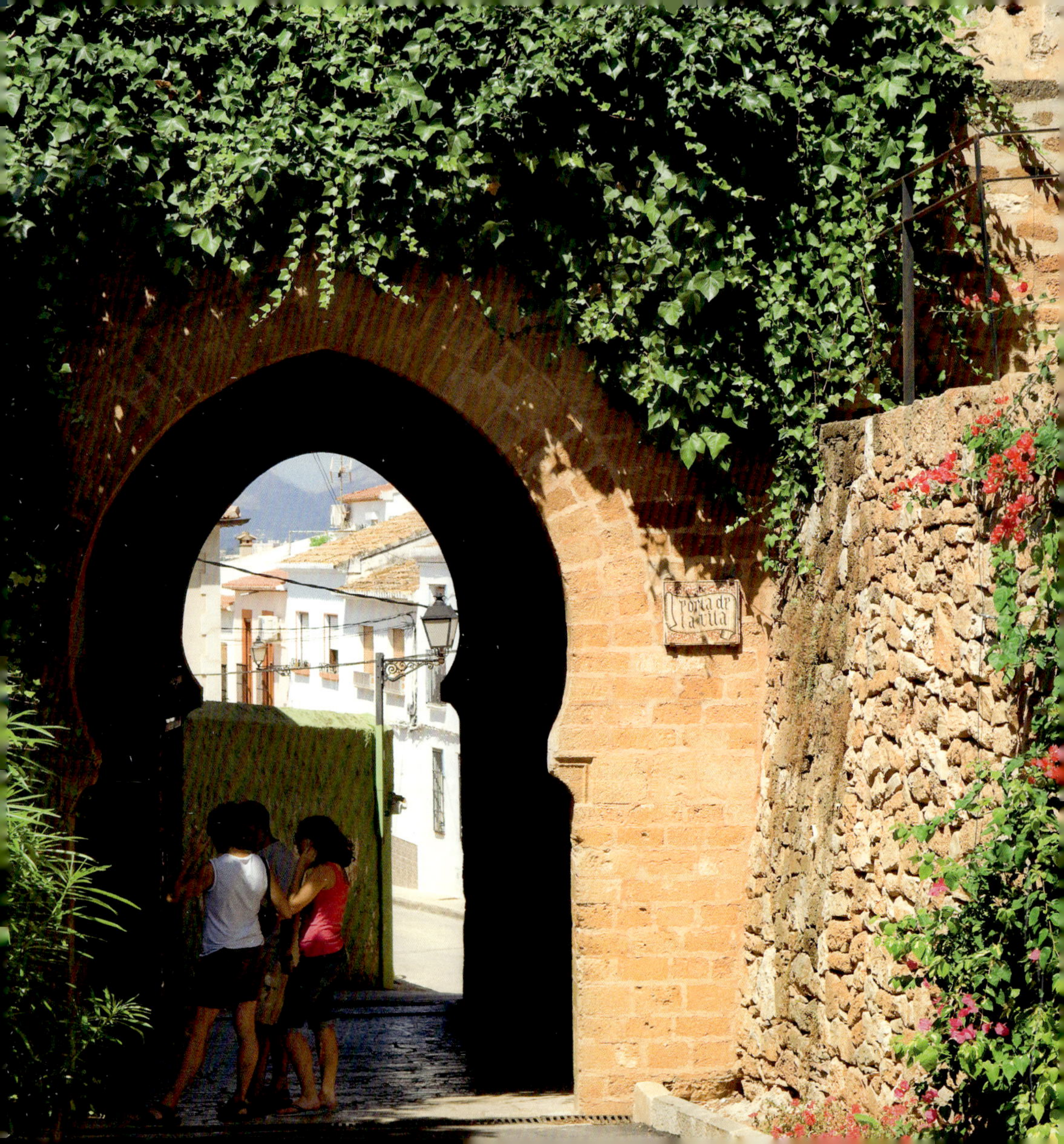
Porta de
la vila

Dénia

Protected by the massif of Montgó, the capital of the Marina Alta was founded by a Greek colony, although it was with the Roman Dianium when it reached its status of city. Devoted to Diana, it was the first to recognise Charles of Austria as king and its capitulation was of major importance during the War of Succession. The route its inhabitants took to escape from the war, in direction Ibiza, is today done the other way. It is the ferries that fill its port loaded with people from the island who come in search of a space on the twenty kilometres of beaches, from the fine sand of the Les Marines to the rocky coves of Les Rotes.

Before the arrival of tourism, the town had experienced its age of splendour in the 19th century, when it became wealthy from the raisin trade, common all over the county and of which there is now hardly any trace of the *riauriaus*, the popular construction of the Marina Alta.

At the foot of the castle and the city wall, the Baix a la Mar fishermen's district houses quite a few rice restaurants in the typical houses with a seafaring atmosphere. The fishermen still arrive at the port and the fish market where the auction is held, although the red prawn is becoming increasingly scarcer, to which Quique Dacosta has raised to the status of art in his restaurant close to Dénia.

When the festival season comes it is the bulls that run through its streets and swim in the port in the traditional Bous a la mar (bulls in the sea).

The neighbouring Jávea is separated by just a few bends. The imposing Montgó, declared National Park, drops down to the water that bathes the cape of San Antonio, a natural barrier between the two towns.

Castle entrance

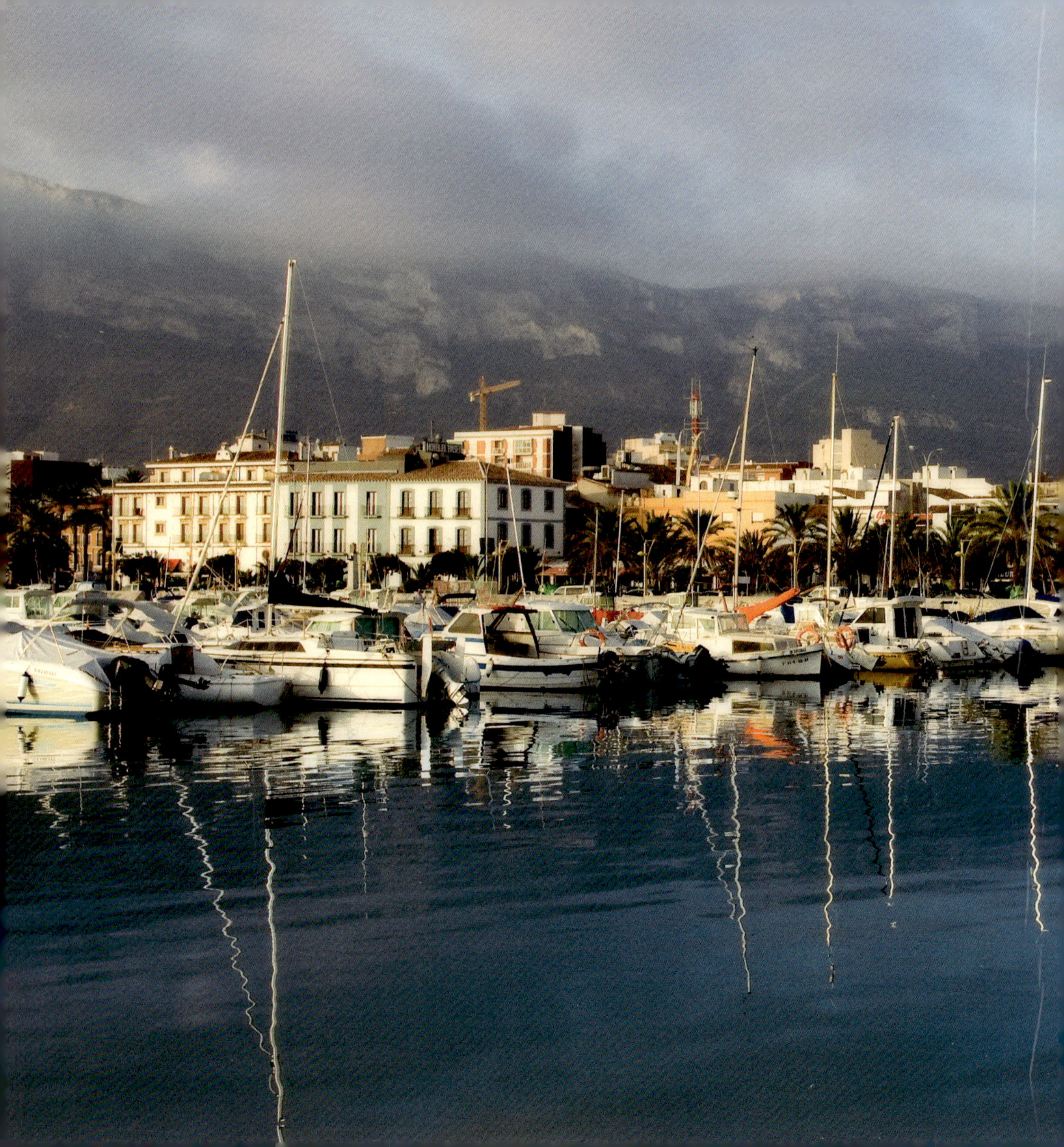

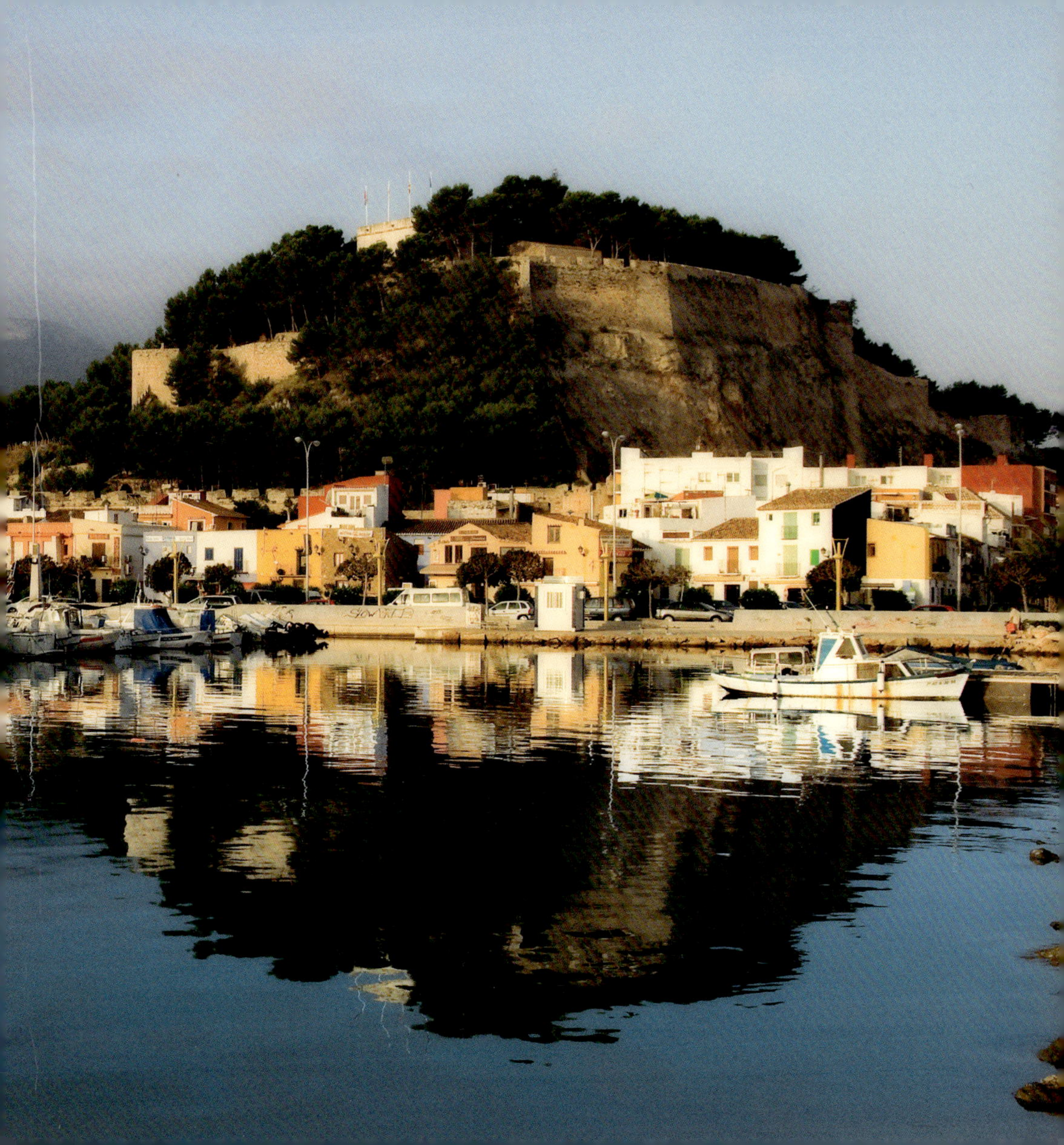

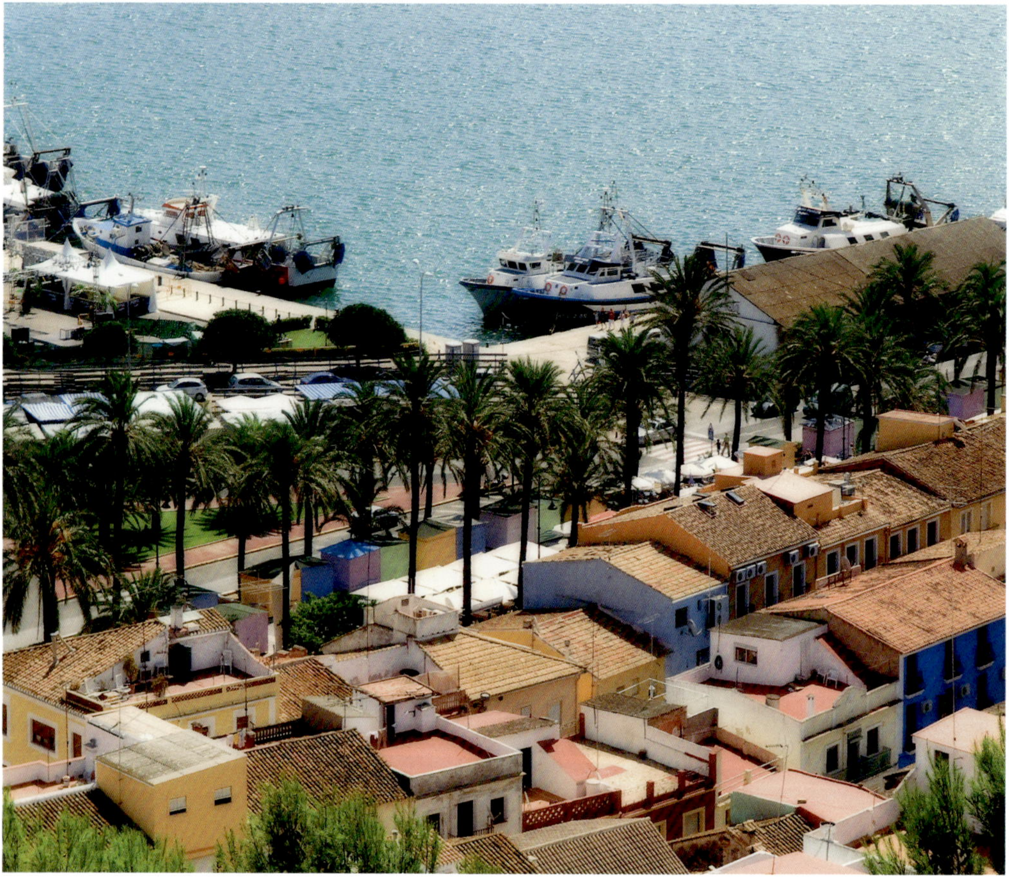

Baix a la Mar district.
Marina of Dénia →

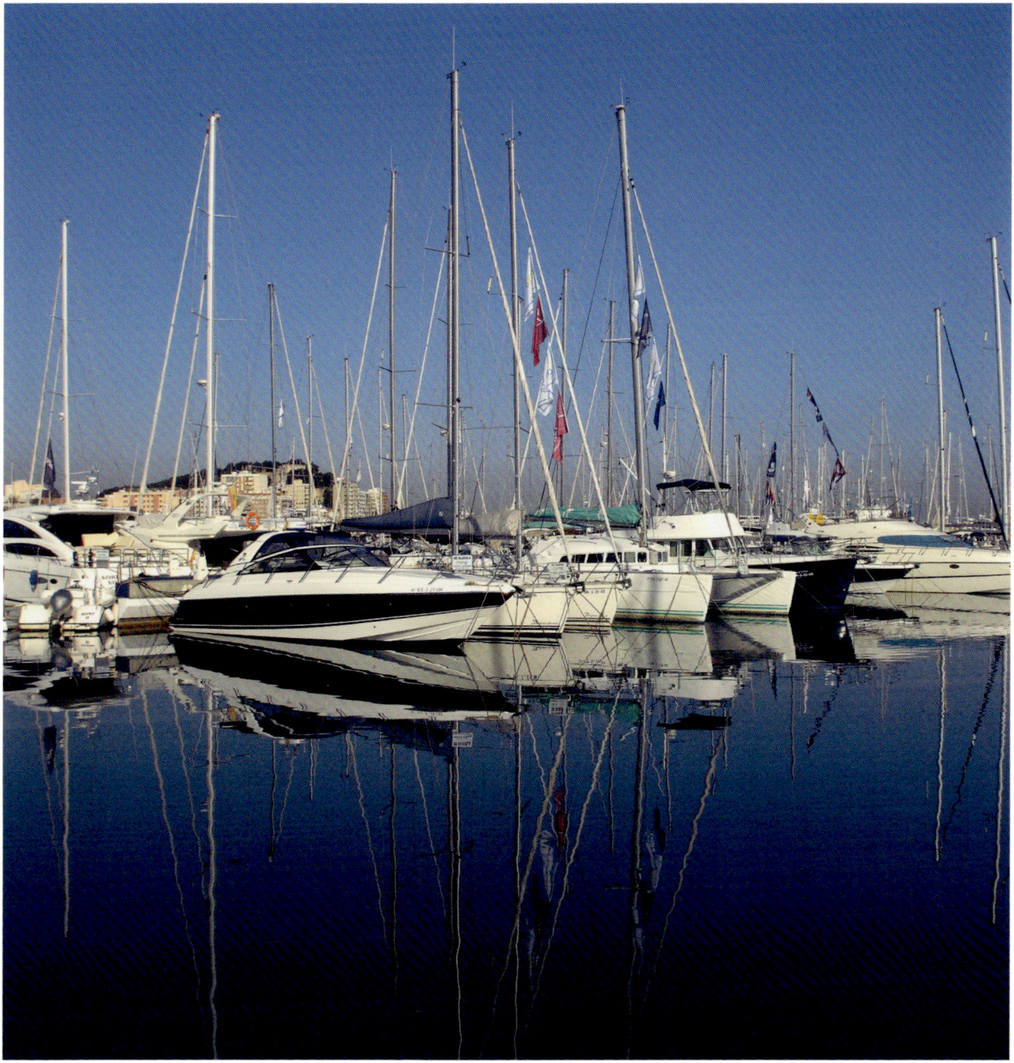

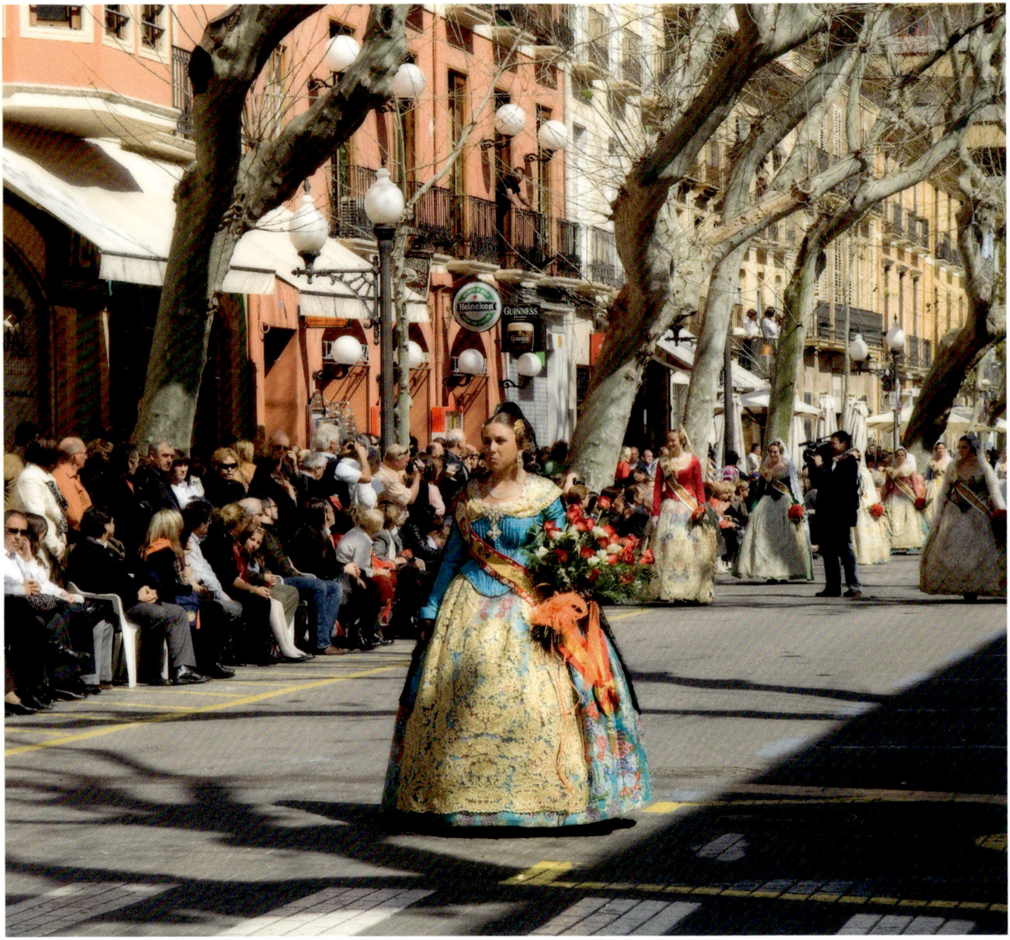

Parade in fallas
"Bous a la mar" →

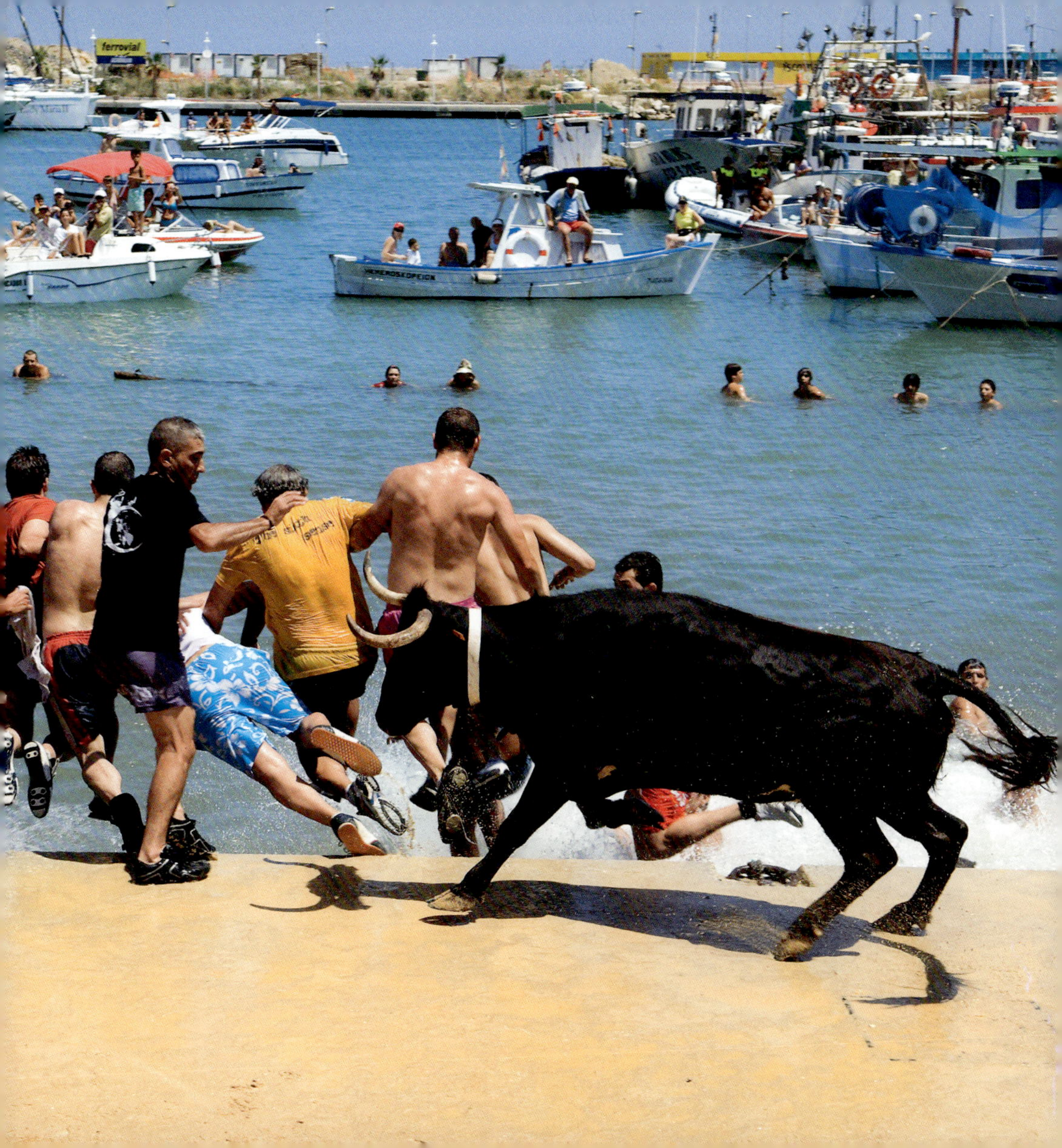
ferrovial

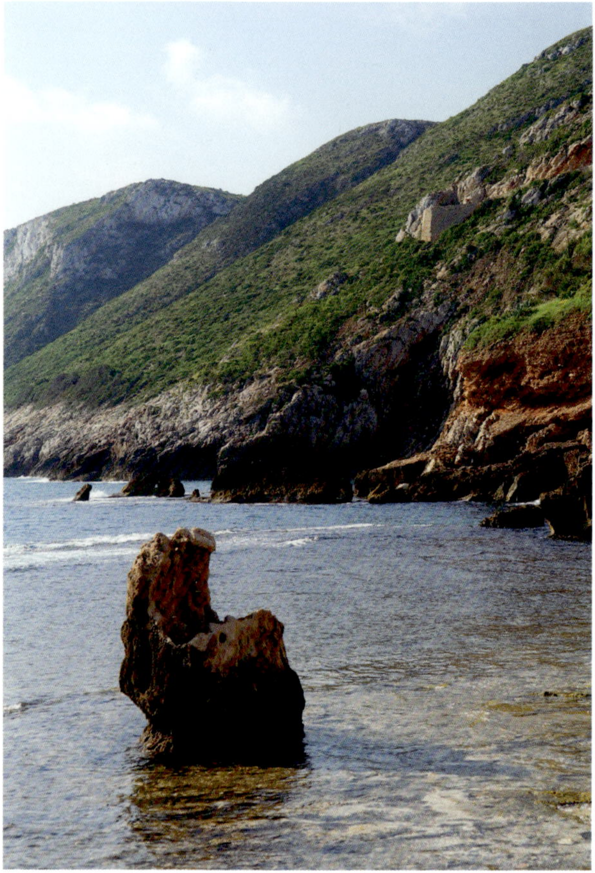

Les Rotes
Old quarter →

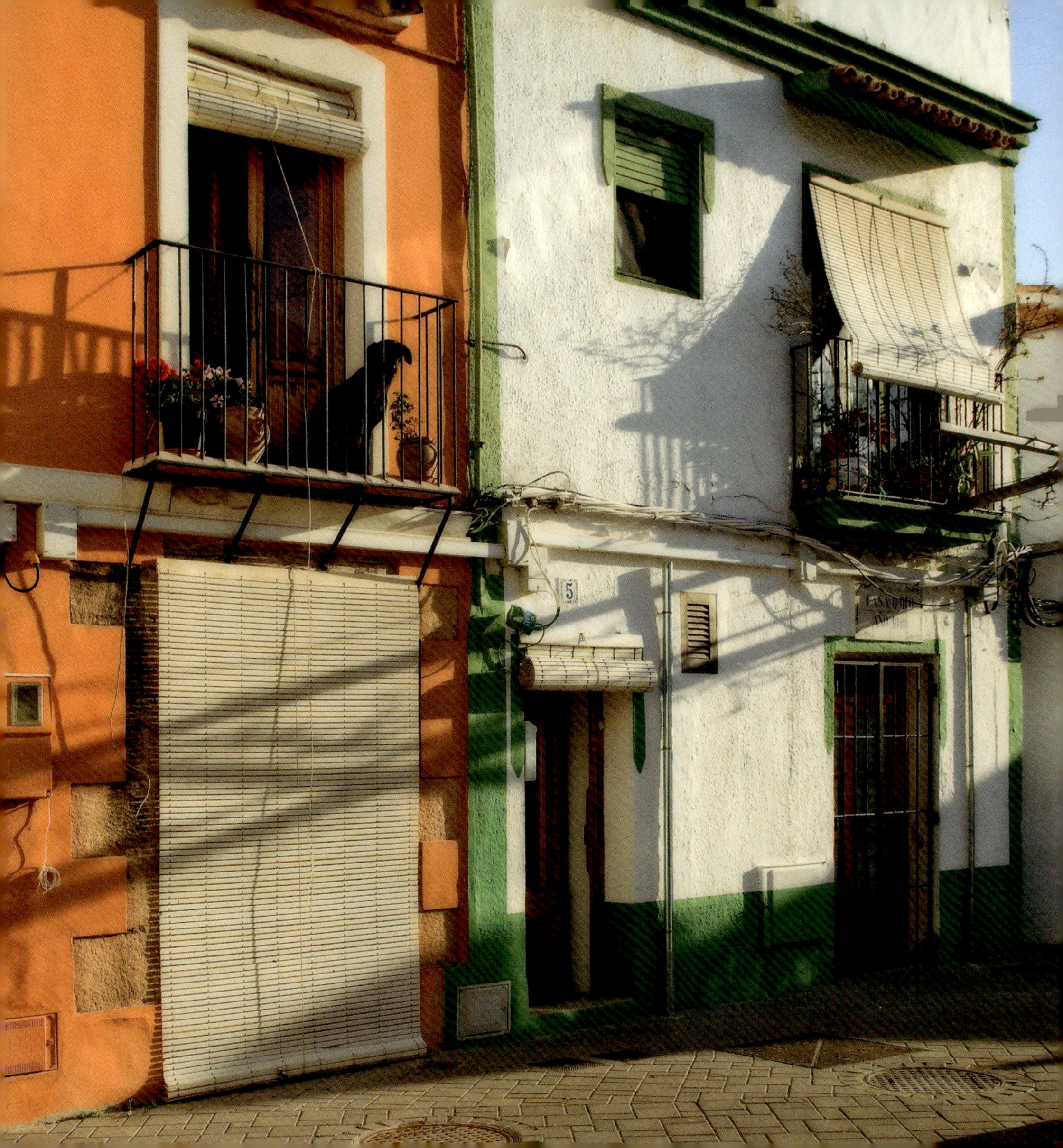
5

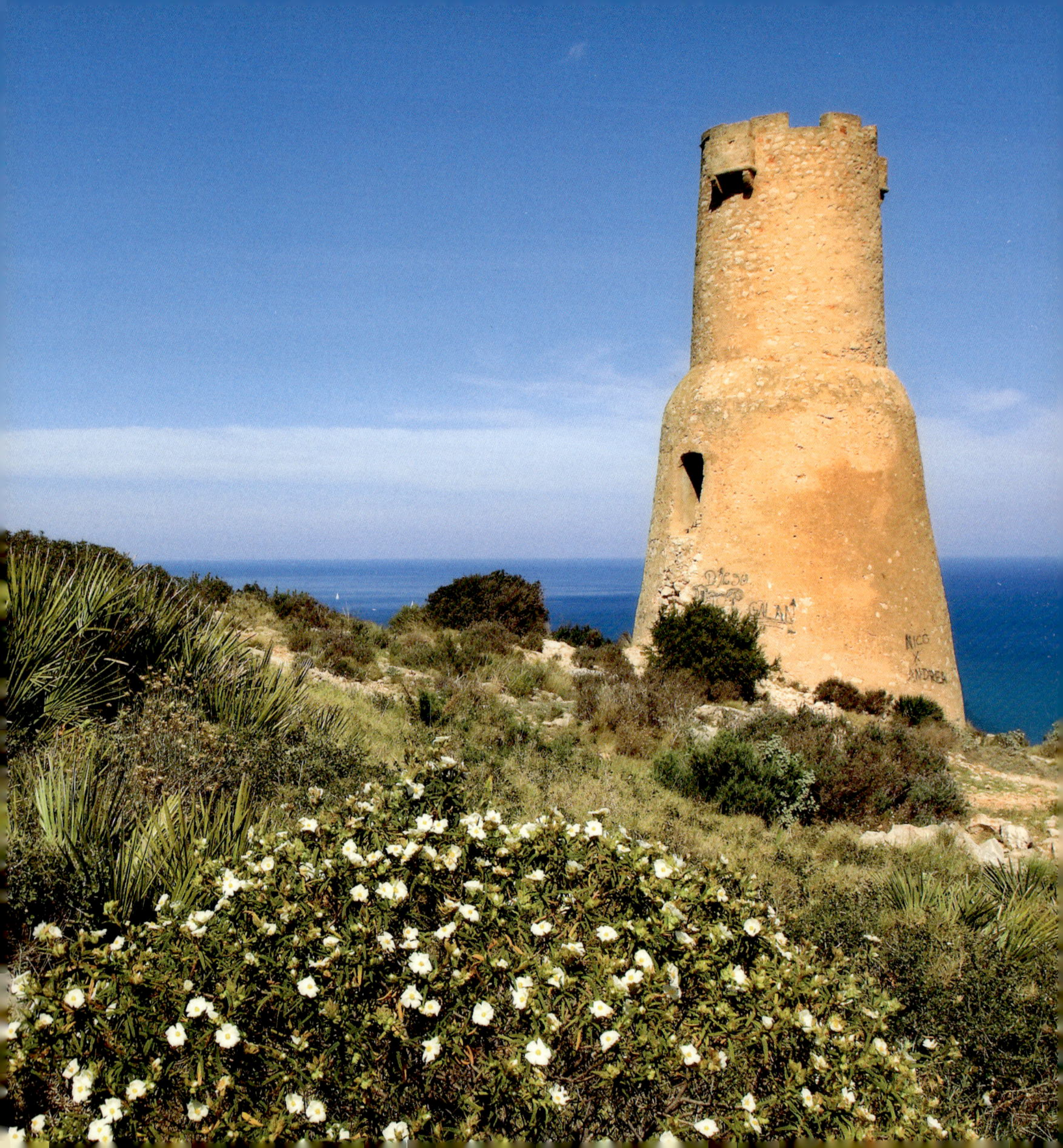

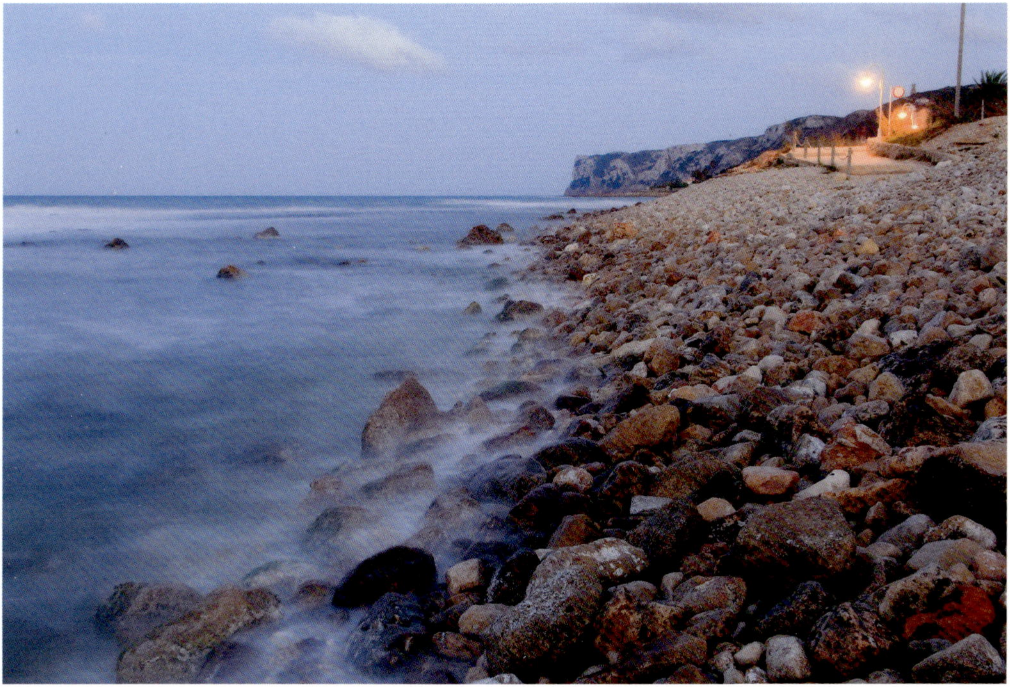

Les Rotes
← *Torre del Gerro*

Xàbia / Jávea

Between the cape of San Antonio and Cala Granadella are some of the most beautiful coves and landscapes of the Costa Blanca.

There was a time in which La Marina existed with its back to the sea, when the people were more concerned with the point of ripening that the grape took to become a raisin, and is one of the most interesting spots in the province. Among the most outstanding buildings is the church of San Bartolomé, of Gothic style, and the nearby market of Abastos (provisions).

From Jávea leads the route of the Miradores, a total of fifteen windows to the Mediterranean and some of its most beautiful coves. The cape of San Antonio, the Roman salted fish factory in Punta del Arenal, the coves called Blanca, Barraca, Granadella and the nudist Ambolo or the cape of La Nau and Punta Falzia, both points with exceptional views towards the island of Portitxol, are some of the essential landmarks on the map of the route.

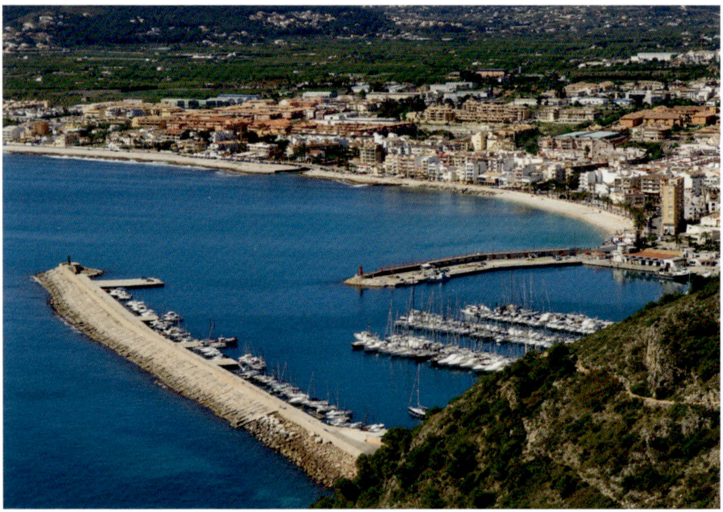

View with church of San Bartolomé →

Cala Barraca also known as Portichol →→

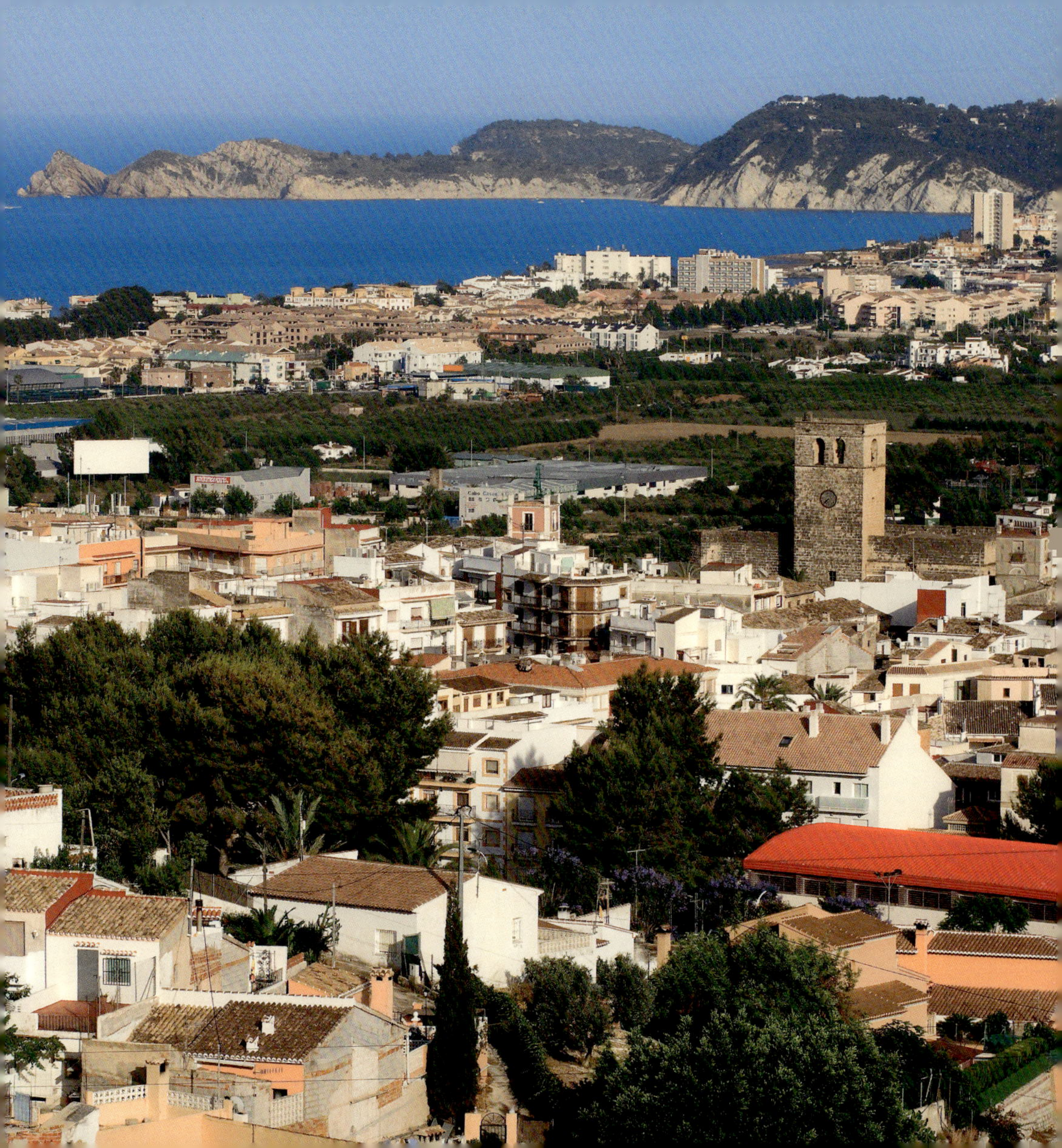

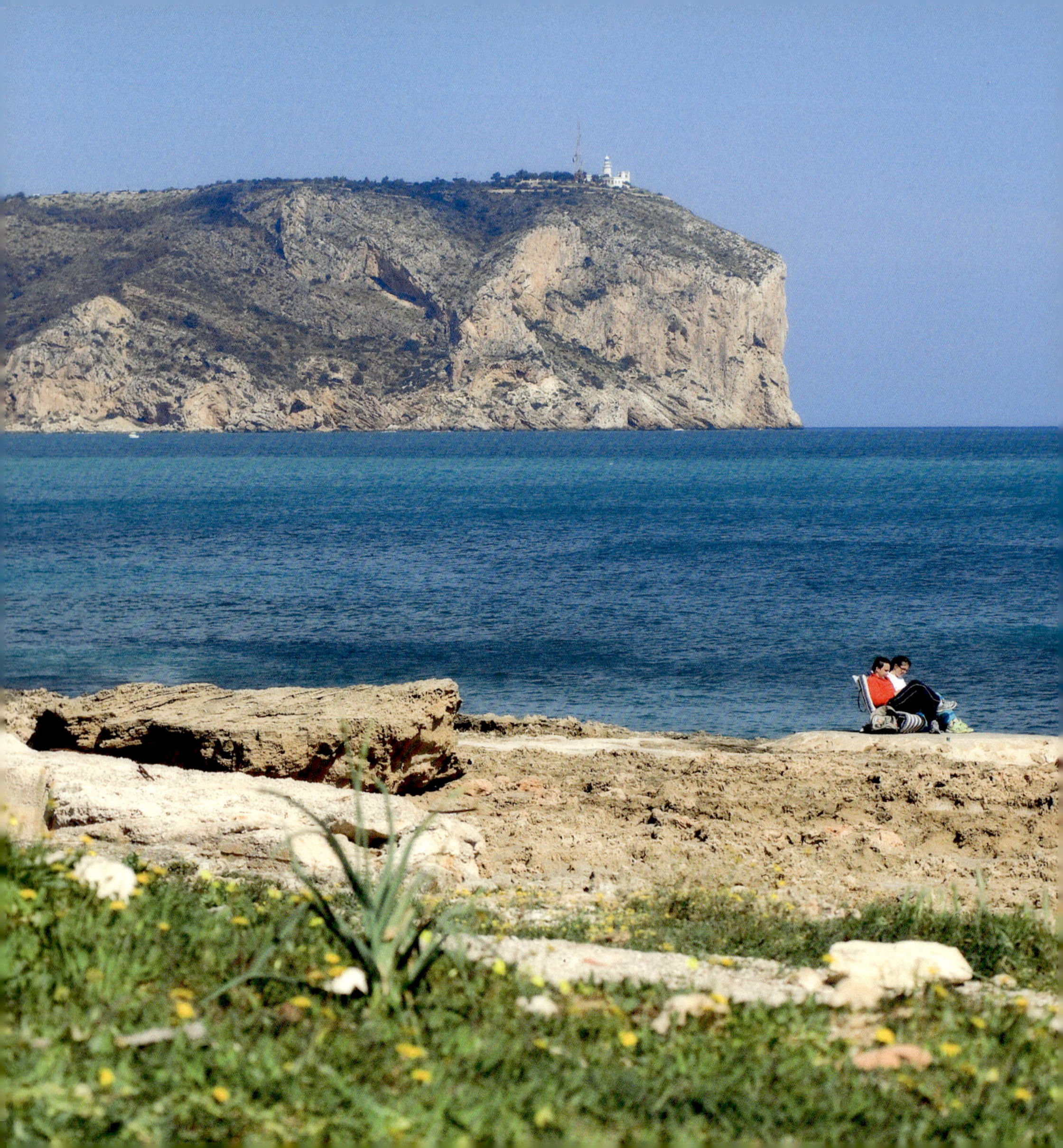

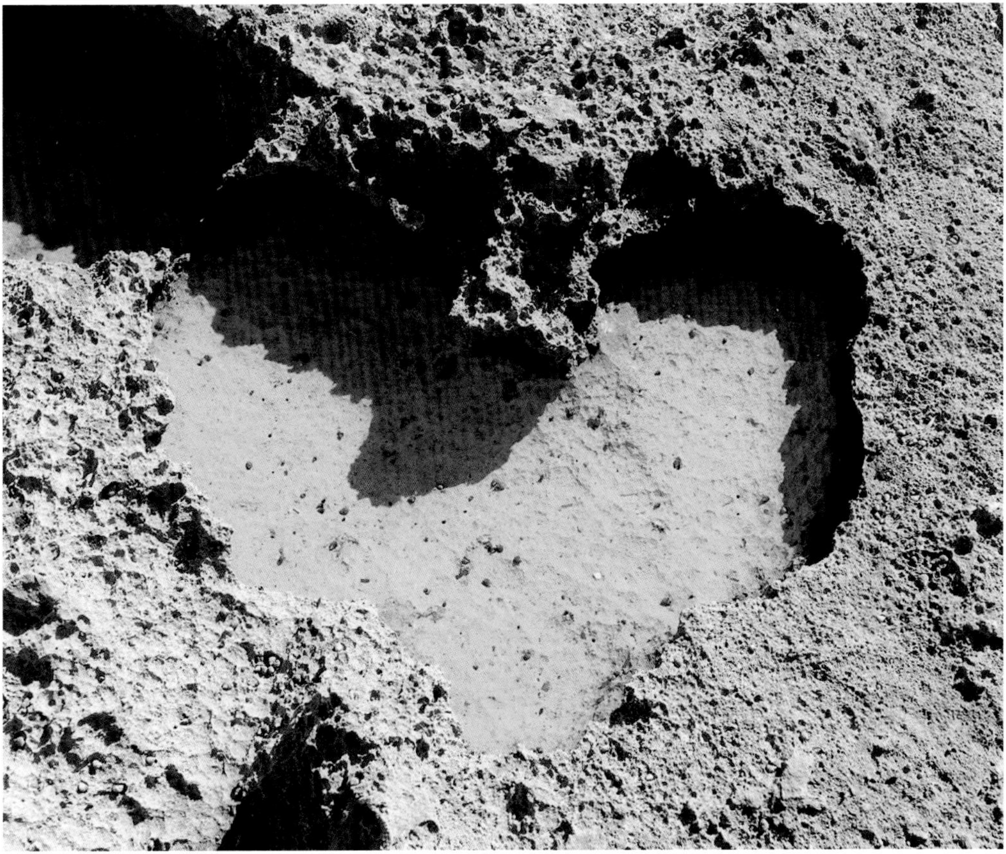

Rocks in Cala Blanca
← Cape of San Antonio

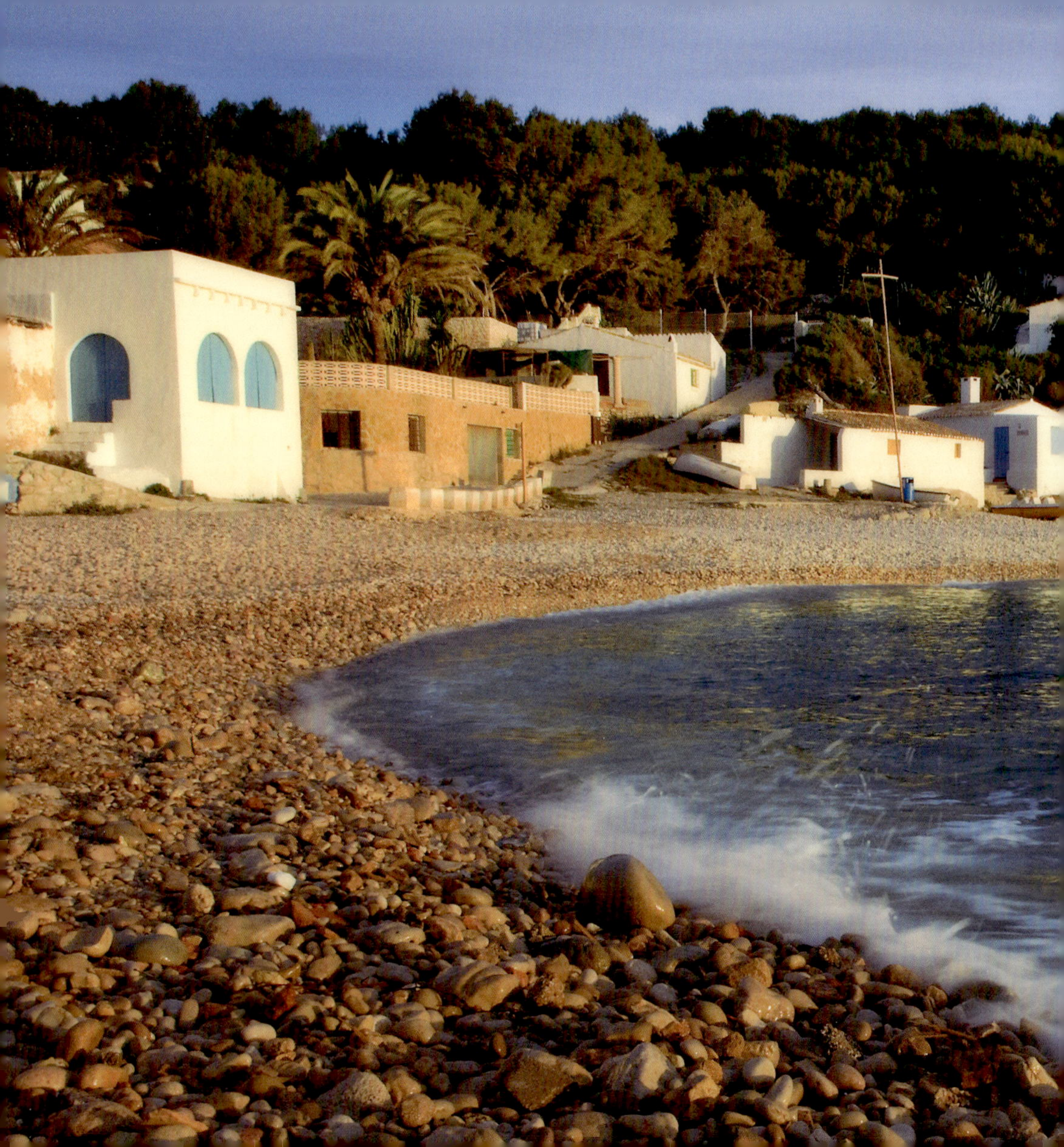

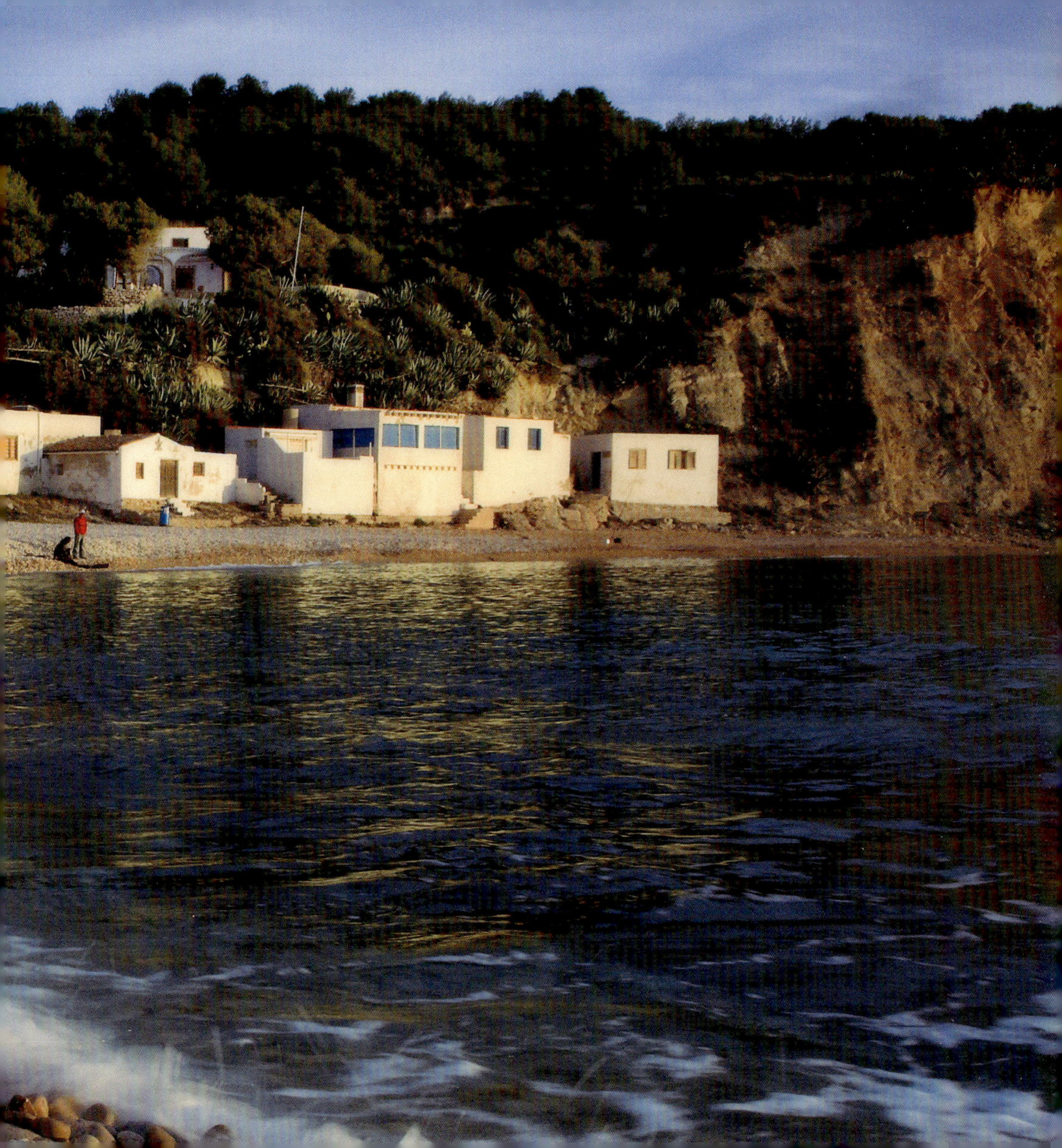

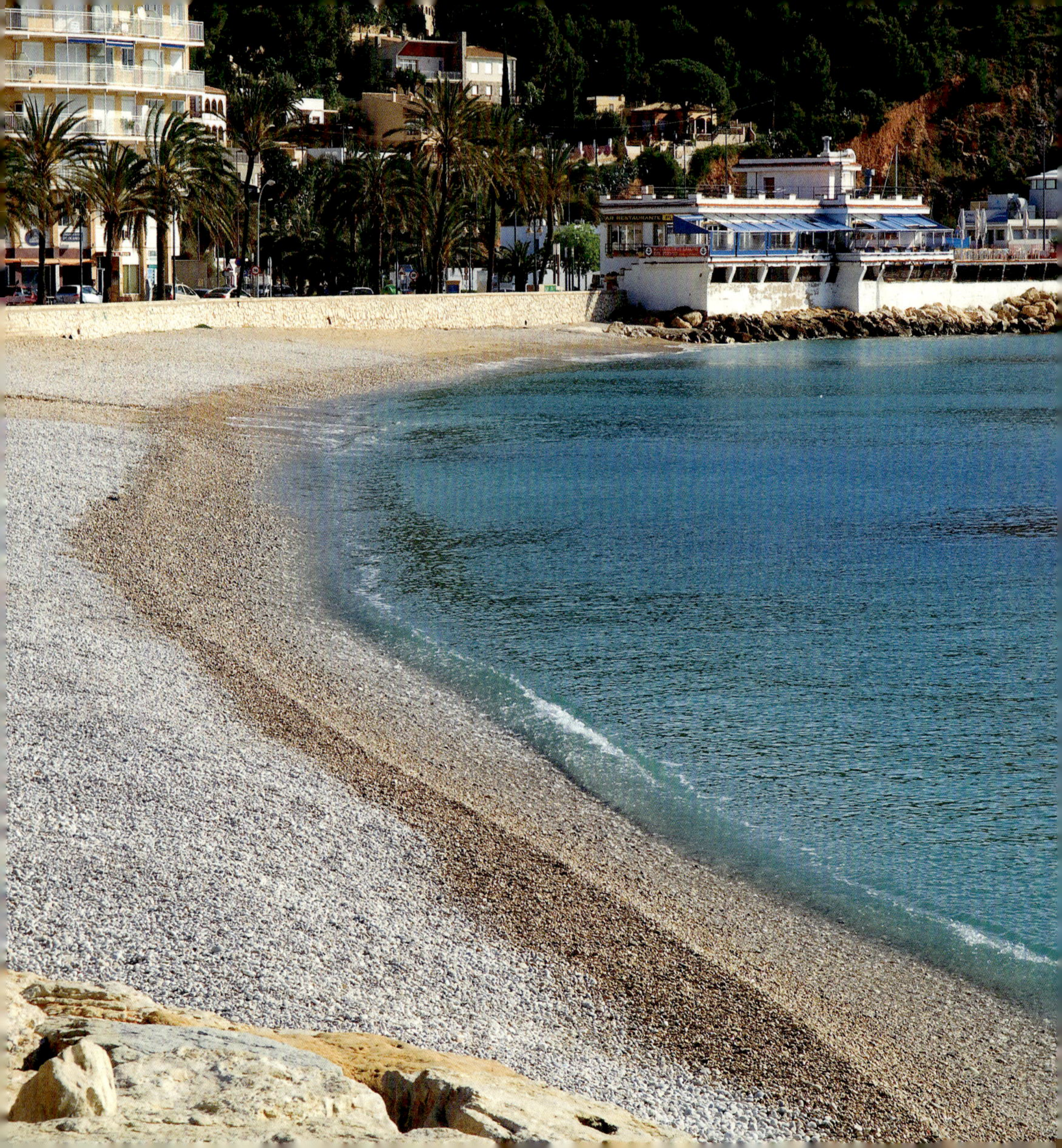

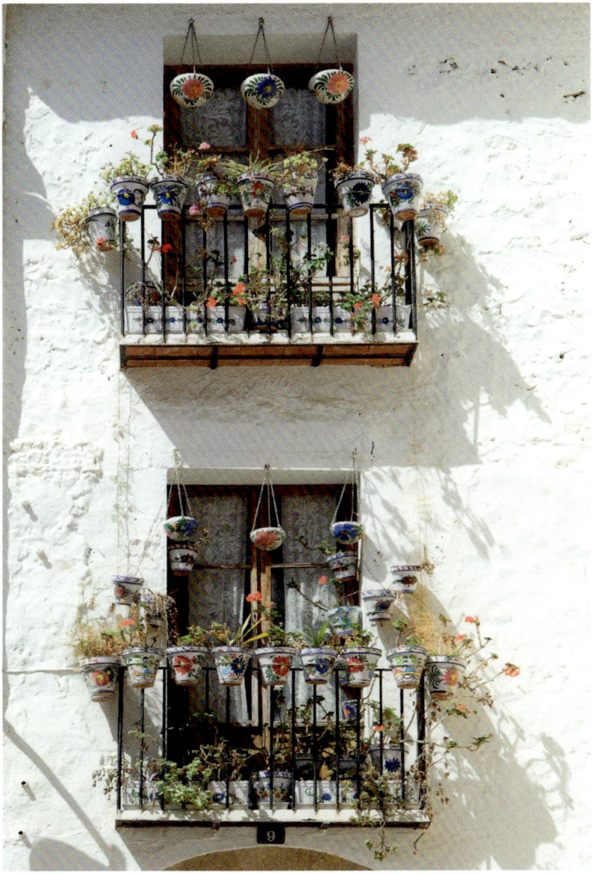

← *Playa Grava*

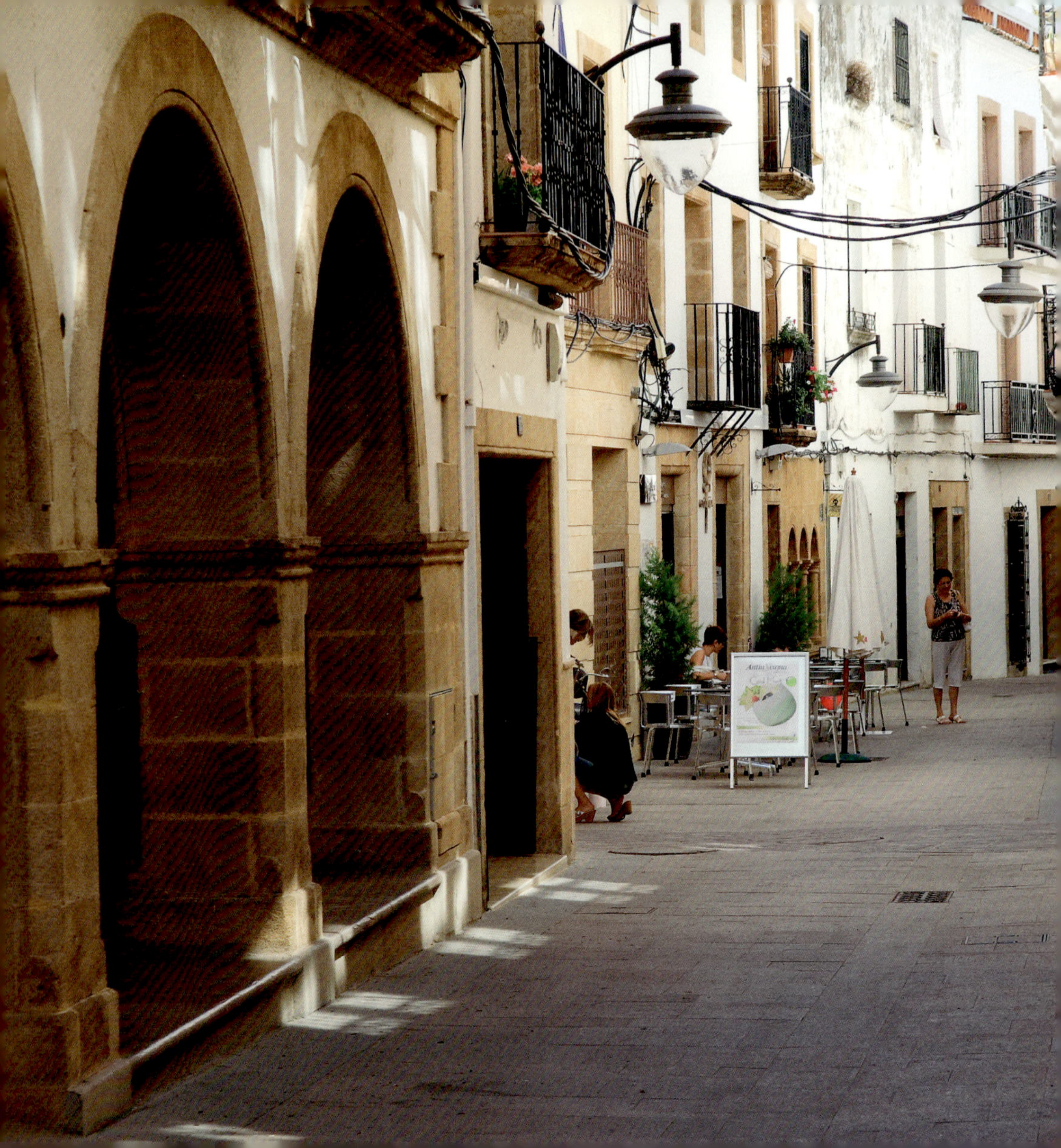

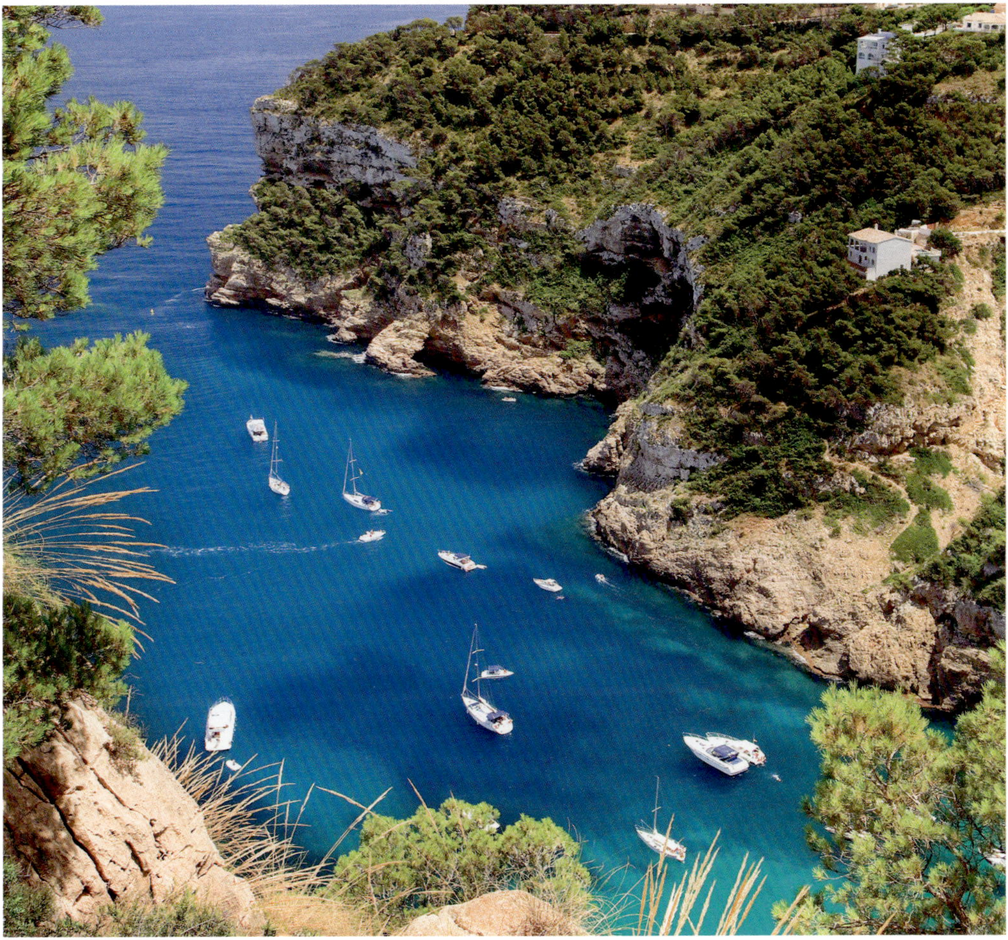

View from the Mirador de la Falzia
← Old quarter
Isle of Portichol from the Punta de Cap Negre →

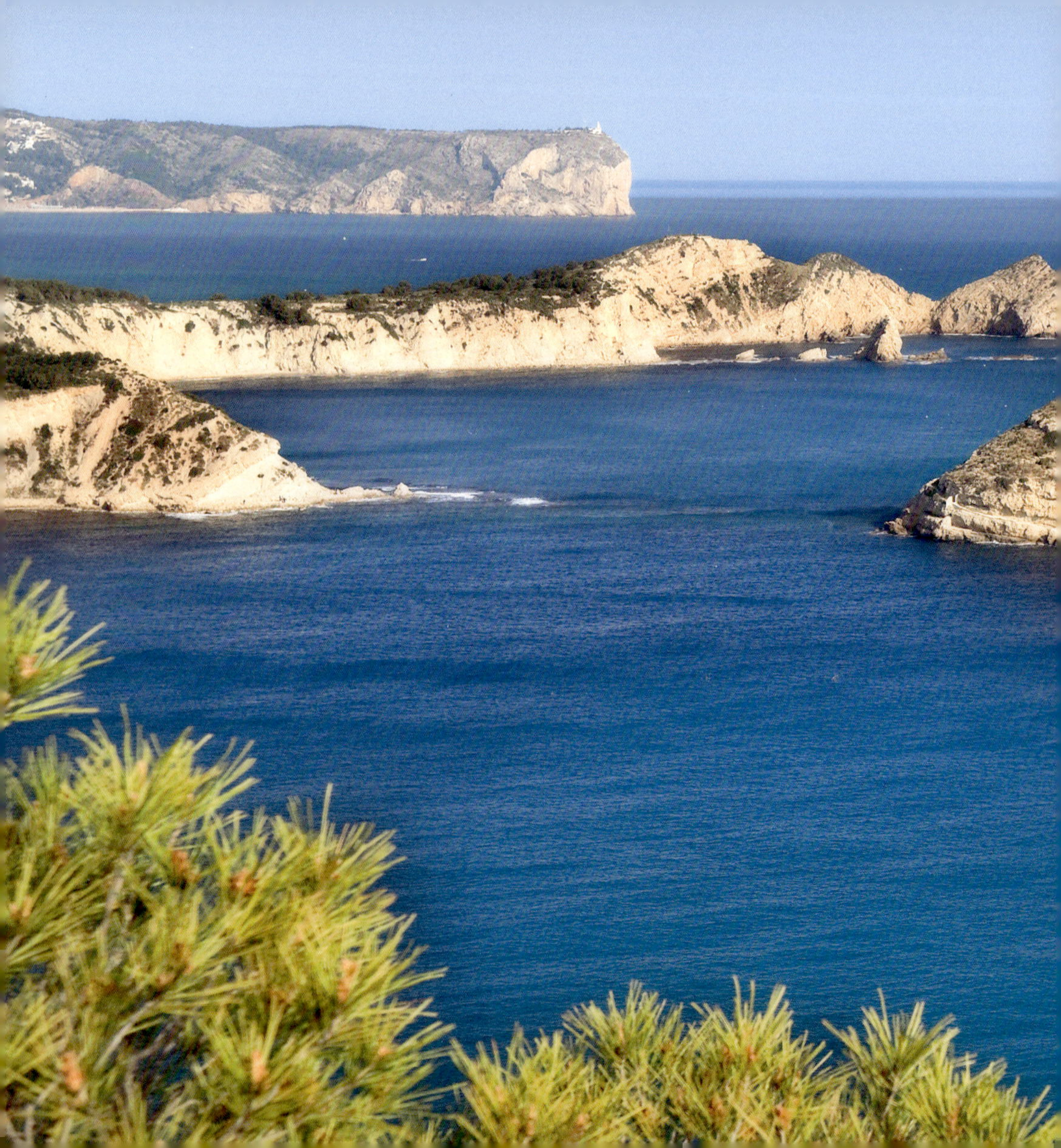

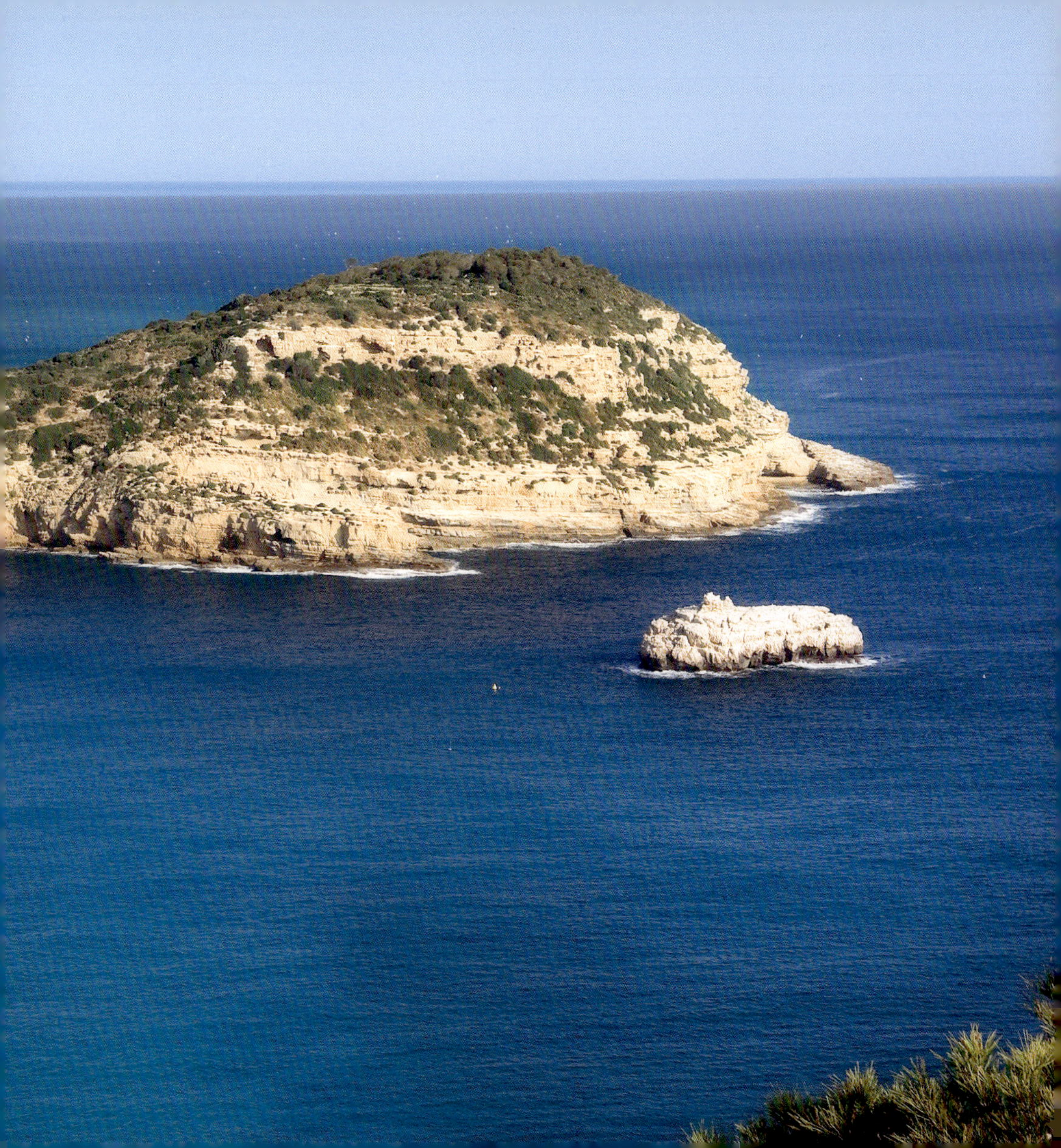

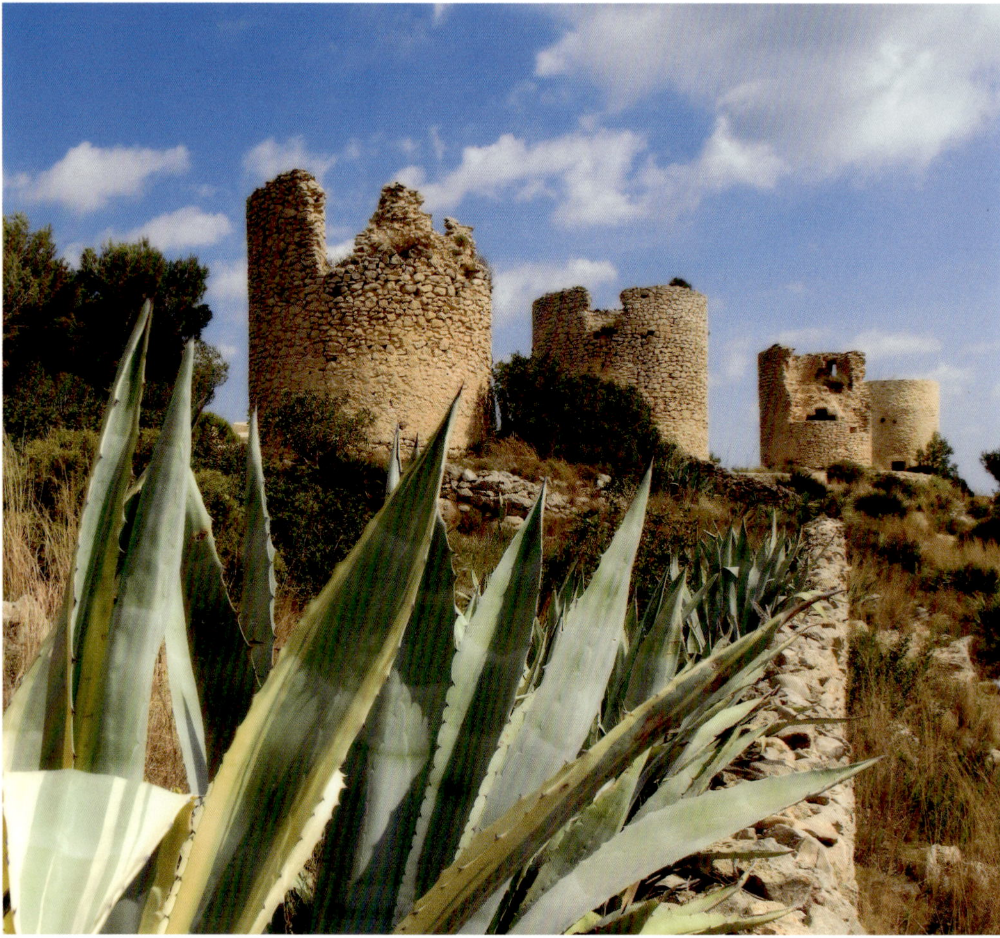

Old mills

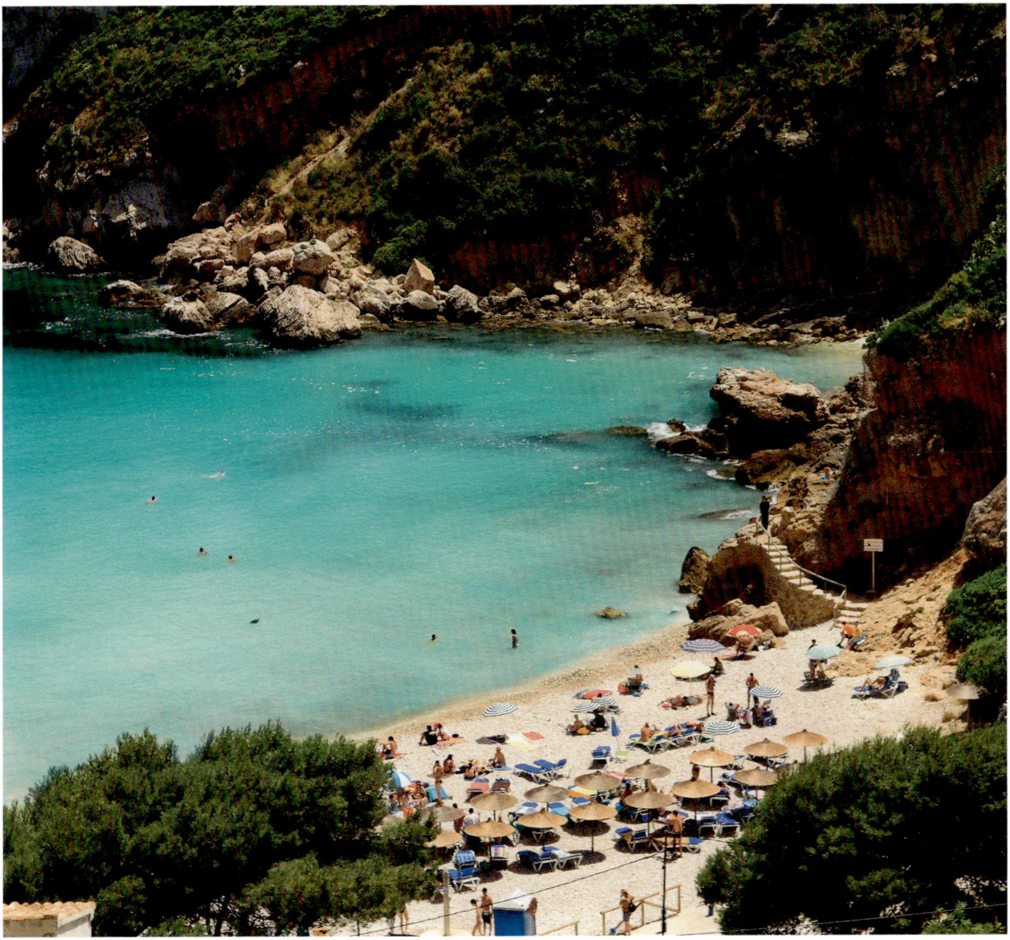

Cala Granadella

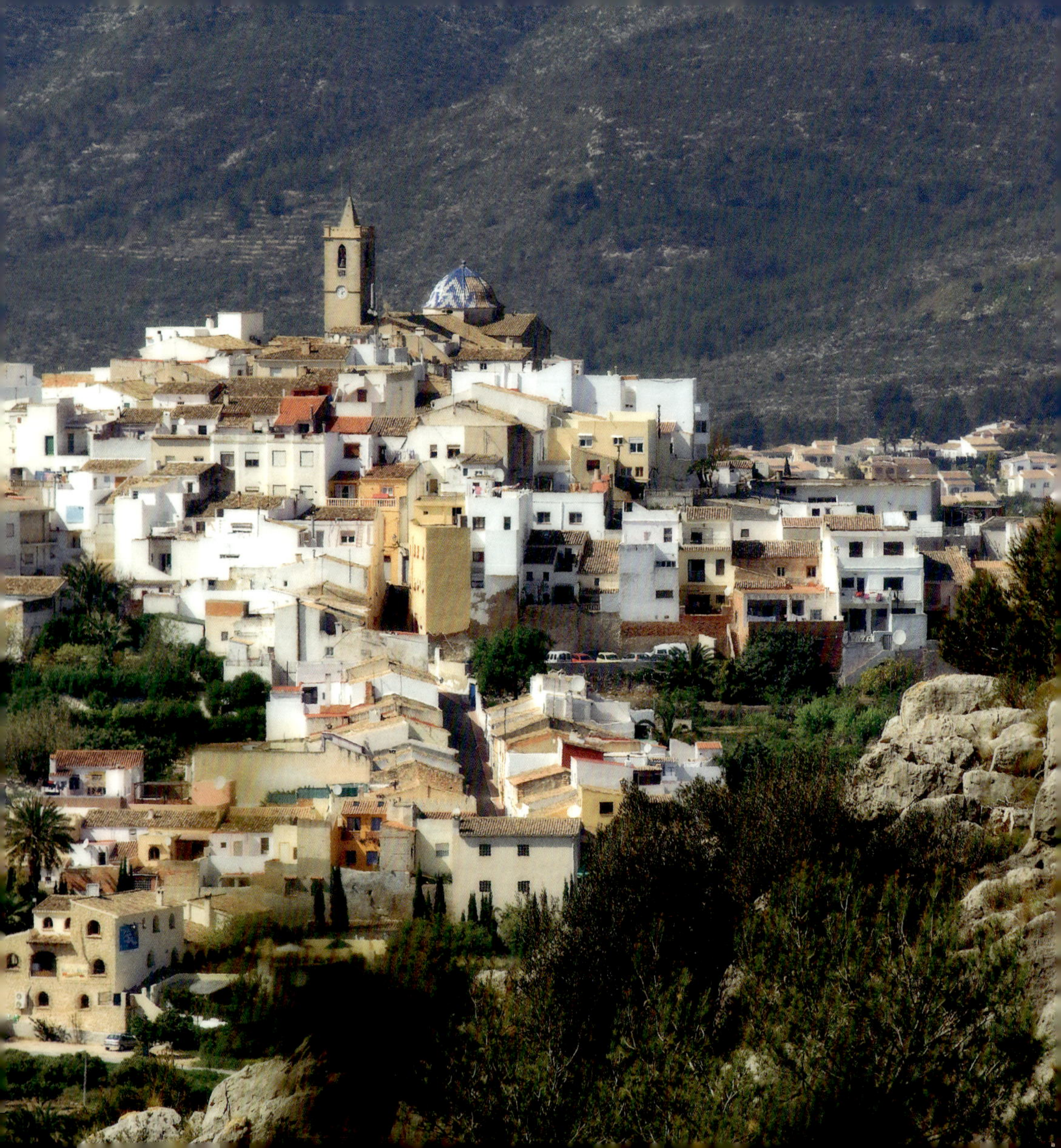

El Poble Nou de Benitatxell / Benitachell

Balancing high up on a hill appears the white village of El Poble Nou de Benitatxell, surrounded by terraces where the Muscat grape is still grown and which brought so much wealth and progress to the county. Roaming through its streets we can still find the identity and character of the traditional village. The locality is separate from its coastal strip, where dizzying cliffs —they reach over one hundred metres in height— protect at their feet beautiful coves such as those of Moraig and Testos, of suggestive crystalline water. The abruptness of the coast led to the brilliance of the fishermen in building the dangerous fisheries, platforms of reeds that hang on the cliffs and are reached via a rope ladder. It is still possible to see some of these constructions from the sea.

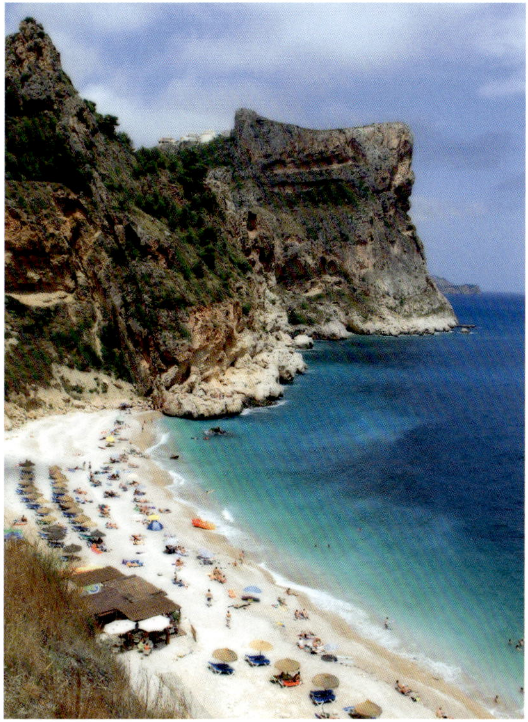

Cala del Moraig

Teulada - Moraira

The Palaeolithic excavation of the Cova de la Cendra is one of the most important in the Mediterranean. Despite this very ancient evidence of human presence in Teulada, its other centre, Moraira, did not develop until the pirates allowed it in the 19th century. The passing of the corsairs is witnessed by the watchtower of the cape of Oro, built in the 16th century. Before any suspicious sighting, the neighbouring towers of Ifach and Granadella were notified in order to warn the population.

Today, the calm of its water is reflected in the beach of El Portet, sheltered by the point of Moraira.

The celebrations that take place every first Sunday of July say that it was Saint Vicente Ferrer who made the water sprout in the hermitage of the Font Santa.

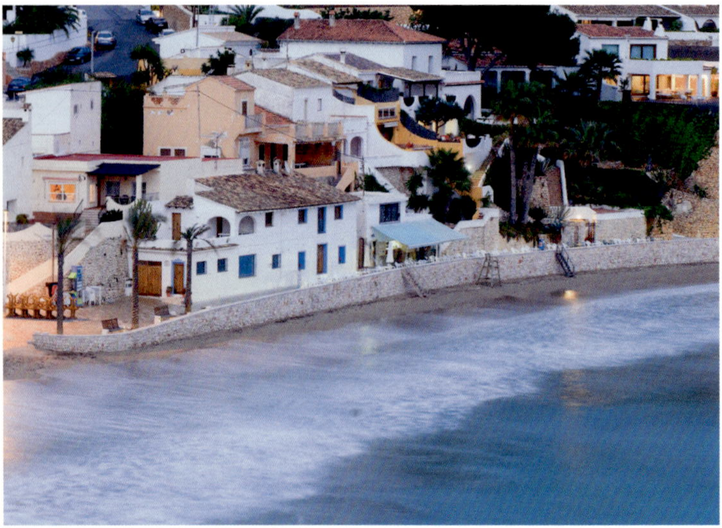

El Portet beach
El Portet de Moraira →

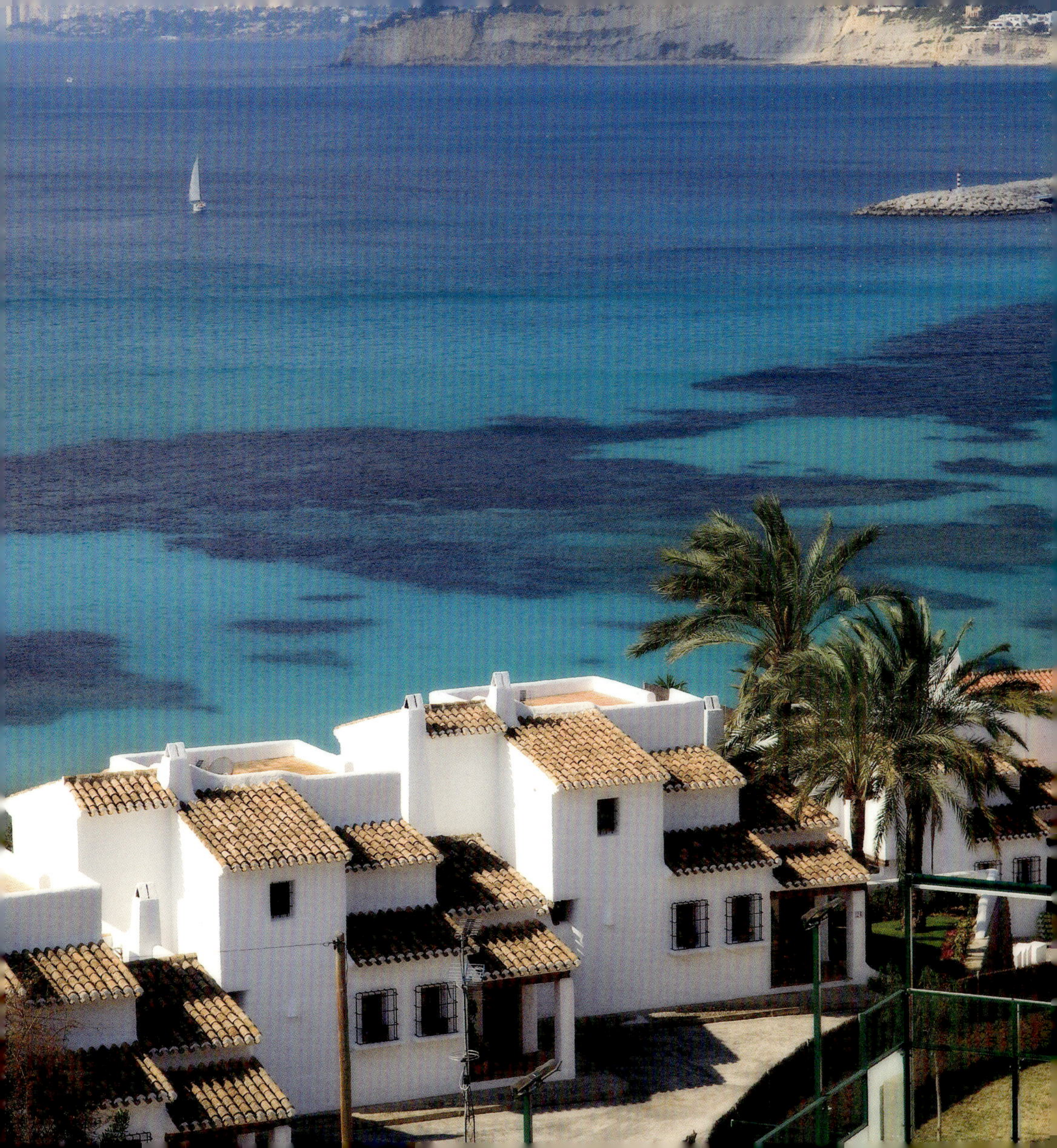

Benissa

The coast of Benissa is a succession of beautiful coves, from the busiest Cala Fustera to Cala Advocat, Pinets and Baladrar, with the pine trees paddling in the water. The fact that the town is cut by the national road has led to it being labelled as a mere passing place on the way to the neighbouring towns of Calpe or Teulada. Nothing could be further from the truth. Among its streets we find beautiful buildings, such as the 16th-century Lonja de Contratación (exchange), which houses exhibitions; the old Hospital de Pobres, headquarters of the Town Council; and the church of the Purísima Concepción or *Xiqueta*, known as the Cathedral of the Marina due to its colossal size.

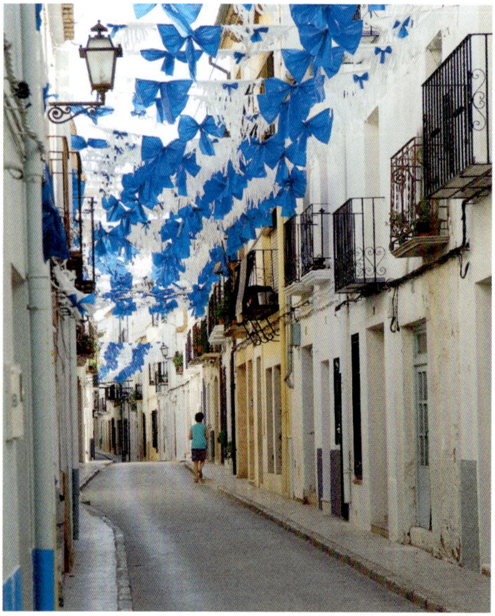

Benissa

Cala Baladrar
In the background the
Peñón de Ifach

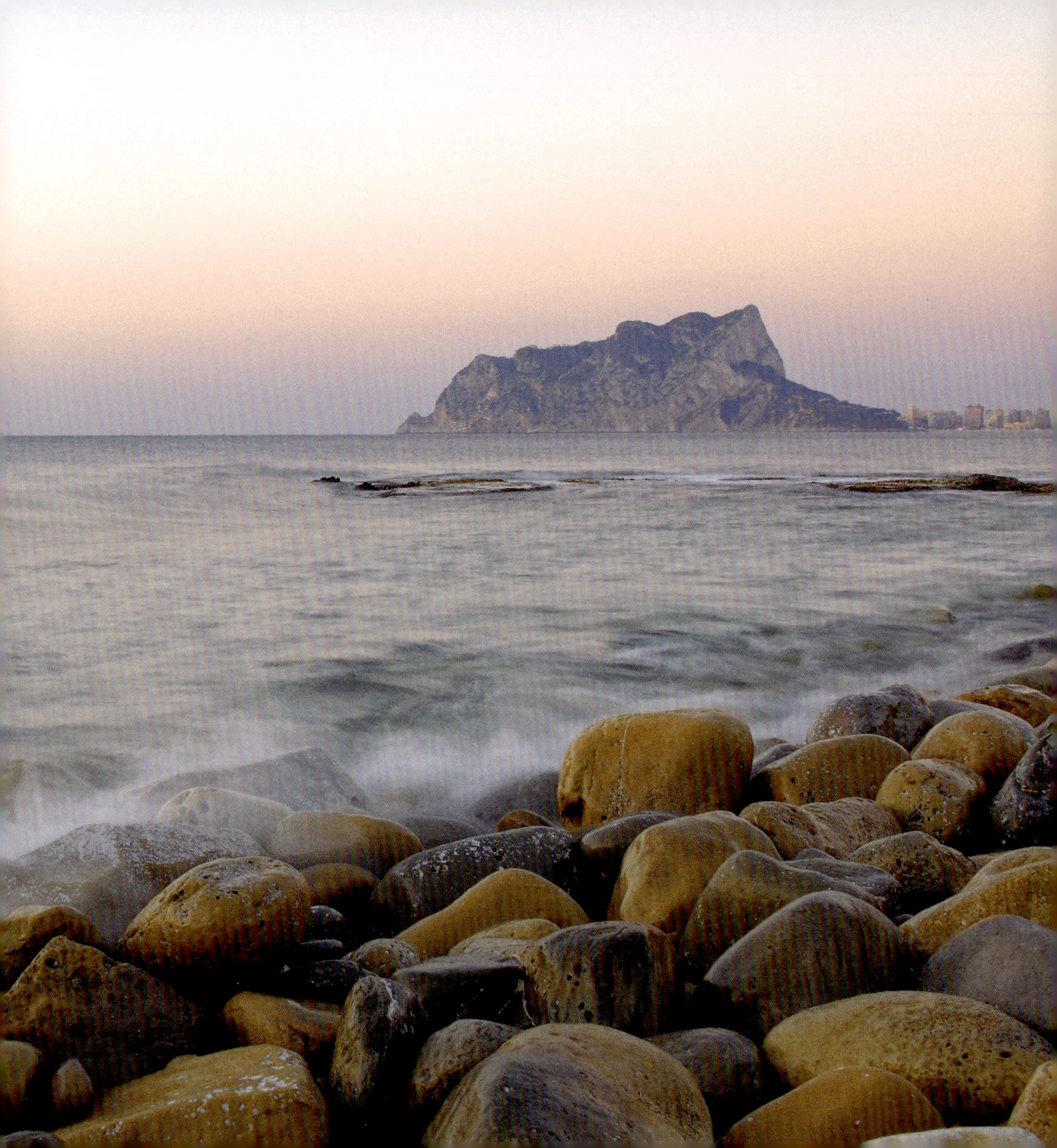

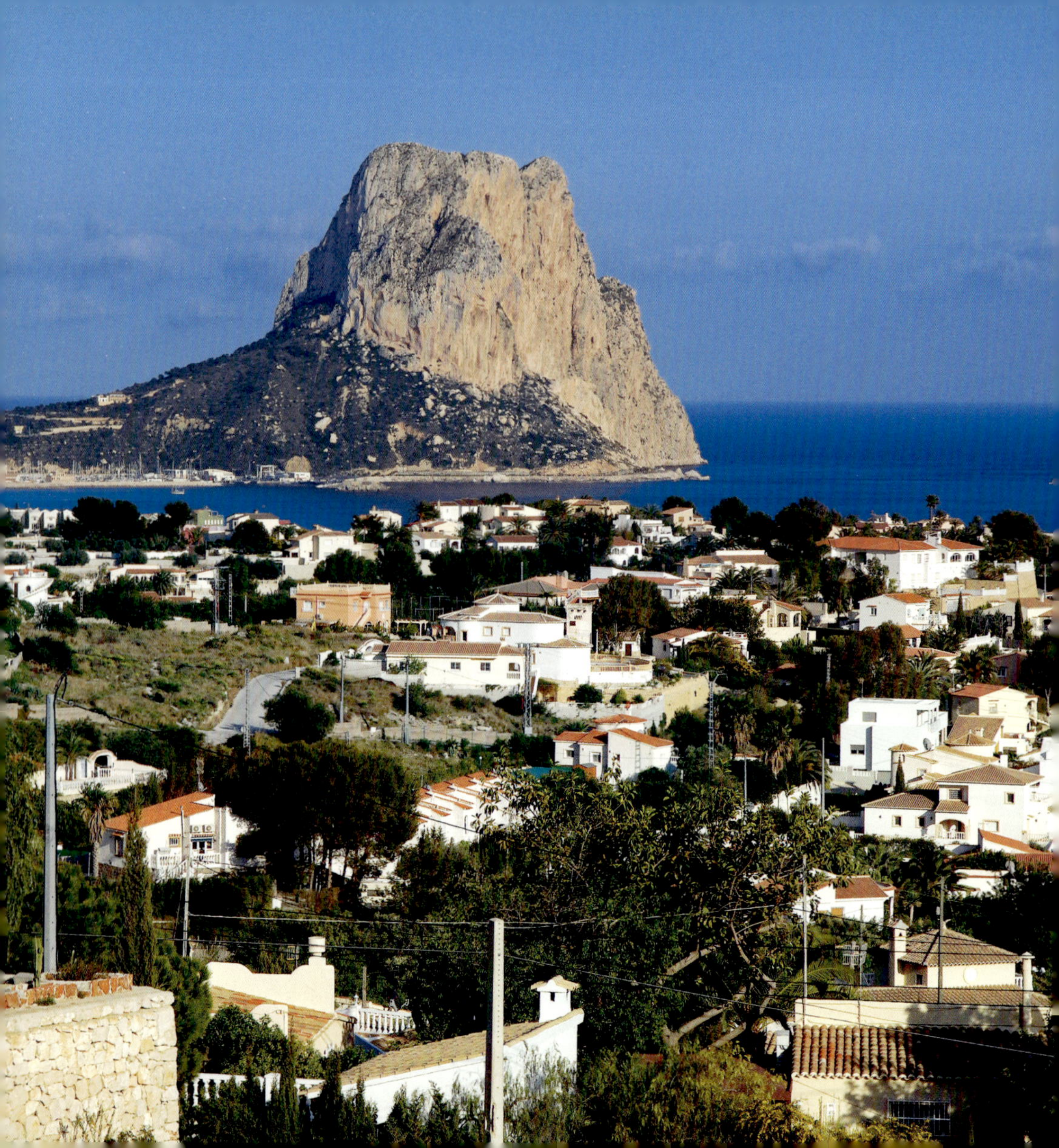

Calp / Calpe

The gigantic bulk of the Peñón de Ifach is one of the icons, one of the most recognisable marks of the Costa Blanca. Azorín wrote of it in a radio play and the writer Gabriel Miró devoted beautiful words to it: "Rocks aflame, cut by the wind. Apse with breast of brig that cuts the waters stilly..." They were not the only figures from the creative world who set their sights on the crag; the composer Óscar Esplá turned the rock into music in his symphony *Los cíclopes de Ifach*. The declaration of the rock as Natural Park, just in time, meant that the construction of other giants, these ones of brick and cement, were halted at the last moment. The Peñón de Ifach, of 332 metres in height and of calcareous origin, divides the beach areas of the town in two, leaving on one side that of Levante and on the other those of Arenal-Bol and Cantal Roig.

The sea procession of the 16th of July, in honour of the Virgin of the Carmen, is one of the best-known in the province.

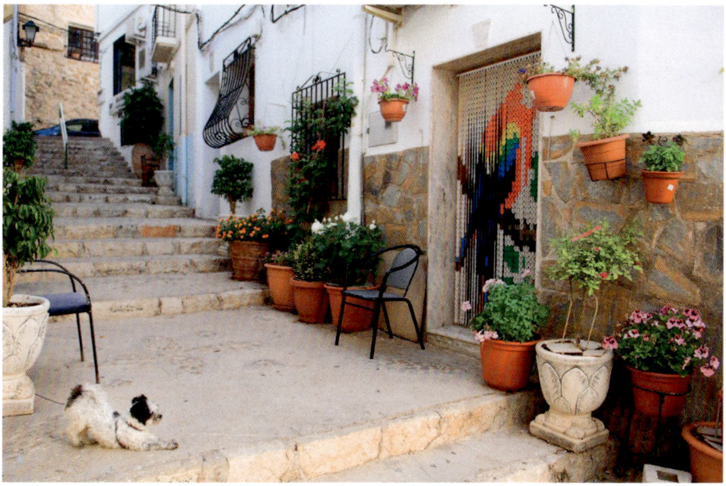

Old quarter
← Peñón de Ifach

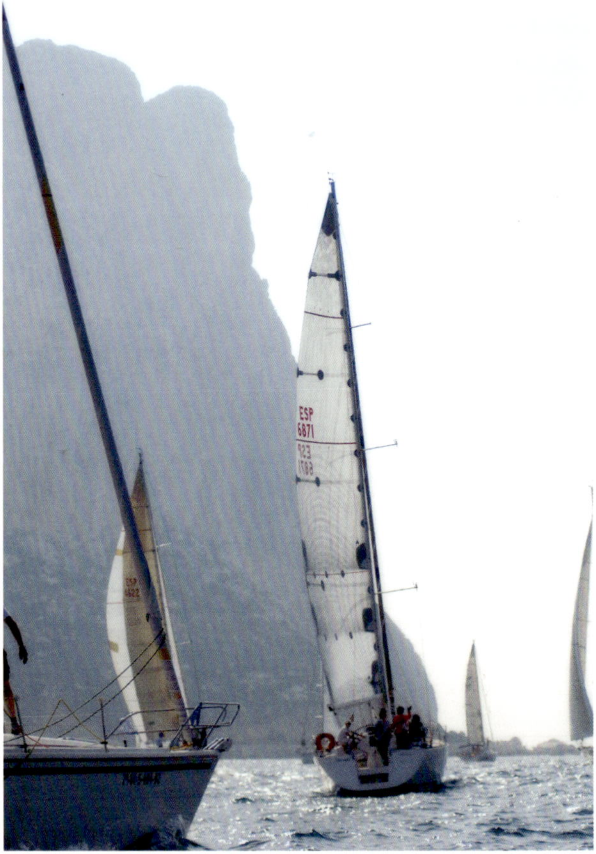

Calp-Formentera Regatta
Peñón de Ifach from the Arenal-Bol beach →

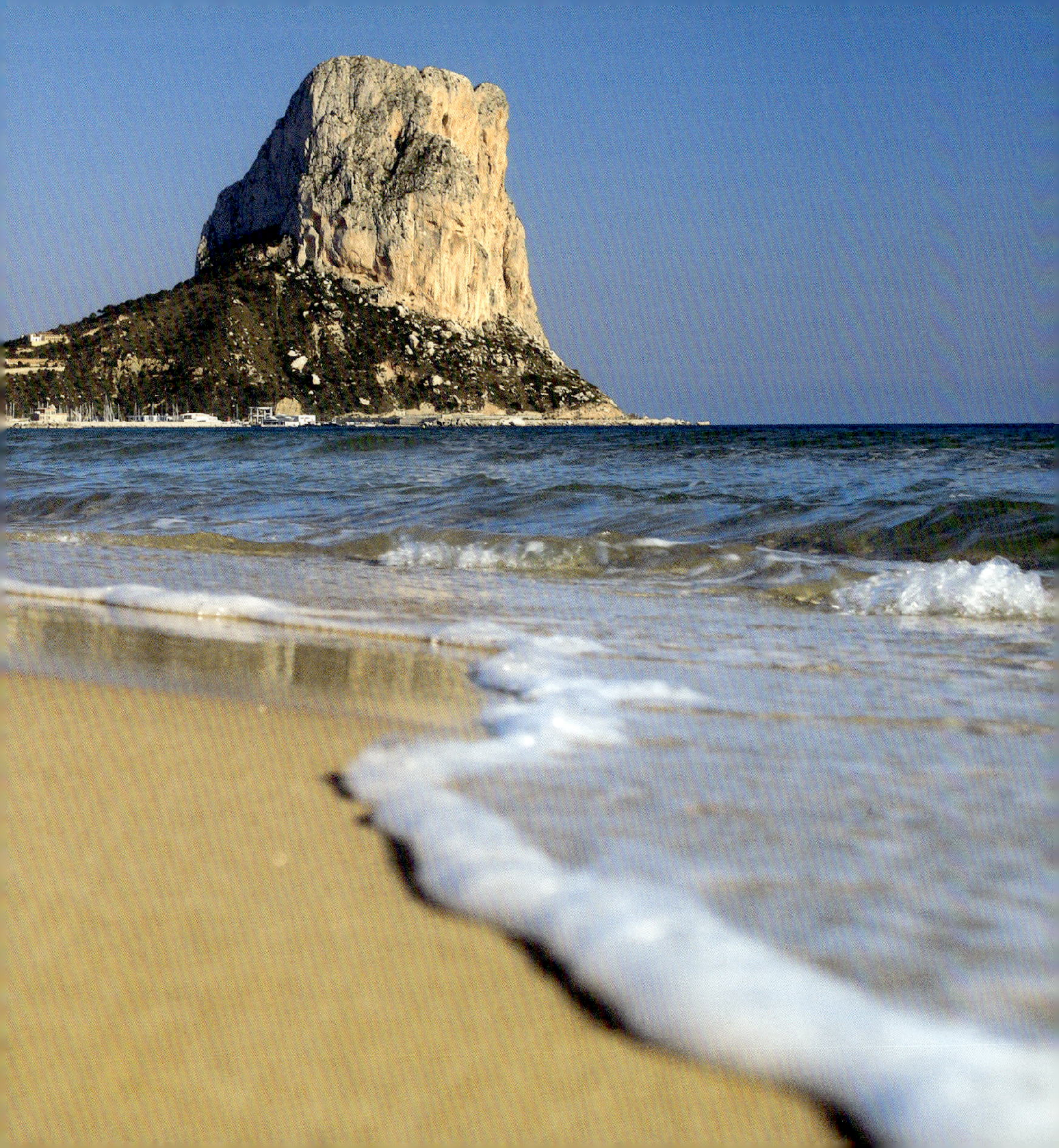

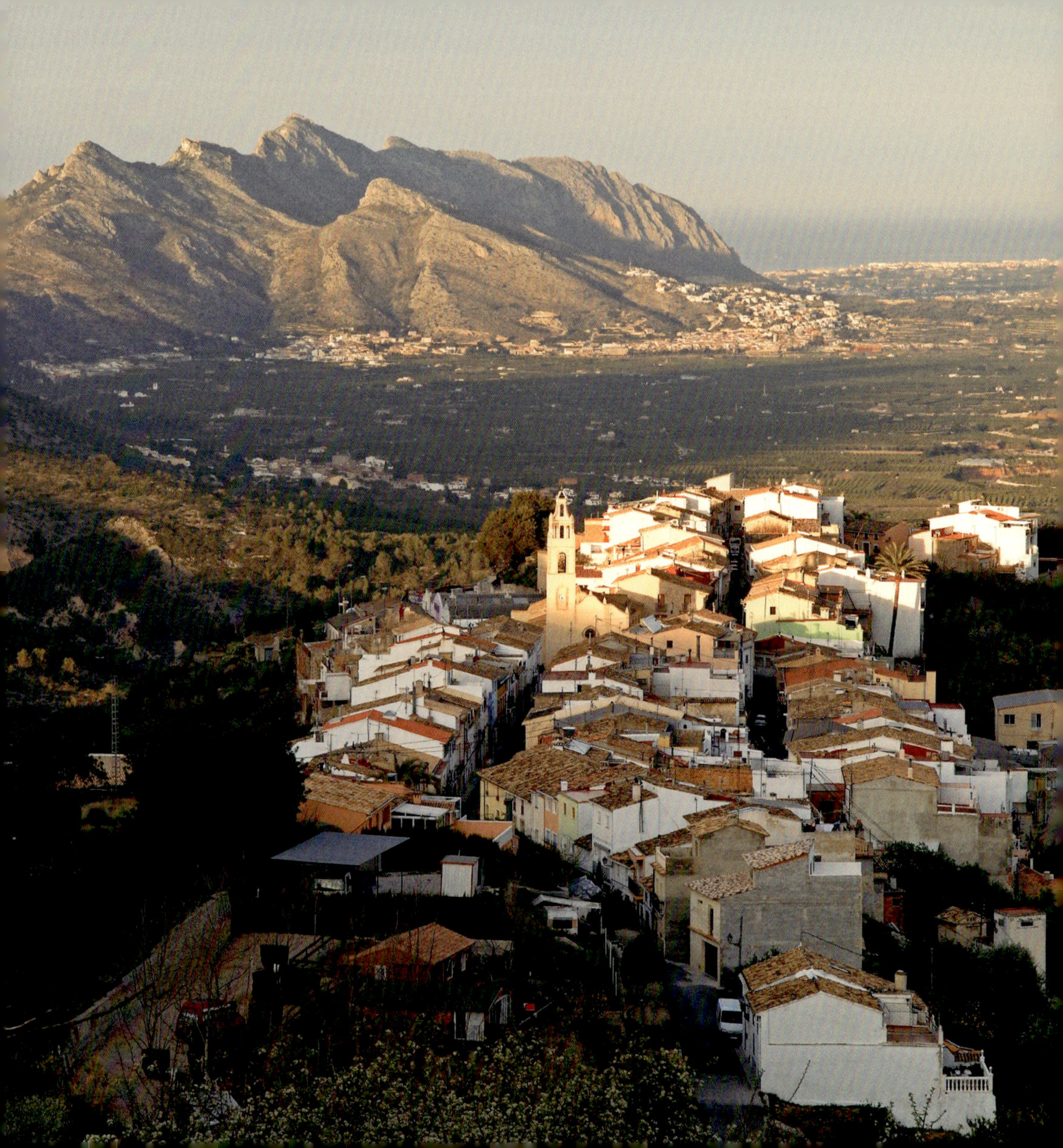

The valleys of La Marina

Inland in the country of the Marina Alta we find a series of valleys with small and charming villages embedded in the foot of the mountains.

In the 13th century, the Muslim leader Al Azraq —the one with the blue eyes— controlled these lands, heading diverse uprisings against Jaume I. The valley of Alcalá was the capital of his fief. Today, there is just a couple of villages remaining in the area, but the surrounding landscapes deserve a visit.

Next to the ravine of Infierno, nicknamed the Cathedral of walking, is the valley of Laguar. The villages of Fleix, Benimaurell and Campell, especially this latter one, are amongst the most picturesque of the inland of the province of Alicante.

When spring arrives, the star turn is the valley of Gallinera with the explosion of beauty of the cherry trees in blossom. Towns such as Alpatró, Alcalalí or Benialí, form the main centre of the DO cherries, Cerezas de la Montaña de Alicante.

The road that goes along the valley of Ebo is well worth the trip on its own due to the panoramic views it offers until reaching the small village of the same name. Another major attraction from the area is the cave of Rull, one of the few of the Levante region that is still forming.

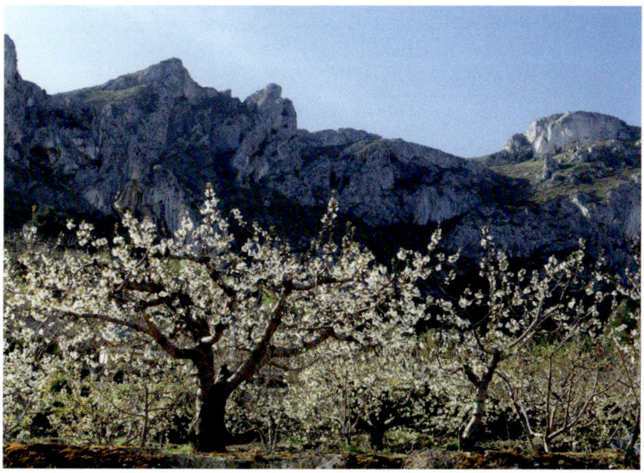

Flowering almond trees in the Alcalà valley
← Laguar valley. Campell

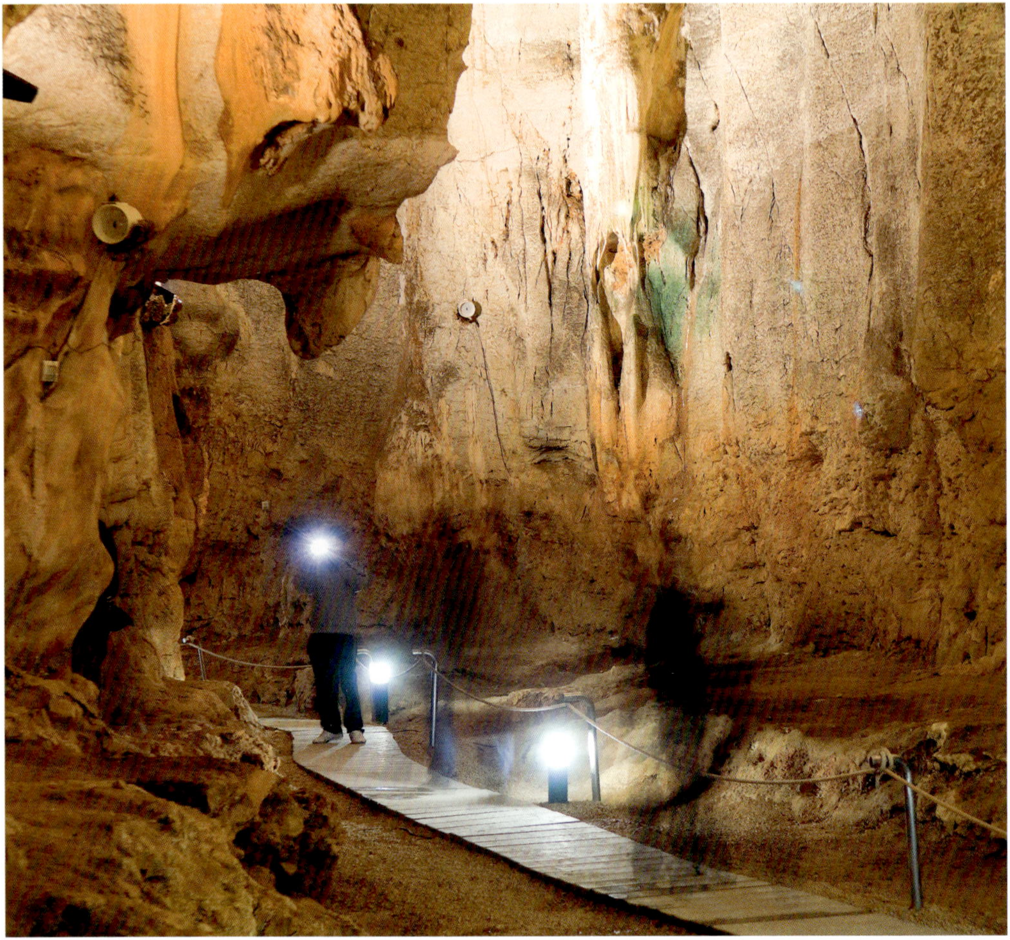

Cave of the Calaveras

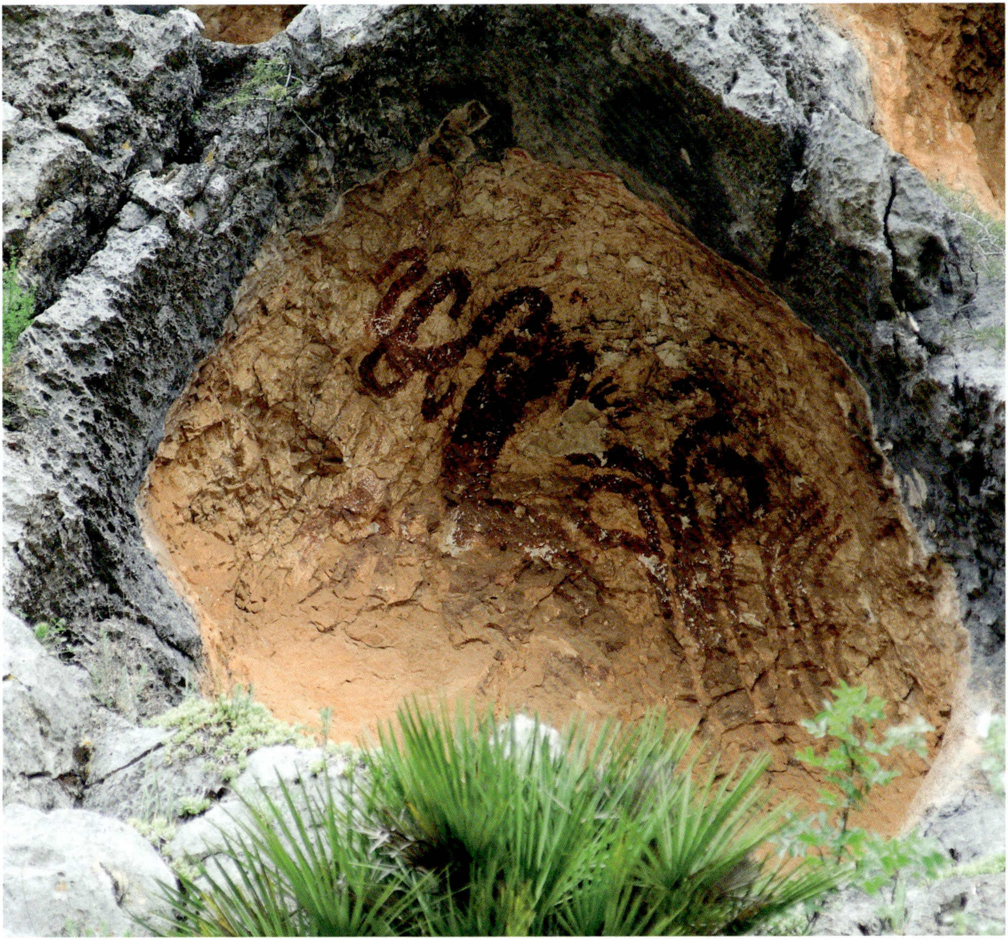

Pla de Petracos, prehistoric paintings

Gata de Gorgos

The craftsmanship of wicker and palm

The skilful hands of the craftsmen of Gata de Gorgos have been weaving wicker and palm for centuries to make the most diverse baskets. The use of palm baskets had its age of splendour when they were used to store and sell raisins, the trade that brought wealth to the whole county.

During the Festivals of San Miguel, at the end of September, the town holds a well-attended craft fair, a good moment to see the work of the craftsmen close-up and check the ductility of the materials they use.

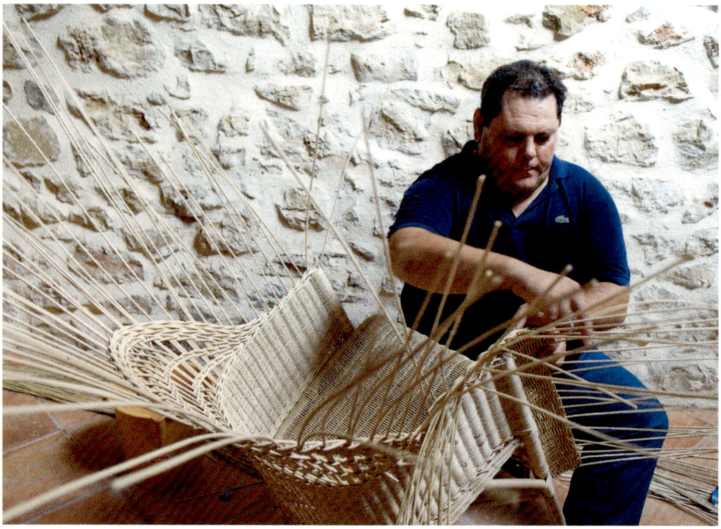

Wickerwork crafts

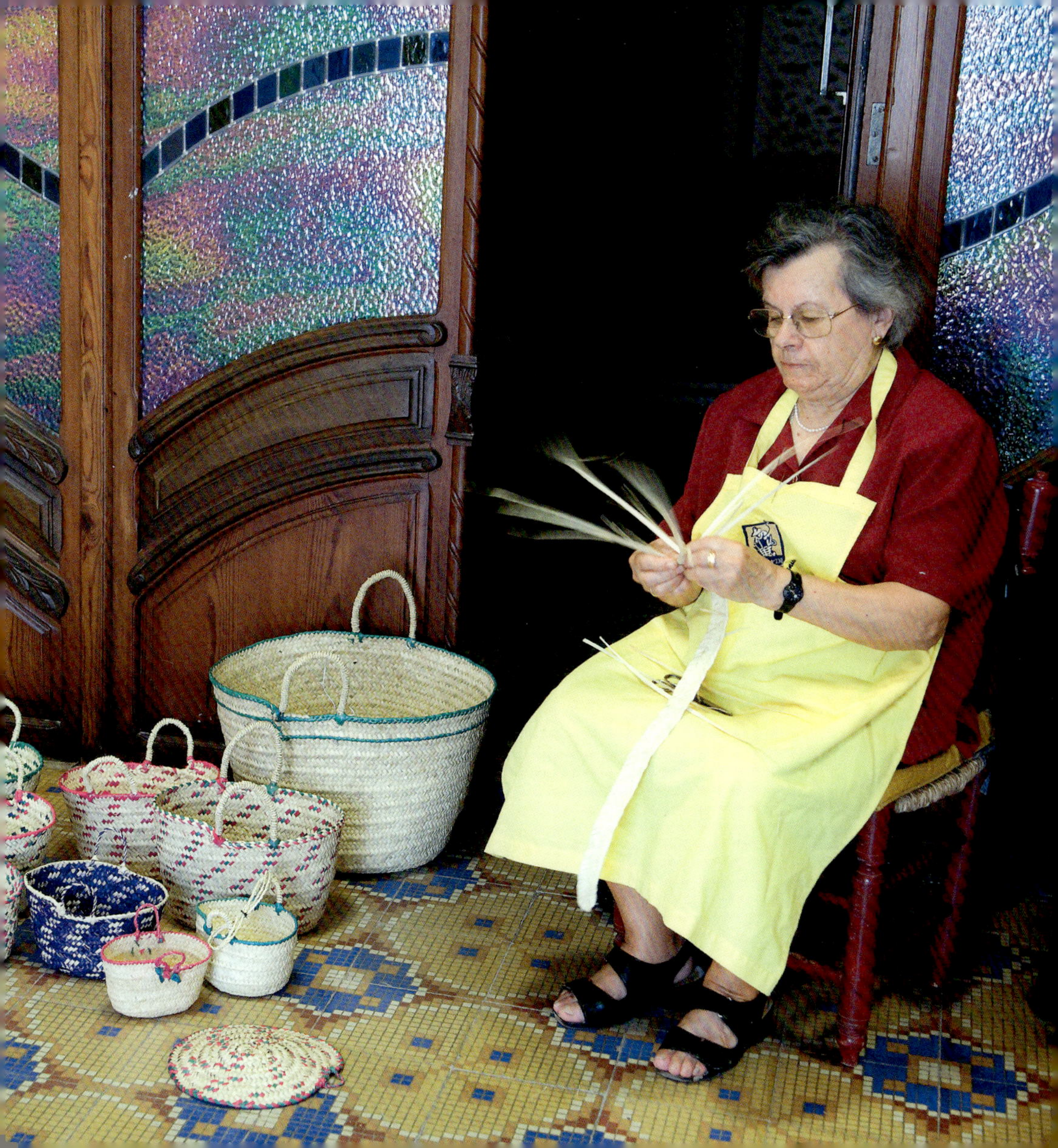

Marina Baixa

Altea
Serra Gelada
Benidorm
La Vila Joiosa / Villajoyosa
The castle of Guadalest
Inland. Mountain Villages

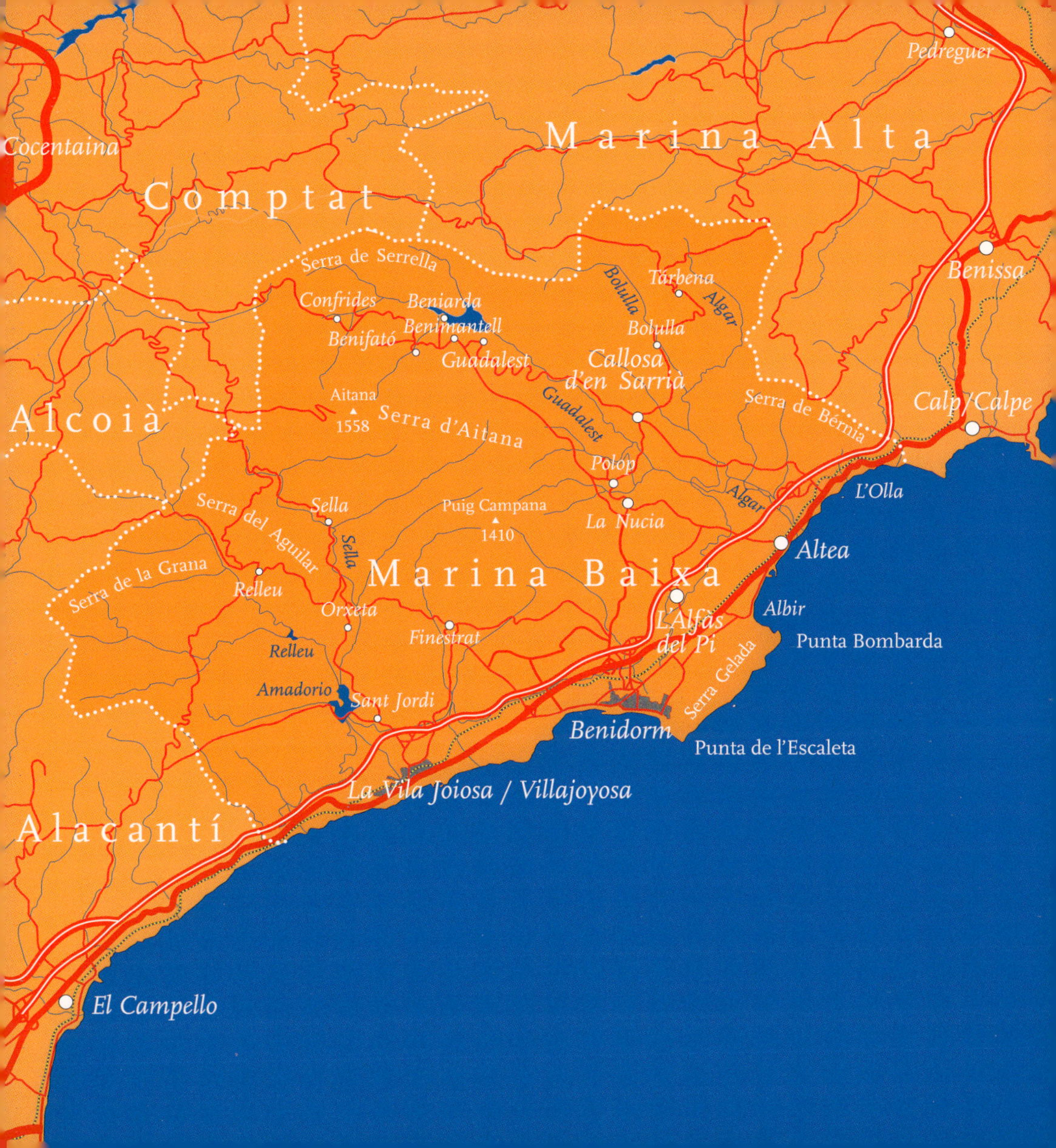
Pedreguer
Cocentaina
Marina Alta
Comptat
Serra de Serrella
Tàrbena
Bolulla
Algar
Confrides
Beniarda
Benimantell
Benifató
Guadalest
Bolulla
Callosa d'en Sarrià
Benissa
Alcoià
Aitana
1558
Serra d'Aitana
Guadalest
Serra de Bèrnia
Calp/Calpe
Polop
L'Olla
Algar
Serra del Aguilar
Sella
Puig Campana
1410
La Nucia
Altea
Sella
Serra de la Grana
Relleu
Marina Baixa
Albir
Orxeta
L'Alfàs del Pi
Finestrat
Punta Bombarda
Relleu
Serra Gelada
Amadorio
Sant Jordi
Benidorm
Punta de l'Escaleta
La Vila Joiosa / Villajoyosa
Alacantí
El Campello

Altea

At the foot of the Bernia mountain range, its silent sentry, appears the most recognisable cupula of the Mediterranean, in Altea. The blue and white tesserae of the church of Nuestra Señora del Consuelo represent a sea that has always been kind to it. A sea from which a special light is born each morning, that for years attracted artists from all over who came to soak themselves in this light and seek the necessary inspiration to create their works.

The whitewashed houses of its old quarter drop down to the sea along cobbled alleys, the geraniums hanging from the balconies and even the hung-up washing seems to want to soak itself in this light and let itself be caressed by the gentle blow of the *llebeig*.

The bay of Altea, from the Morro del Toix to the Punta del Albir, is covered by a series of beaches where the rounded pebble dominates. In one of them, on the Saturday closest to Saint Lorenzo's day —10th of August—, the Castell de l'Olla is held, a spectacular firework display with fireworks launched from the sea that flood the whole bay with colour. Next to the church is held one of the most popular art and craft street markets of the Costa Blanca.

Altea →

View with the church of the Virgen del Consuelo →→

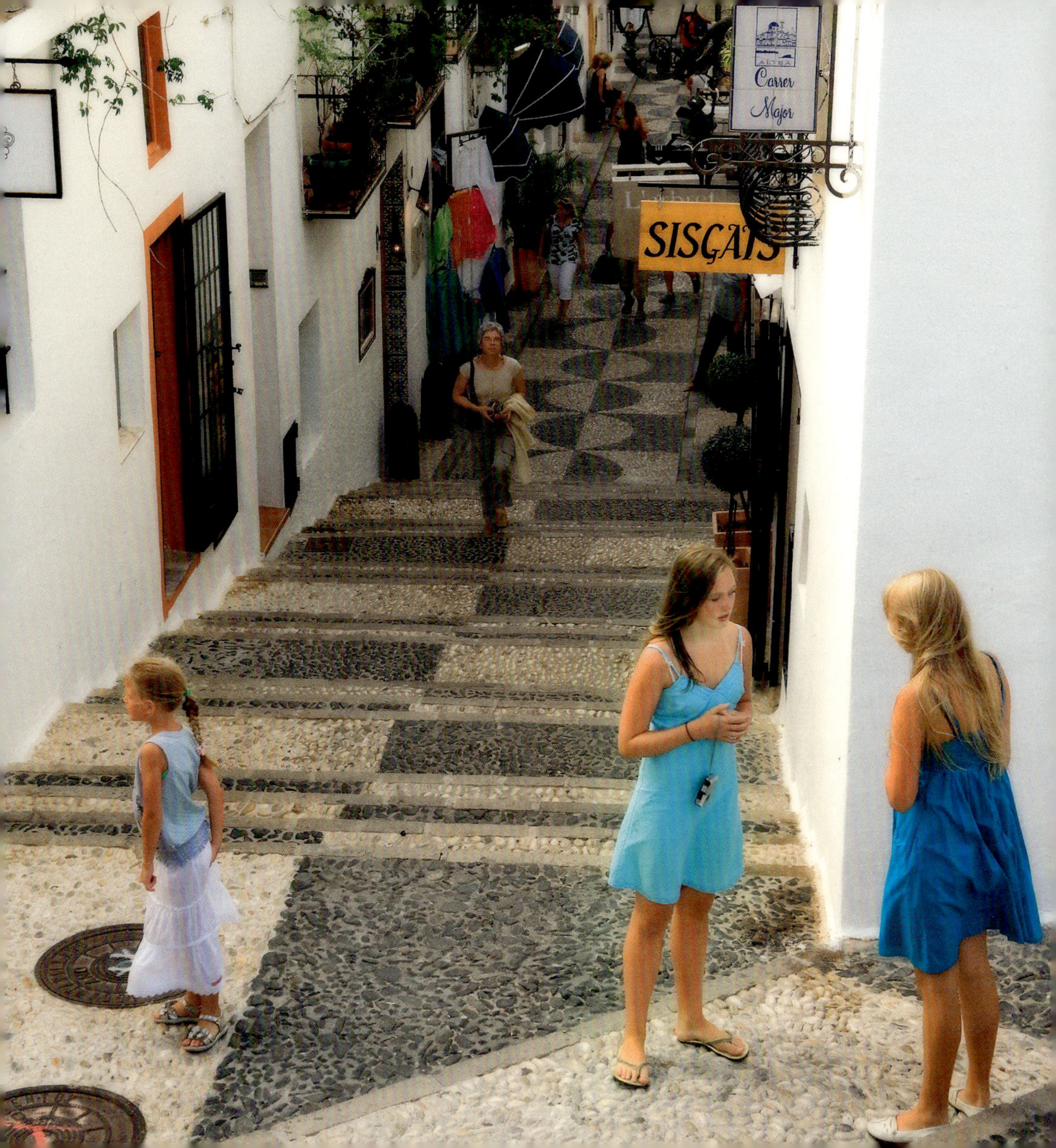
ALTEA
Carrer
Major
SISÇATS

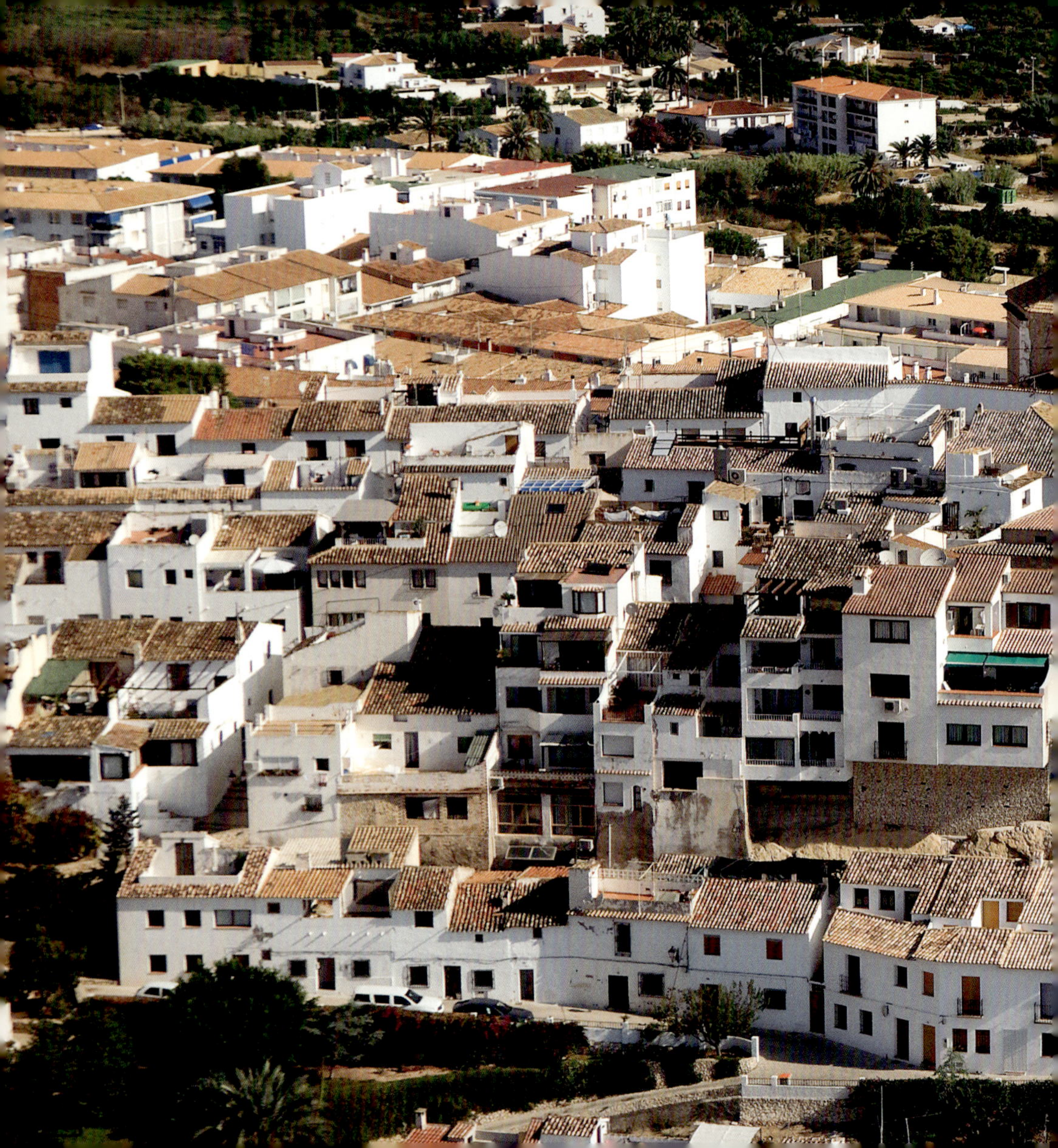

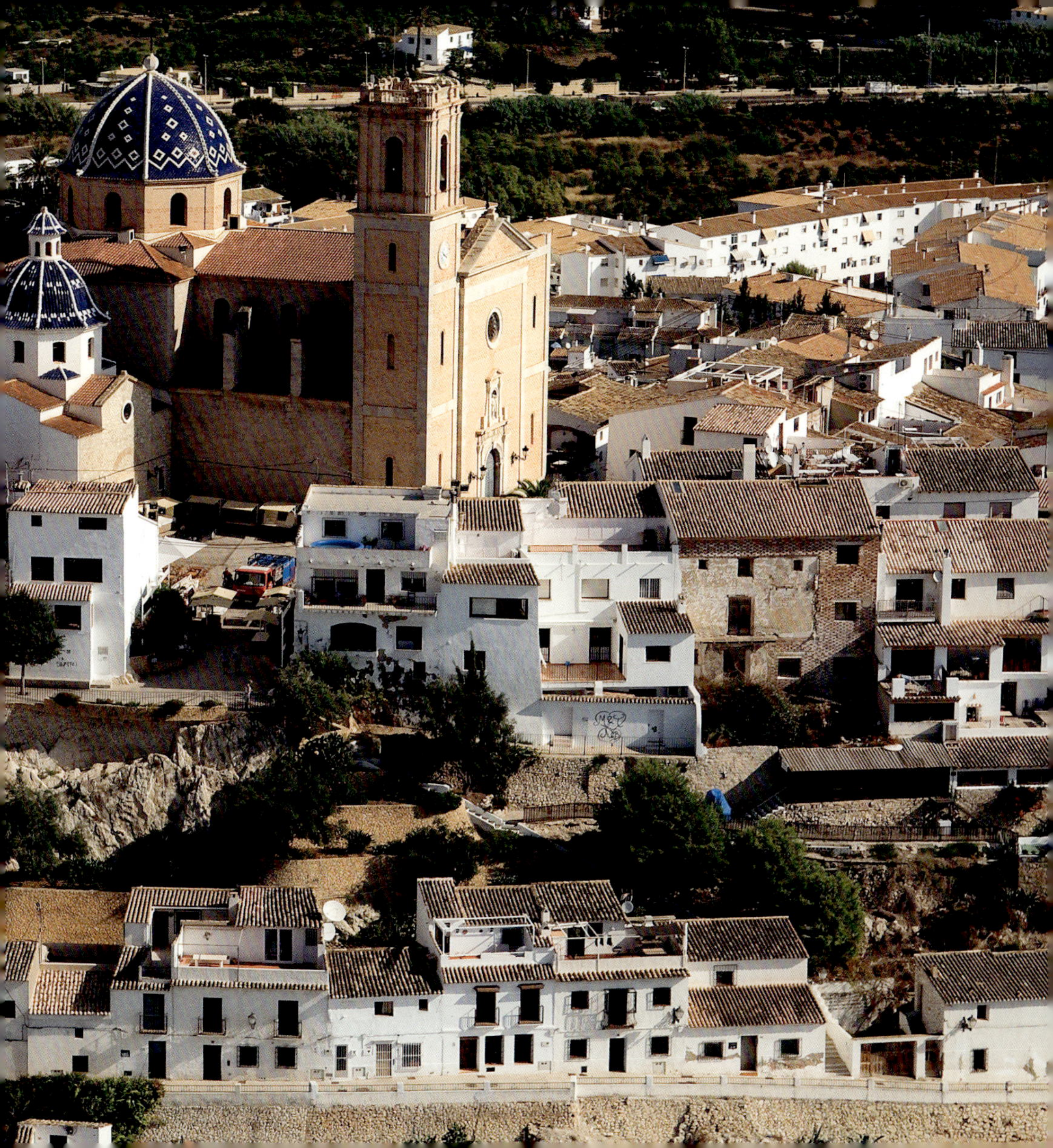

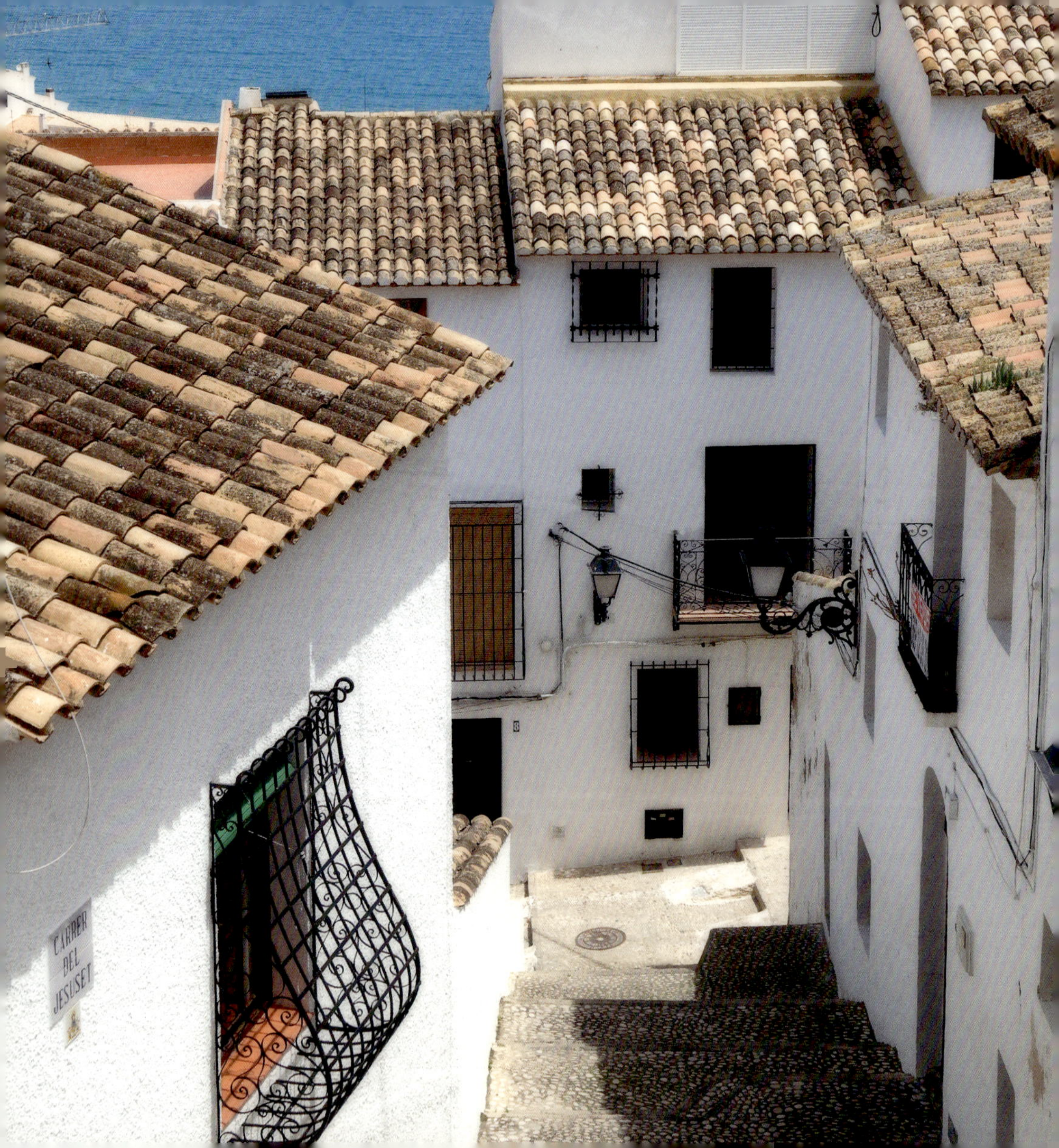
CARRER
DEL
JESUSET

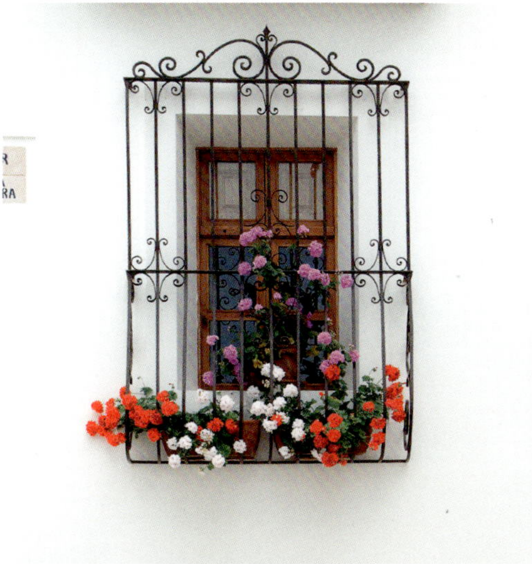

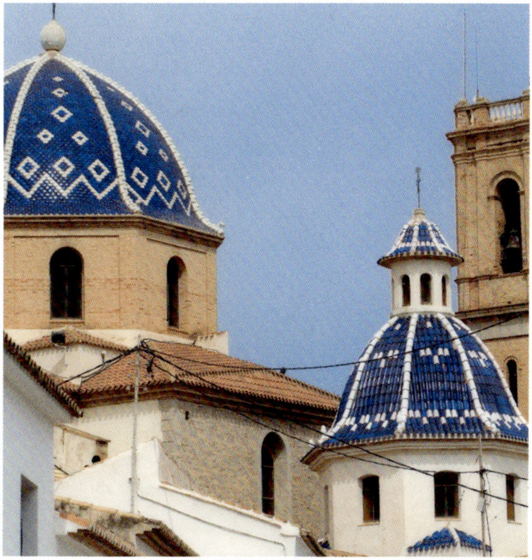

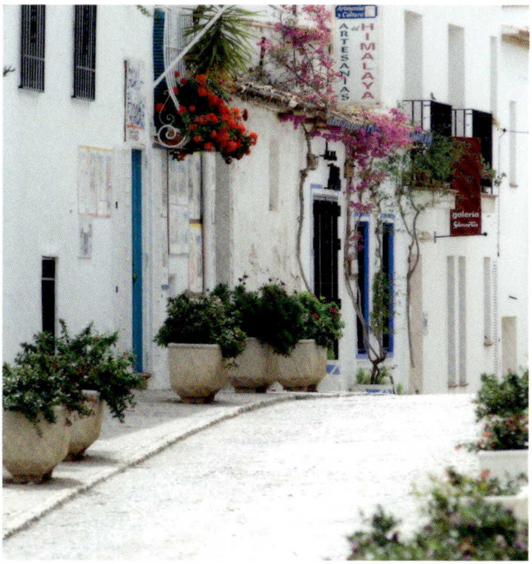
ARTESANIAS
HIMALAYA
galeria

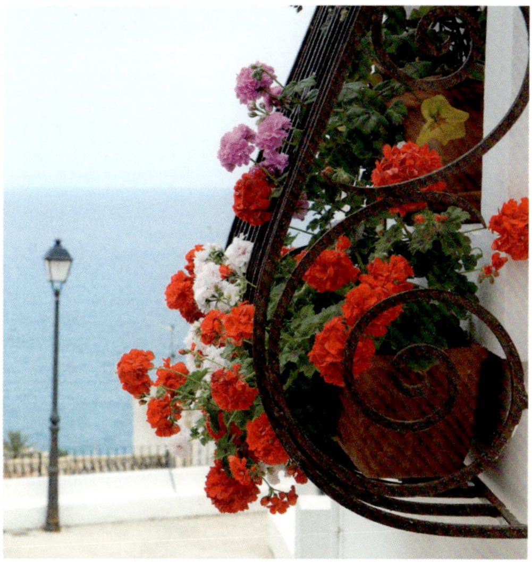

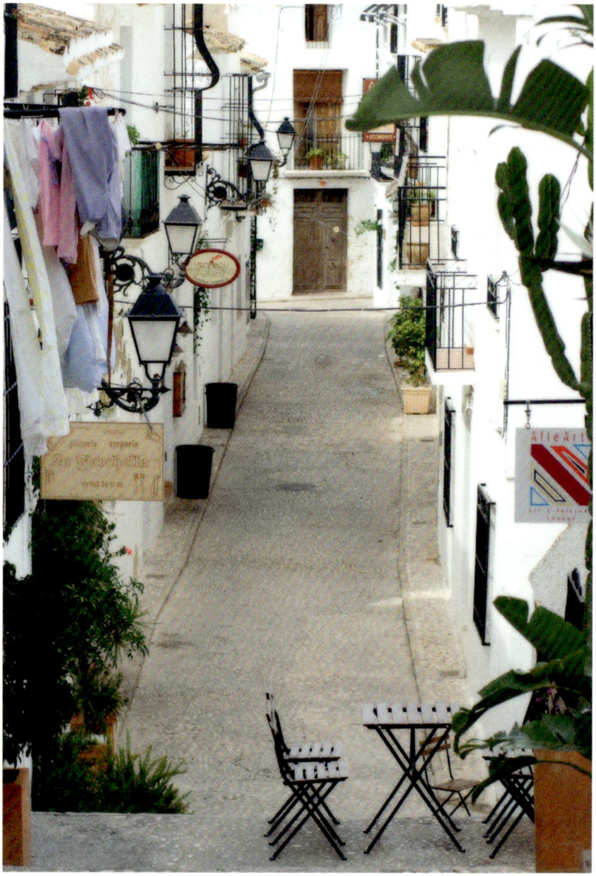

Church of the Virgen del Consuelo. In the background, the Peñón de Ifach →

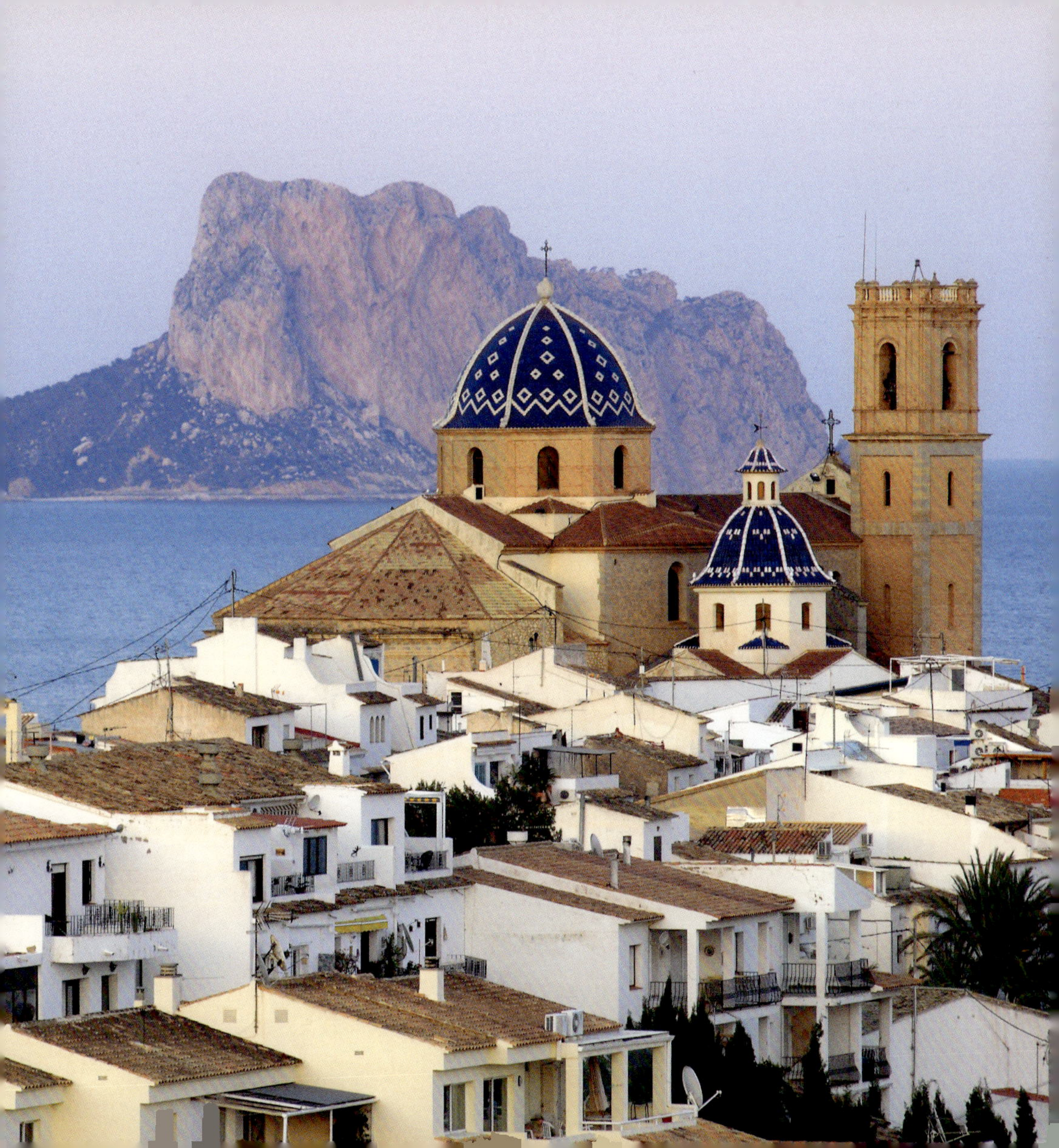

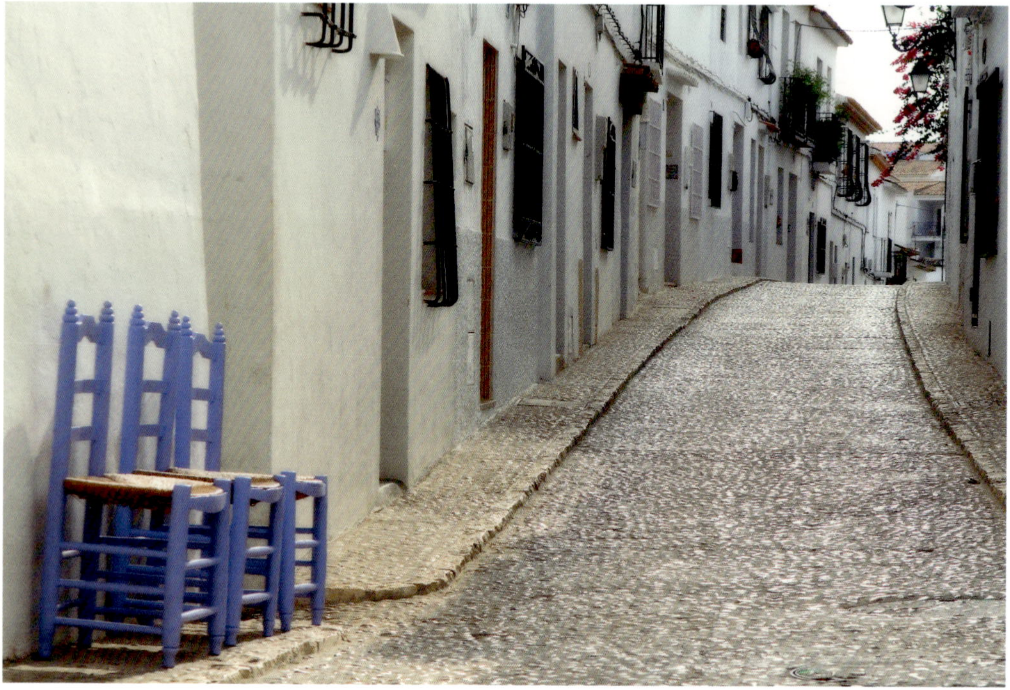

Typical cobbled streets of Altea

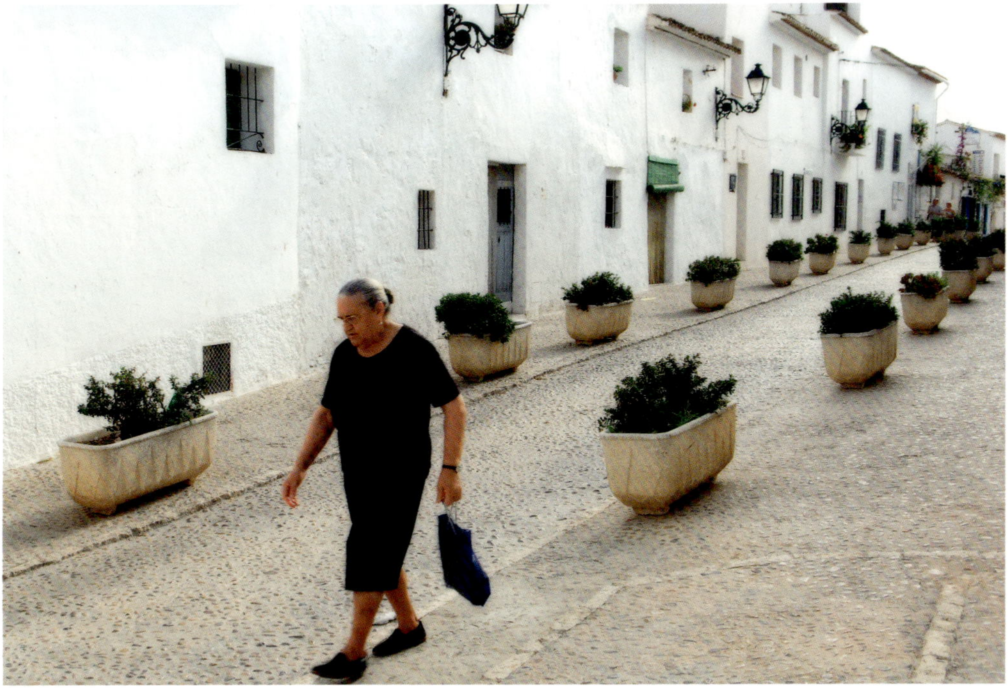

The old part features whitewashed façades

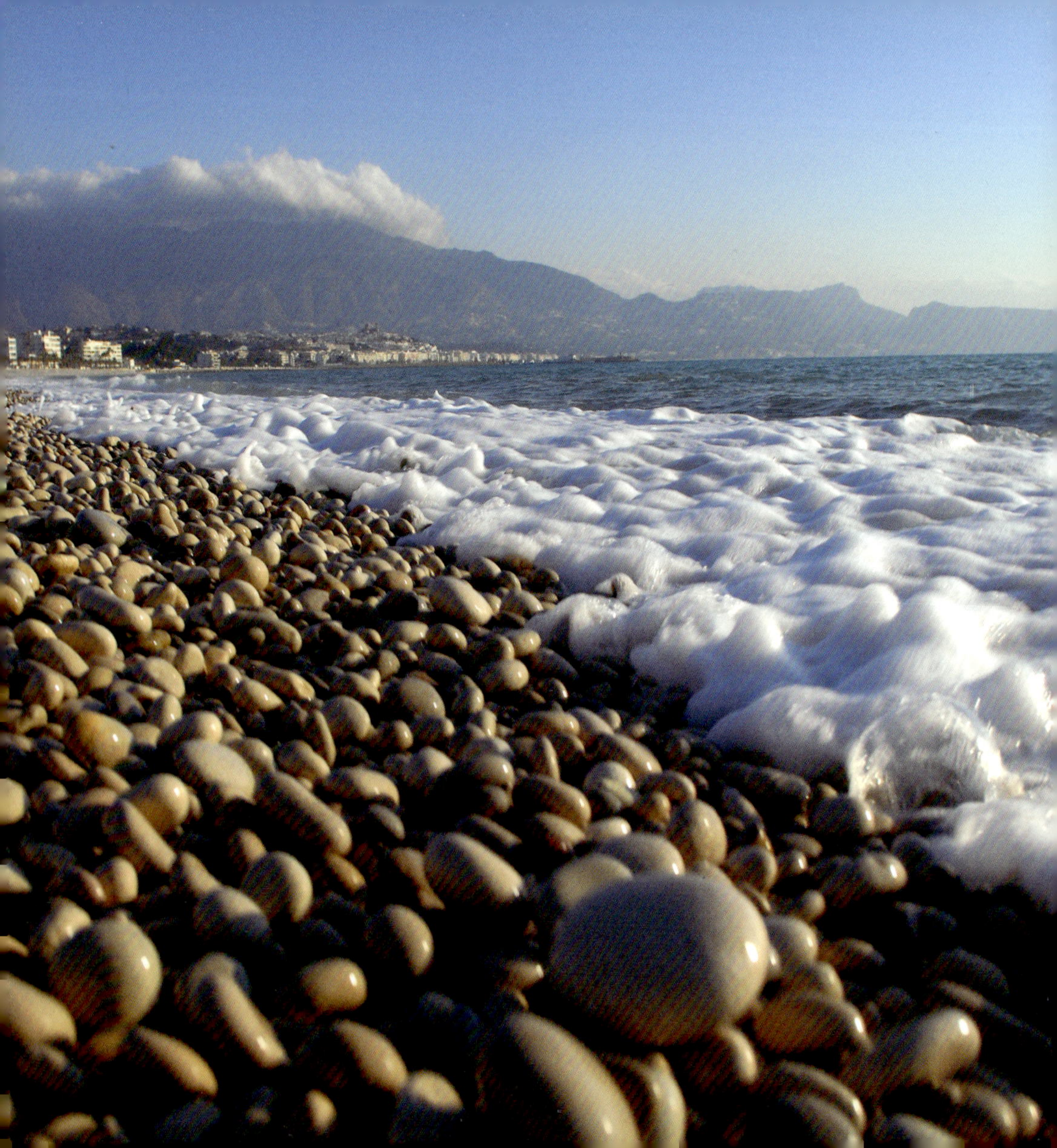

L'Alfàs del Pi

Hardly three kilometres separate the town of L'Alfàs del Pi from its most famous beach, the Albir. It is a beach of perfectly rounded stones and crystalline water, and its position at the foot of the Serra Gelada makes it perfect for starting the walks through the natural space. The pleasant walk to the lighthouse has the reward of the impressive views along the coast of the Marina Baja. The Paseo de las Estrellas, next to the beach, has engraved the names of those honoured in the International Film Festival that is held every July. In L'Alfàs del Pi is the Enrique Mendoza bodega, producer of some of the best wines in the Valencia Community.

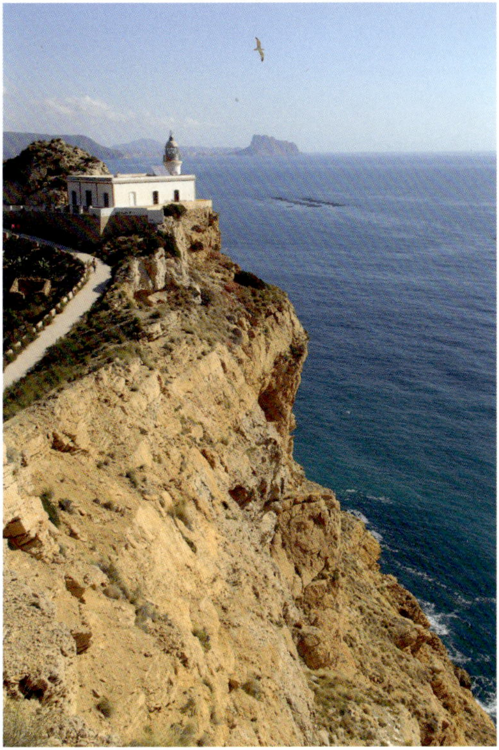

L'Albir beach

L'Albir lighthouse on the Serra Gelada ↗

Serra Gelada

Serra Gelada has been a Natural park since 2005. A succession of cliffs, some of them more than 400 metres high, act as a natural barrier between the bays of Altea and Benidorm. The different routes around the park, well signposted, are a good opportunity to be in contact with and discover Mediterranean nature. There are very simple routes, for all publics, such as that which leads to the Lighthouse of L'Albir; and other more demanding ones that go along the different mountain crests, walking among white pine trees, without losing sight of a sea so crystalline that you can even make out the marine meadows of posidonia seagrass. They say that the range gets its name from the reflections that the moon produces on the limestone cliffs and which makes them look like ice.

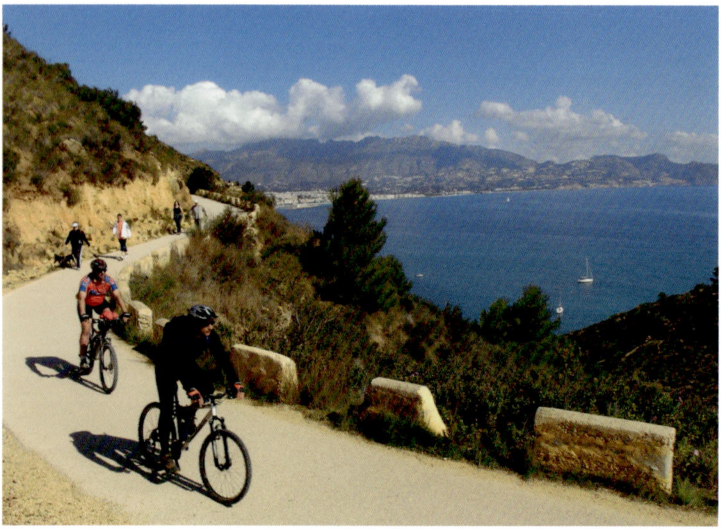

Natural Park of the Serra Gelada

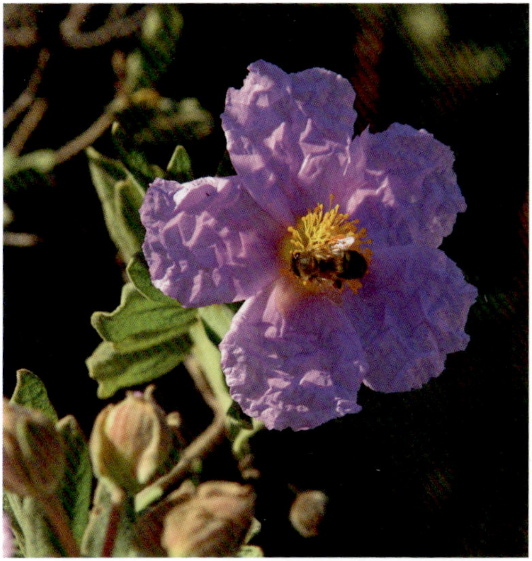
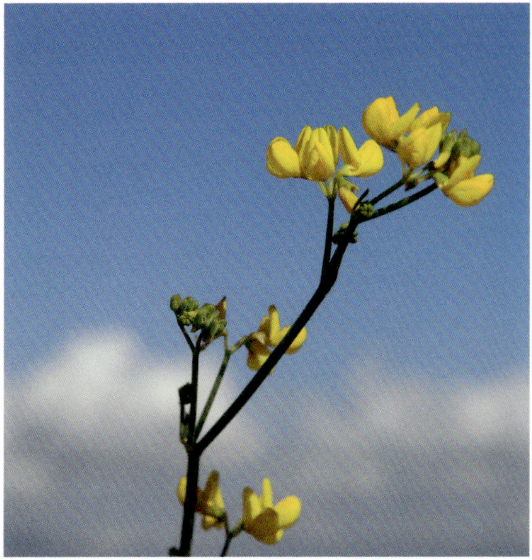
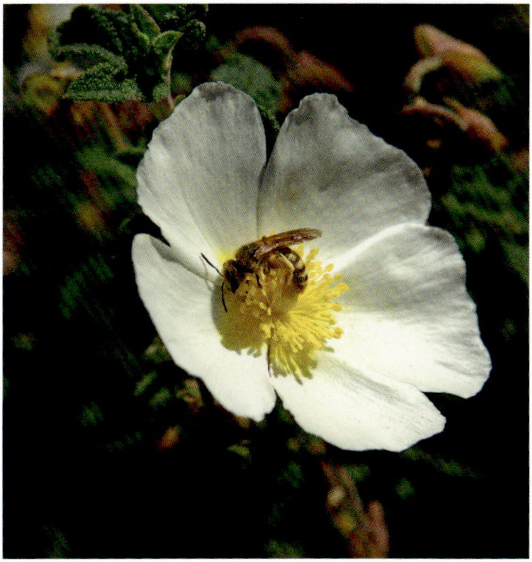
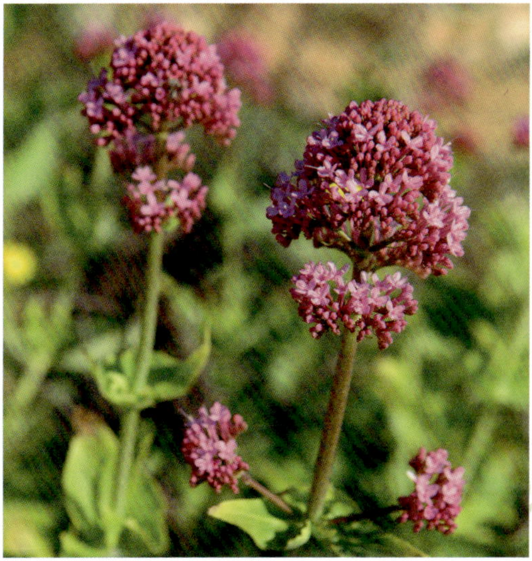

Benidorm

It was in 1953 when a visionary mayor, Pedro Zaragoza, faced the dictator Franco to explain to him his idea of converting the Benidorm of boats and orchards into a combination of sun and sand that would arouse the desire of the rest of Europe. With his insistence going from fair to fair selling bottled sun, he turned a small town into a kind of Babel in bikini. Little remains of that small village, but Pedro Zaragoza showed the appropriateness of a model of tourism and urban planning that is still valid today. On building upwards, the magnificent natural spaces that surround Benidorm, such as Serra Gelada, were saved.

Benidorm was the resort, the first tourist promoter of the province. Making the most of its particular microclimate, it continues offering a very particular tourist model, but which functions throughout the year. The beach of Levante is among the best urban beaches in the world. The other major beach of Benidorm, that of Poniente, was renovated with the construction of the new Seafront Esplanade, the work of the architects Carlos Ferrater and Xavier Martí. From all the sandy area there are views of another stone icon, next to the Peñón de Ifach, of the Costa Blanca: the island of Benidorm, also known as the island of the Journalists.

The city has been able to adapt to the new times and complement the leisure offer with parks such as Mundomar or Terra Mítica and top-quality hotels such as the Barceló Asia Gardens.

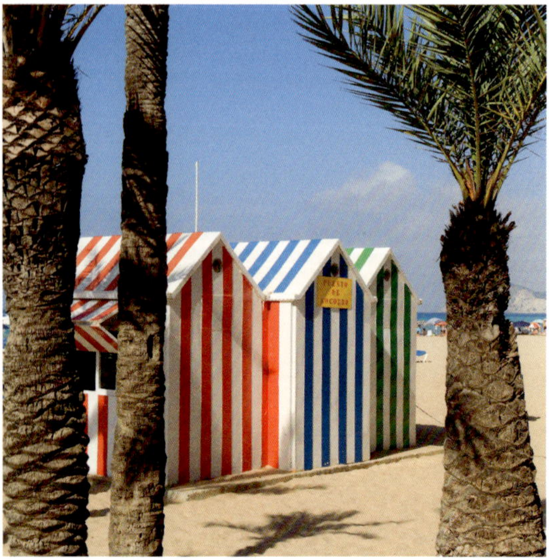

Levante Beach

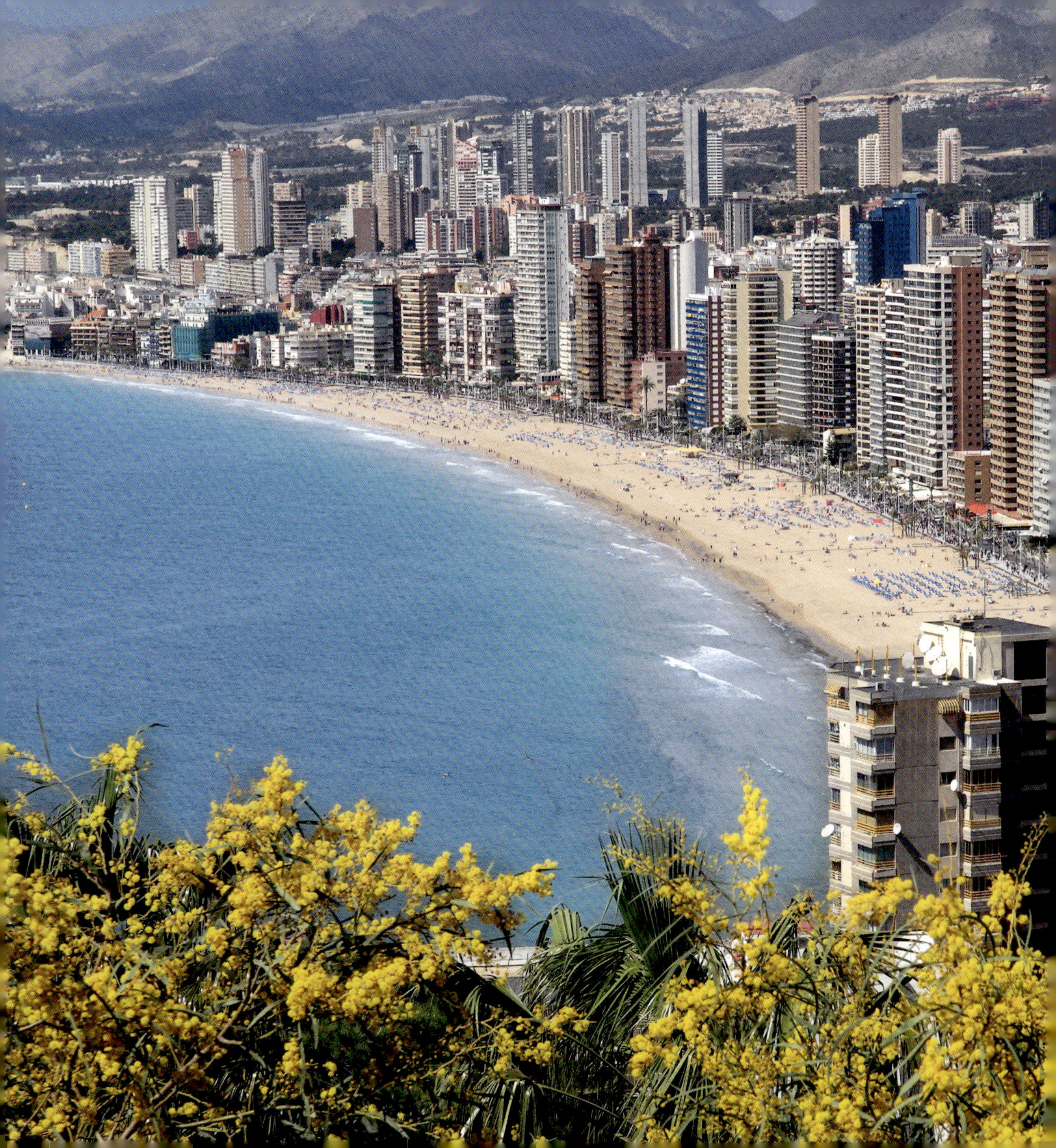

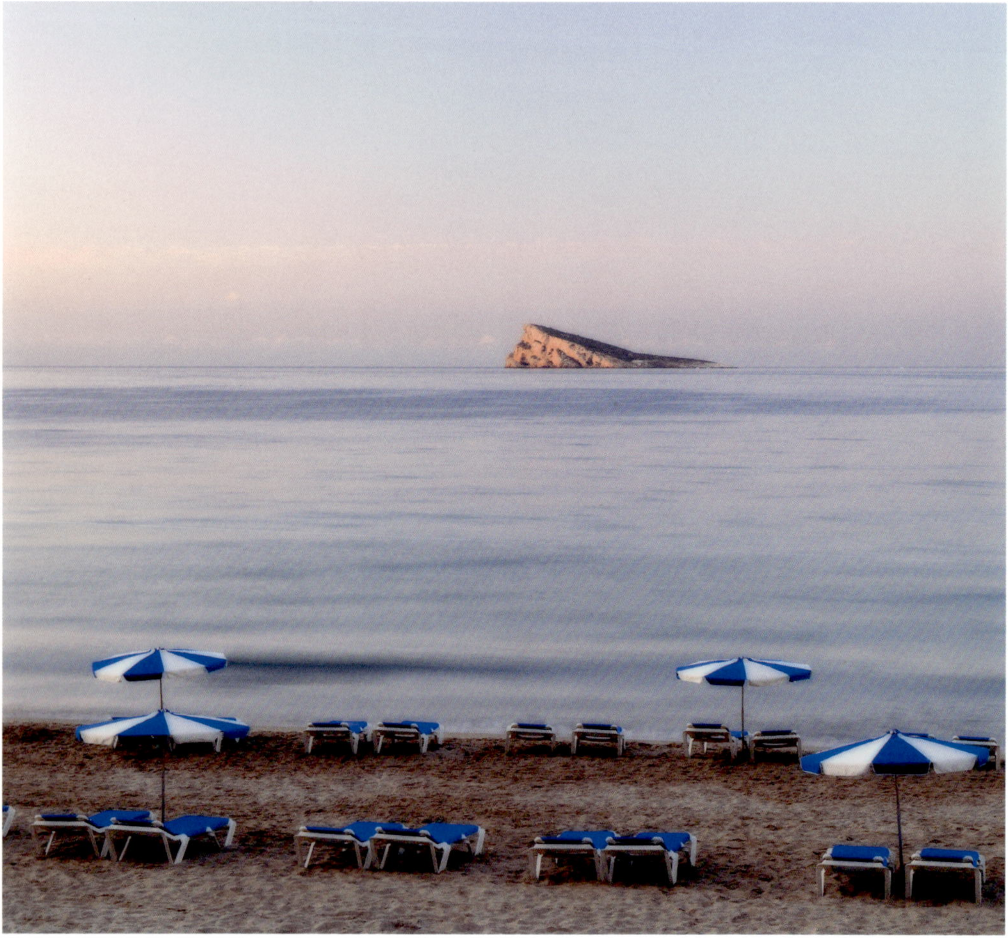

Island of Benidorm. Poniente Beach

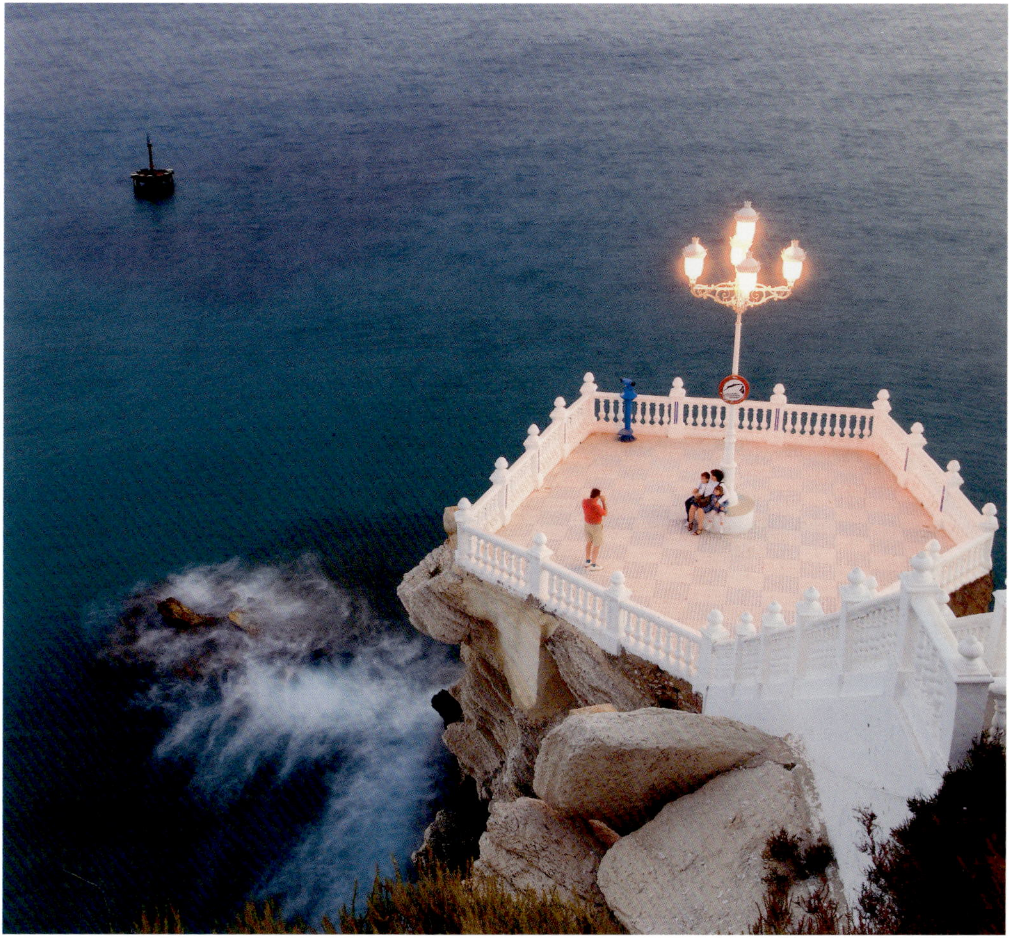

Castle

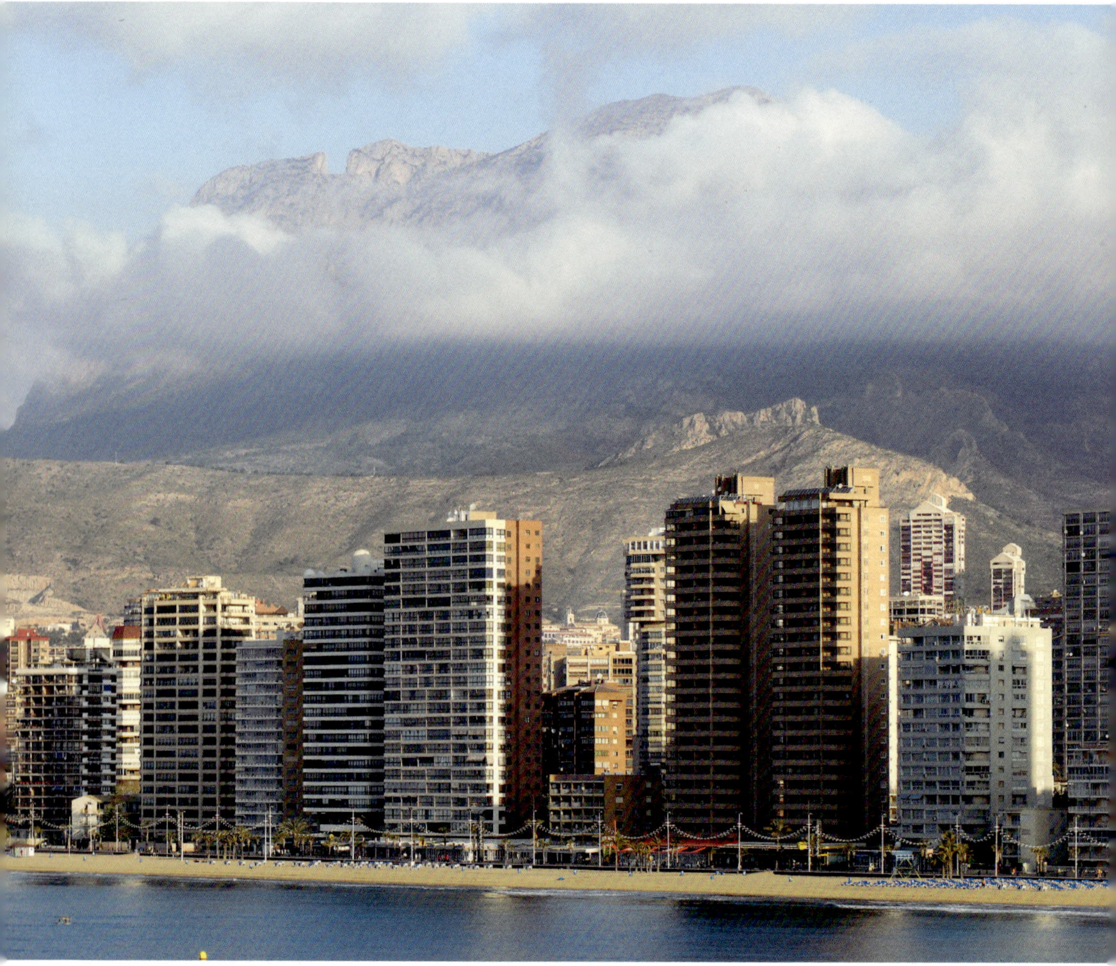

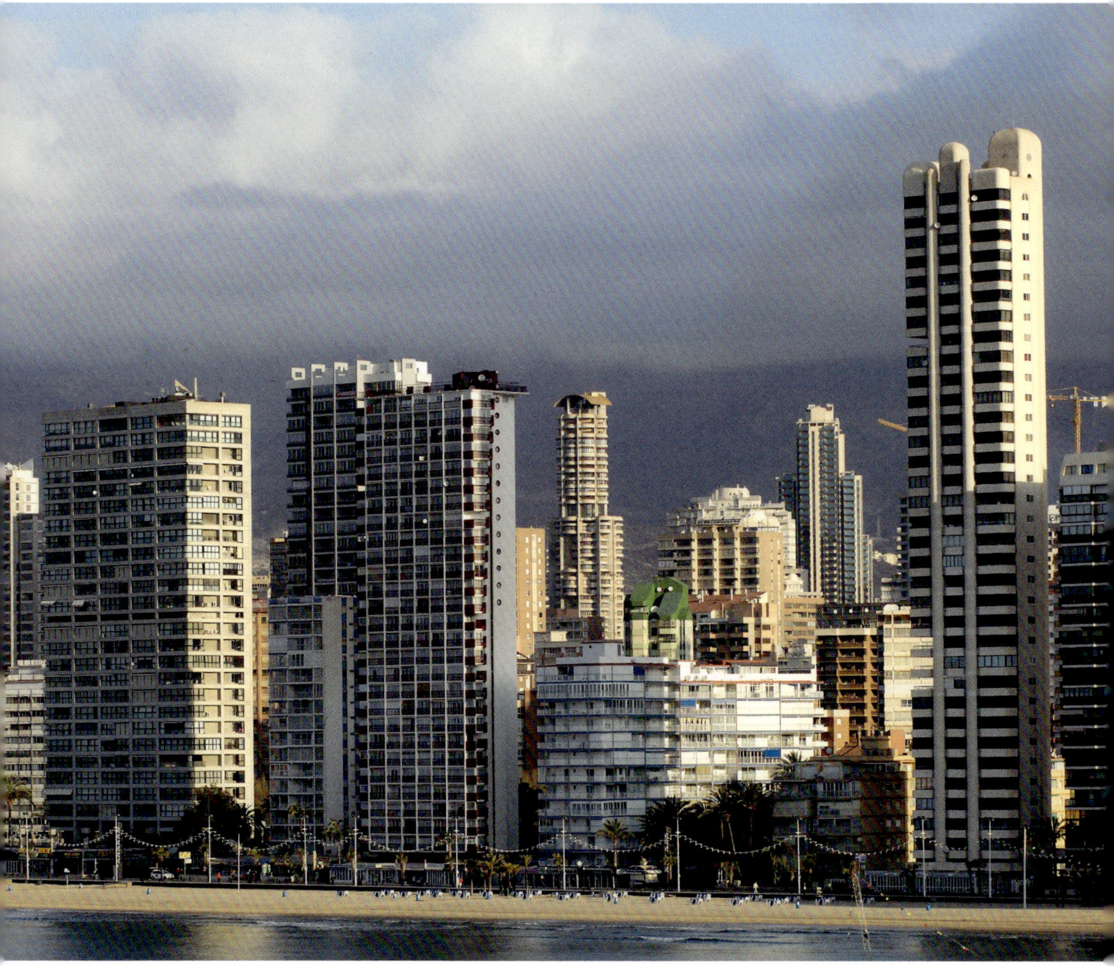

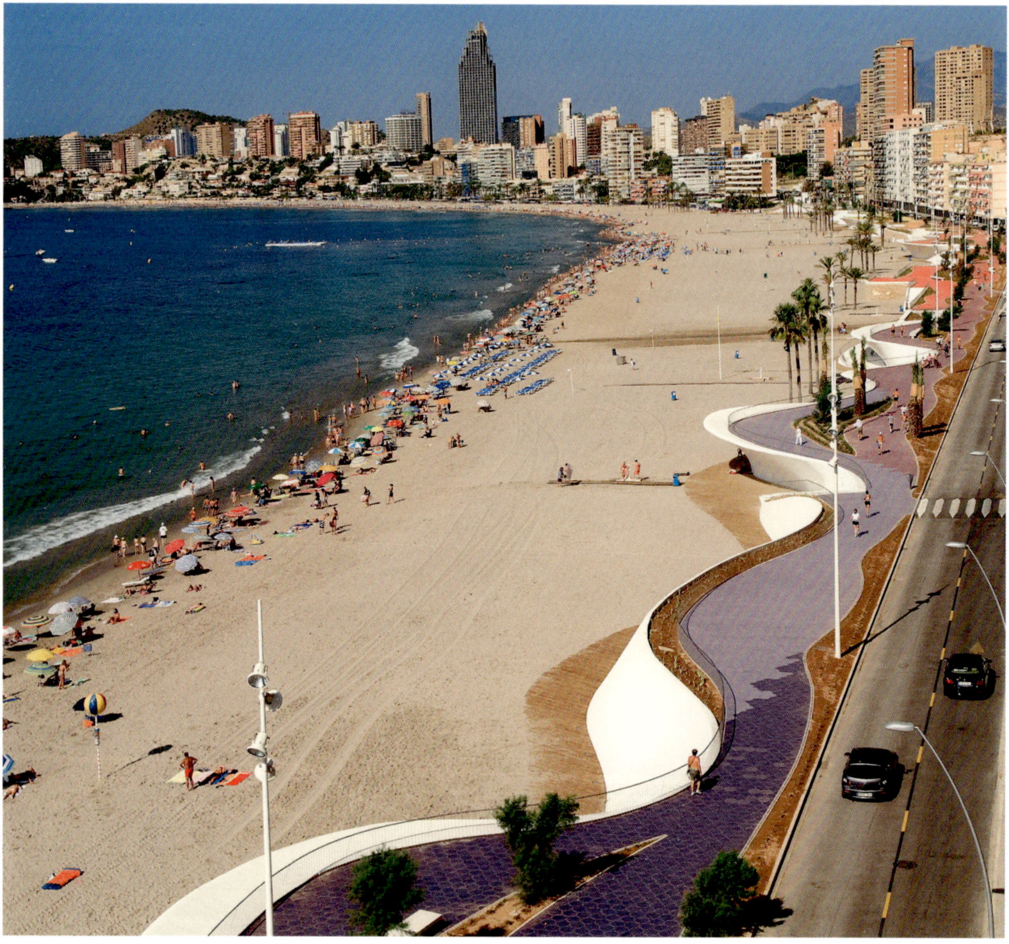

Poniente beach and the new Paseo Marítimo seafront

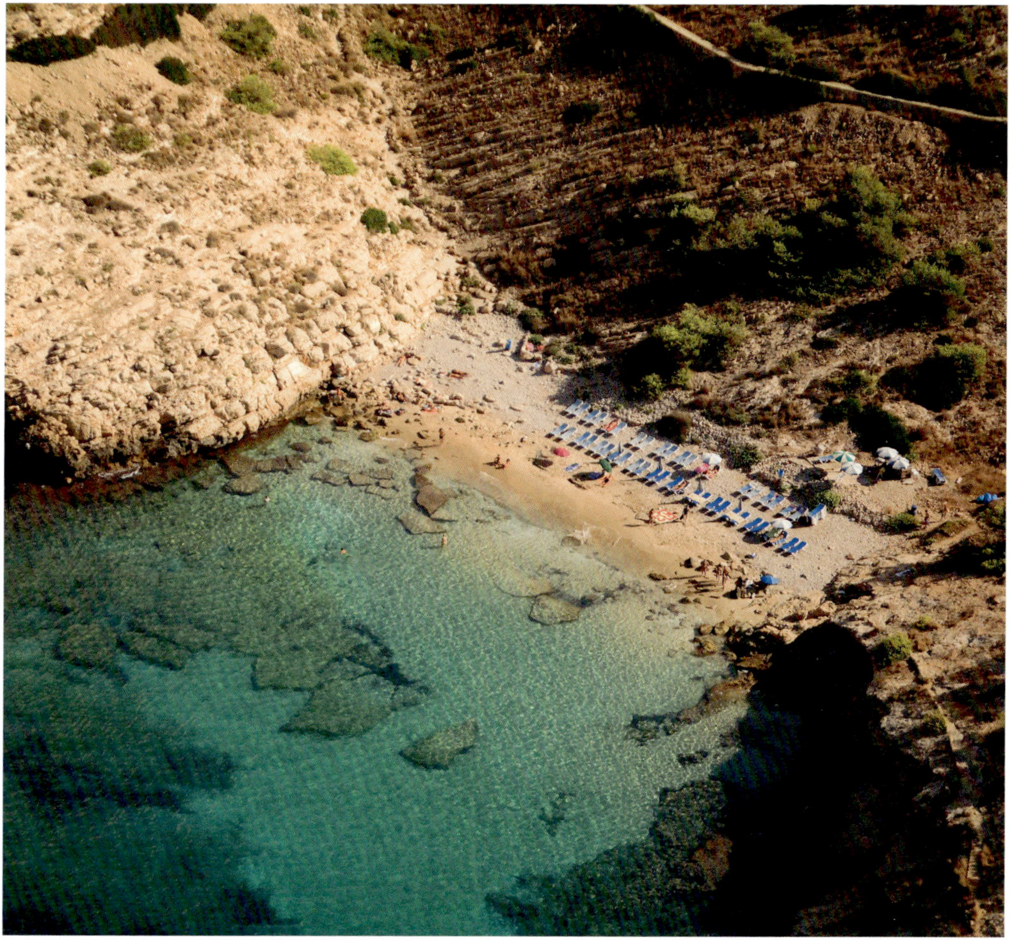

Cala Tio Ximo

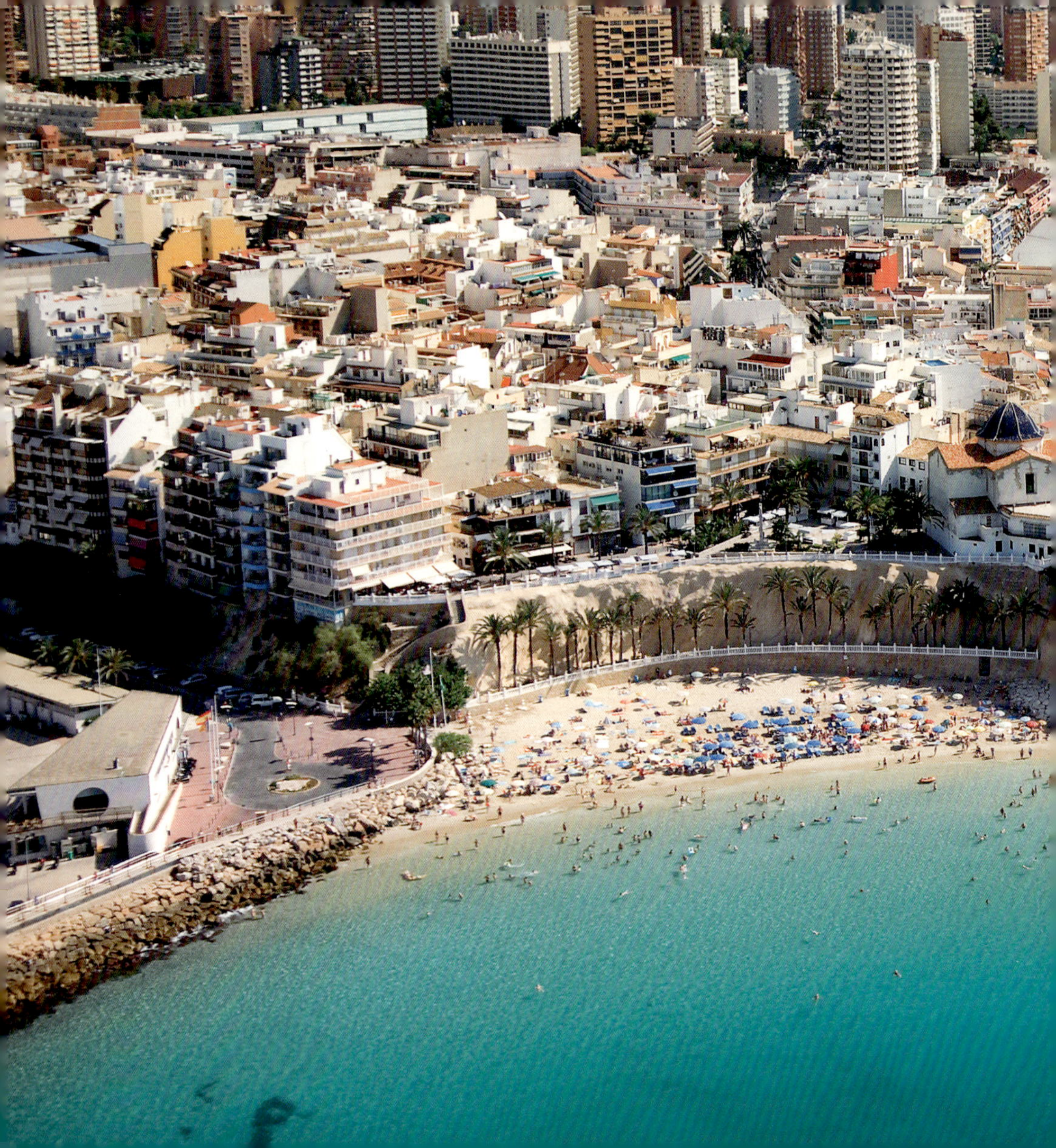

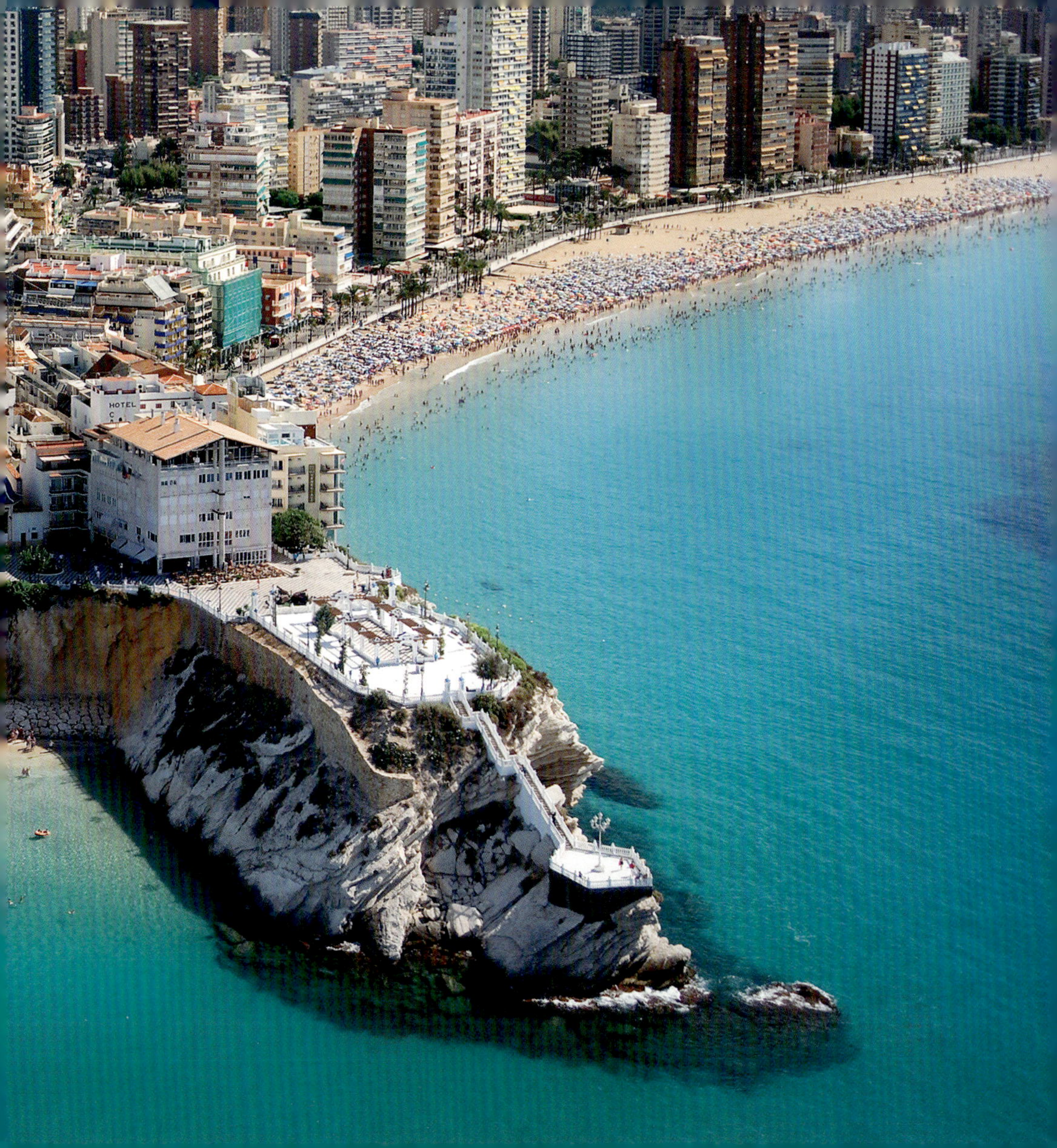
HOTEL

La Vila Joiosa / Villajoyosa

The maritime façade of the capital of the Marina Baja gives a note of colour to the coastline of the Costa Blanca. They say that the fishermen painted their houses in colours in order to recognise them when they returned home after working at sea. Parallel to the fishing activity, the chocolate industry was developed, of which the Valor brand is its leading representative. In the Valor factory you can visit an interesting museum dedicated to chocolate, and discover details about its production, the advertising produced throughout history and curiosities about the product. However, if Villajoyosa is known for something it is for the festivals of Moors and Christians. The mediation of Saint Martha in an attack by Berber pirates resulted in the celebrations in her honour. The parades of the respective *filaes* of Moors and Christians, on the 25th and 26th of July, come before the key moment of the festival: the Disembarkation, which takes place in the early hours of the 28th of July. The Moorish boats arrive at the coast and take over the castle. In the afternoon, the break in negotiations ends with the victory of the Christian troops who return the Moors to the sea.

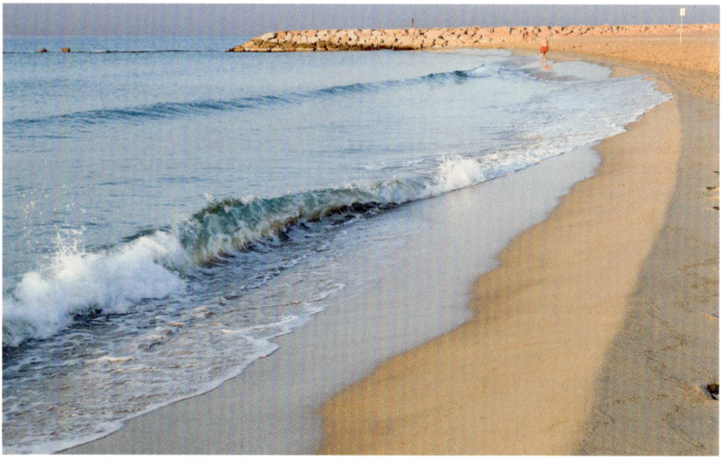

Colourful houses in the old city →

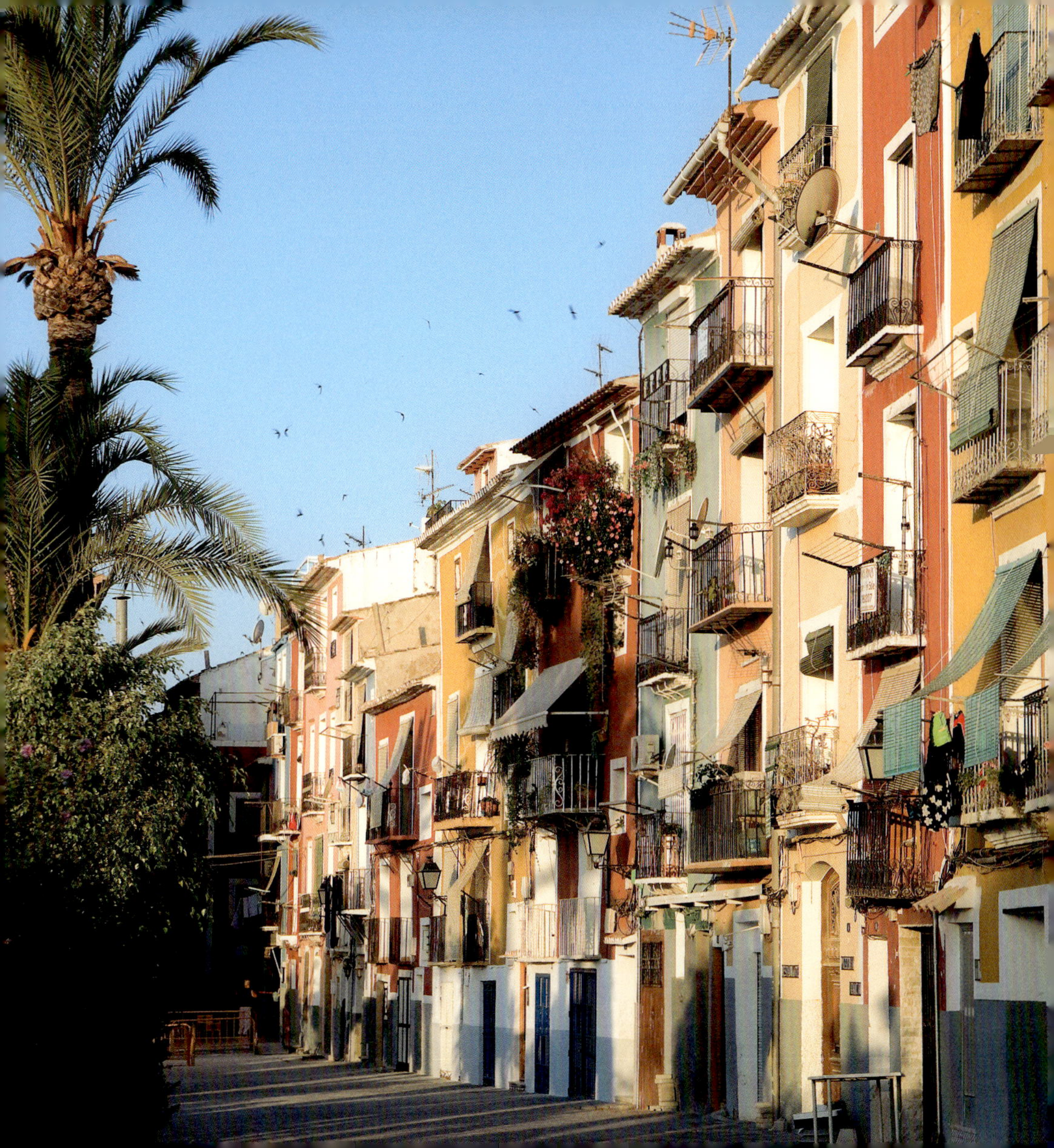

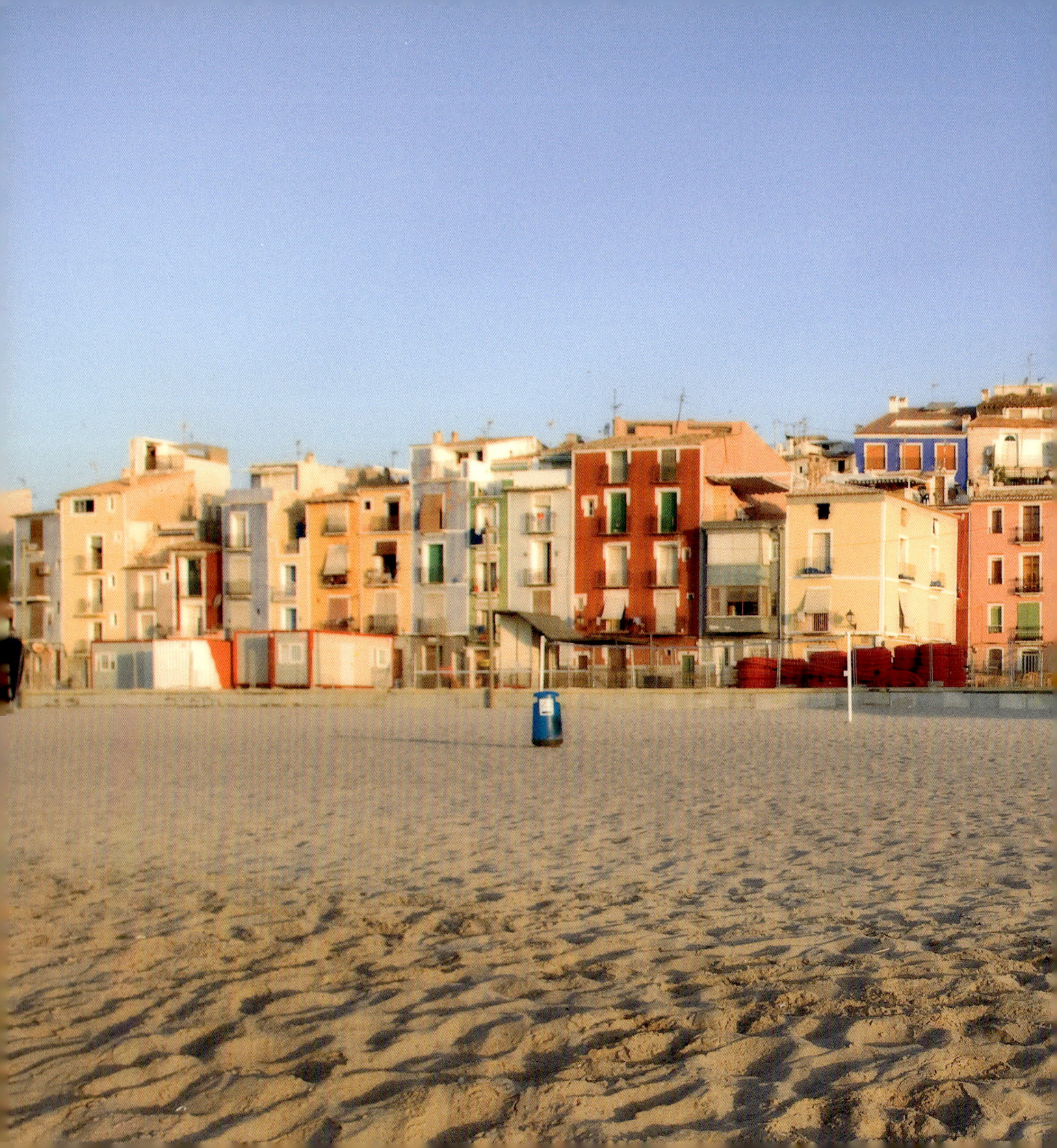

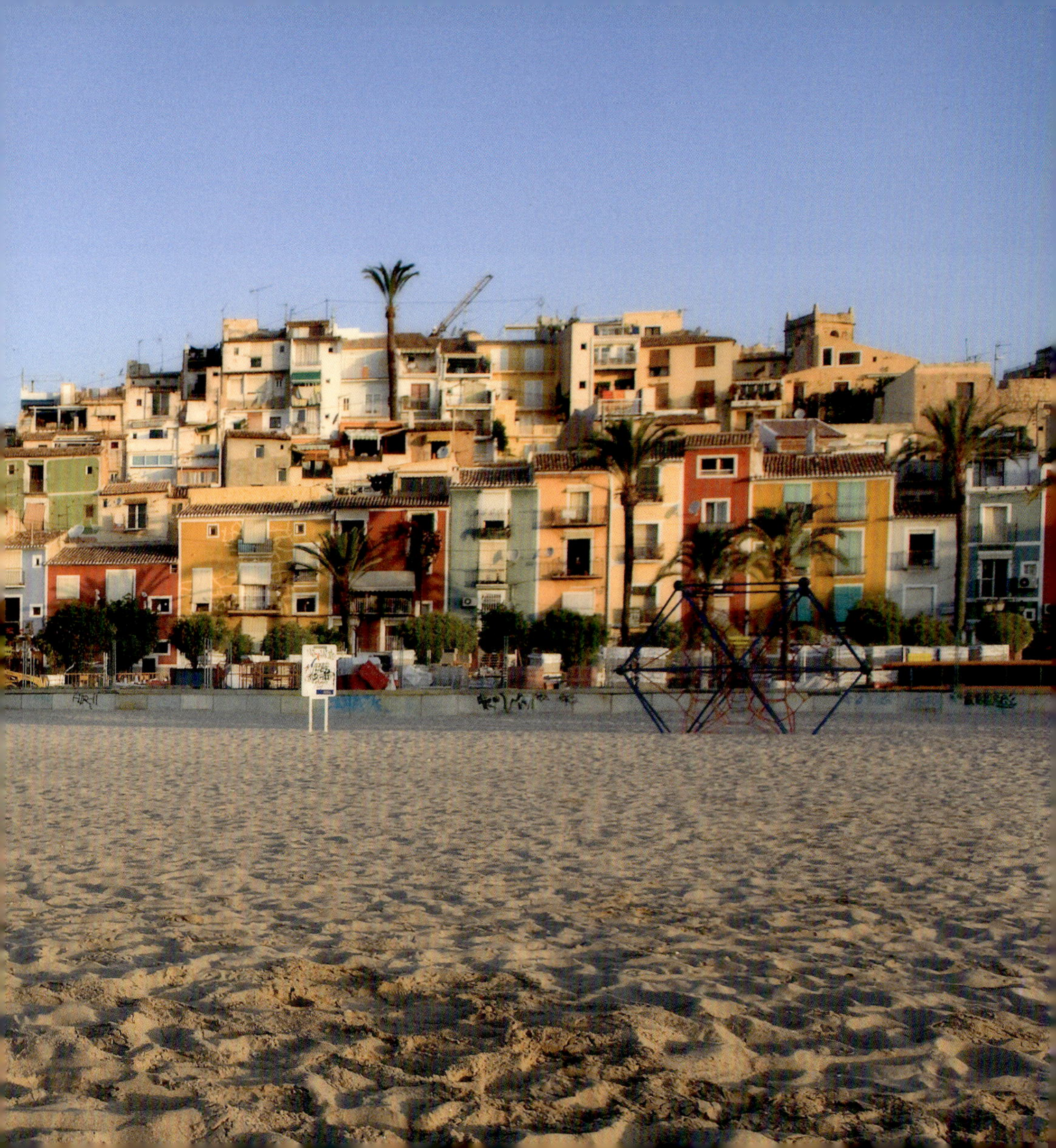

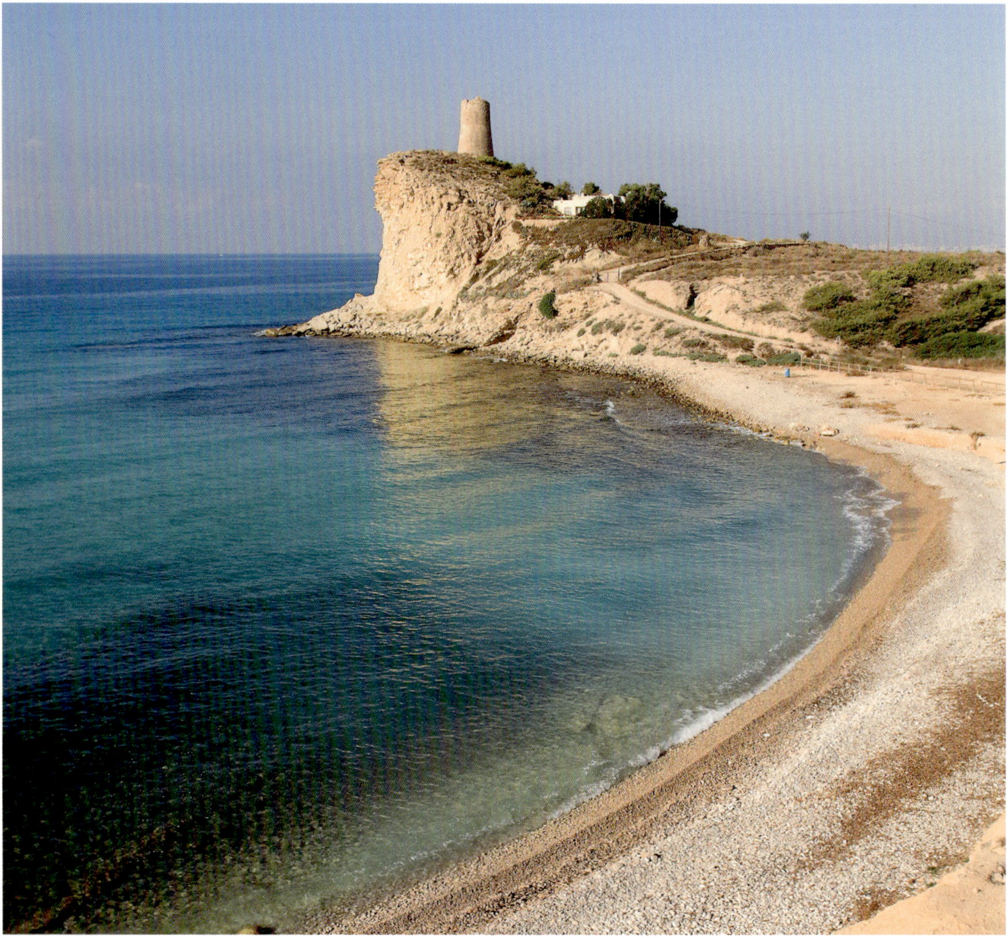

Cala del Xarco

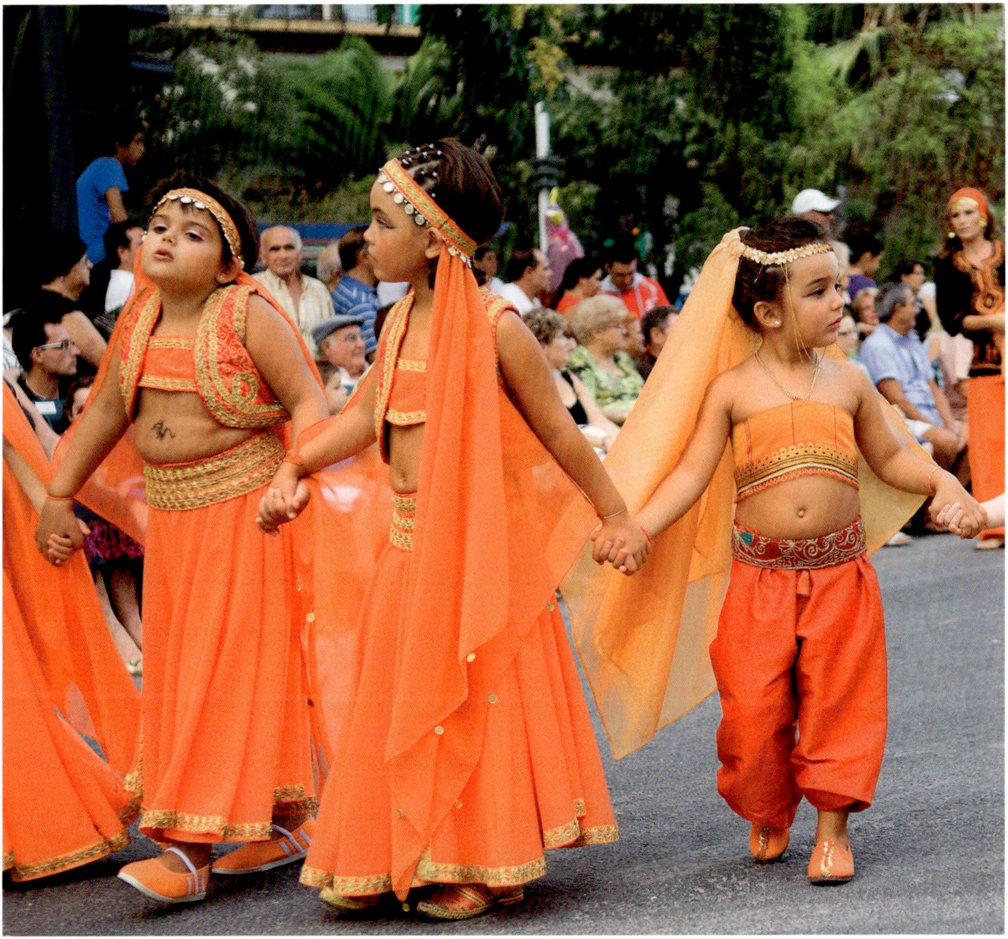

Festivals of Moors and Christians

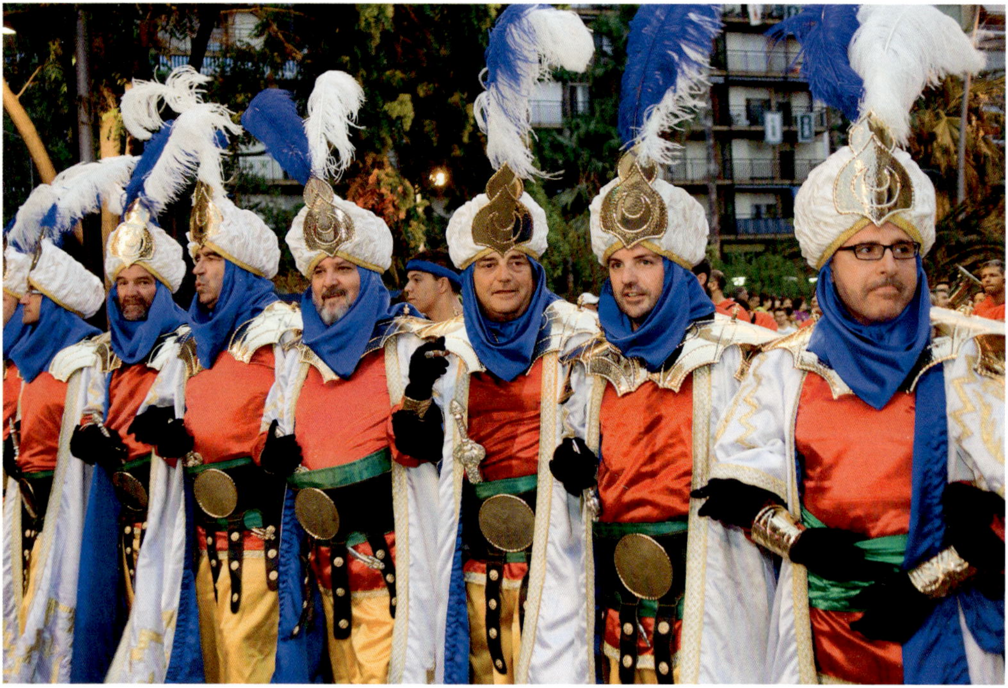

"Filaes" of Moors

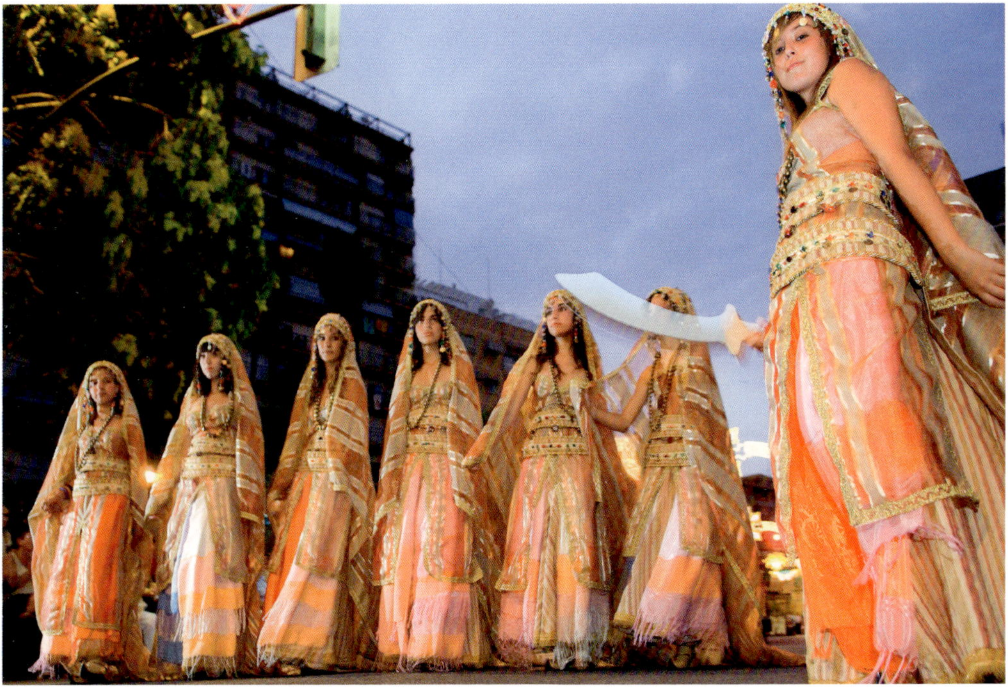

The Disembarkation →

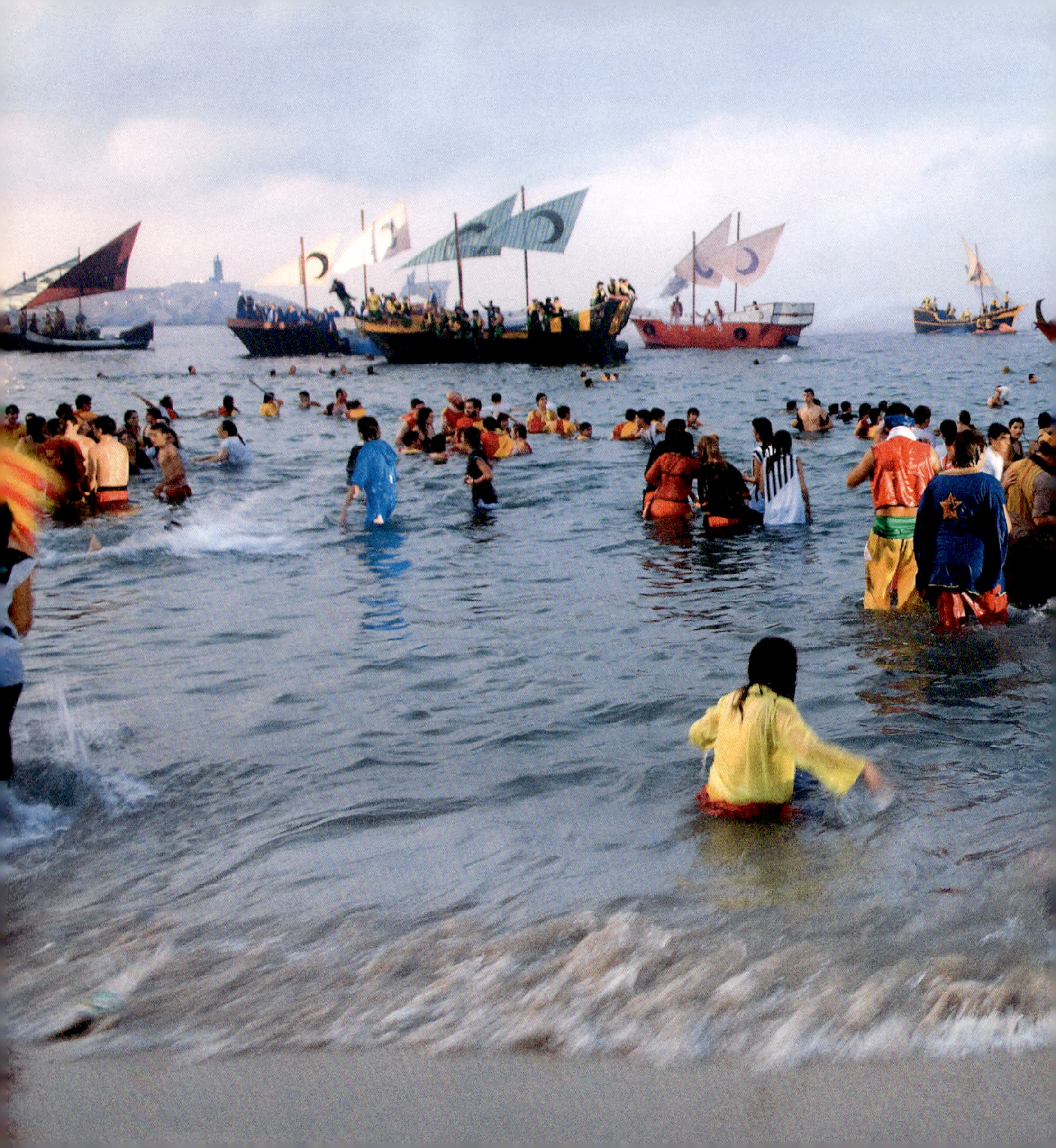

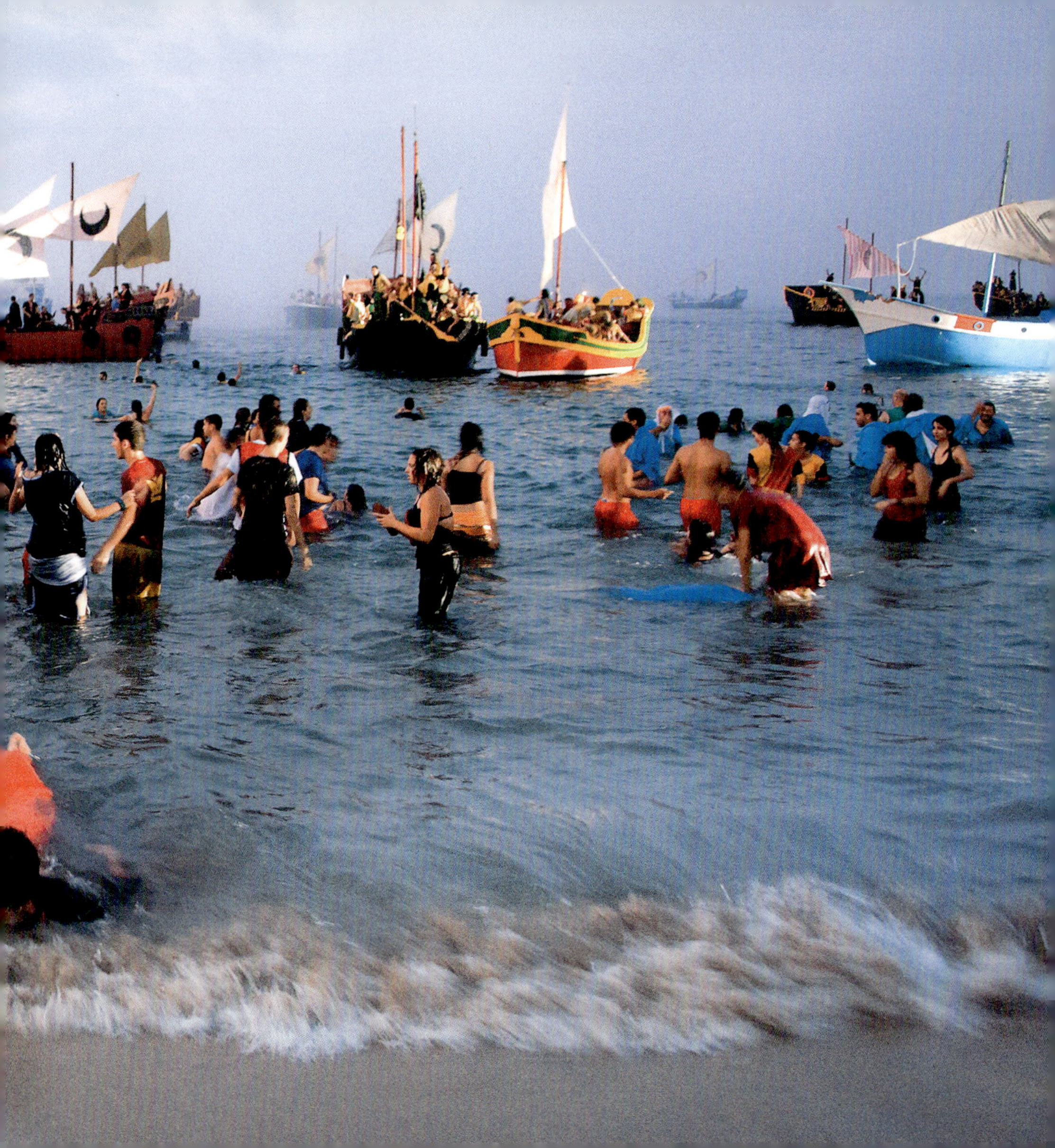

The Castle of Guadalest

Surrounded by the Aitana, Serrella and Xortà ranges, the Castle of Guadalest stands on a small hill. The castle of San José and the fortress of the Alcozaiba, from the 11th century and of Muslim origin, form, together with the reservoir, one of the most singular aspects of the county. The only entrance to the town is through a cavity in the rock over which it rests. The construction of the reservoir of Guadalest, to collect the water from the river of the same name, was completed in 1971 and changed the physiognomy of the landscape completely. The home inhabited by one of the wealthiest families in the history of the town, that of the Orduña, today houses the interesting Municipal Museum.

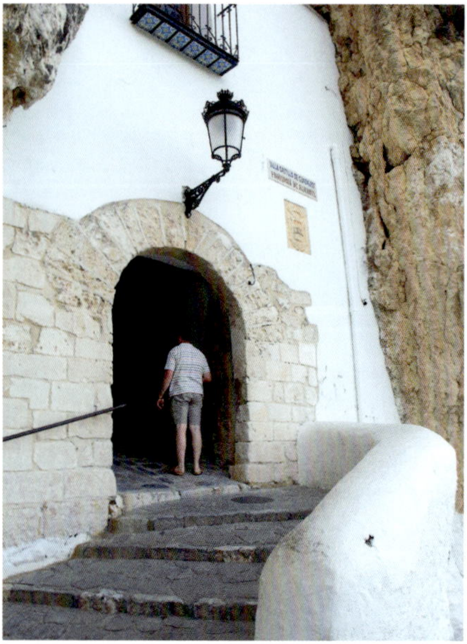

Entrance to the town

The Castle of San José and the fortress of Alcozaiba

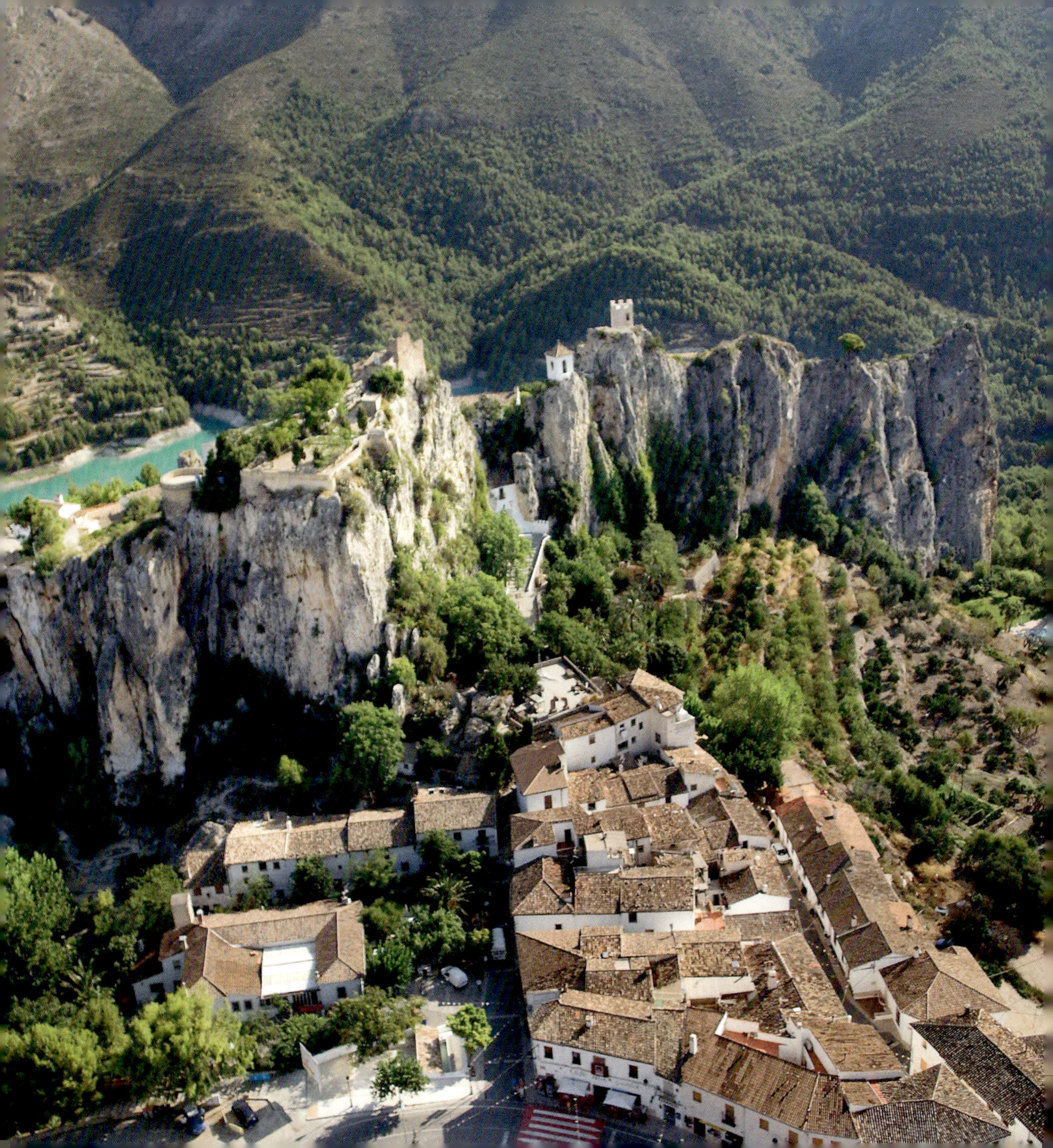

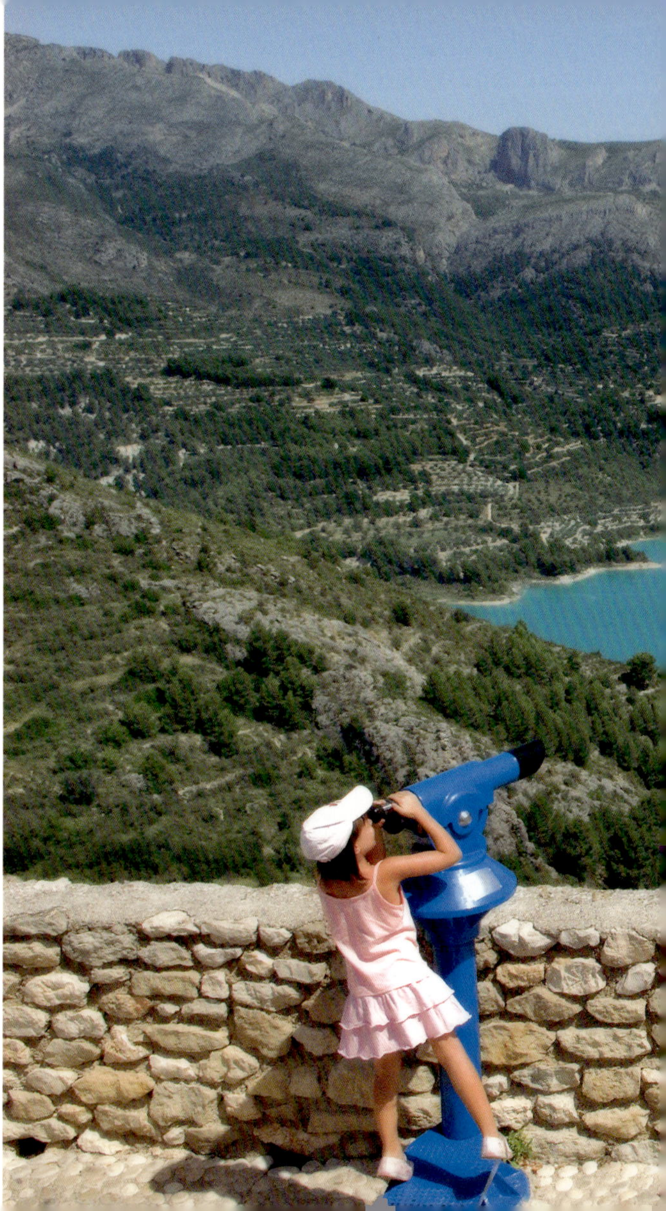

View of the Guadalest reservoir

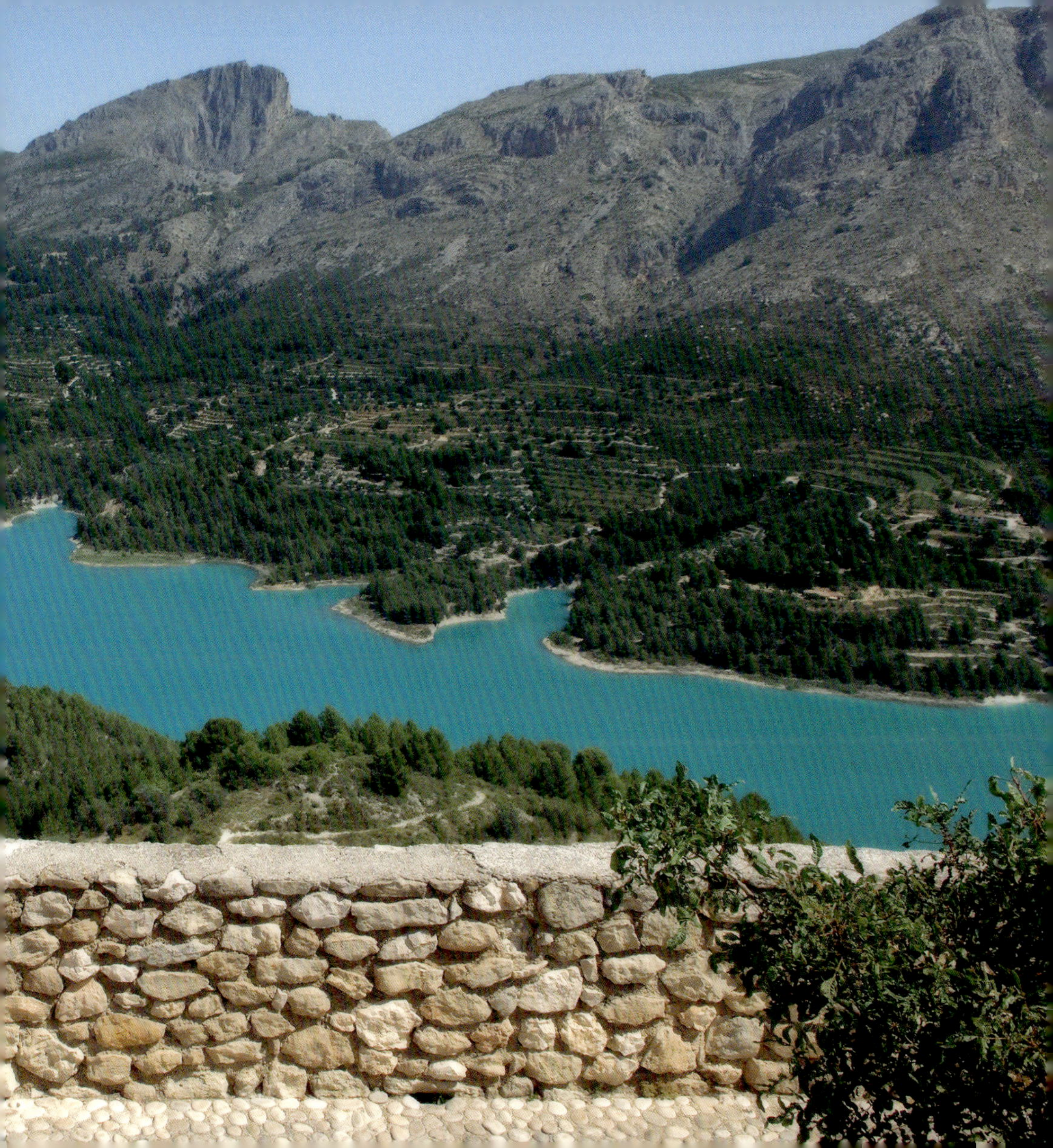

Inland. Mountain Villages

Towards the interior of the Marina Baja the orography becomes abrupt, the landscape gradually climbs to craggy peaks, the highest of the province. The Aitana range, that of Bernia and Puig Campana are the lookouts, the watchtowers, of a province accustomed that the fame of its water does not let its mountains be seen. At their feet are the villages of brick and clay, with strong-handed settlers used to battling with the land. As examples of the rural architecture of the county we have the villages of Polop, which has one of the most beautiful aspects of the Alicante interior: Callosa d´en Sarrià, famous for its medlars and for the springs of the Algar; Beniardà, at the foot of the Reservoir of Guadalest; Relleu or Tàrbena. The mountainous landscape offers adventure sports lovers quite a few options: climbing in Sella, canyoning in Bolulla and walking to the peaks from where everything looks tiny. The legend tells that the Frenchman Roland was responsible for the fissure of Puig Campana, with his sword Durandal, a characteristic trait of this mountain visible from a large part of the county. At the foot of Puig Campana is Finestrat, which paddles in a charming cove that takes the name of the village.

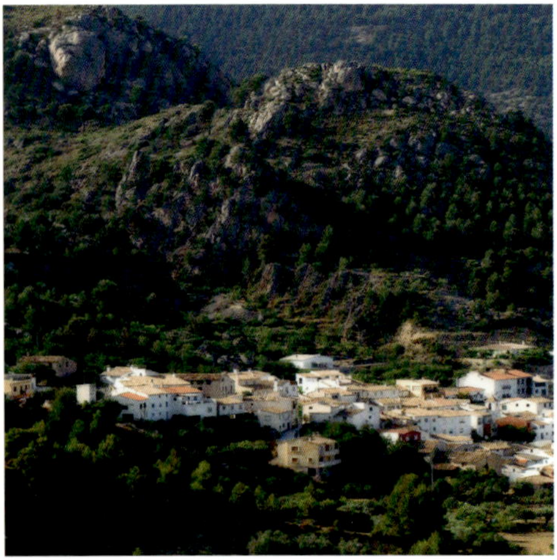

L'Abdet

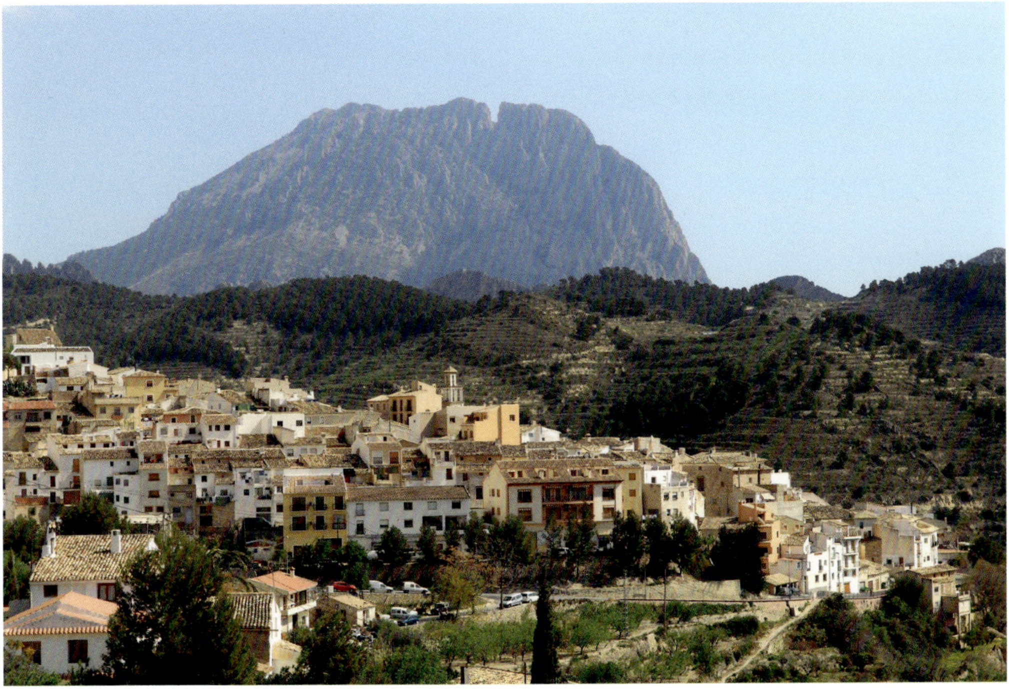

Sella. In the background, the Puig Campana
Polop de la Mariana →

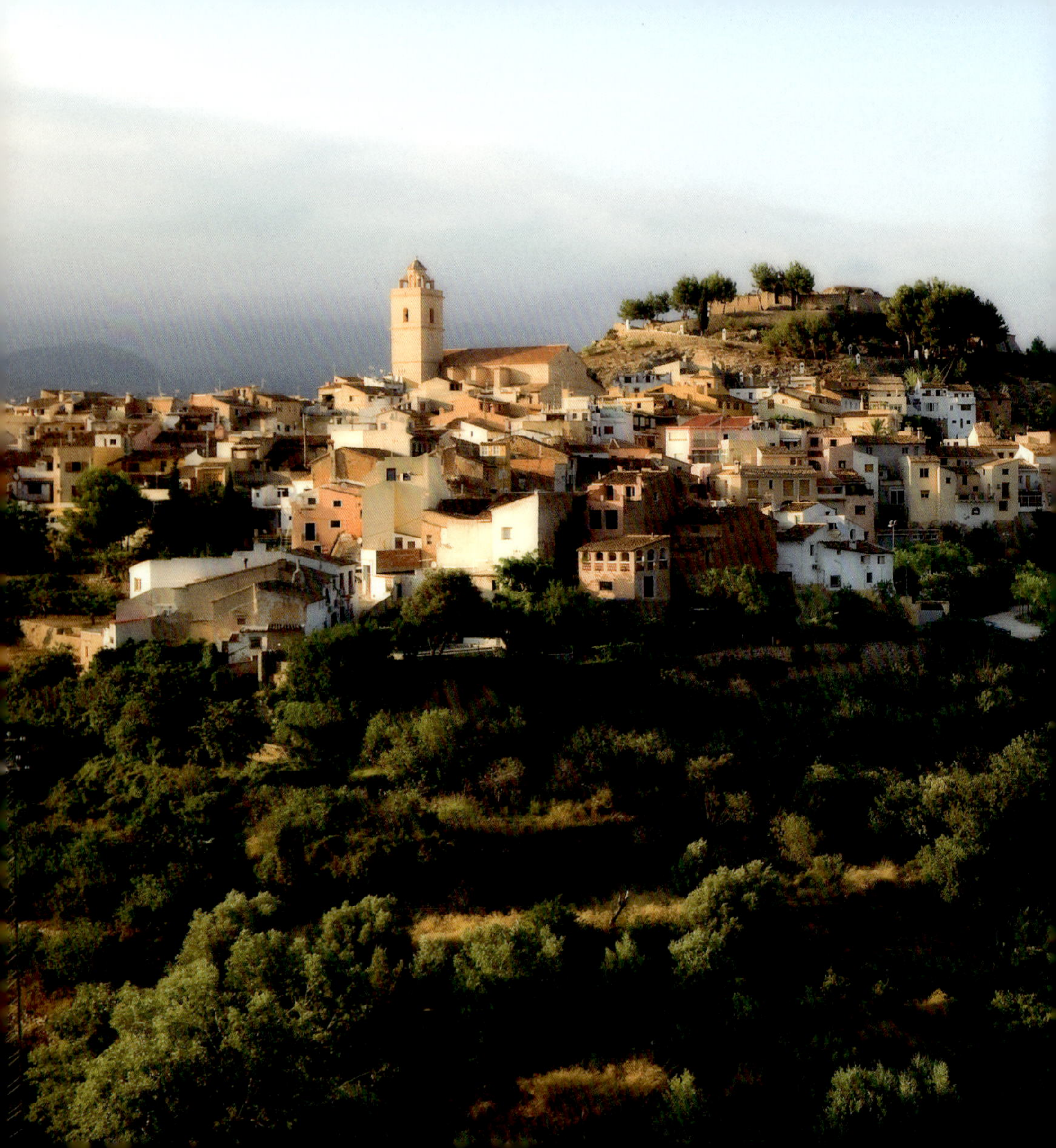

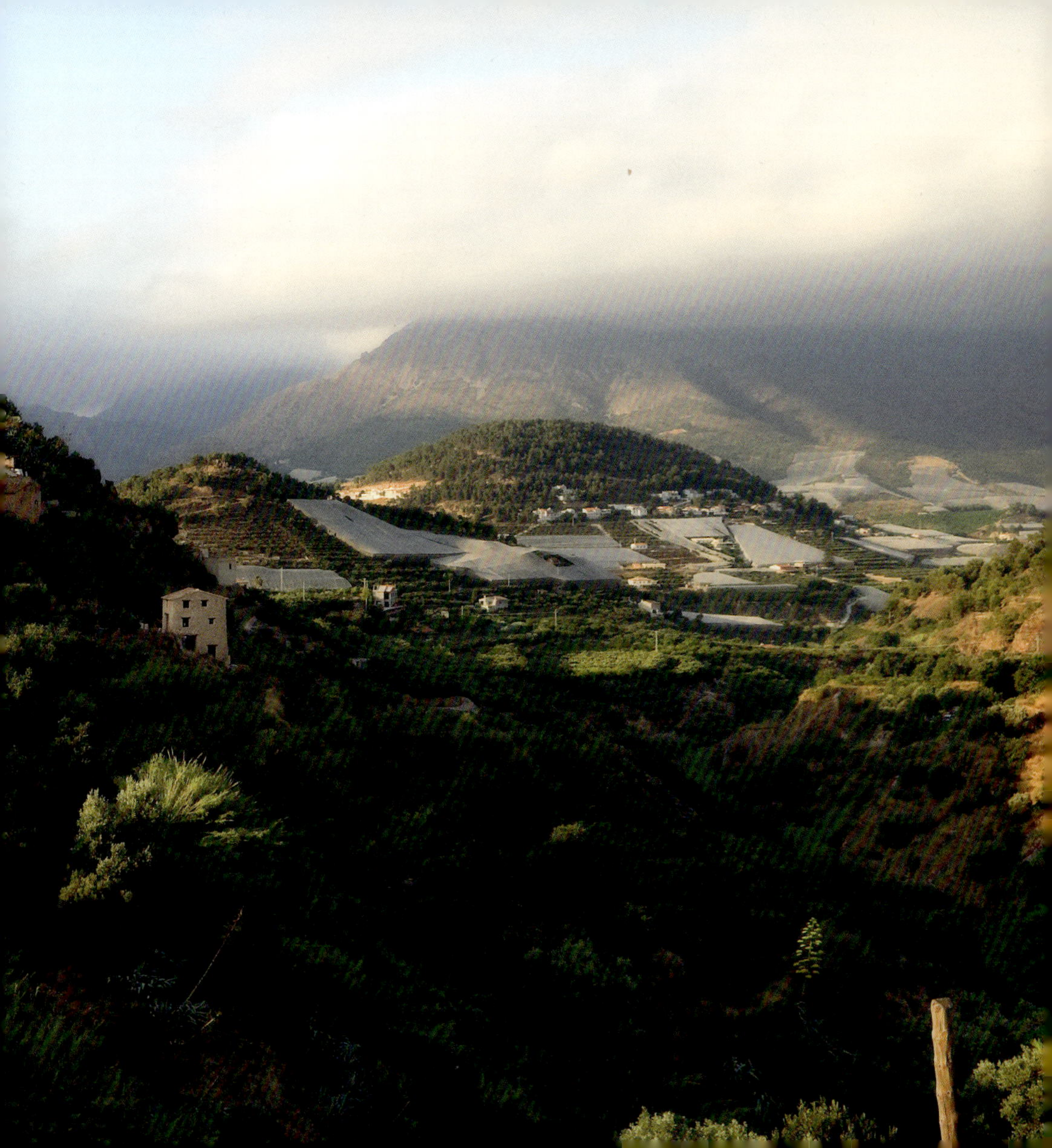

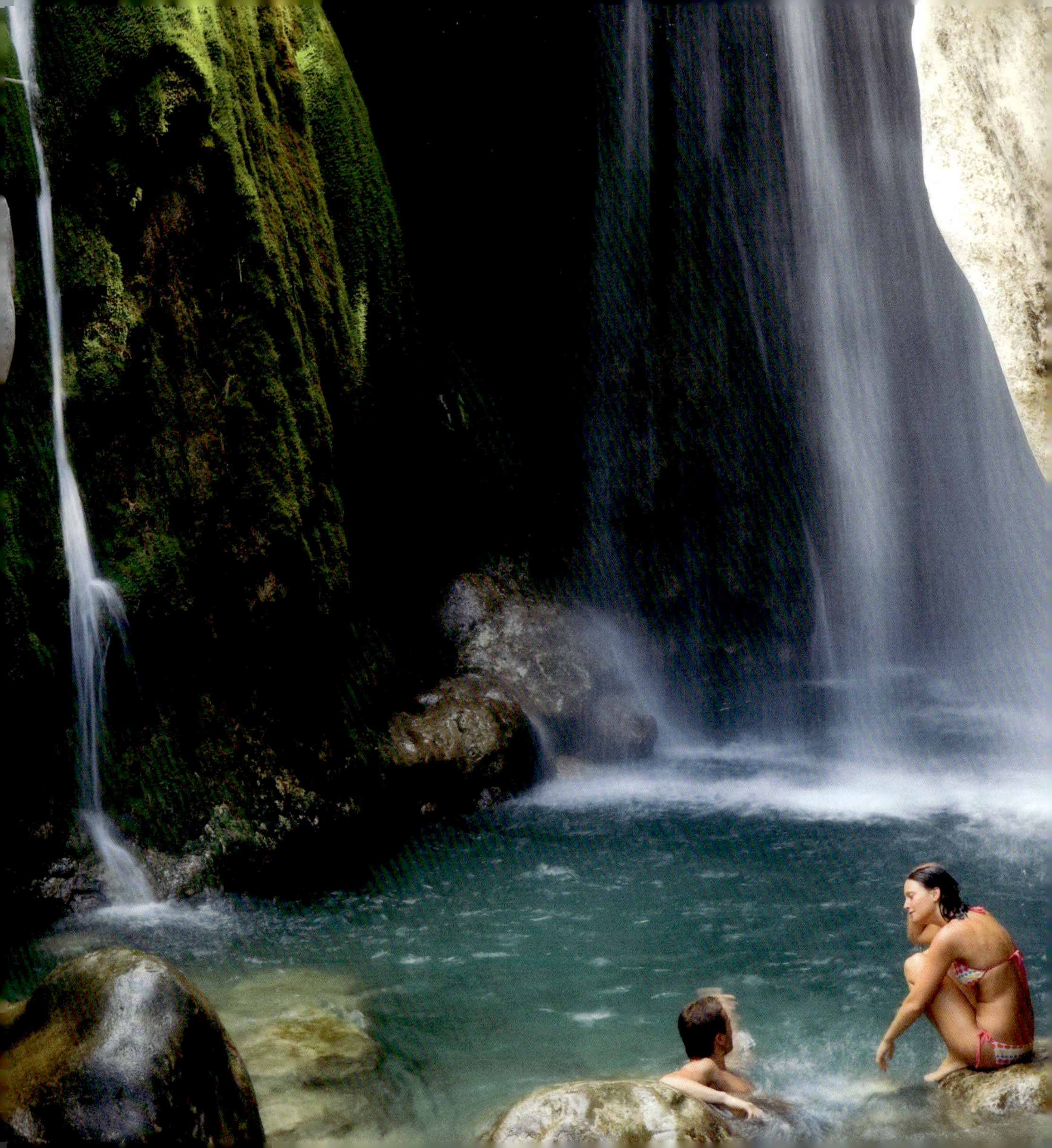

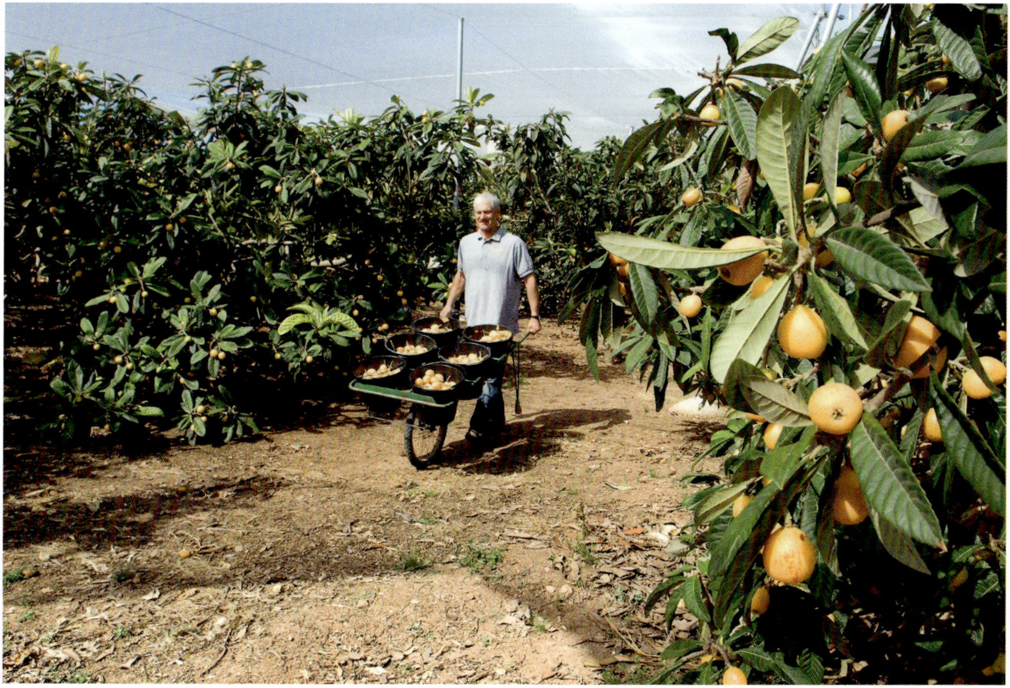

Callosa d'en Sarrià, collecting medlars
← *Fuentes de L'Algar*
Sierra Aitana →

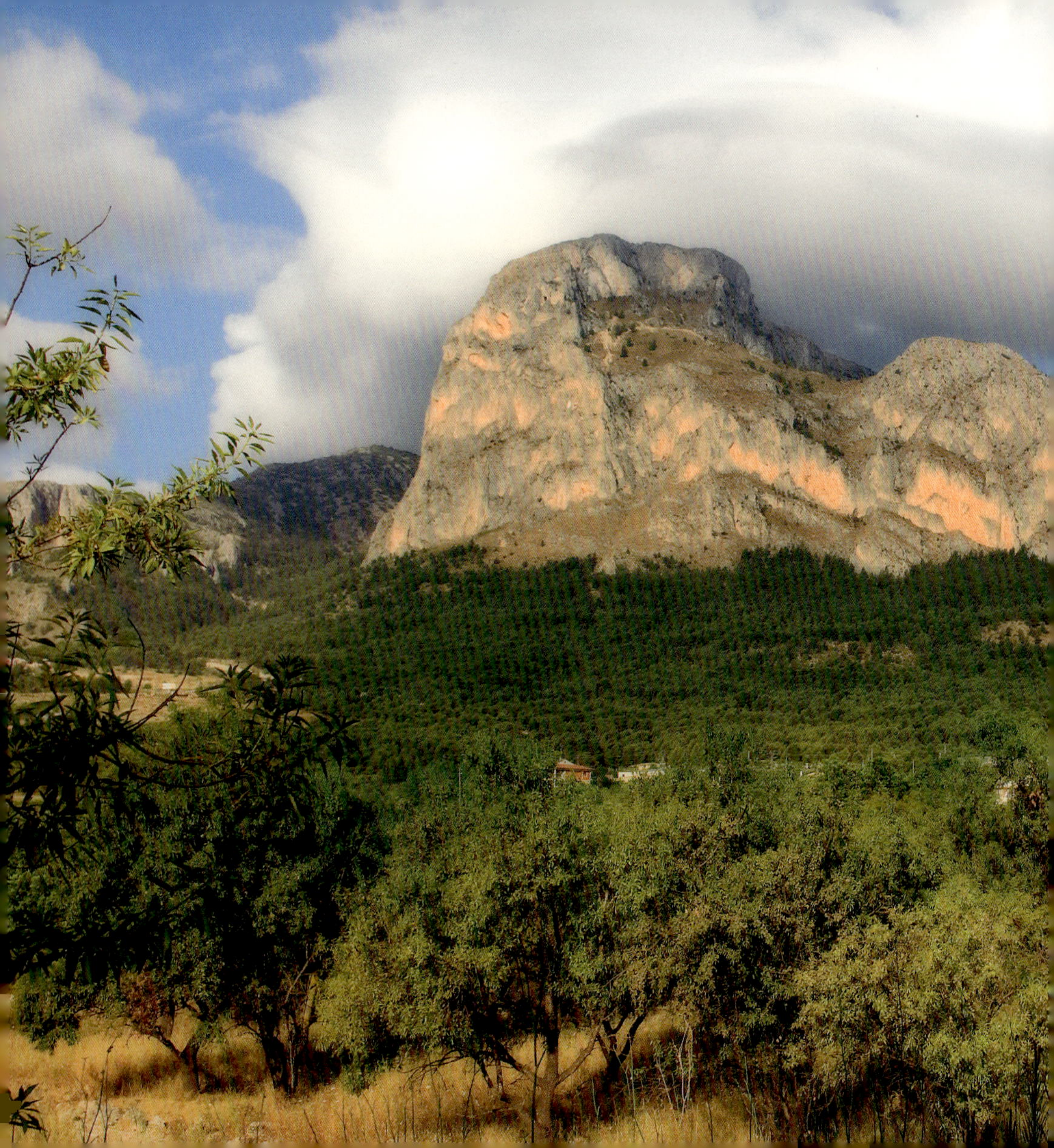

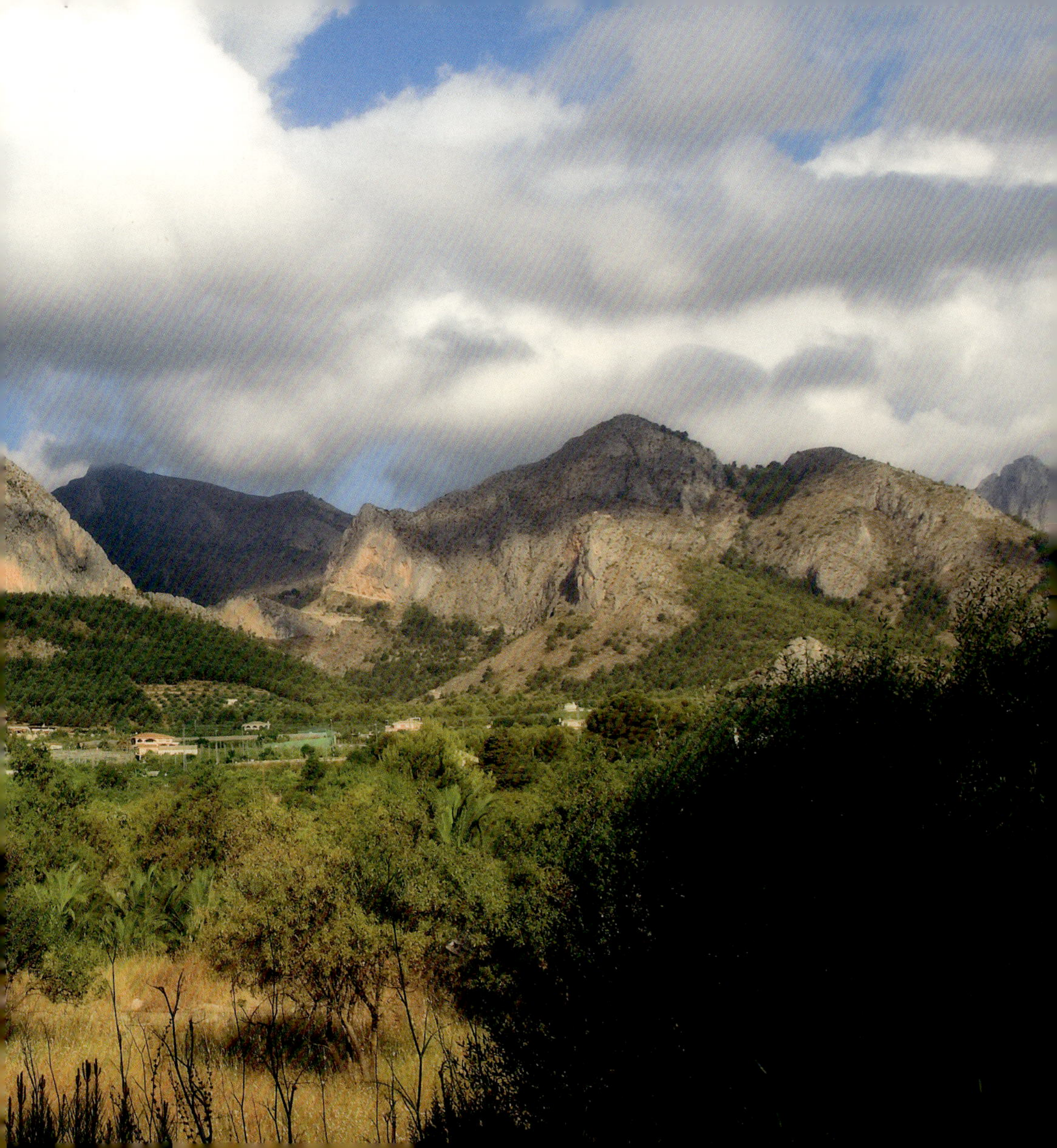

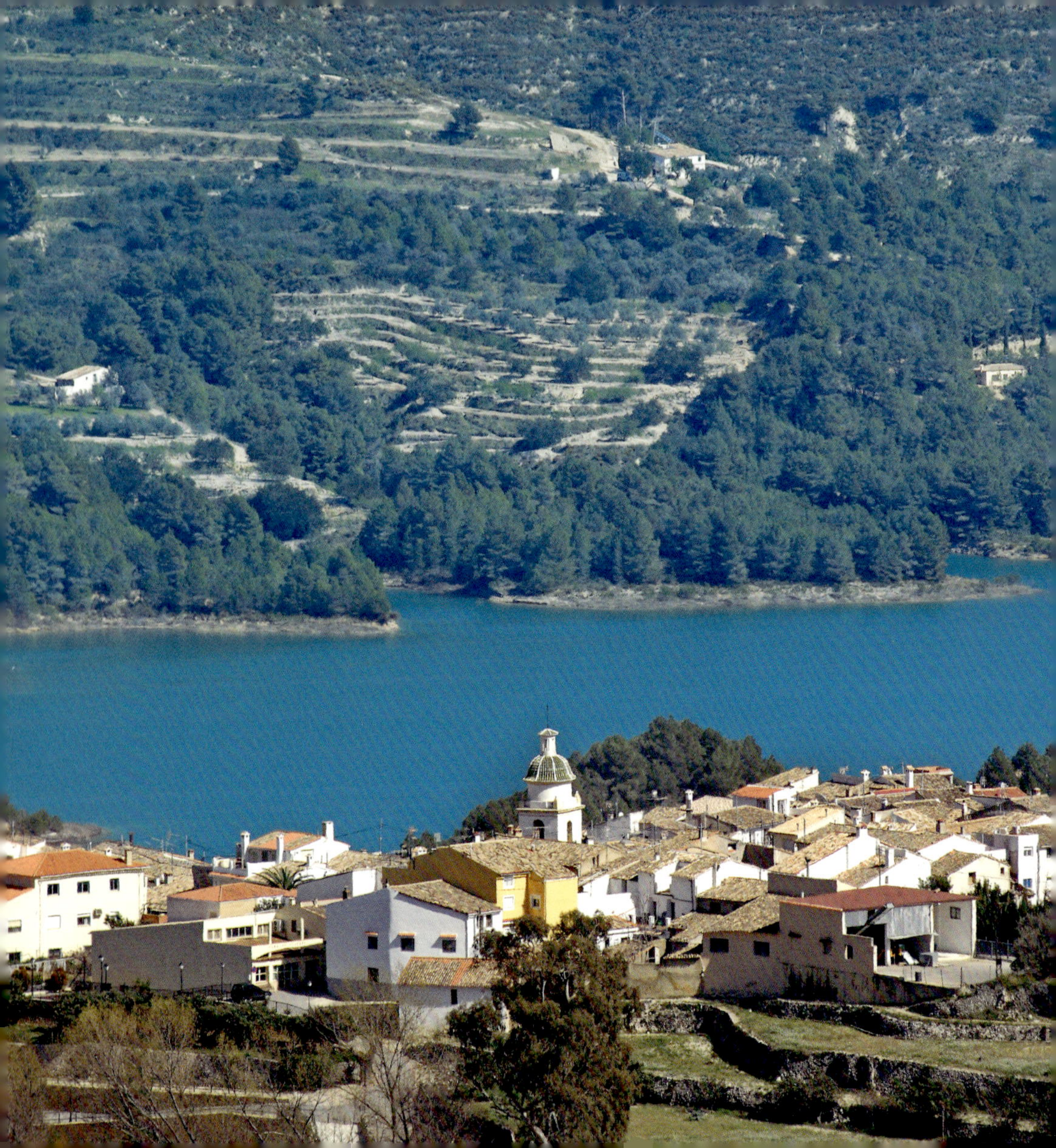

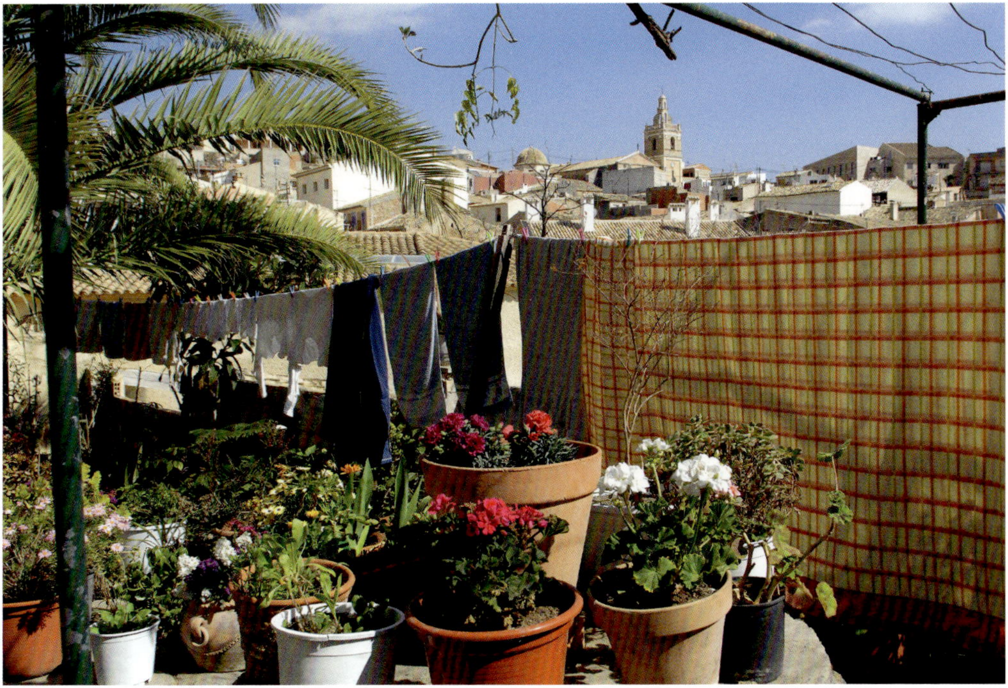

Relleu
← Beniardà and the Guadalest reservoir

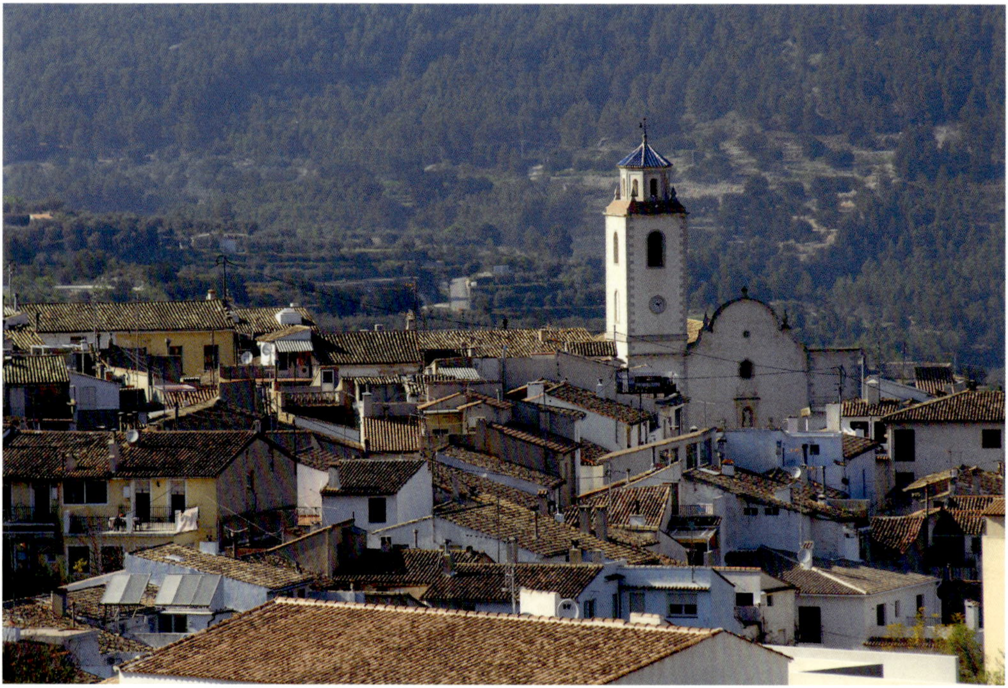

Benimantell
Gully descent in the Bolulla ravine →

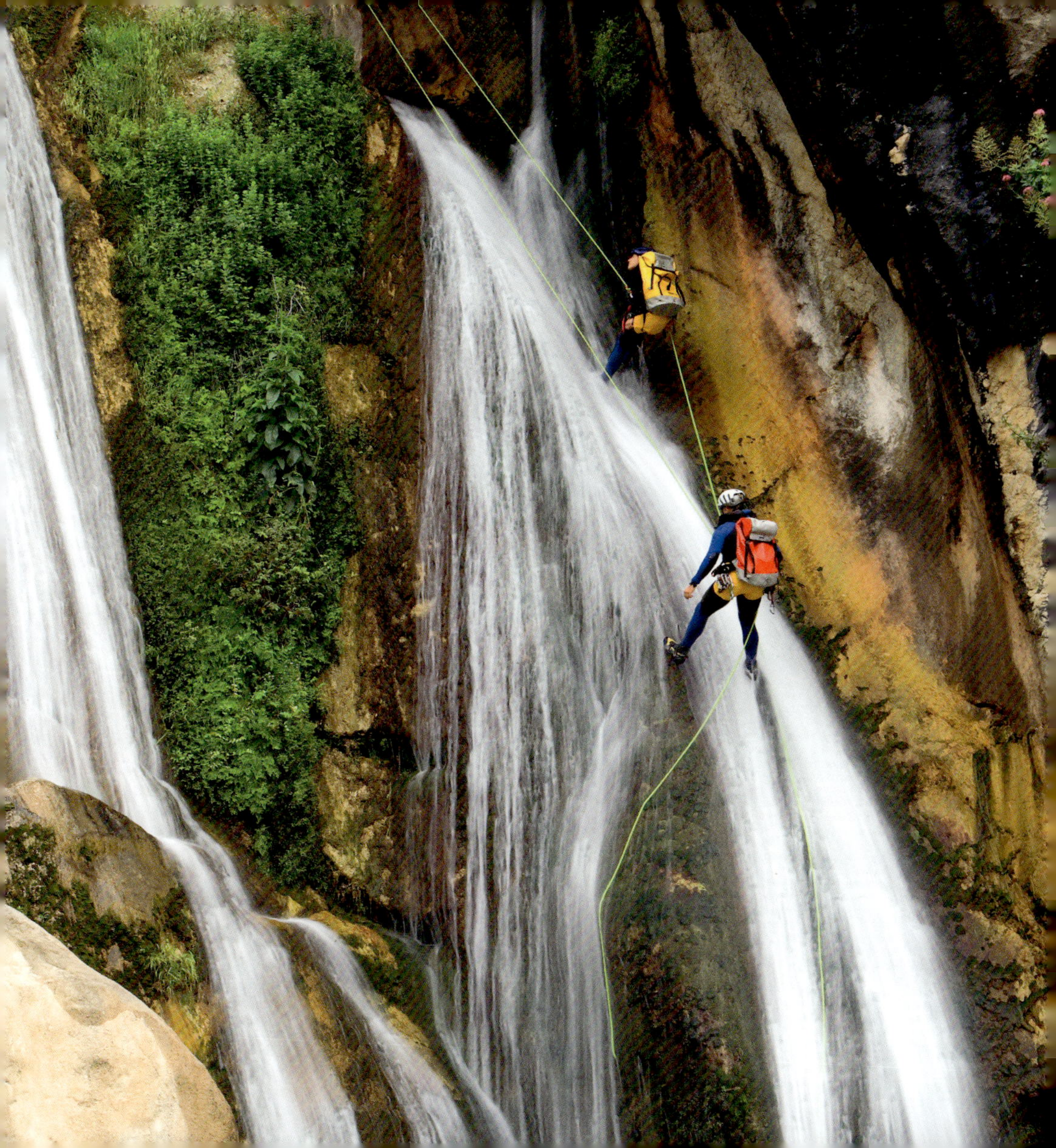

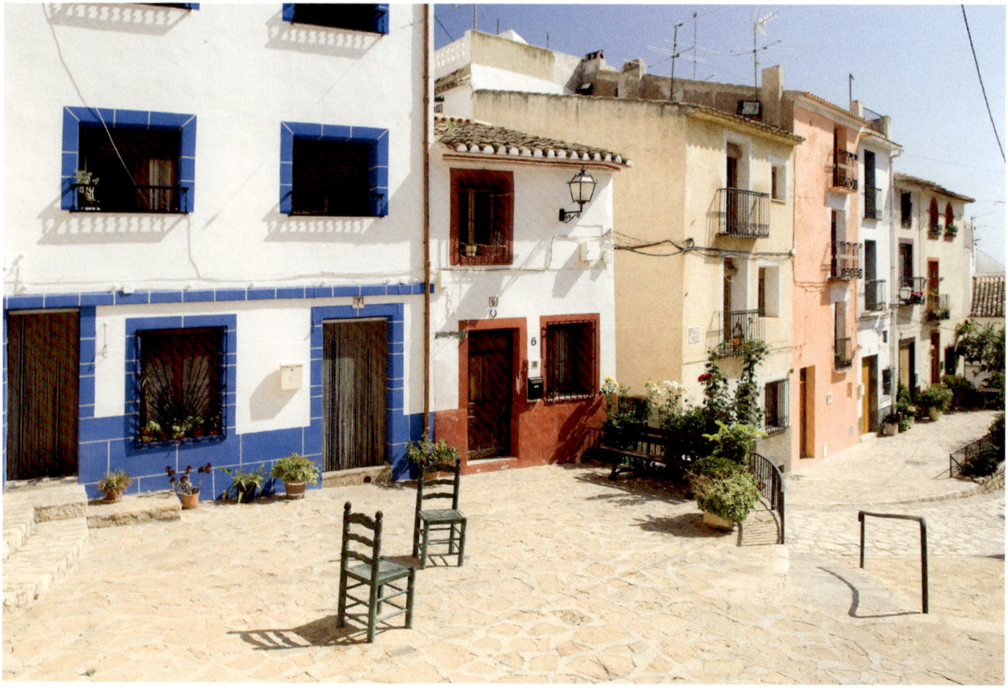

Finestrat
Finestrat beach →

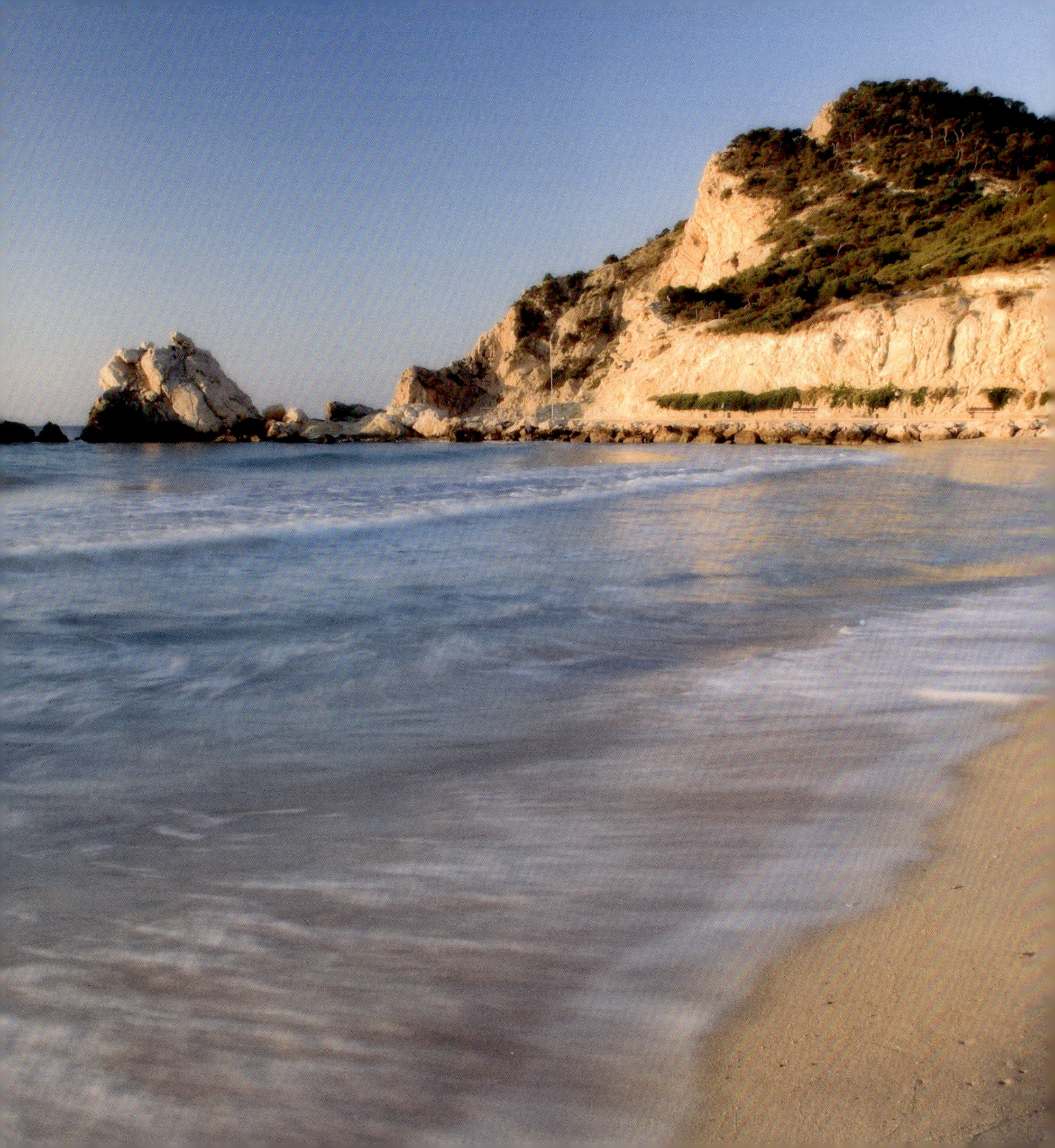

L'Alacantí

Alacant / Alicante
Tabarca
El Campello
Agost
Busot
Xixona / Jijona

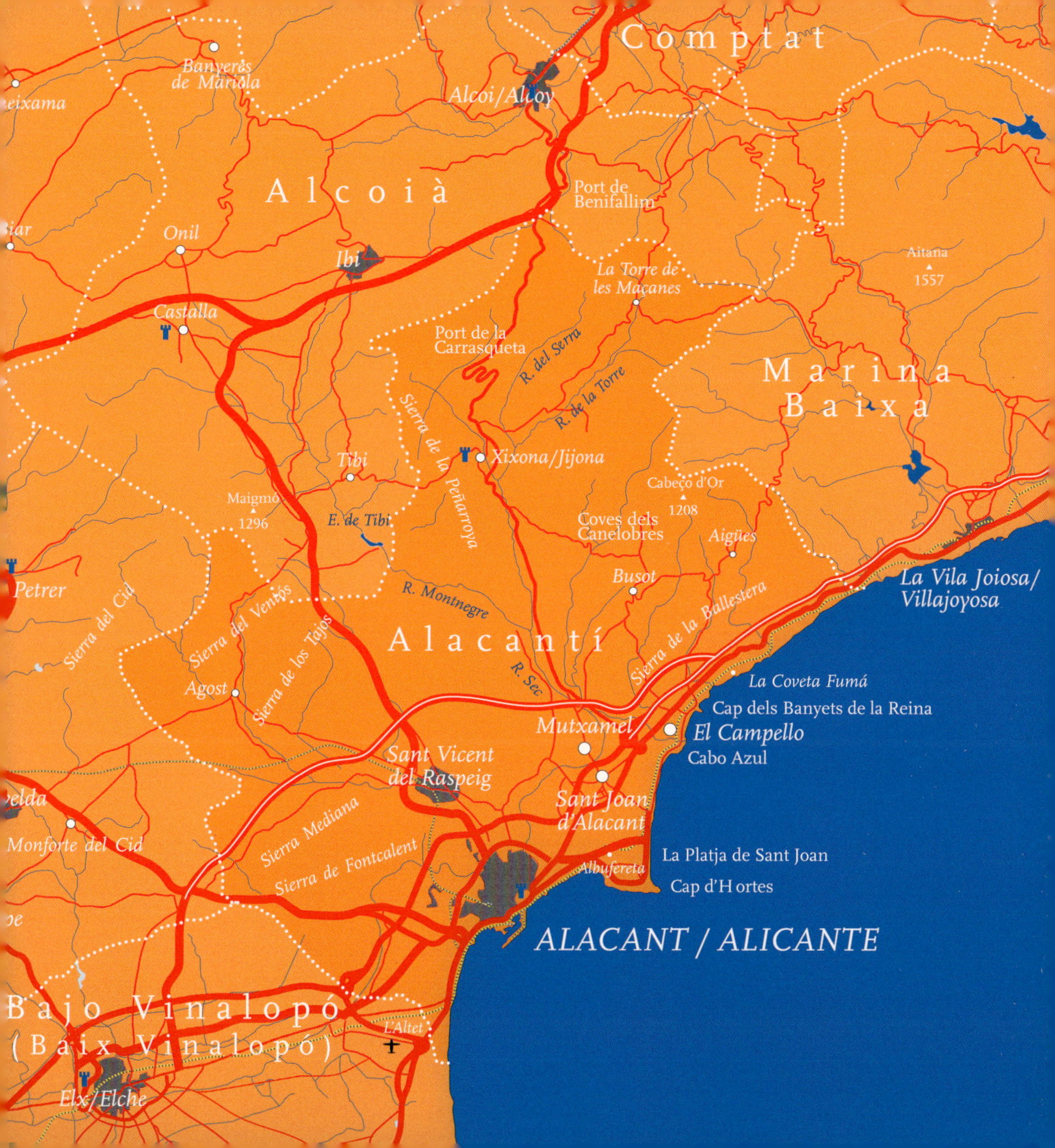
Comptat
Banyeres de Mariola
Alcoi/Alcoy
Alcoià
Port de Benifallim
Onil
Ibi
Castalla
La Torre de les Maçanes
Aitana
1557
Port de la Carrasqueta
R. del Serra
R. de la Torre
Marina Baixa
Sierra de la Peñarroya
Xixona/Jijona
Tibi
Maigmó
1296
E. de Tibi
Cabeço d'Or
1208
Coves dels Canelobres
Aigües
Petrer
Busot
R. Montnegre
La Vila Joiosa/ Villajoyosa
Sierra del Cid
Sierra del Ventós
Sierra de los Tajos
Alacantí
Sierra de la Ballestera
R. Sec
Agost
La Coveta Fumá
Cap dels Banyets de la Reina
Mutxamel
El Campello
Cabo Azul
Sant Vicent del Raspeig
Sant Joan d'Alacant
Monforte del Cid
Sierra Mediana
Sierra de Fontcalent
La Platja de Sant Joan
Albufereta
Cap d'Hortes
ALACANT / ALICANTE
Bajo Vinalopó
(Baix Vinalopó)
L'Altet
Elx/Elche

Alacant /Alicante

Alicante is a type of jar that encloses all the essences of the Costa Blanca: many hours of sun, good beaches, an interesting cultural offer, well-conserved heritage, popular festivals and high gastronomy.

The city has different types of beaches: next to the cape of the Huertas we come across rocky coves; the beaches of Postiguet and Albufereta, in contrast, are of fine sand and crystalline water.

The Town Hall building, at sea level, is a reference for measuring the altitudes of other points of Spain. Behind the administrative building are the first houses of the old quarter. Along its streets we find civil buildings converted into a museum, such as the Palacio Gravina, home of the Gravina Fine Art Museum (MUBAG); religious buildings, such as the basilica of Santa María or the co-cathedral of San Nicolás; and pleasant alleys in the district of Santa Cruz. Without doubt, however, the most recognised image of the city is the castle of Santa Bárbara crowning the Benacantil. To discover the deep history of Alicante we recommend you visit the Provincial Archaeological Museum (MARQ), one of the best museum spaces in Spain on this question.

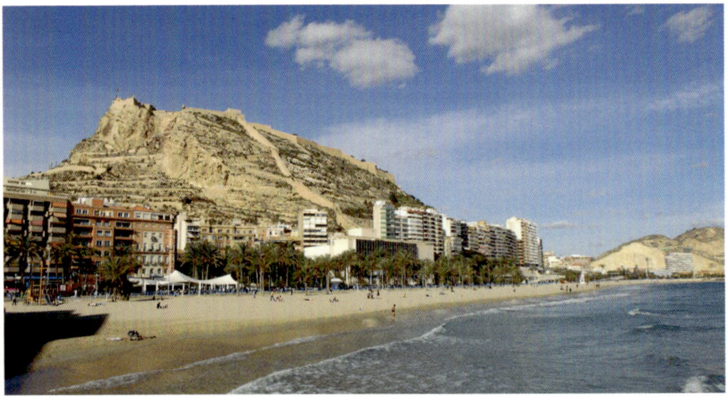

Postiguet beach and castle of Santa Bárbara

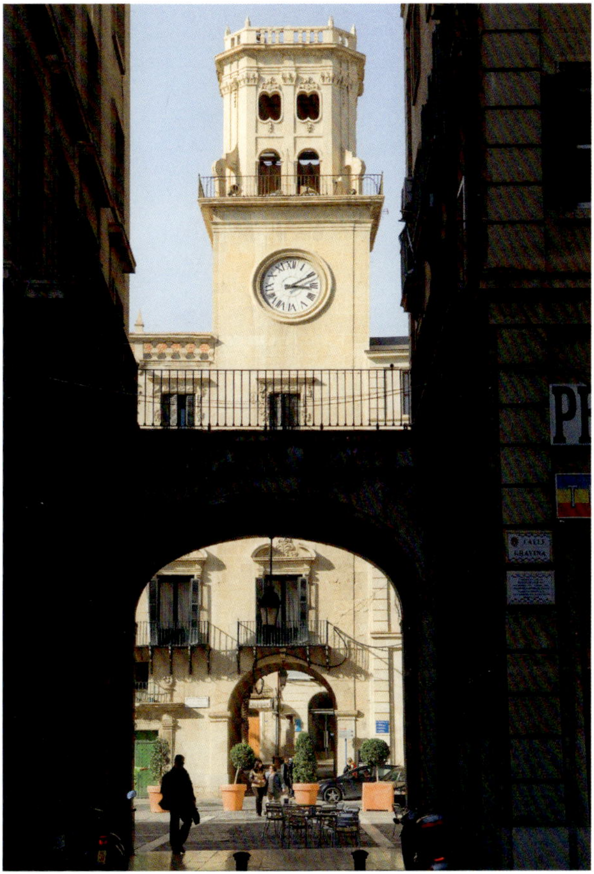

Town Hall Tower
View of the city and the castle →
Port of Alicante →→

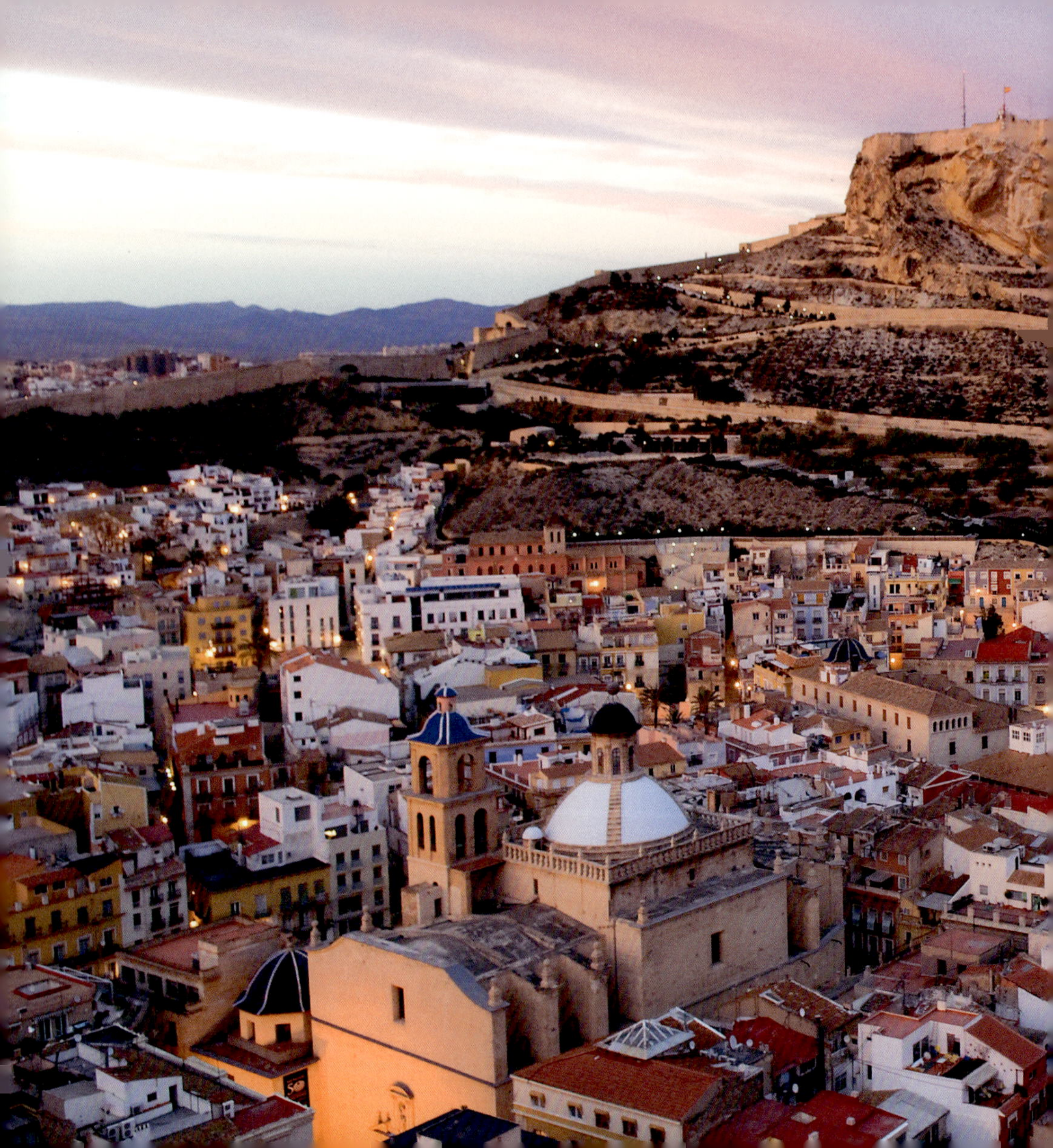

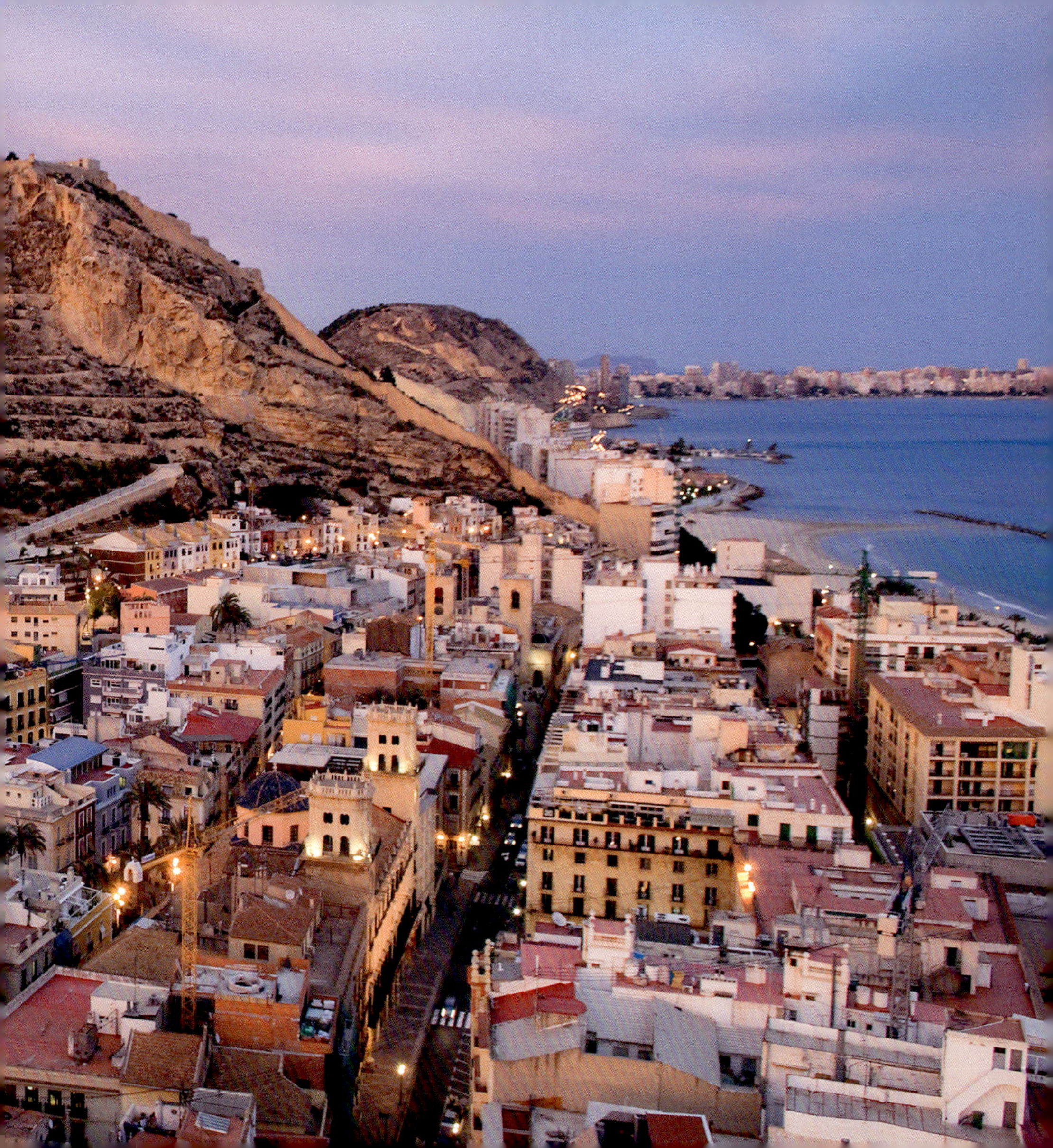

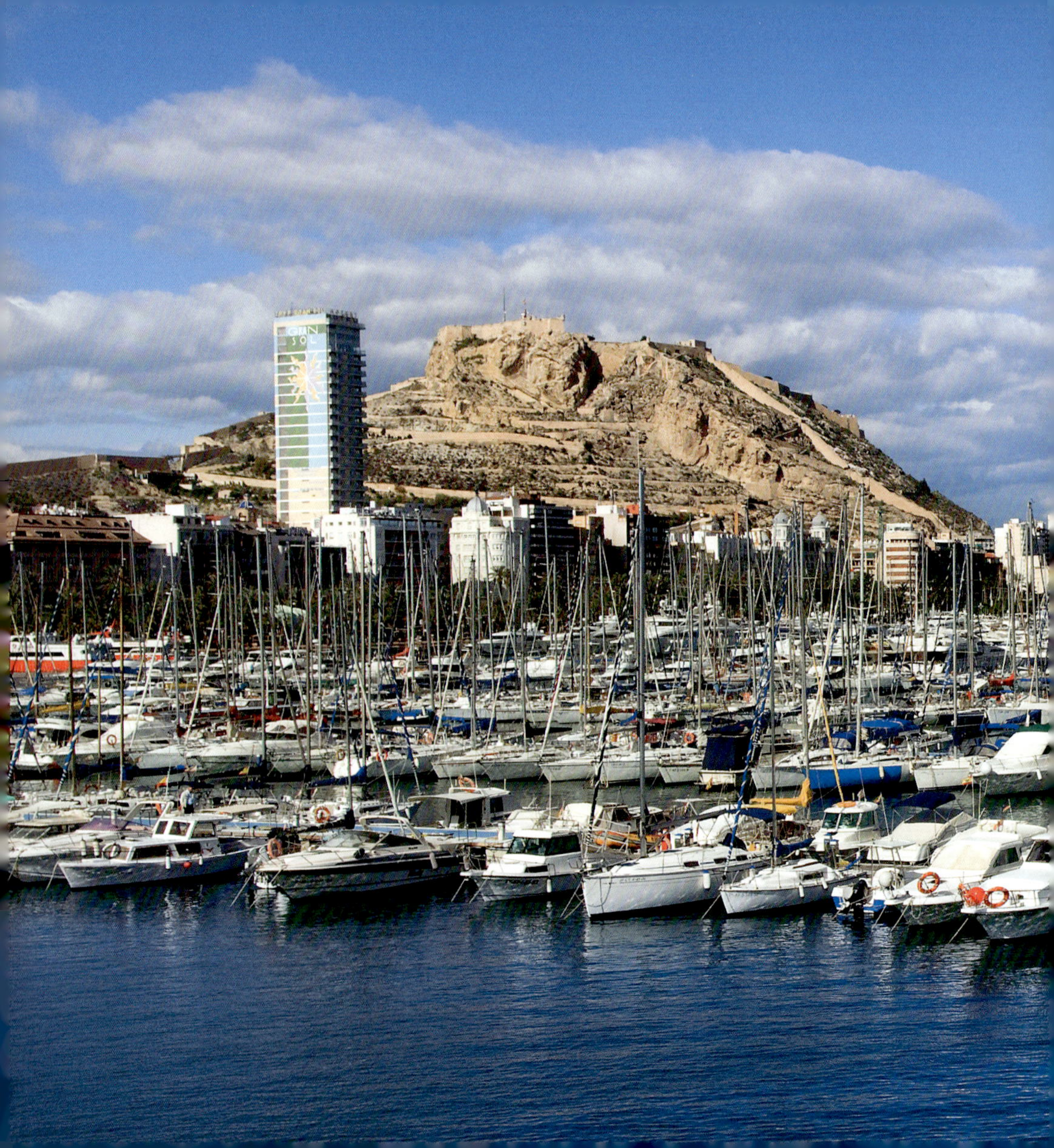
GRAN SOL

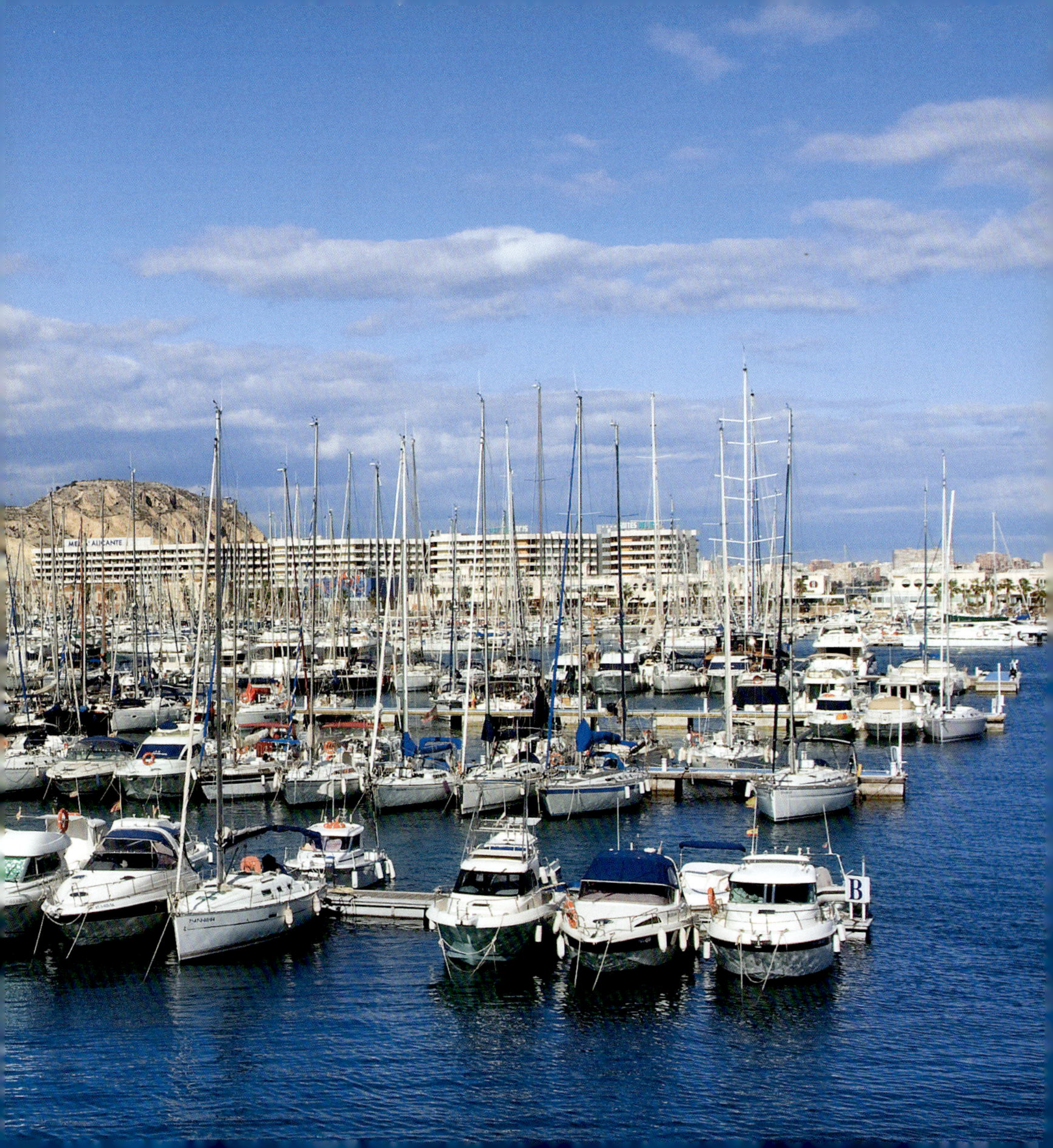
ALICANTE
B

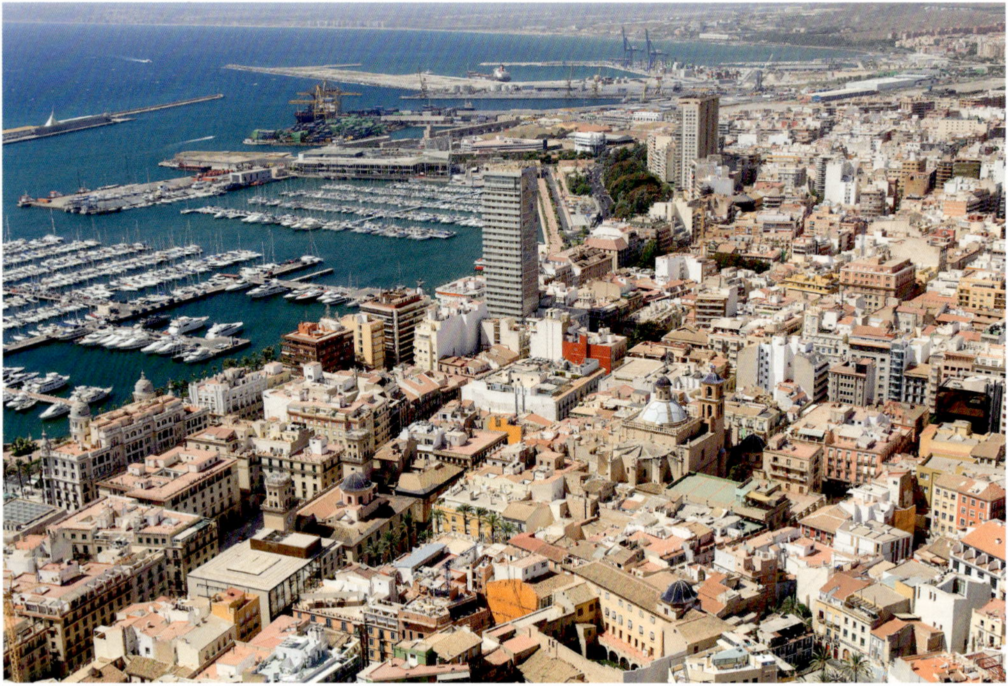

View from the castle

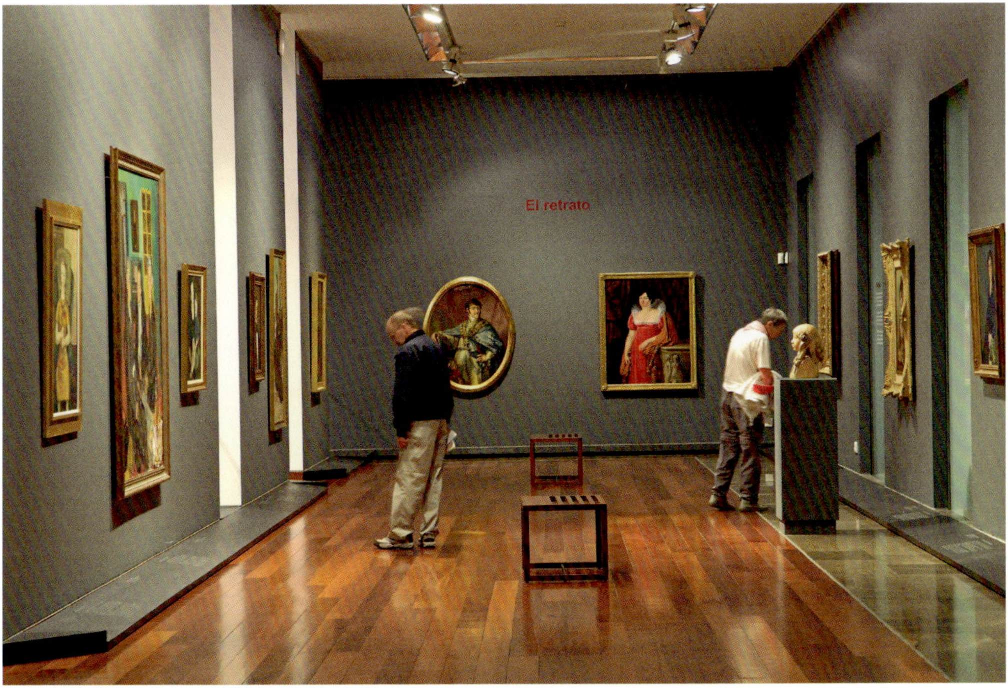

Gravina Fine Arts Museum (MUBAG)

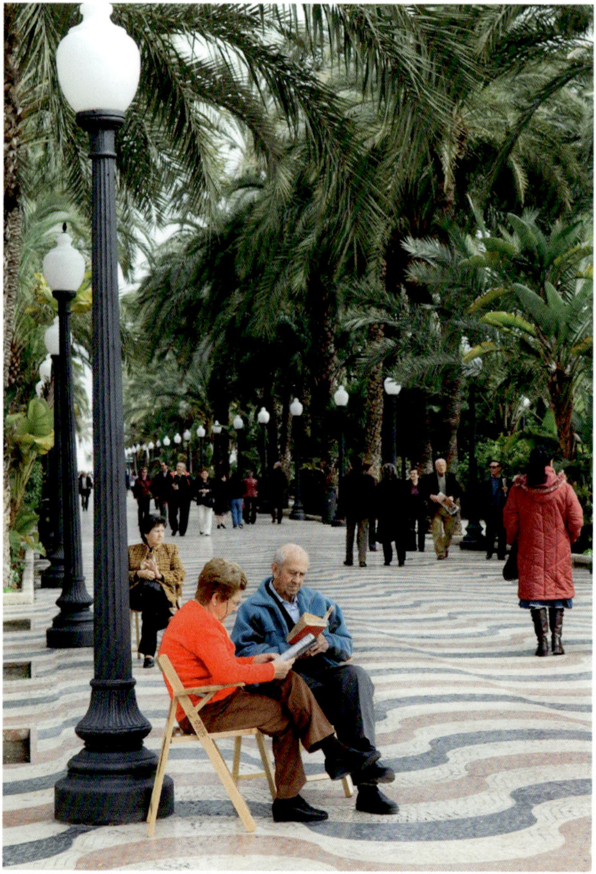

Explanada de España

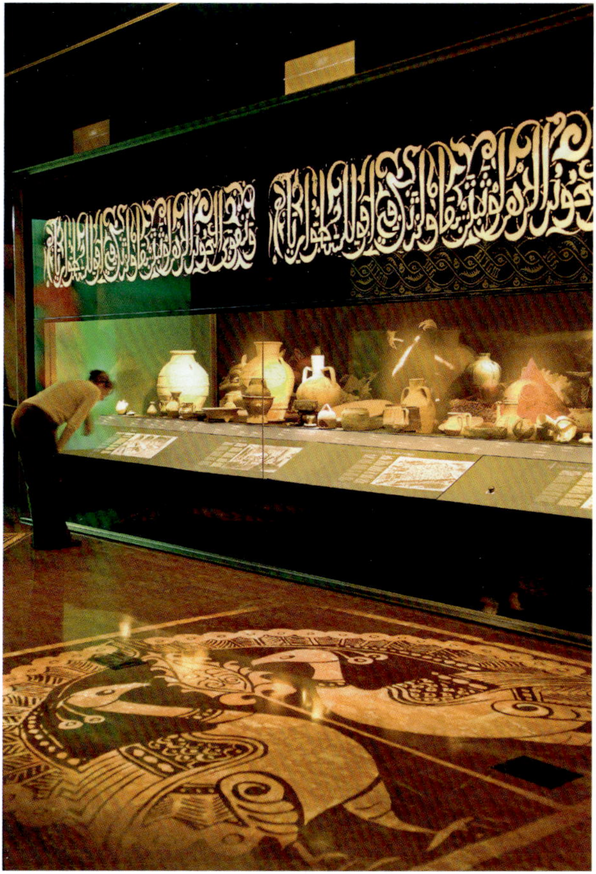

Provincial Archaeological Museum of Alicante (MARQ)

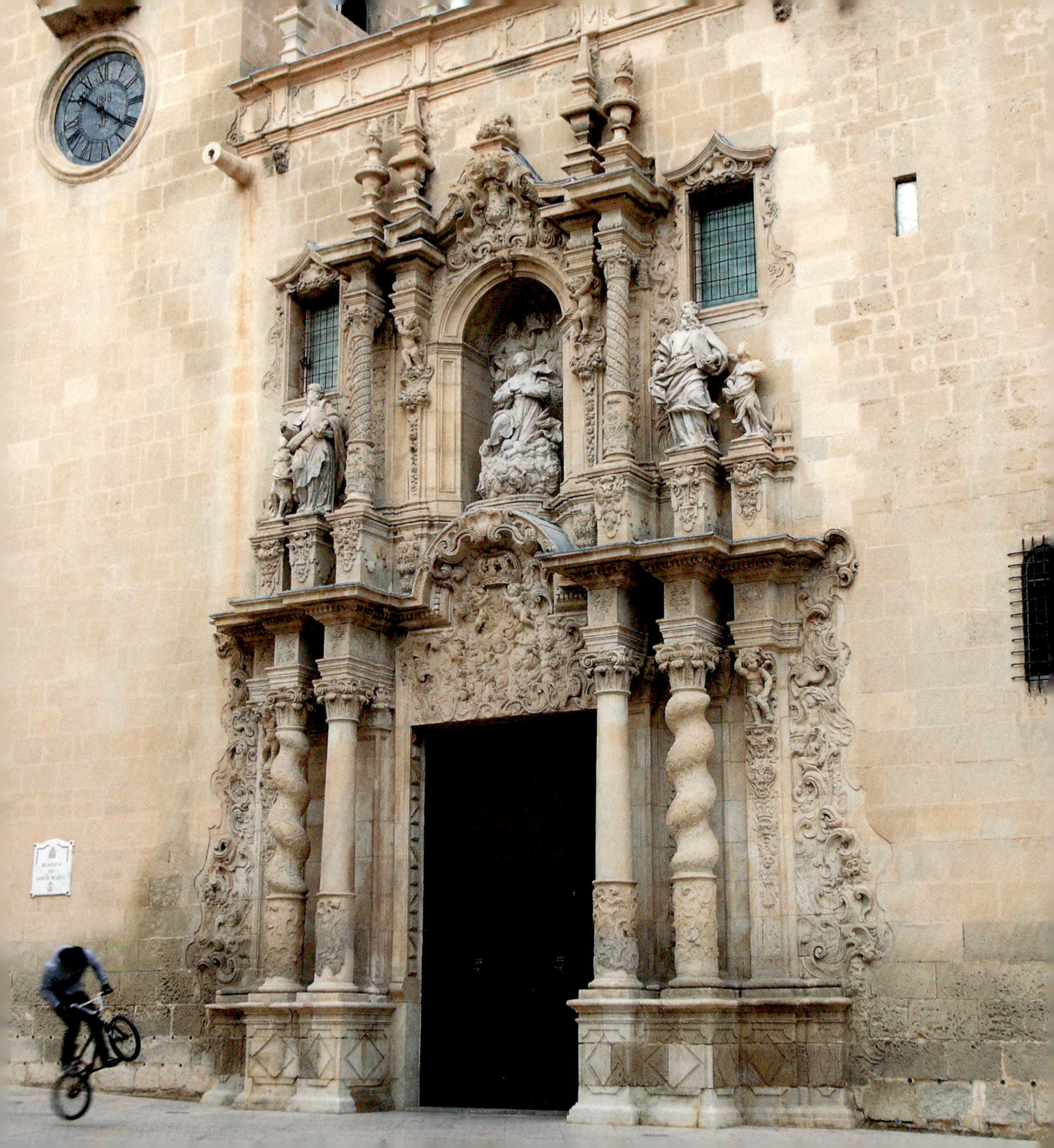

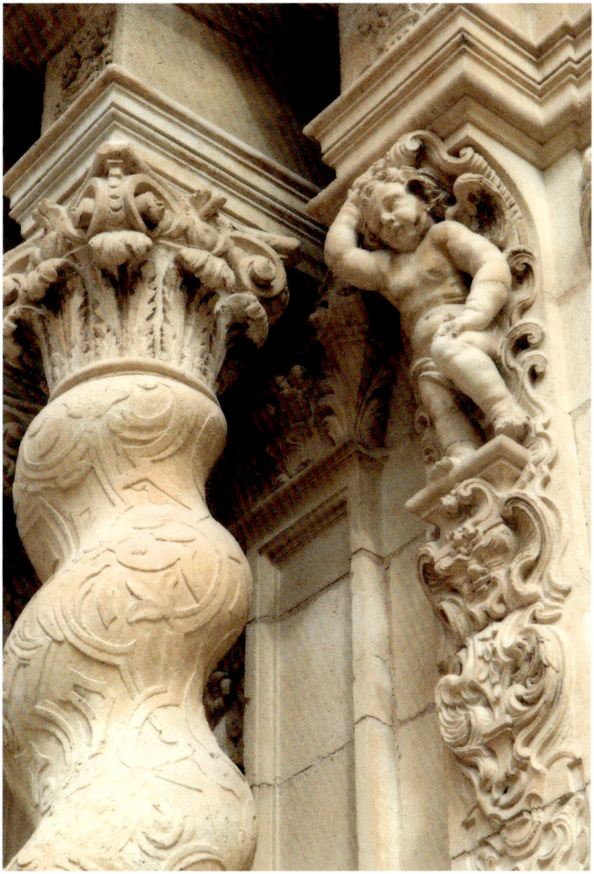

Basilica of Santa Maria

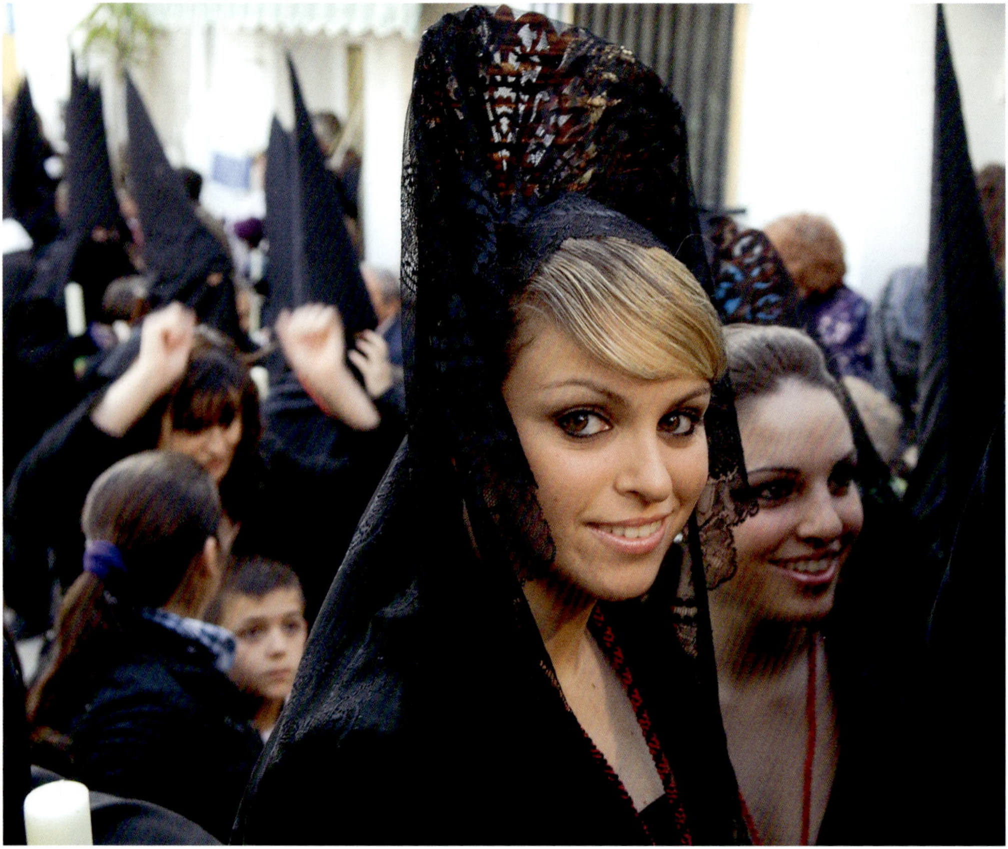

Two of the key elements in the Mediterranean festivals cannot be missed in Alicante. Passion flows through the streets of the district of Santa Cruz during the Wednesday procession of Easter and fire is the leading player in the Hogueras (bonfires) on the night of St John.

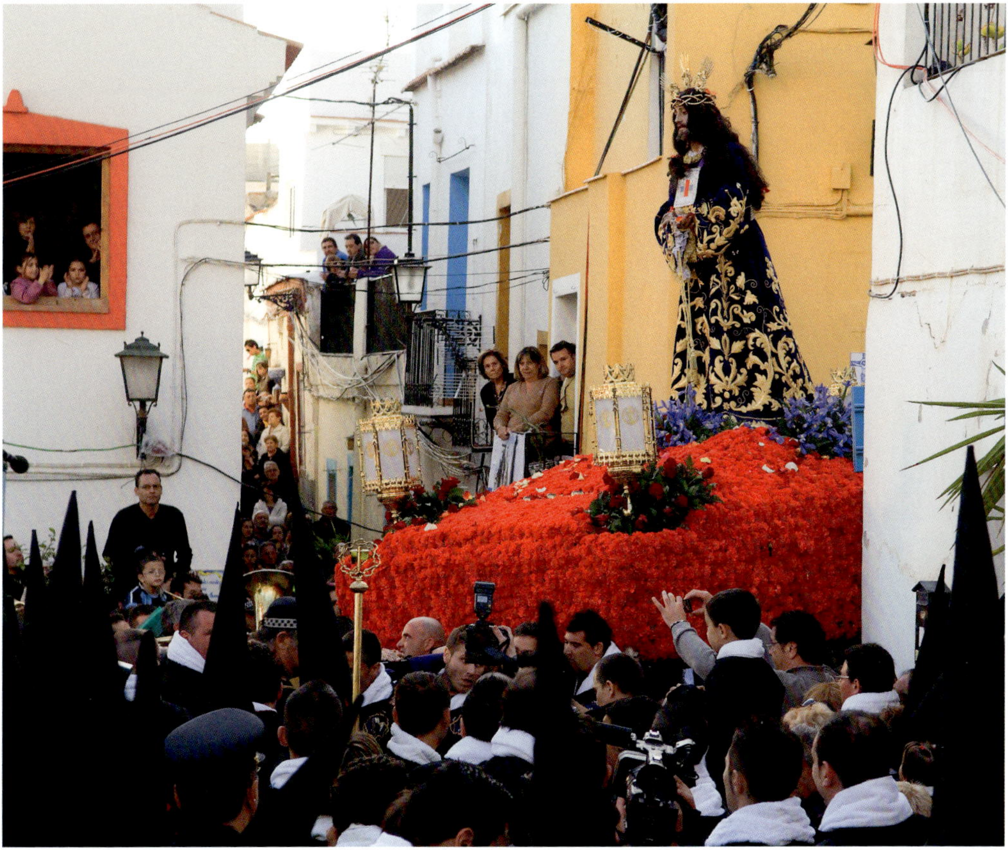

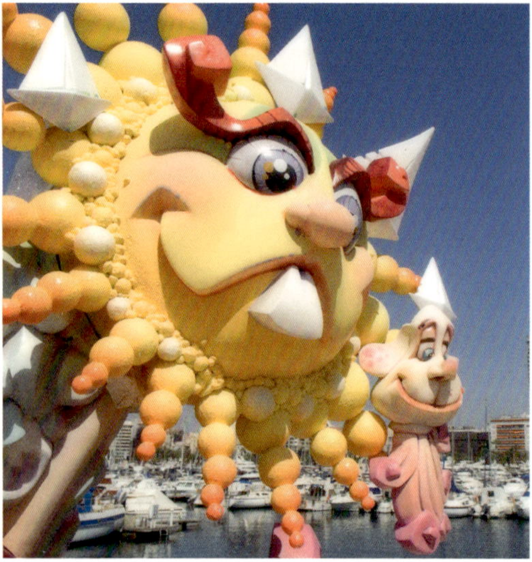

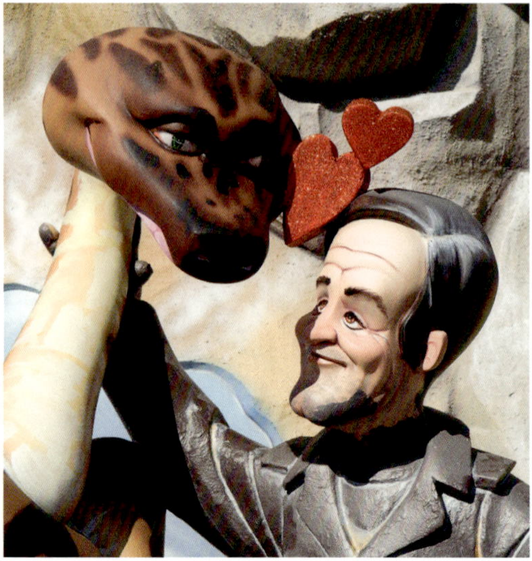

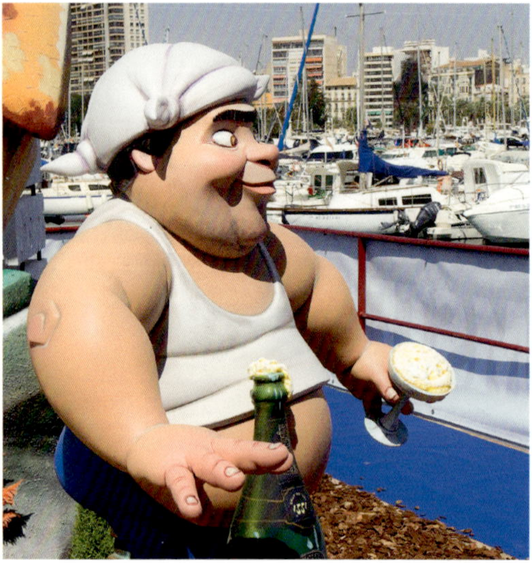

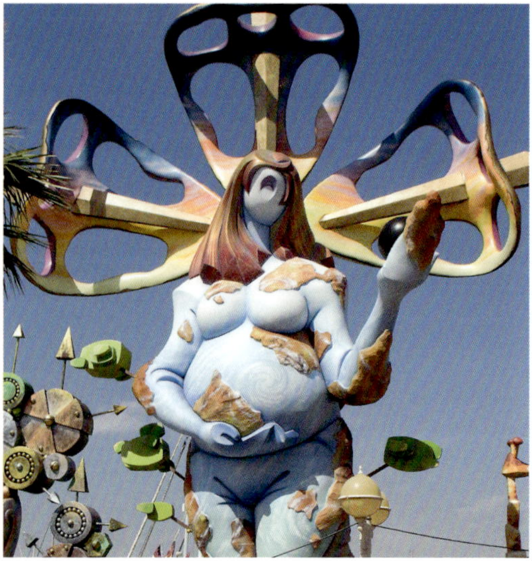

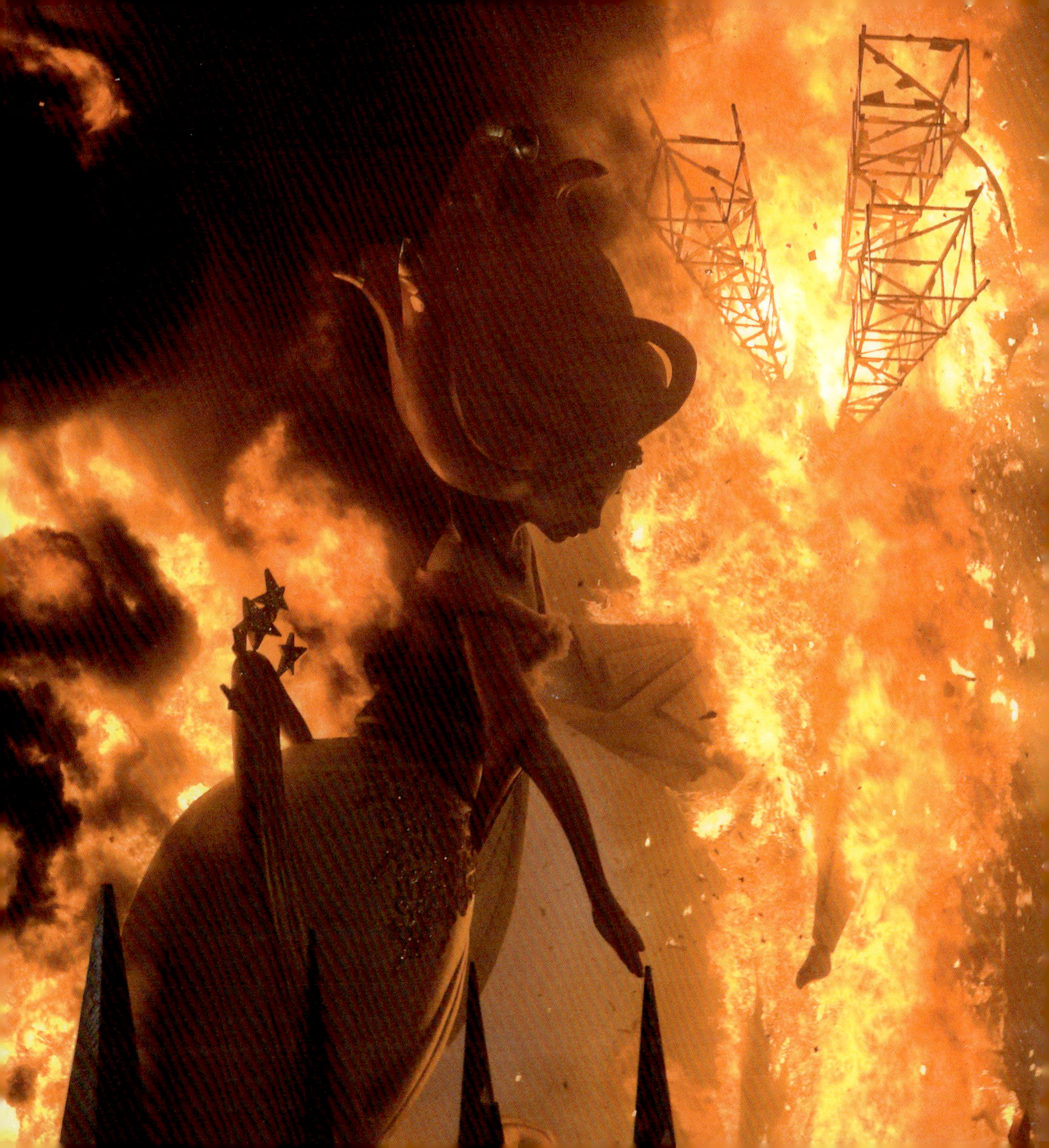

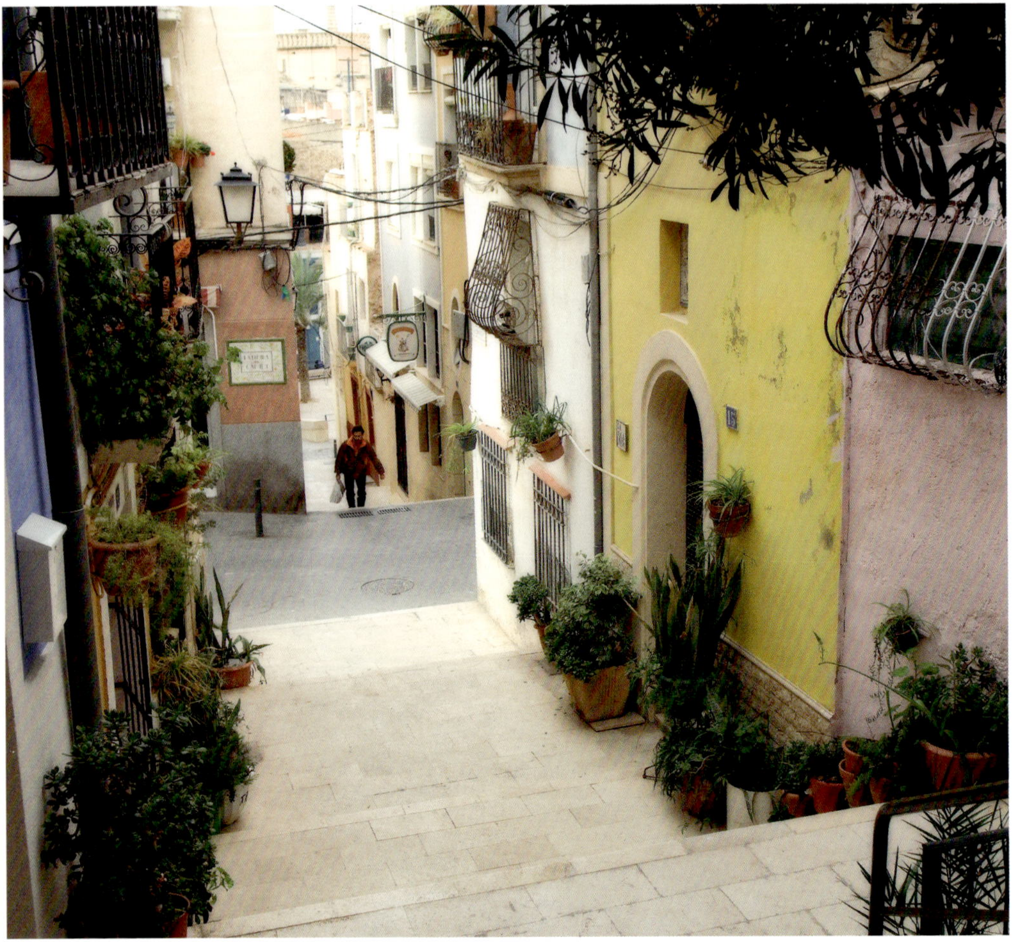

Old quarter

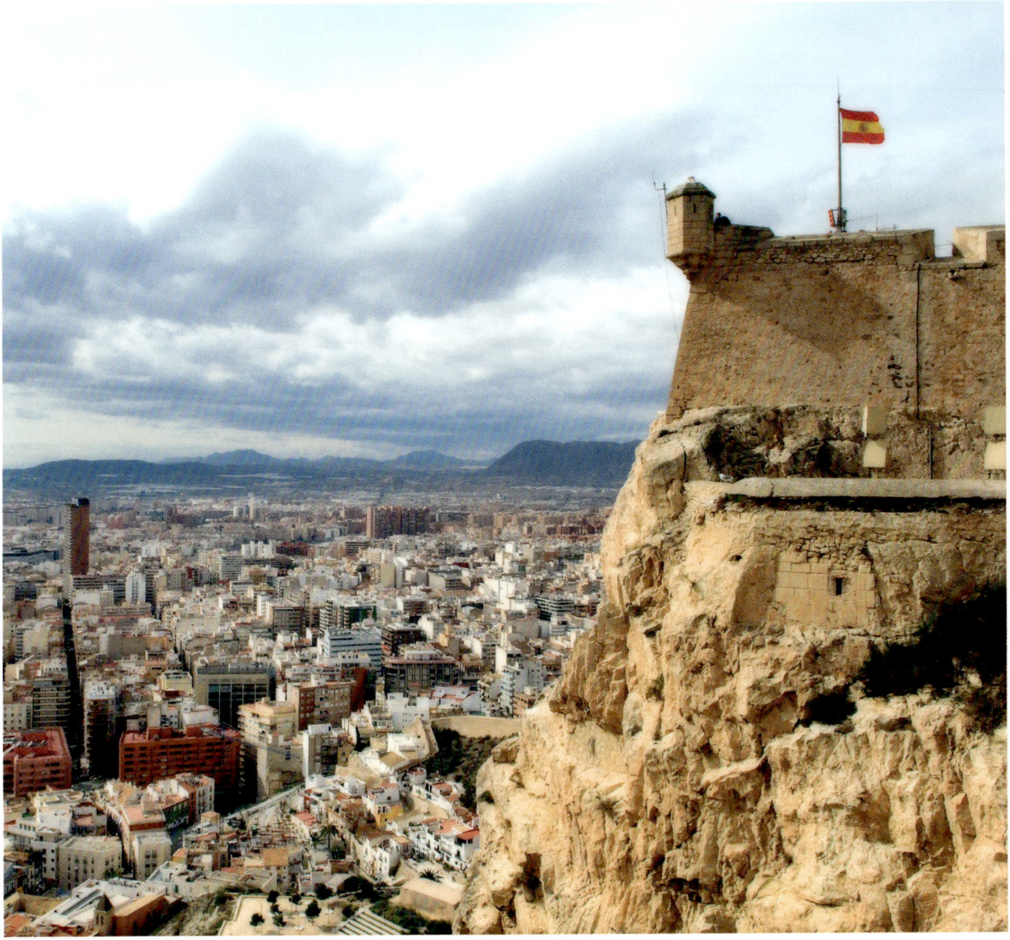

Castle of Santa Bárbara
MedCup Regatta →

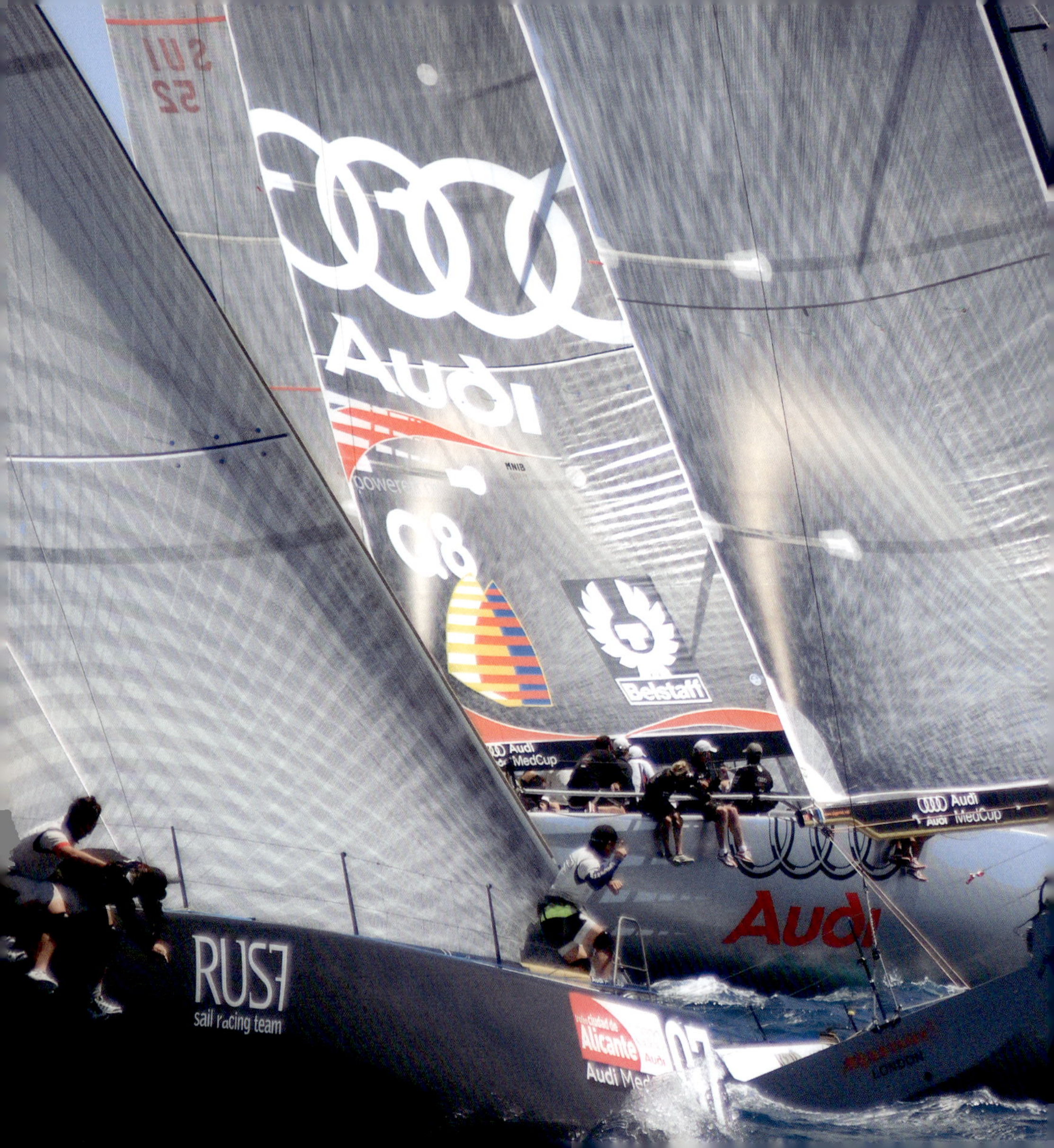

Audi
Q8
Belstaff
Audi MedCup
Audi
RUS7
sail racing team
Alicante

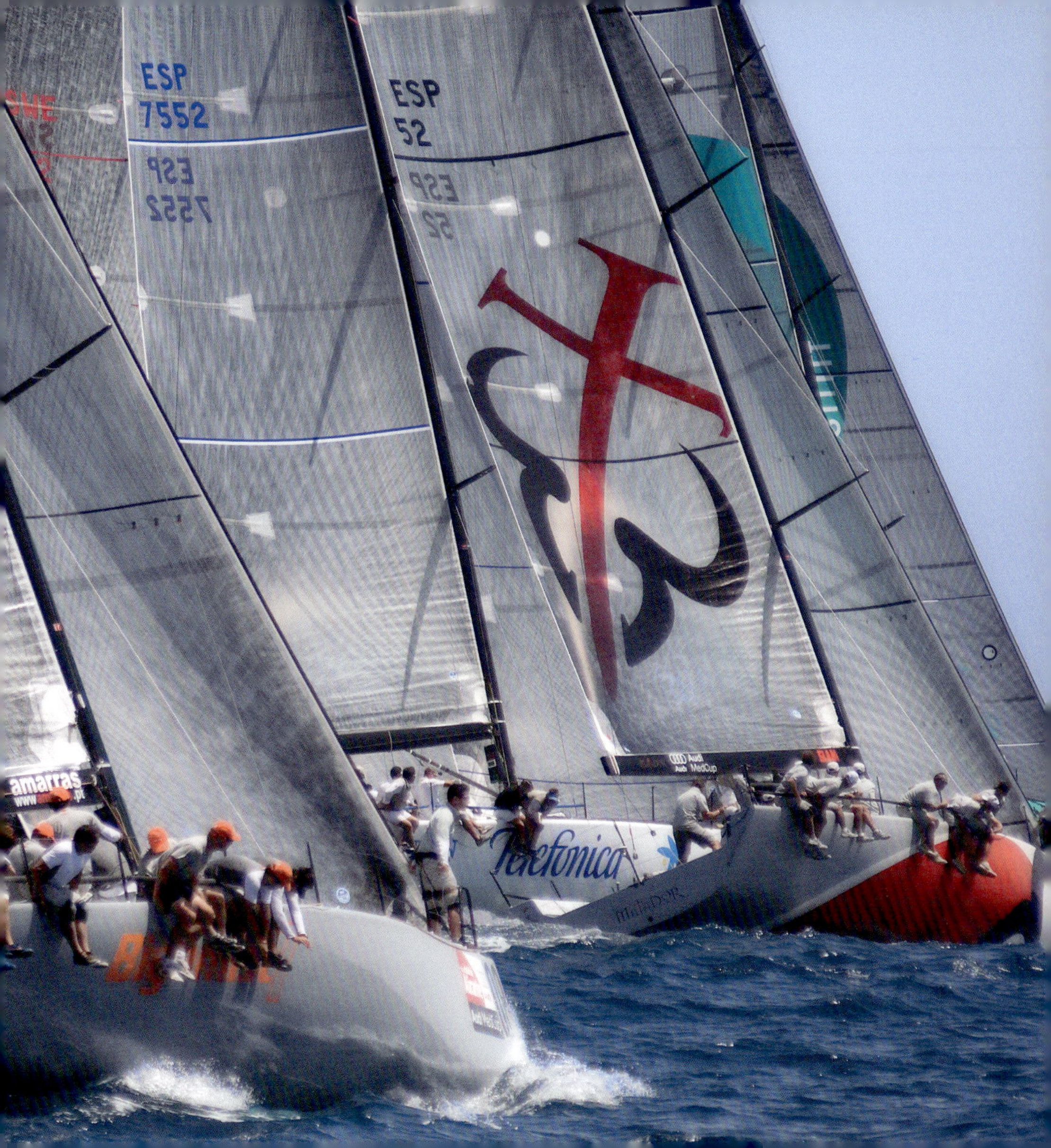
ESP
7552
ESP
52
amarras
Telefonica
Audi MedCup

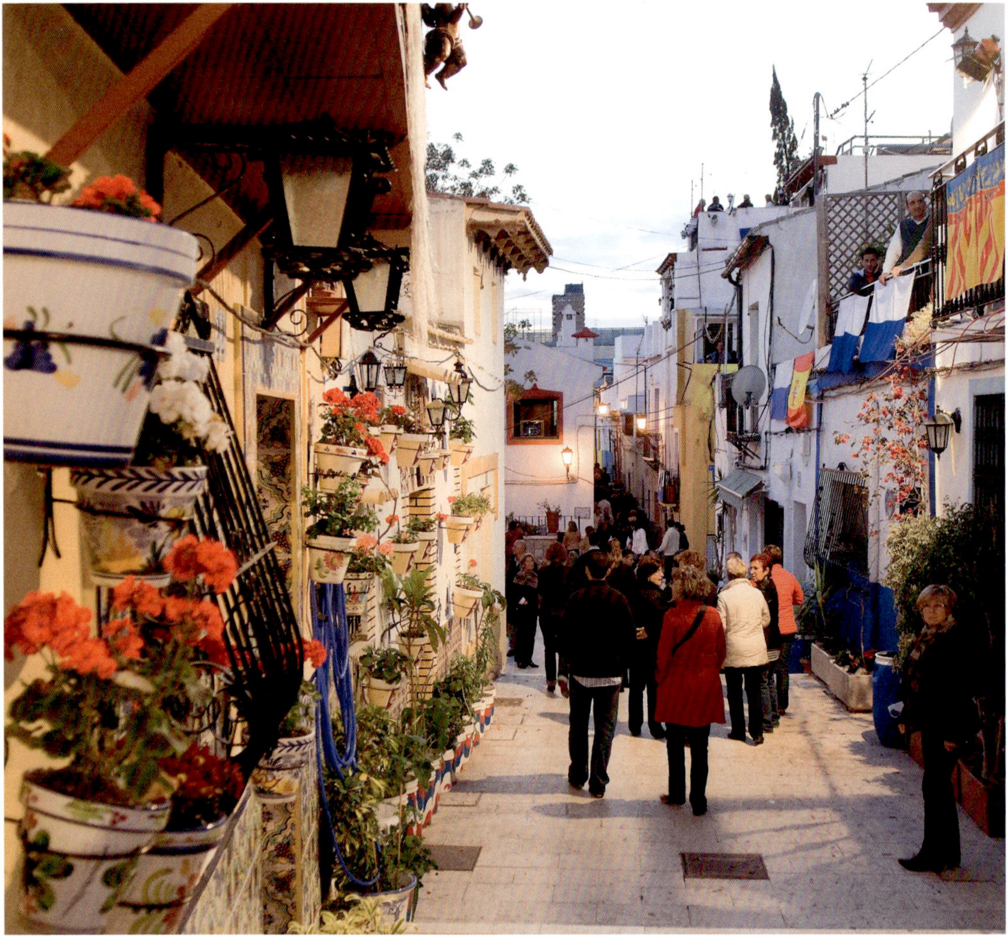

Santa Cruz district

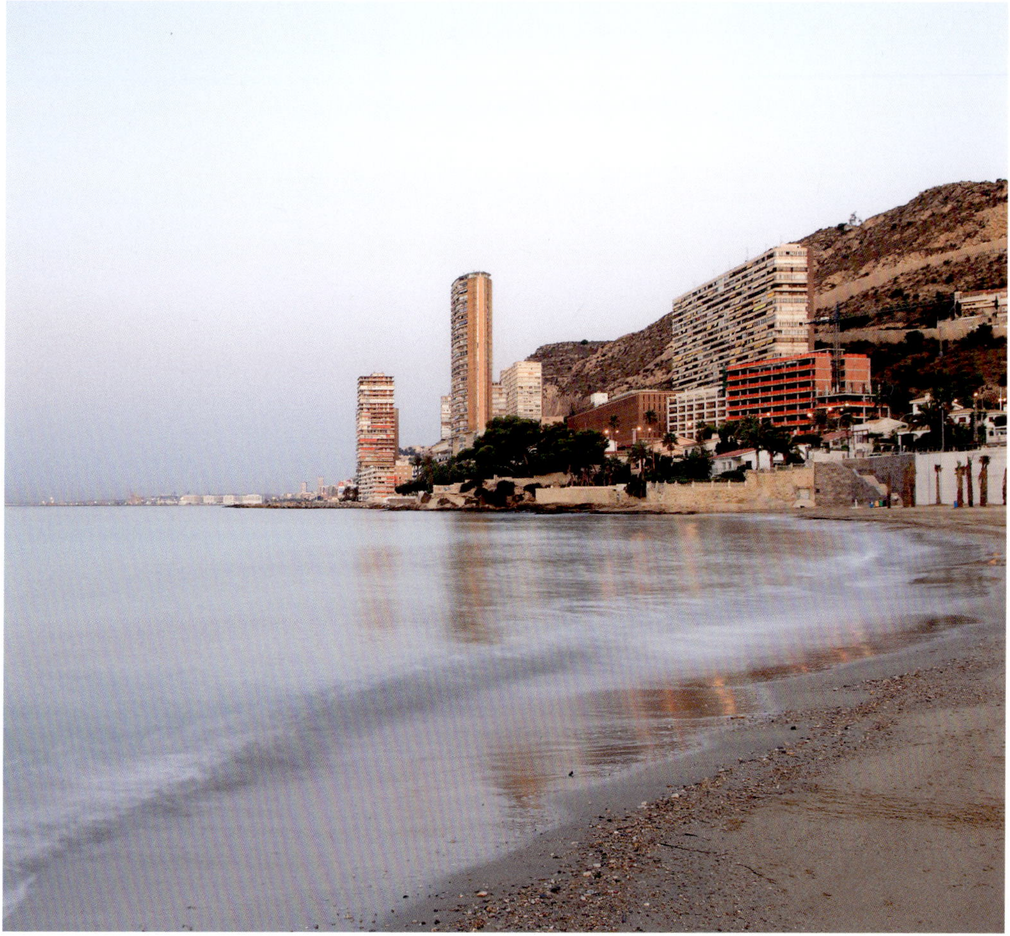

Albufereta beach

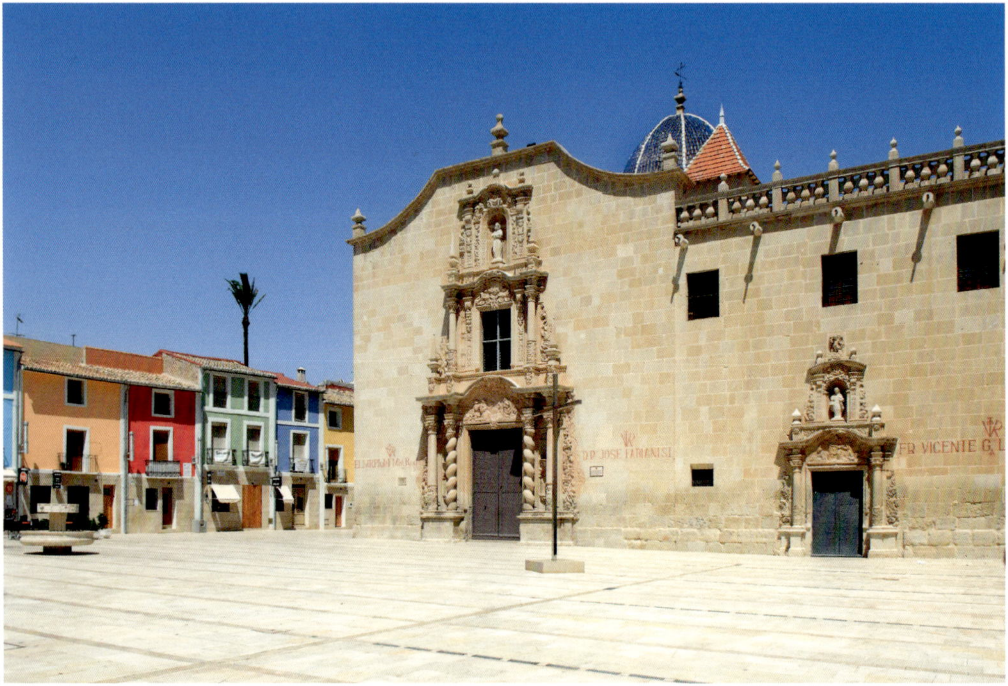

Church of the Santa Faz

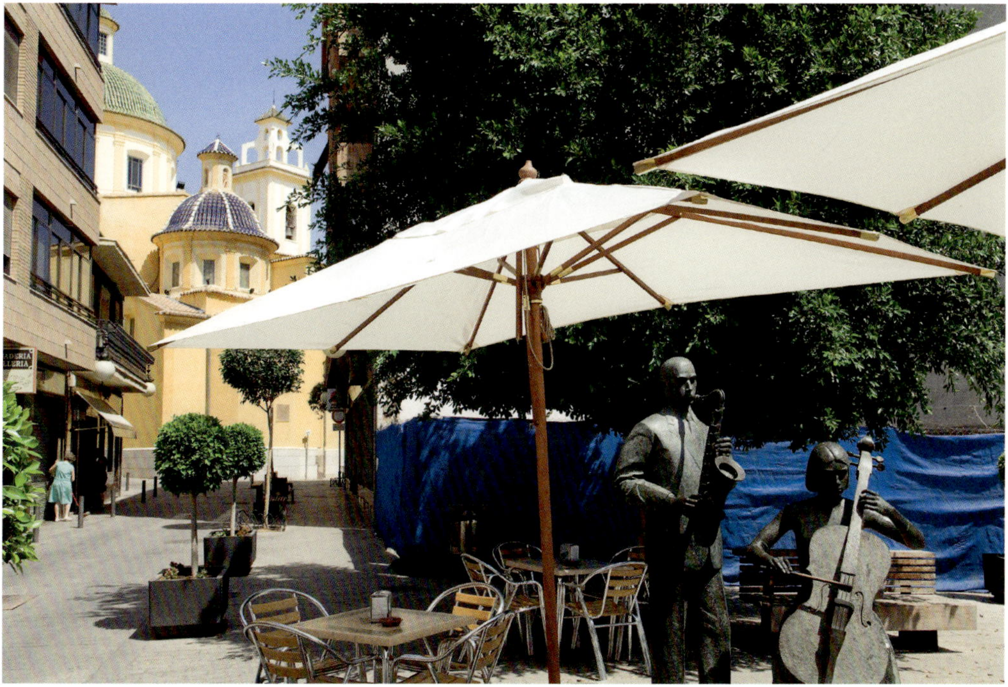

Sant Vicenç del Raspeig

Tabarca

Ptolemy and Pliny already mentioned the island, calling it Planesia, to later be known as Isla Plana due to its hardly six metres of average altitude. In 1769 it took on the definitive name of Nueva Tabarca by mediation of Carlos III, who fortified the island and sent the families of the Ligur people there, who had been enslaved by the Algerians on the isle of Tabarka, located on the Tunisian coast. One of the gates of the wall, that of San Gabriel, still conserves part of an inscription in Latin that when complete read: "Carlos III King of the Spains did it and built it".

The inhabited zone of the island is in the inside of the precinct, walled in the 18th century, a series of old fishermen's houses around two main streets. Here we can see the Baroque church of San Pedro y San Pablo, and the Governor's house. During the medieval and modern age, the island was an operational base for Berber pirates and smugglers due to its strategic position facing the coastline. The cave of the *Llop Marí* is the origin of several legends about these incursions.

The island as a whole has been declared a Marine Reserve. In its uninhabited part, there are other points of interest, such as the tower of San José, which was a prison in the 19th century, the lighthouse or the cemetery that stands alongside Punta Falcó.

The storm of 1980 increased the economic decline that began in 1960, with the end of the tunny fishery activity that had maintained the majority of inhabitants, descendants of the first Genovese who populated the island —they intermarried and, even today, the most common surnames are Pianelo or Parodi, among others—.

The traditional dish of Tabarca is the broth, made with fish such as gurnard, sea bass or greater amberback.

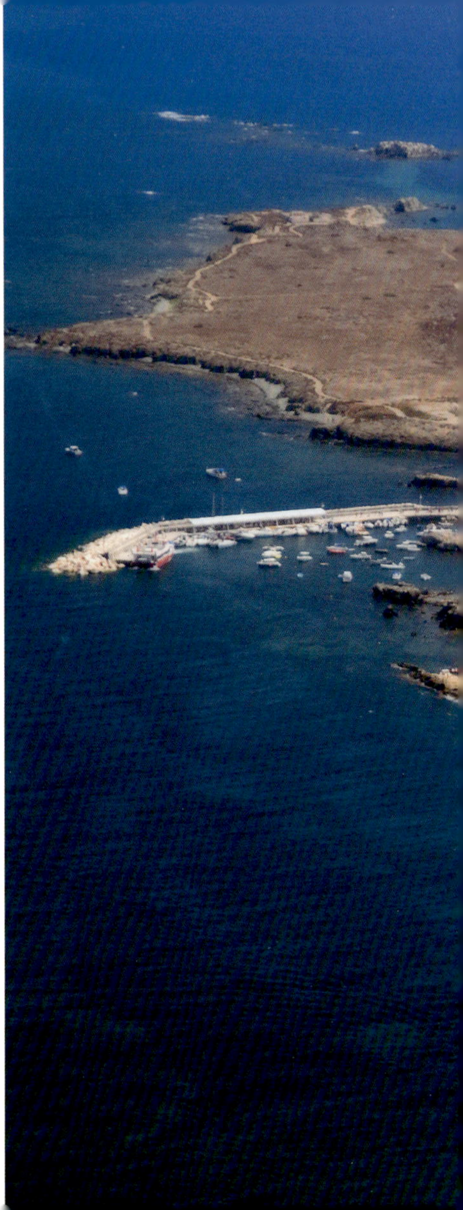

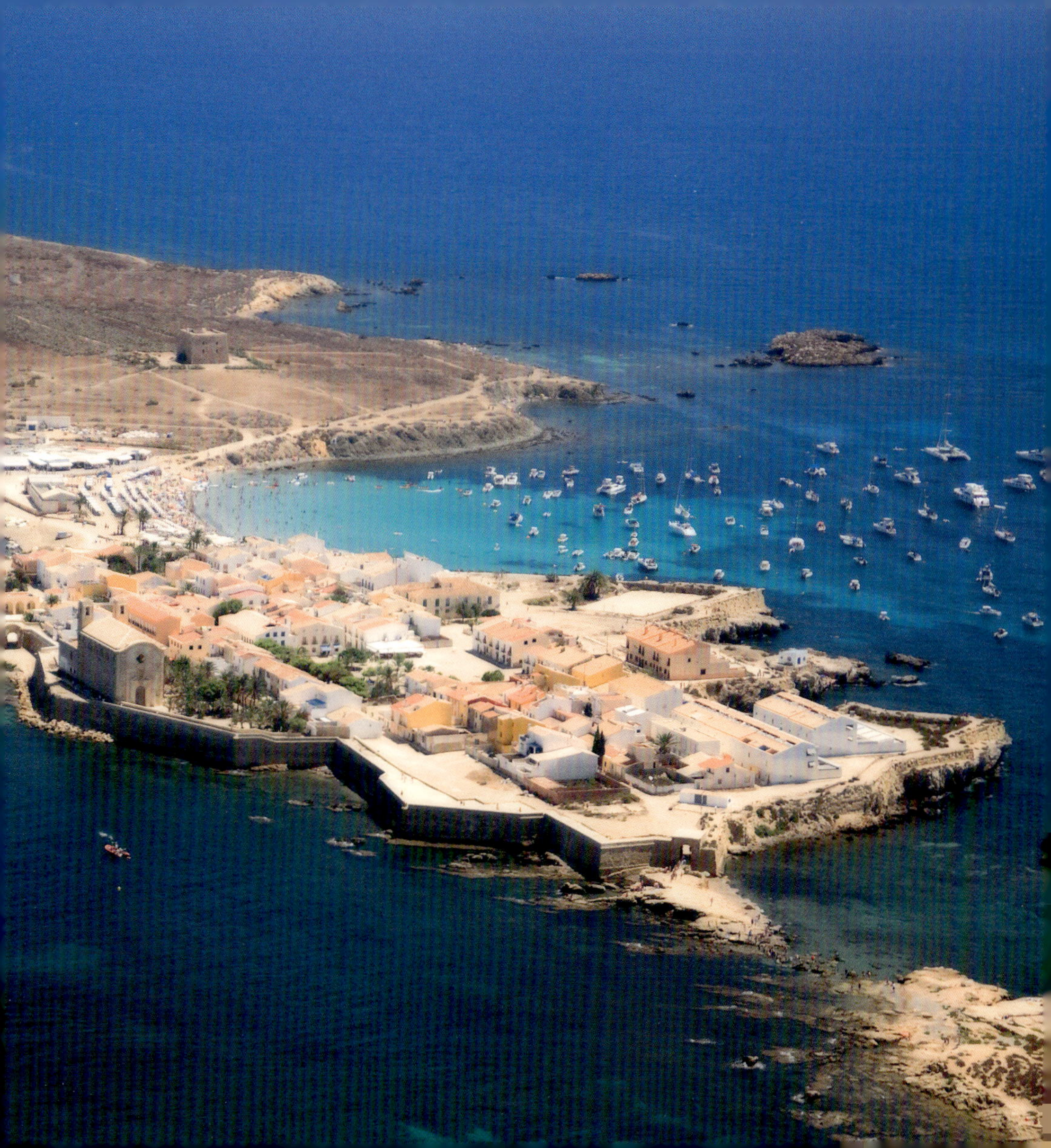

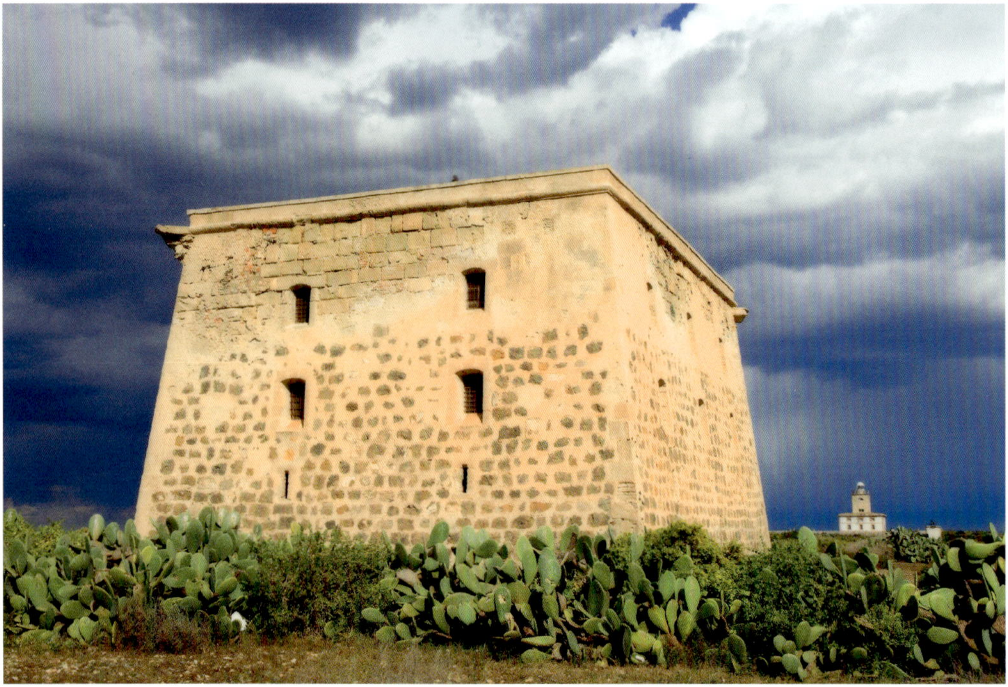

Tower of San José. In the background, the lighthouse

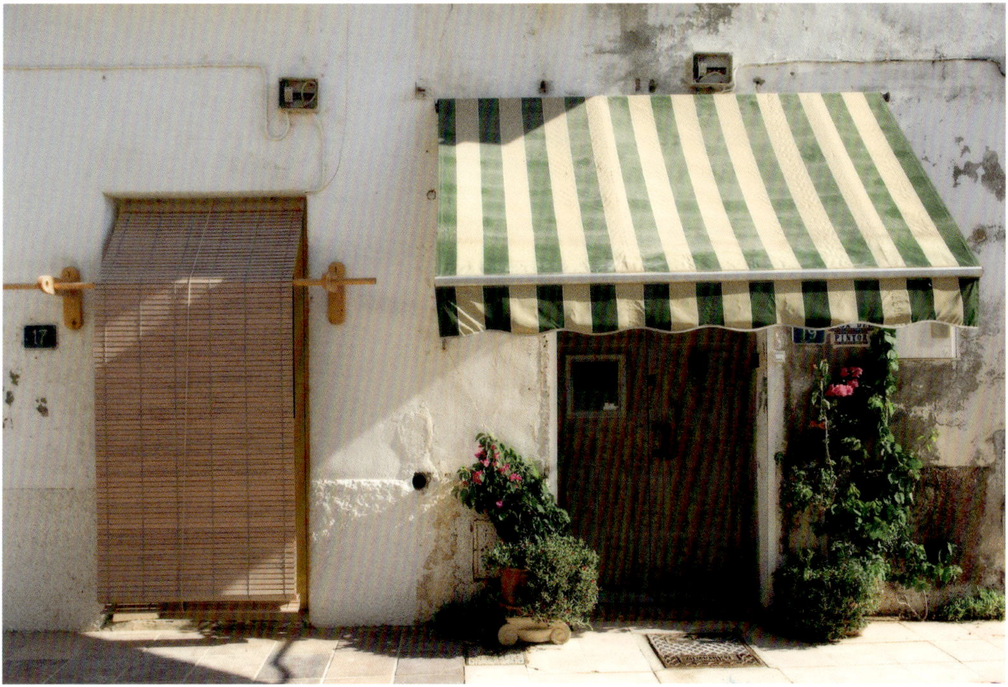

Tabarca

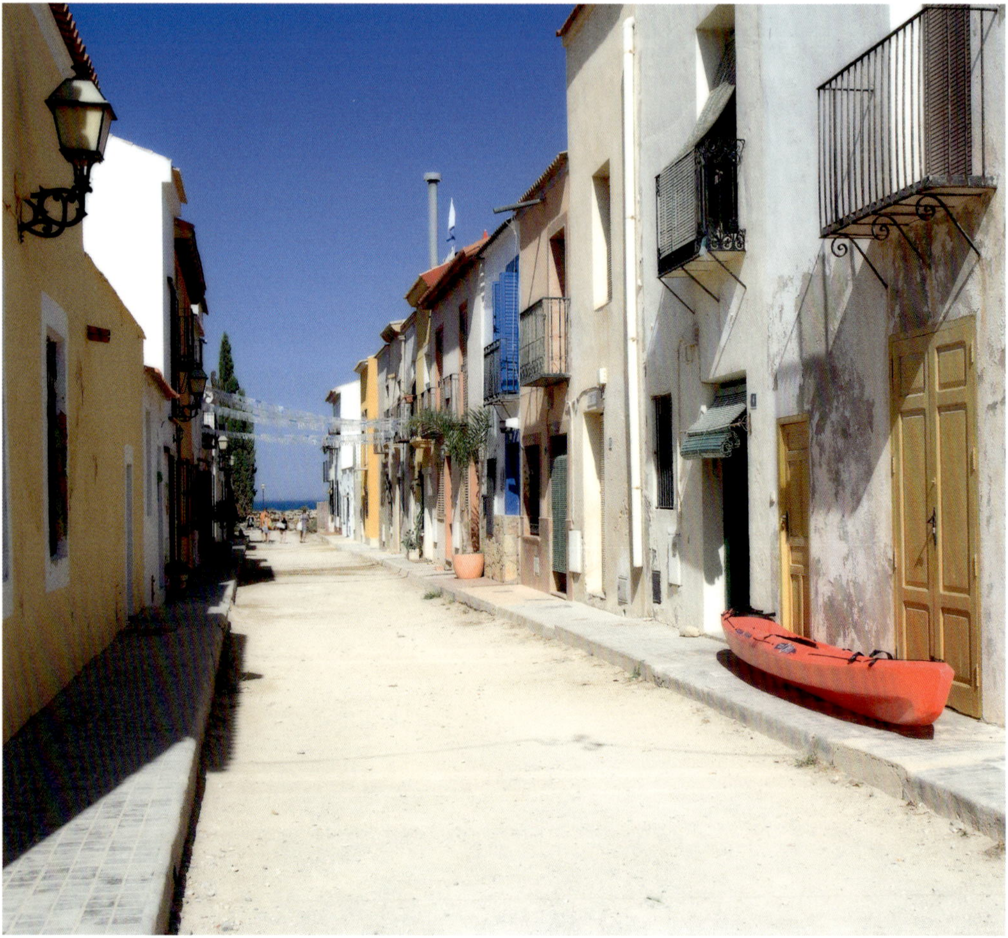

Old fishermen's houses

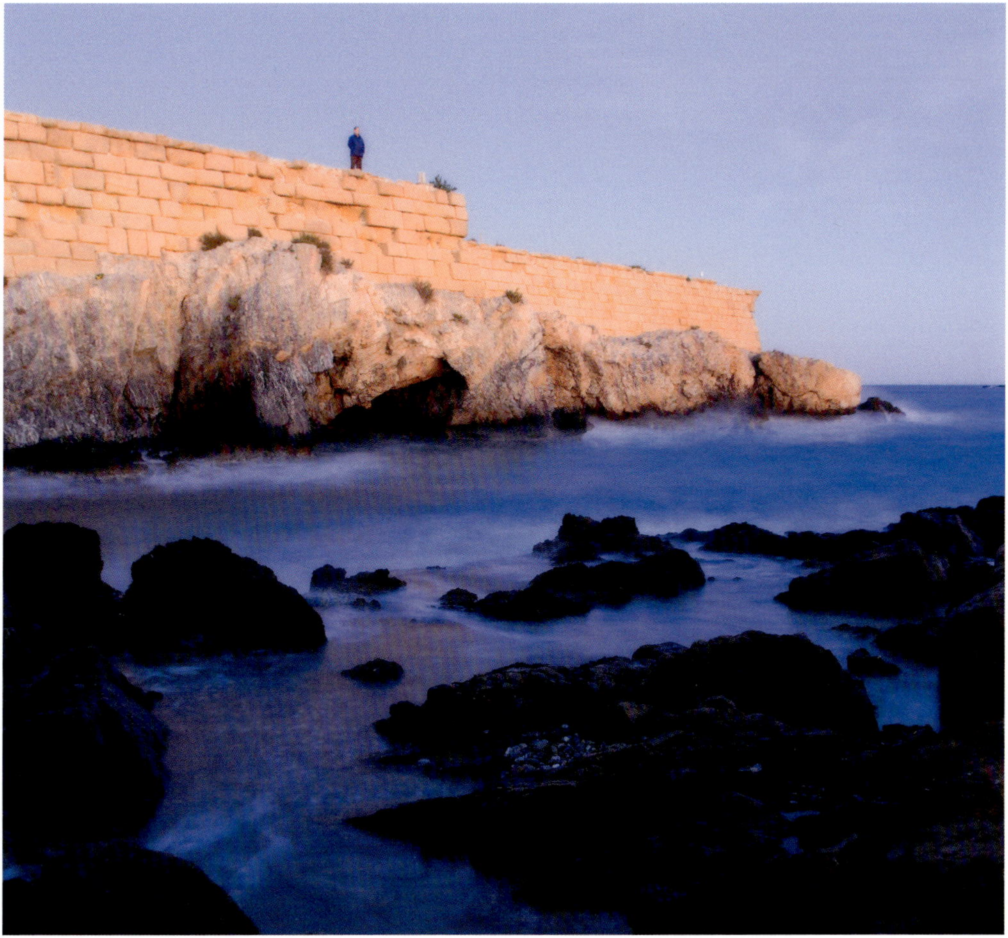

Remains of the city wall of Tabarca

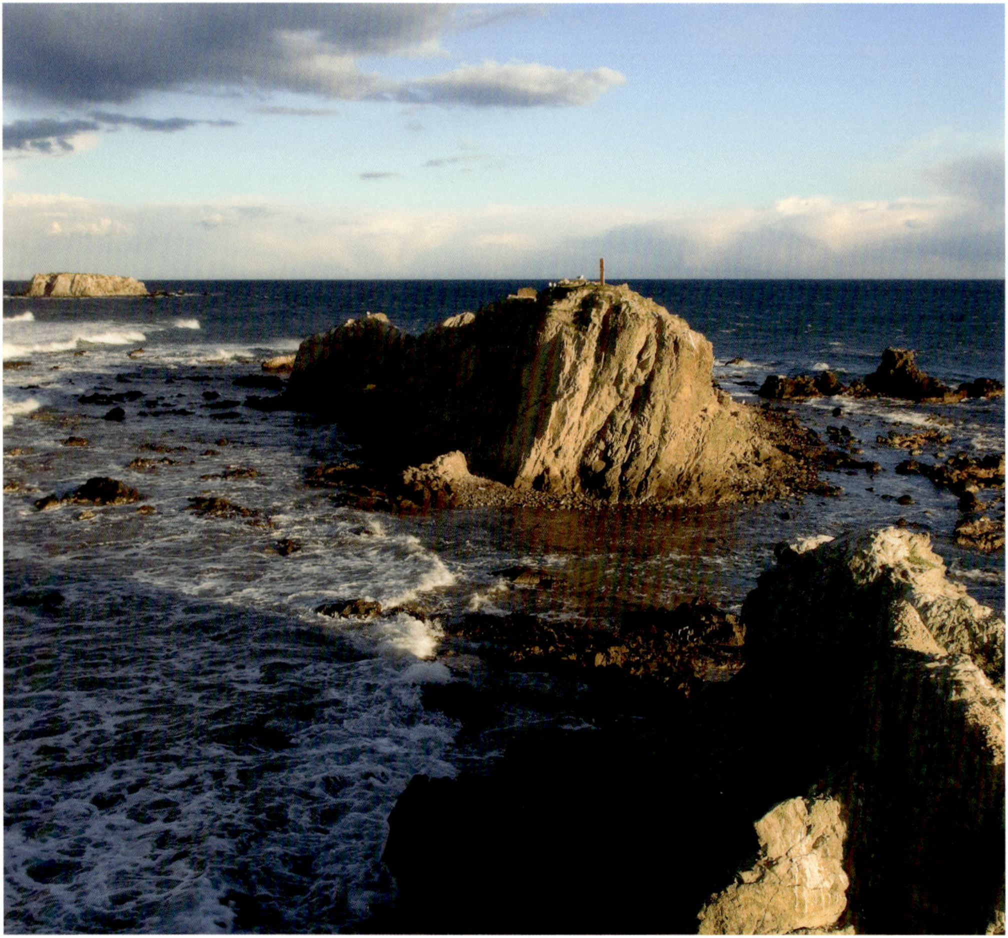

Punta Falcó

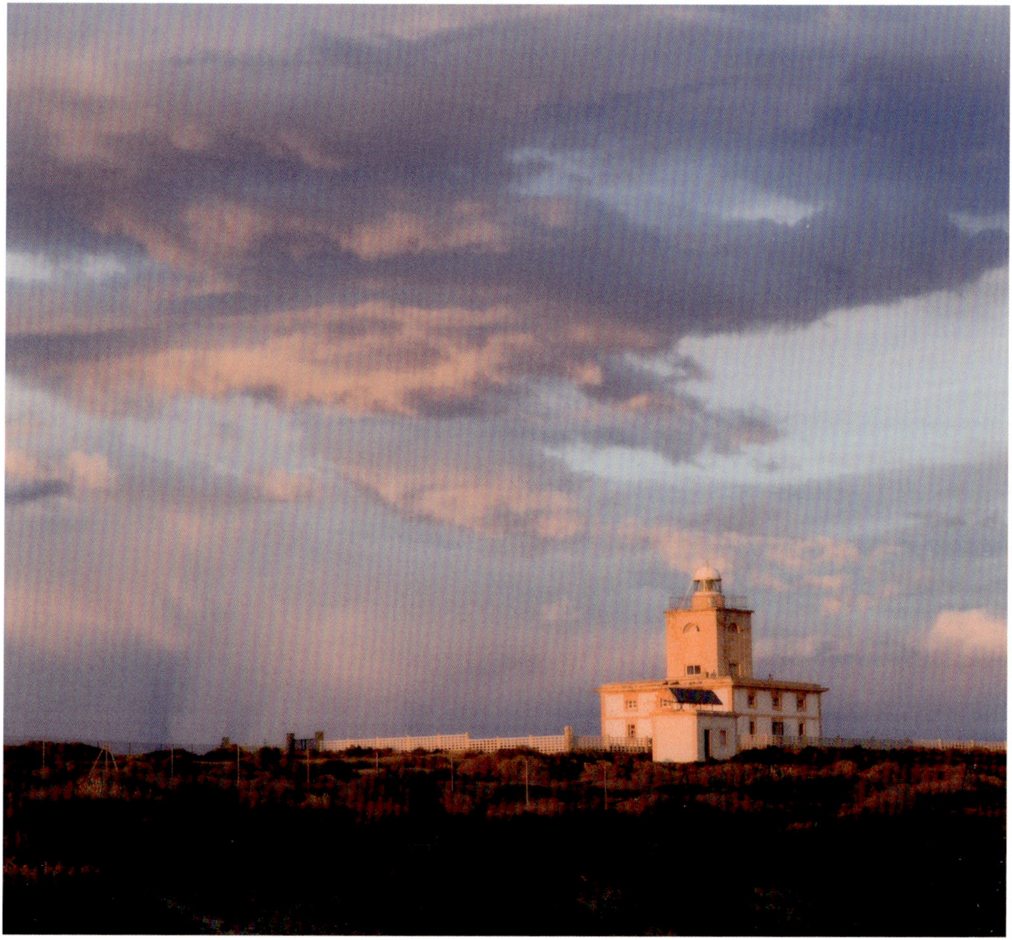

Lighthouse of the island of Tabarca

El Campello

On reaching El Campello, the coastline has dropped brusquely. Behind us are the cliffs of the counties of La Marina. The flat orography leads to interminable beaches of fine golden sand. A feint silhouette is all that remains of the mountains, that of the Cabezón de Oro, in the background of more than six kilometres of the beaches of Muchavista and the neighbouring beach of San Juan. The Calle del Mar beach, in the town centre, is also very popular. Next to these beaches, the seafront promenade and its palm trees invite one to stroll.

The town is one of the passing points of the popular TRAM, affectionately renamed *El trenet,* the little train.

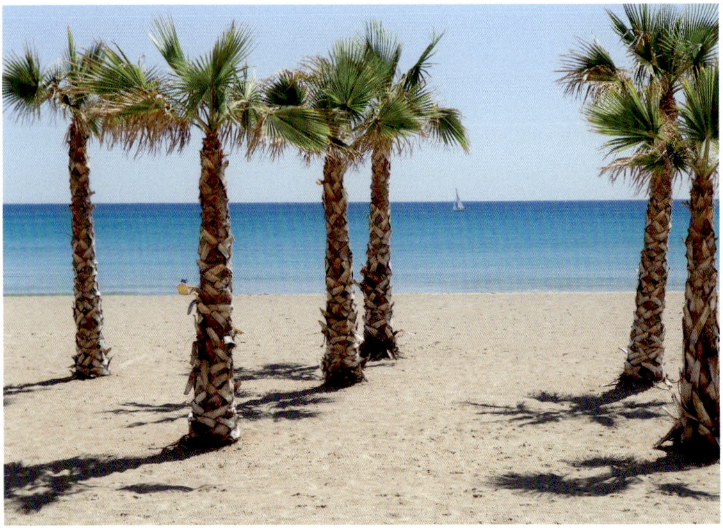

Carrer de la Mar beach

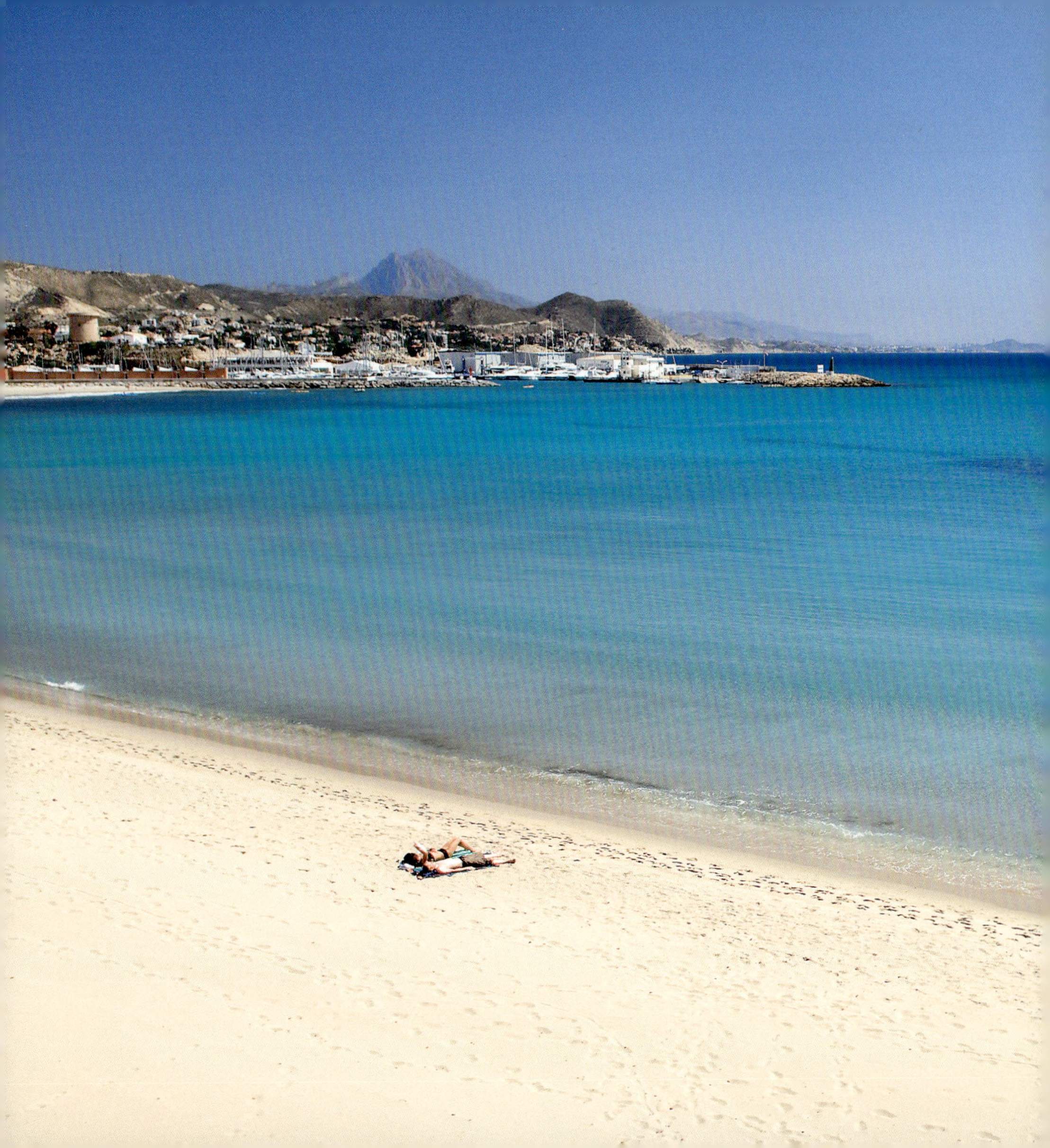

Agost

The beginning of the pottery tradition in Agost dates back to the 18th century. Until the middle of the last century, the economy of the town of Agost was based on the production of pottery items, mainly the white jug that keeps the water fresh and gives it that very particular flavour. Today hardly half a dozen potters remain, who continue traditional production, firing in wood-fired Moorish kilns.

The interest in tourism has led to the production to those known as "Sunday" novelties or souvenirs. In the interesting Pottery Museum we can discover the history, the process and see old pieces of such a deeply-rooted art.

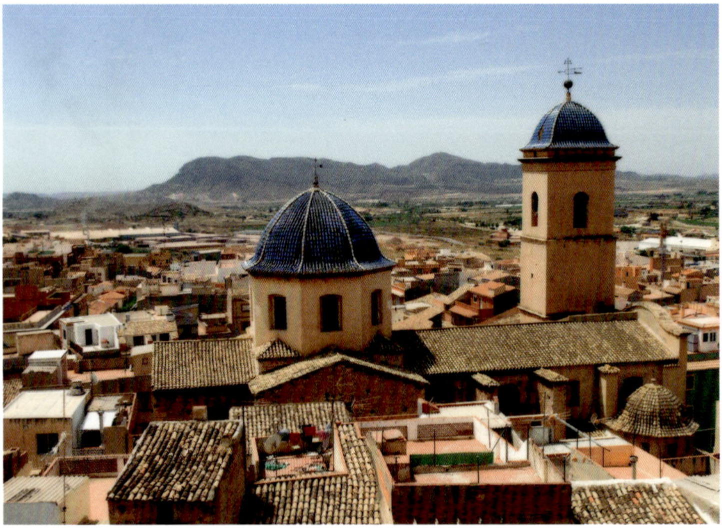

Traditional pottery

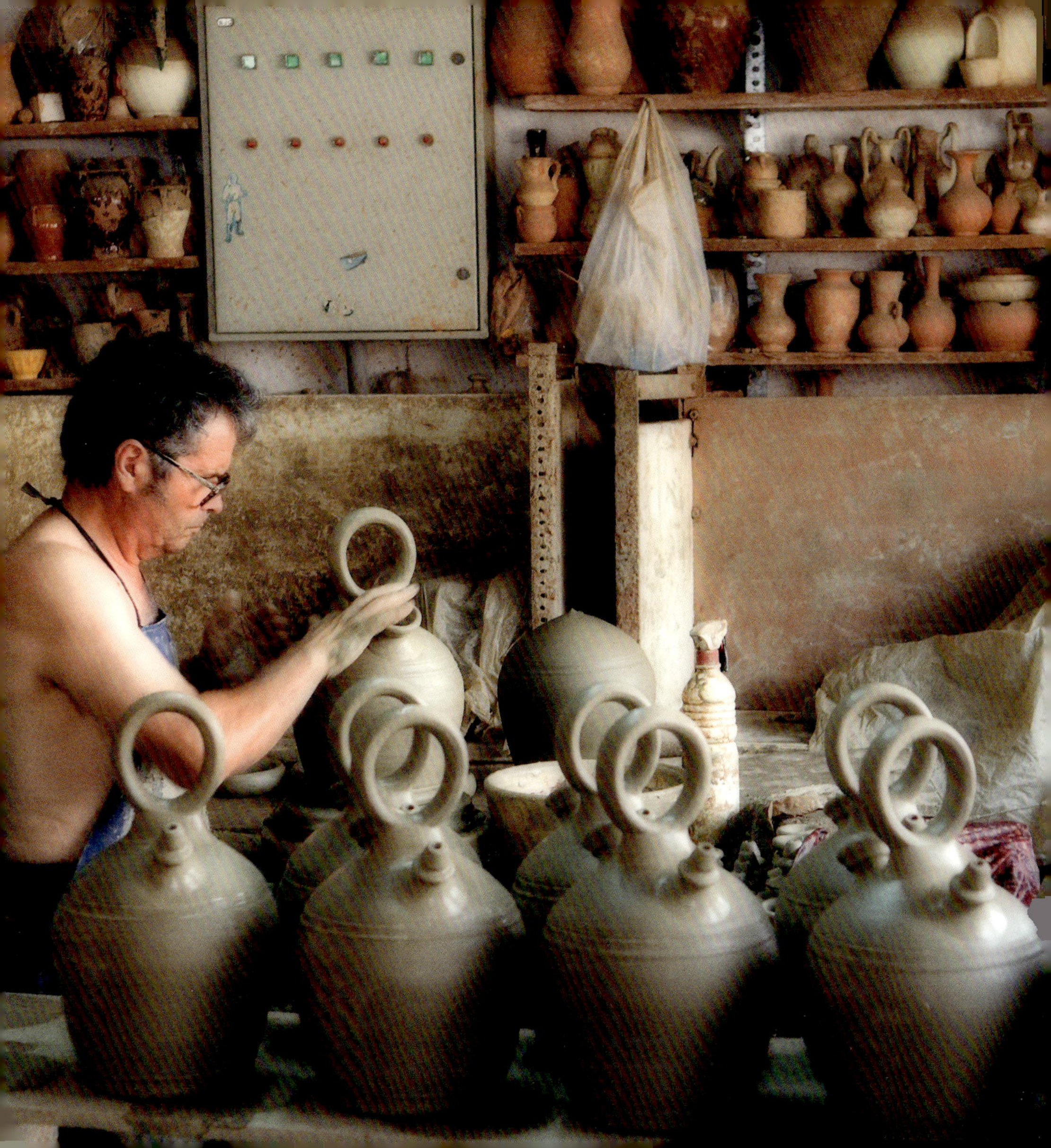

Busot

On the southern slope of the Cabezón de Oro range appears this small village of Muslim origin, as the remains of its castle bear witness. The village's main attraction are the caves of Canelobre. Its interior is similar to a cathedral, with one of the highest vaultings in Spain. During the visit we suggest a type of game in order to discover the fanciful shapes that the rocks acquire: candelabras, organs or the series known as the Sagrada Familia. The exceptional acoustics of the place have been used on occasions for holding concerts and other types of musical events.

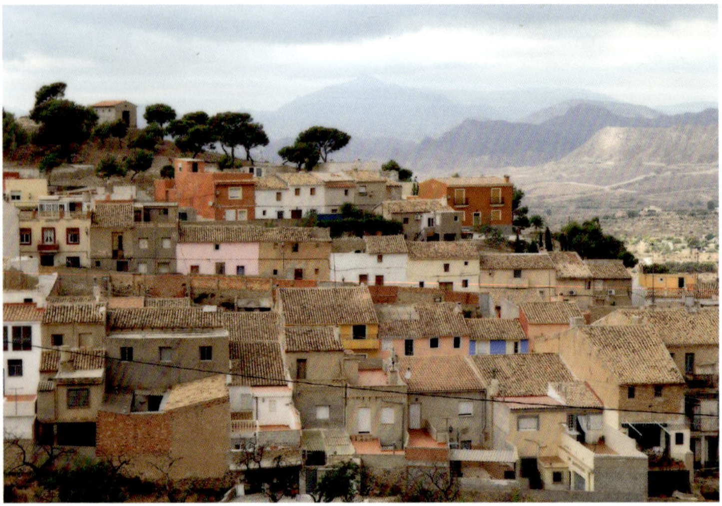

Canelobre caves

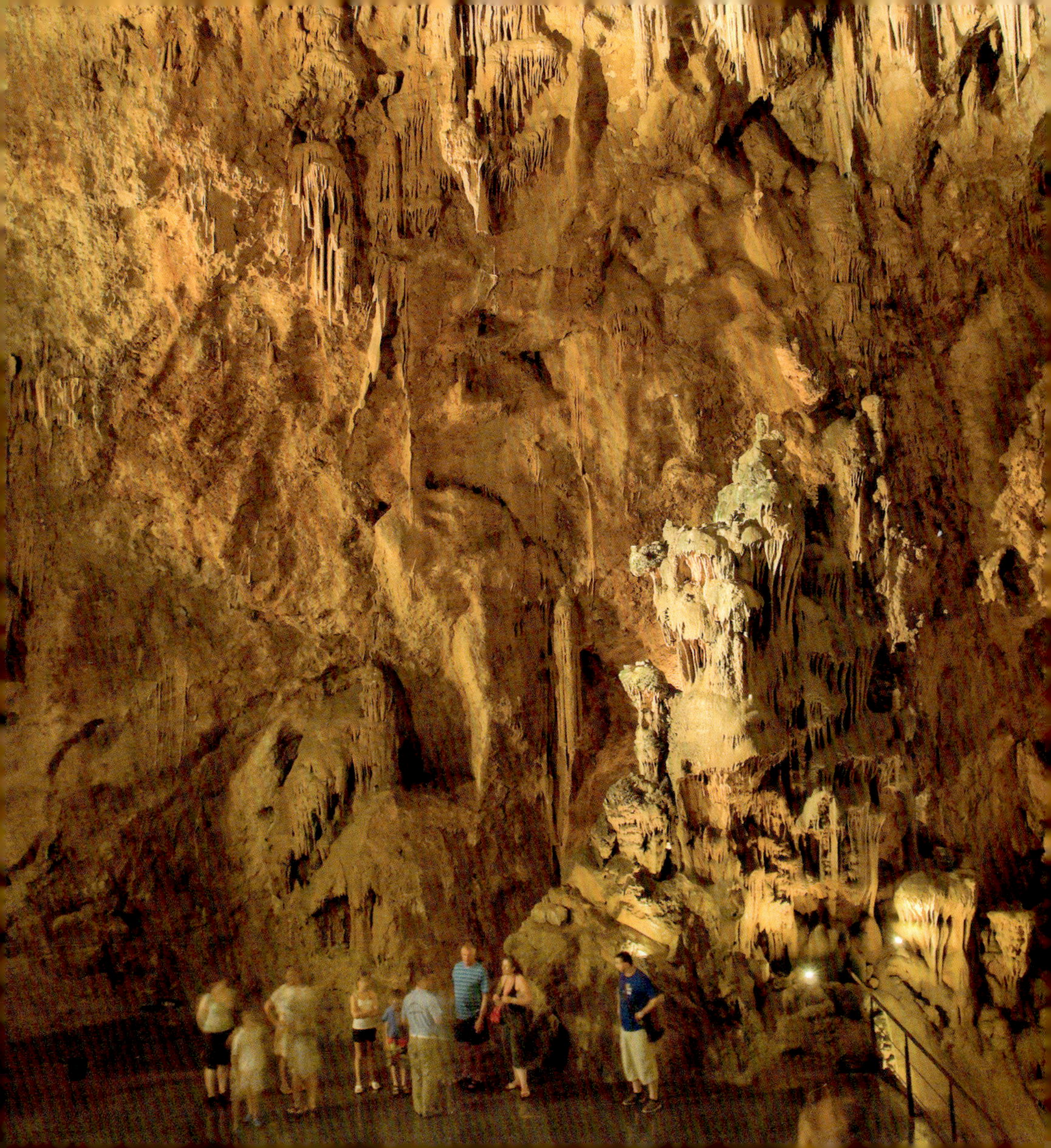

Xixona / Jijona

The town of Jijona, on the slopes of the Peña Roja, is known world-wide for the production of nougat. Sugar, honey, almond and eggs, the ingredients for an essential product on the table during the Christmas celebrations. Of uncertain origin —they speak of the Middle Ages—, nougat is still made using the traditional recipe. According to the process that the almond passes through, we have the hard nougat from Alicante or the soft variety from Jijona. The Nougat Museum shows us the history and the relationship the town has with this so famous sweet.

In the Carrasqueta range is conserved the snow well of Surdo, where snow was stored to turn into ice.

Snow well

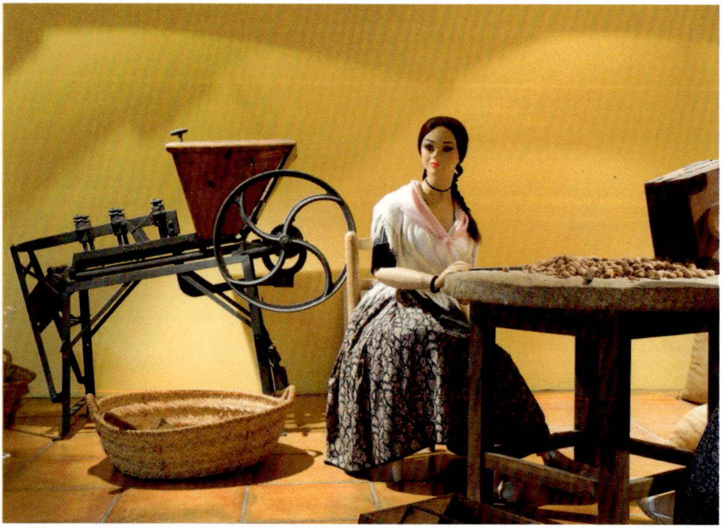

Turrón Museum

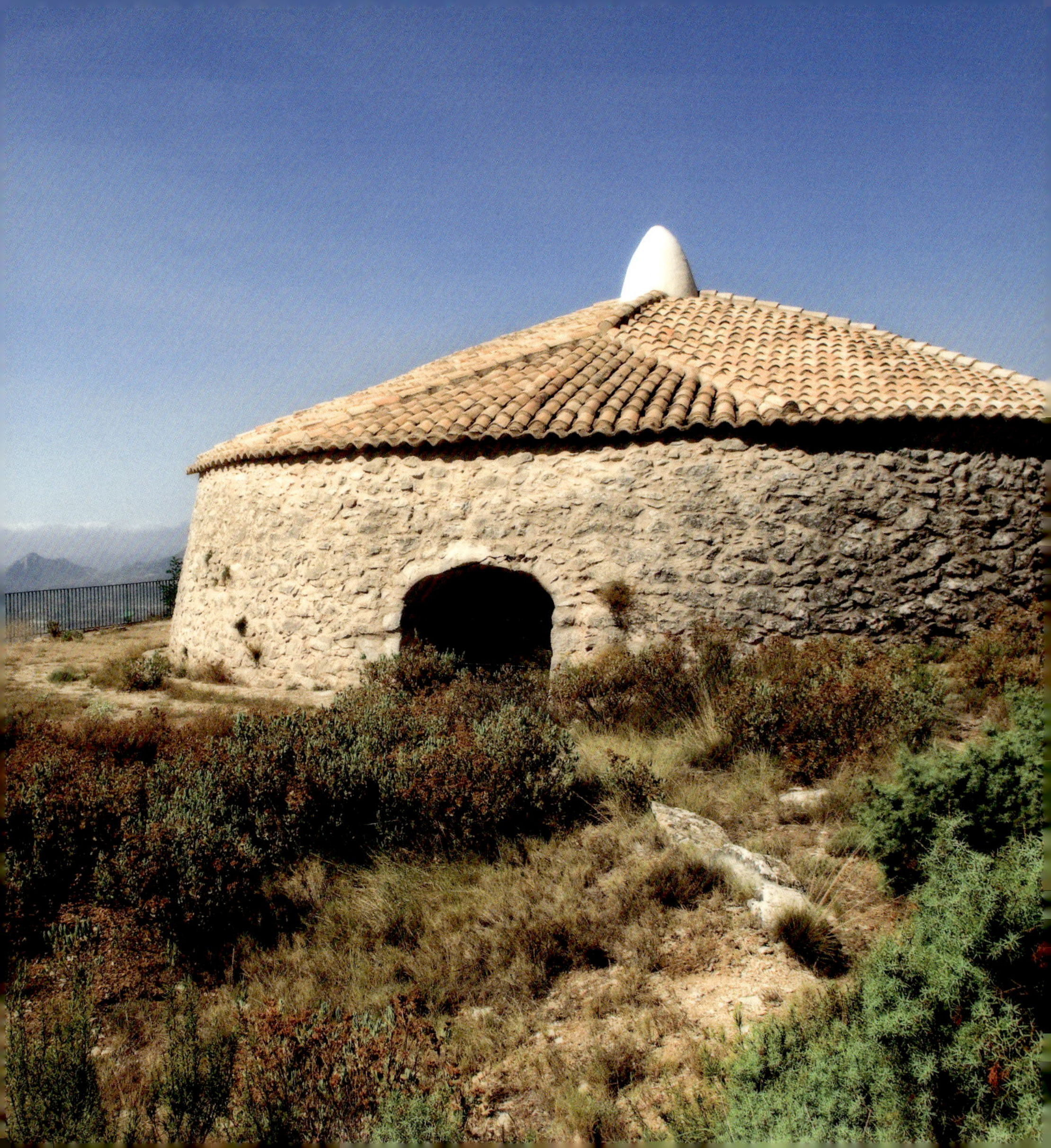

Vega Baja del Segura

Callosa de Segura
Torrevieja
Pilar de la Horadada
Orihuela
Guardamar del Segura

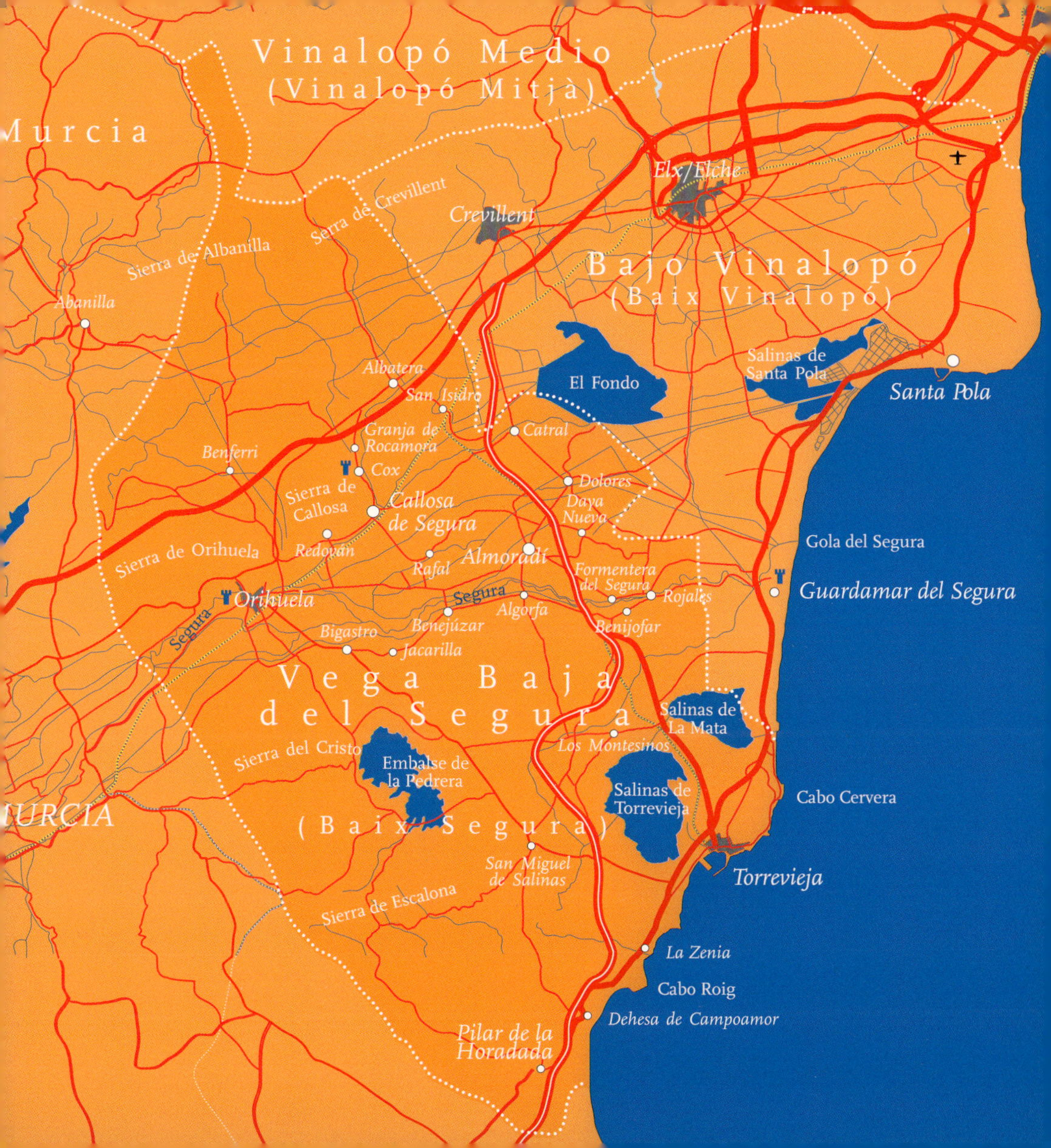

Vinalopó Medio
(Vinalopó Mitjà)
Murcia
Elx/Elche
Serra de Crevillent
Crevillent
Sierra de Albanilla
Abanilla
Bajo Vinalopó
(Baix Vinalopó)
Albatera
San Isidro
El Fondo
Salinas de Santa Pola
Santa Pola
Catral
Granja de Rocamora
Benferri
Cox
Dolores
Sierra de Callosa
Callosa de Segura
Daya Nueva
Redován
Sierra de Orihuela
Almoradí
Rafal
Gola del Segura
Formentera del Segura
Guardamar del Segura
Orihuela
Segura
Rojales
Algorfa
Benejúzar
Benijofar
Bigastro
Jacarilla
Vega Baja del Segura
Salinas de La Mata
Los Montesinos
Sierra del Cristo
Embalse de la Pedrera
Salinas de Torrevieja
Cabo Cervera
(Baix Segura)
Torrevieja
San Miguel de Salinas
Sierra de Escalona
La Zenia
Cabo Roig
Dehesa de Campoamor
Pilar de la Horadada

Callosa de Segura

The county of La Vega Baja del Segura is a tapestry of extremely fertile lands that have the deserved fame as the orchard of the province of Alicante.

The title of city was awarded to Callosa de Segura by grace of Alfonso XIII. The old city centre conserves the medieval layout and its cobbled streets which had already received the monarch in his stays there.

On a small hill appears the sanctuary of San Roque with its colonial façade and the figure of the hermit San Roquero, the person who was in charge of watching over the place. From this height you can make out a fine panoramic view of the province. It is no coincidence that this spot is known as the balcony of Vega Baja.

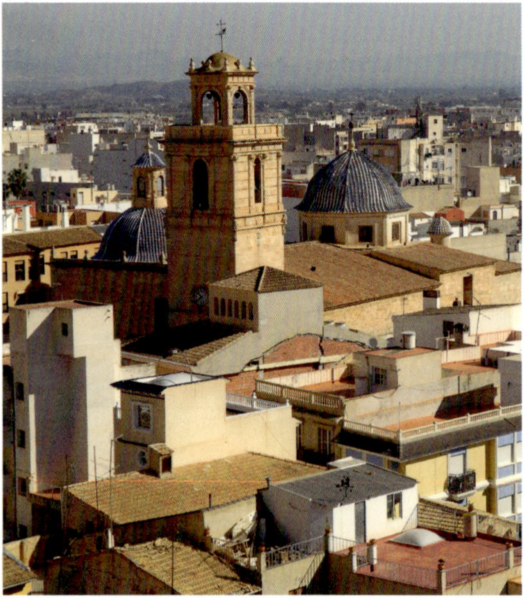

Church of San Martín

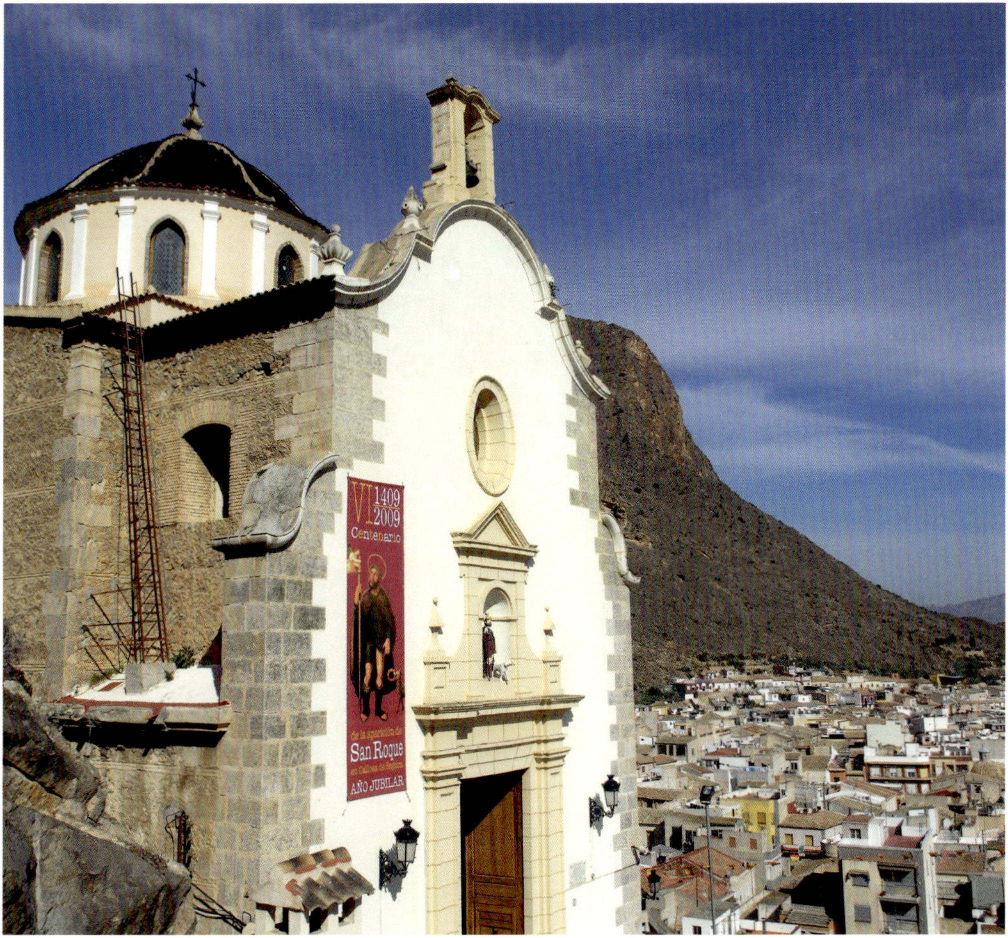

Sanctuary of San Roque

Torrevieja

You are bewitching, / song of loves / peaceful dream / for he who seeks / to dream alongside the sea. This is how the best-known shanty song or *habanera* of the city ends, the work of Ricardo Lafuente.

During recent decades, people have come to Torrevieja attracted by its beaches, by that sea to dream alongside. Before the arrival of tourism the city was particularly significant in the salt trade from the nearby exploitations. The saltworks of La Mata-Torrevieja are protected under the figure of Natural Park.

Two internationally recognised events place the cultural note on the calendar. Firstly, the International Event of Shanty Songs and Polyphony is held in July in Las Eras de la Sal, and old deposit and salt jetty. And secondly, the Ciudad de Torrevieja novel prize, the second biggest in economic reward after the Planeta prize.

Acequión beach

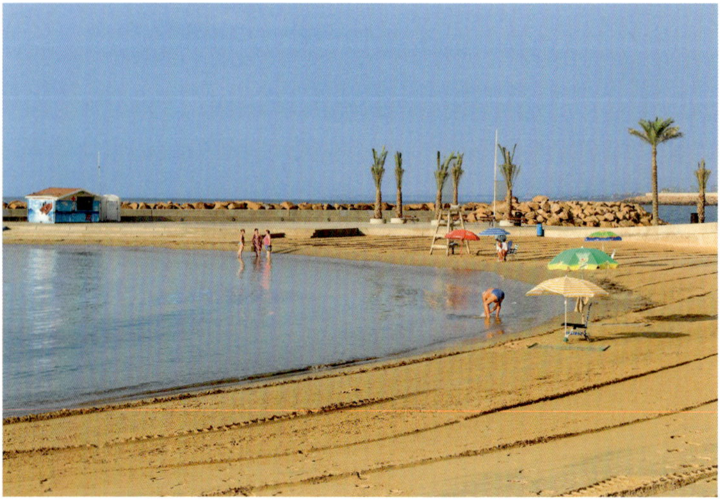

Cura beach

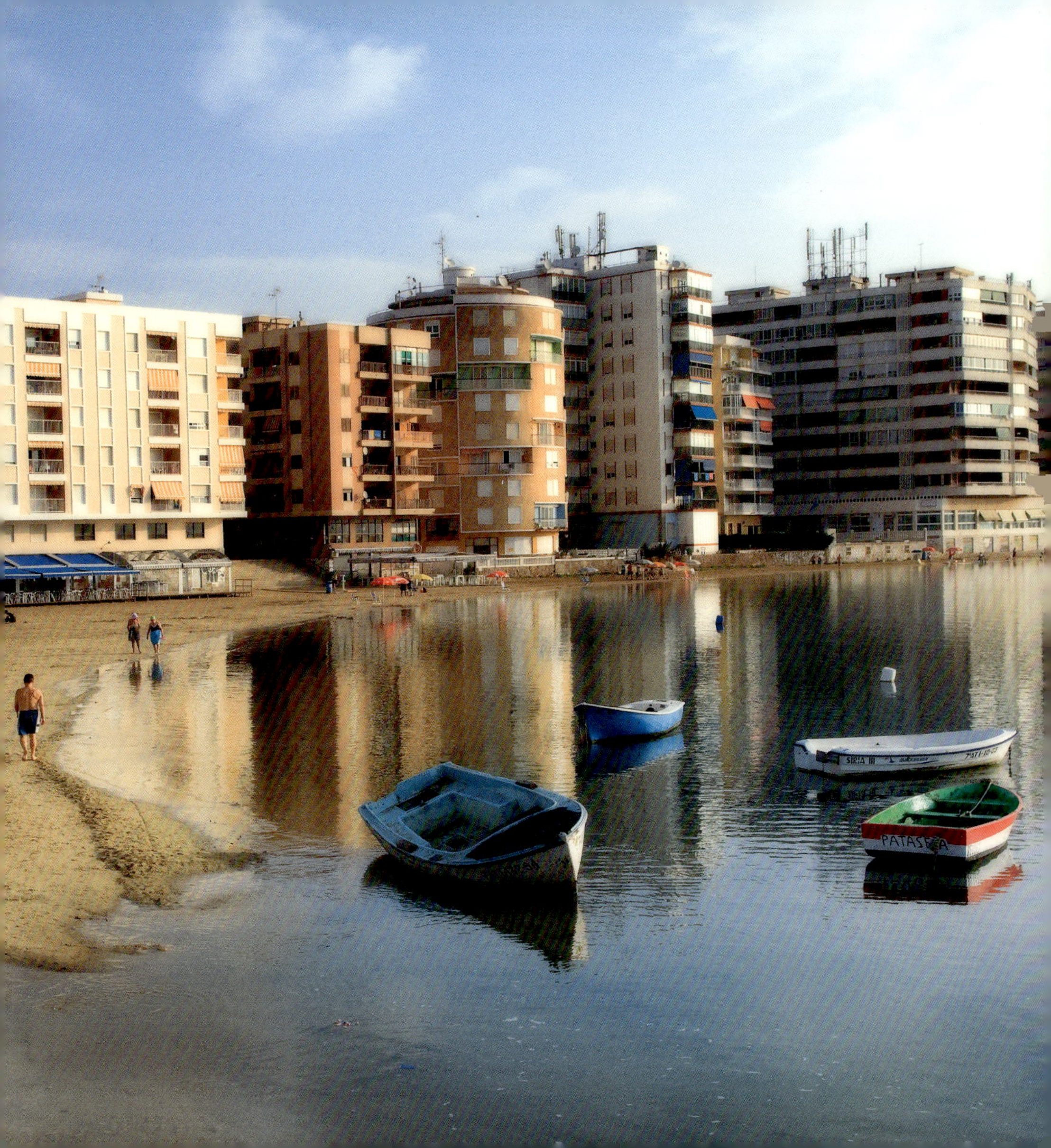

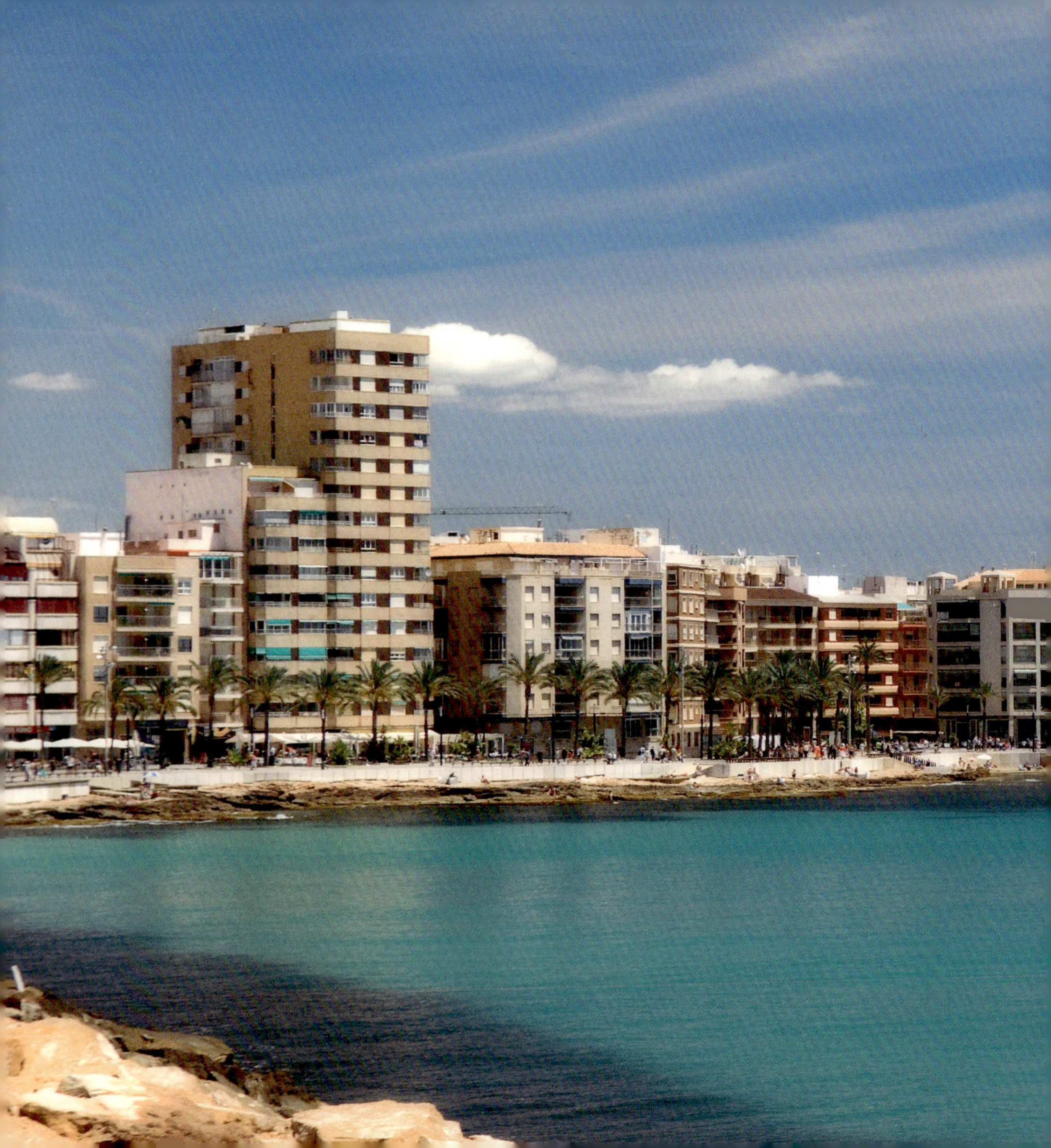

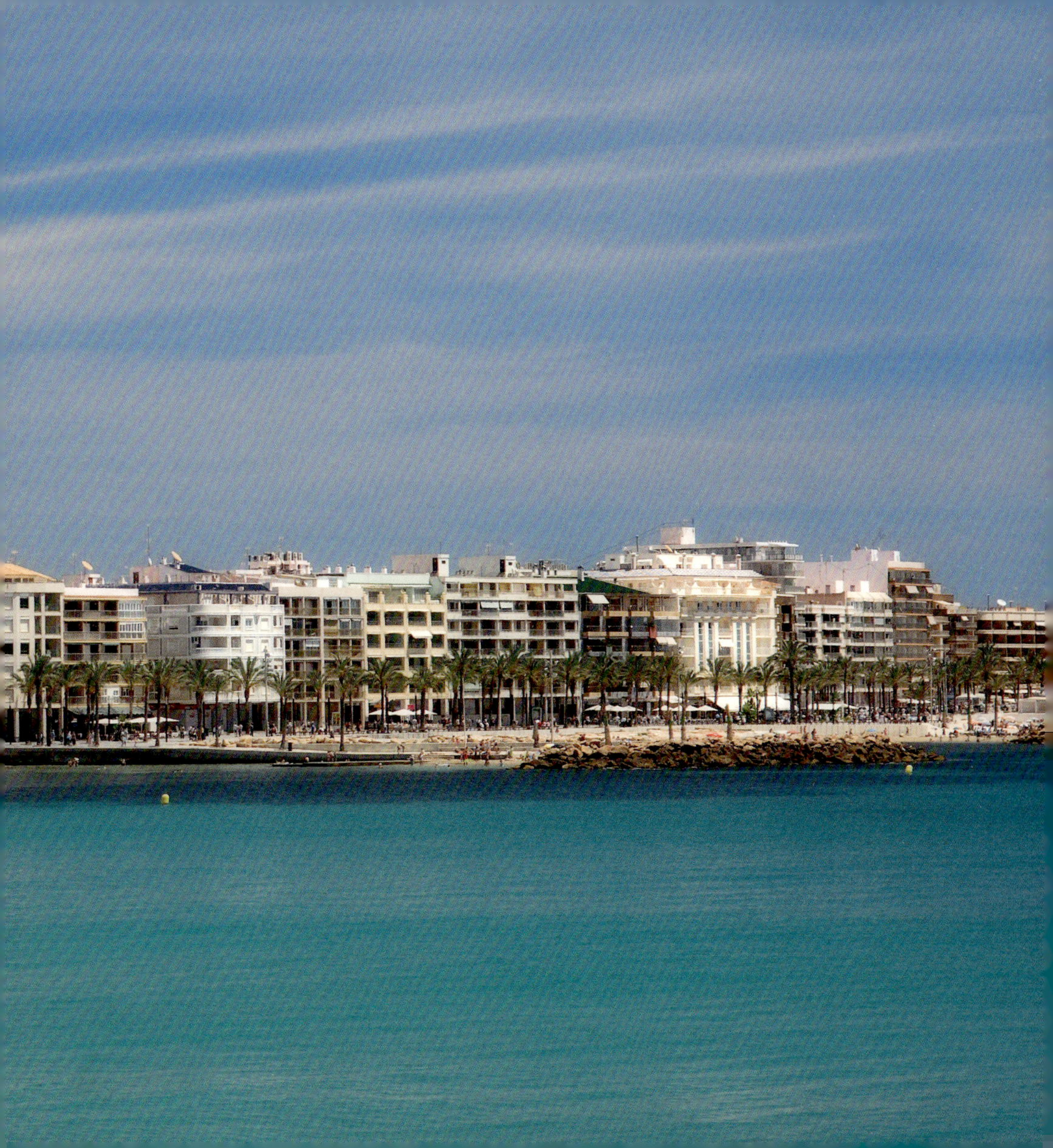

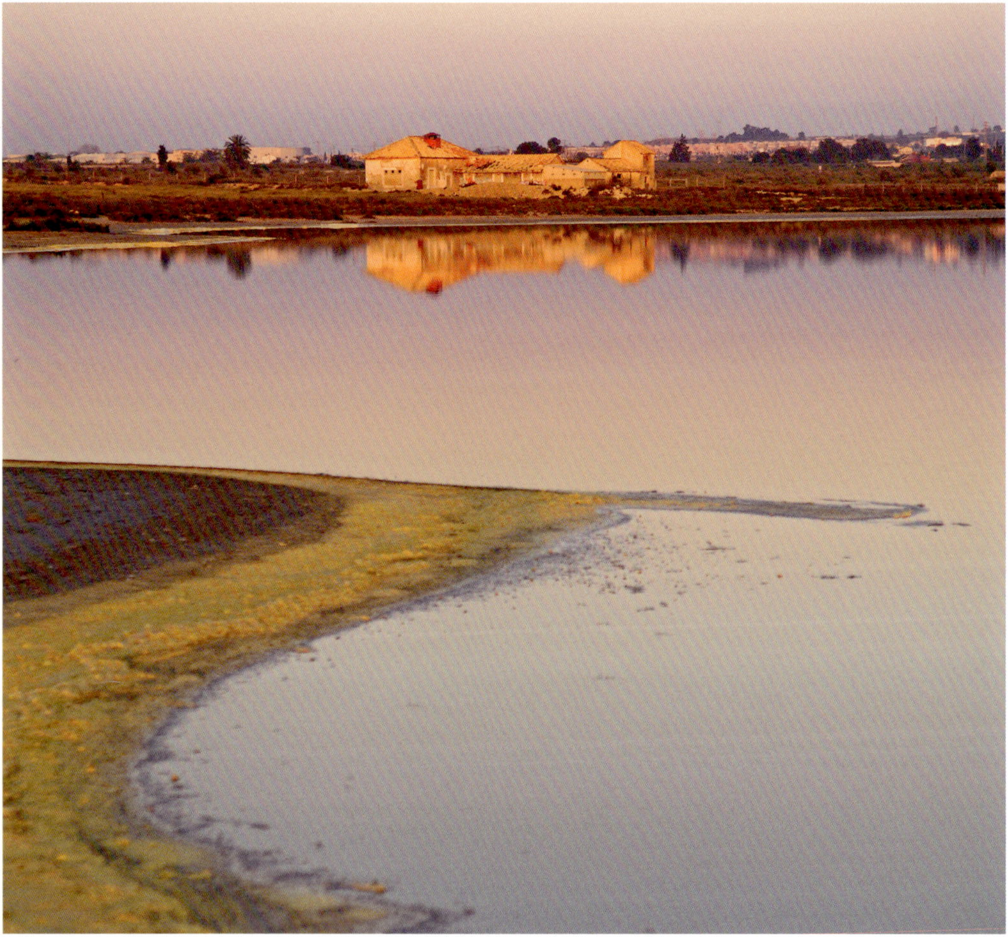

Natural Park of Lagunas La Mata-Torrevieja

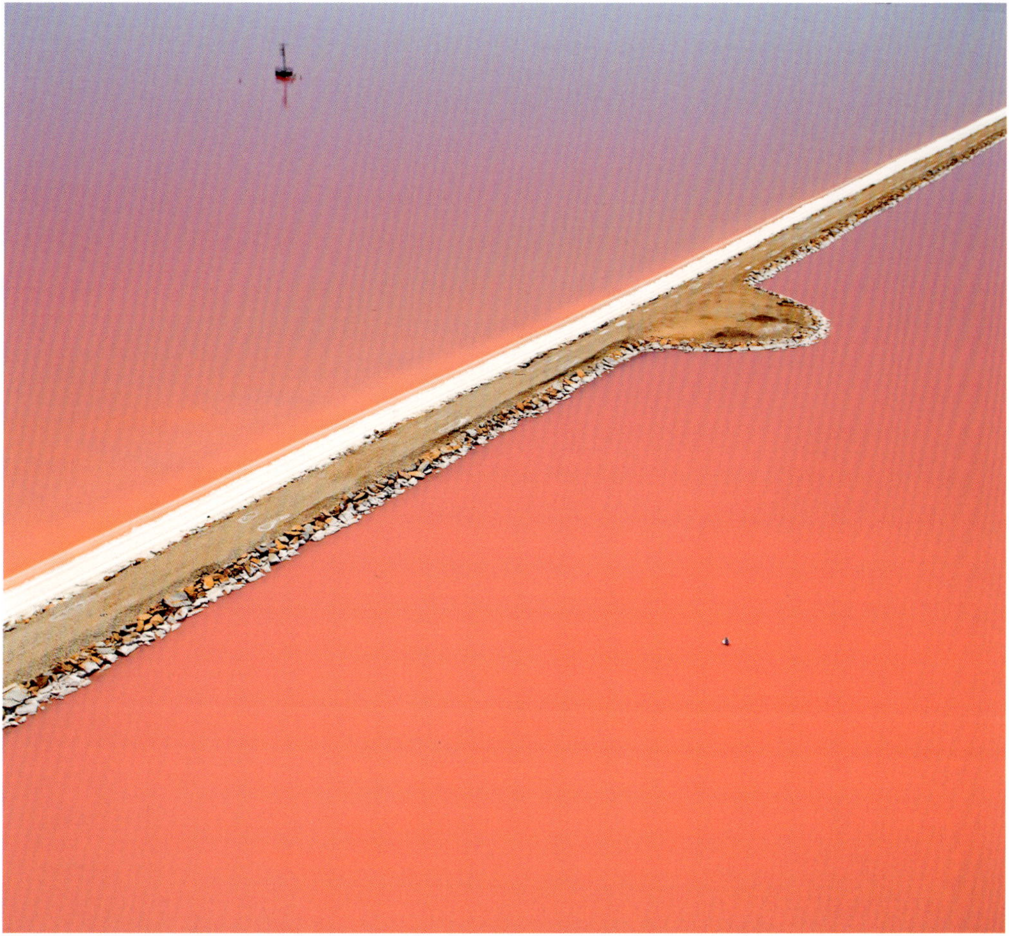

Saltworks of Torrevieja
Natural Park of Lagunas La Mata-Torrevieja →

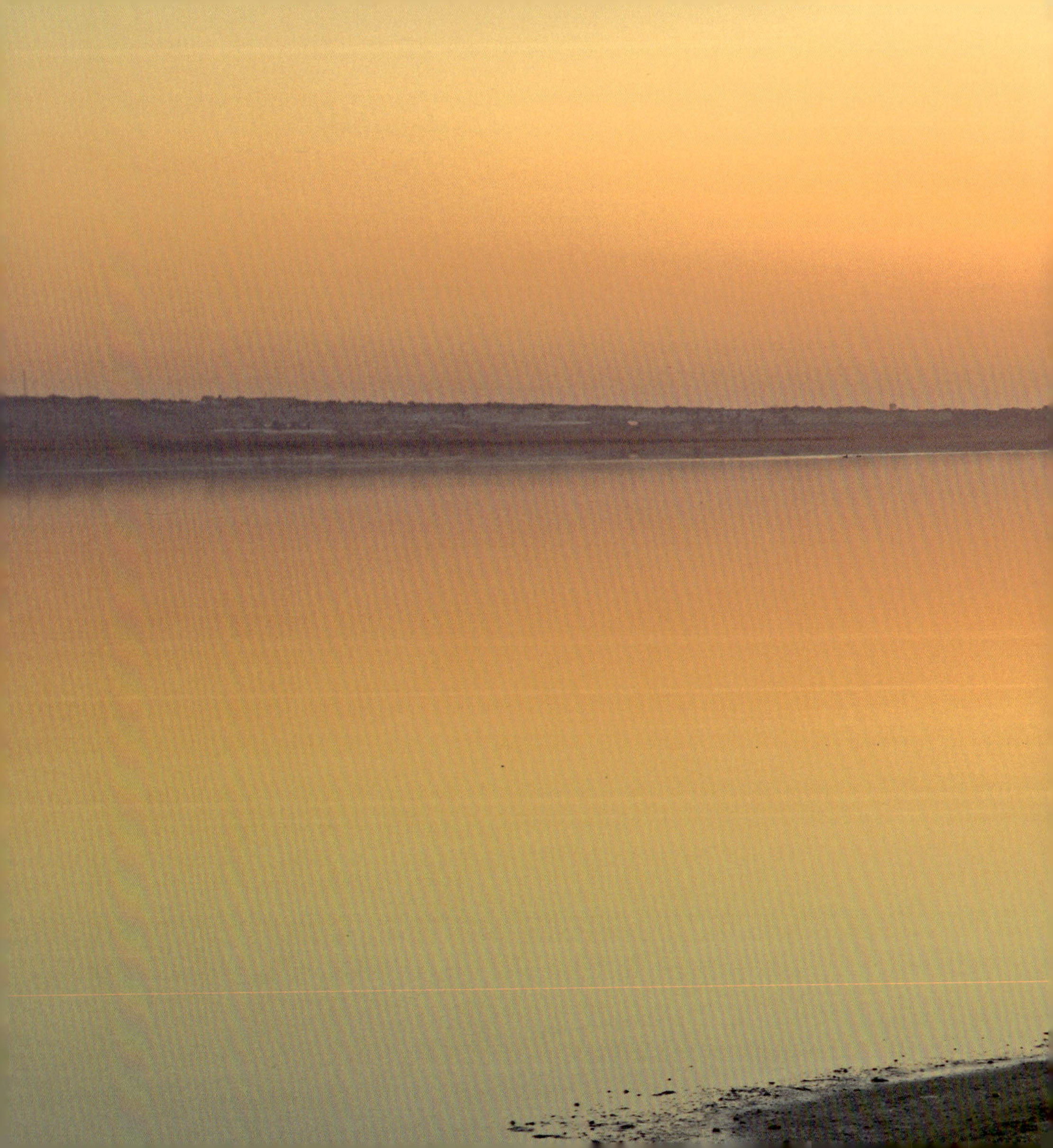

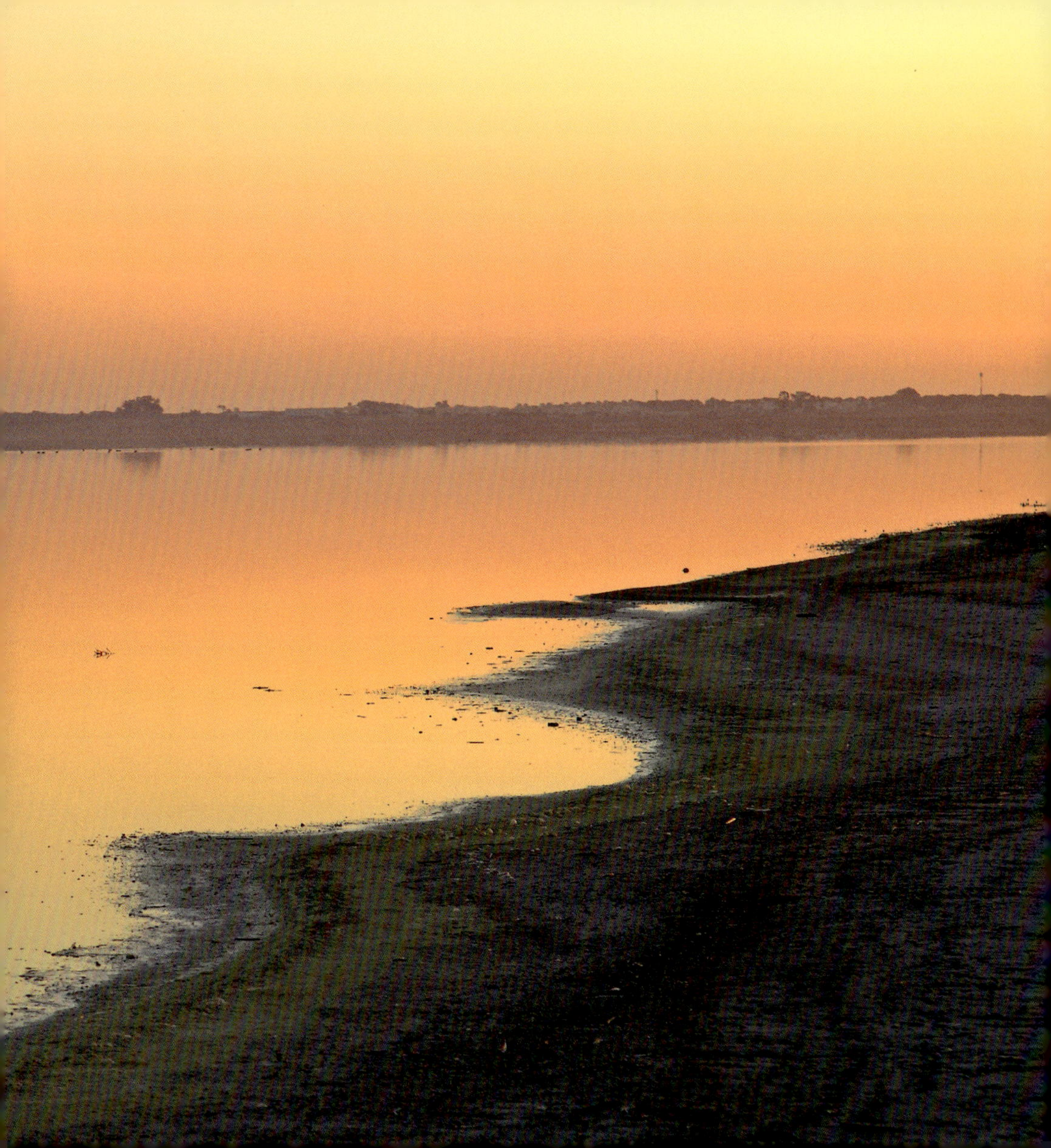

Pilar de la Horadada

The ancient Thiar, in Roman times, was a passing point along the Via Augusta between the current towns of Elche and Cartagena. When pirate incursions were common all along the coastline, a series of watchtowers were built due to the need to warn the population of those hostile approaches. Out of all of them, the one best-conserved is the Torre Horadada, thus named for the holes that were used for communication between the guards. The coastline of Pilar de la Horadada is a succession of quiet beaches among which stand out those of Conde, Higuericas, Mil Palmeras and the small coves of Rocamar.

Rocamar coves →

Conde beach in Torre de la Horadada →→

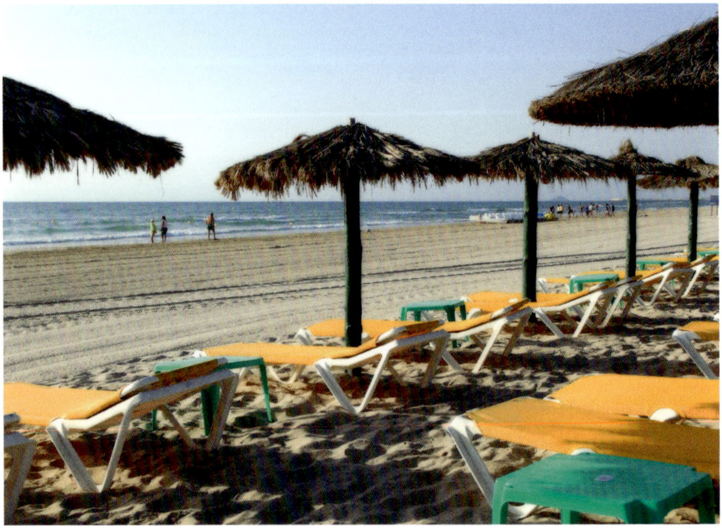

Las Higuericas beach

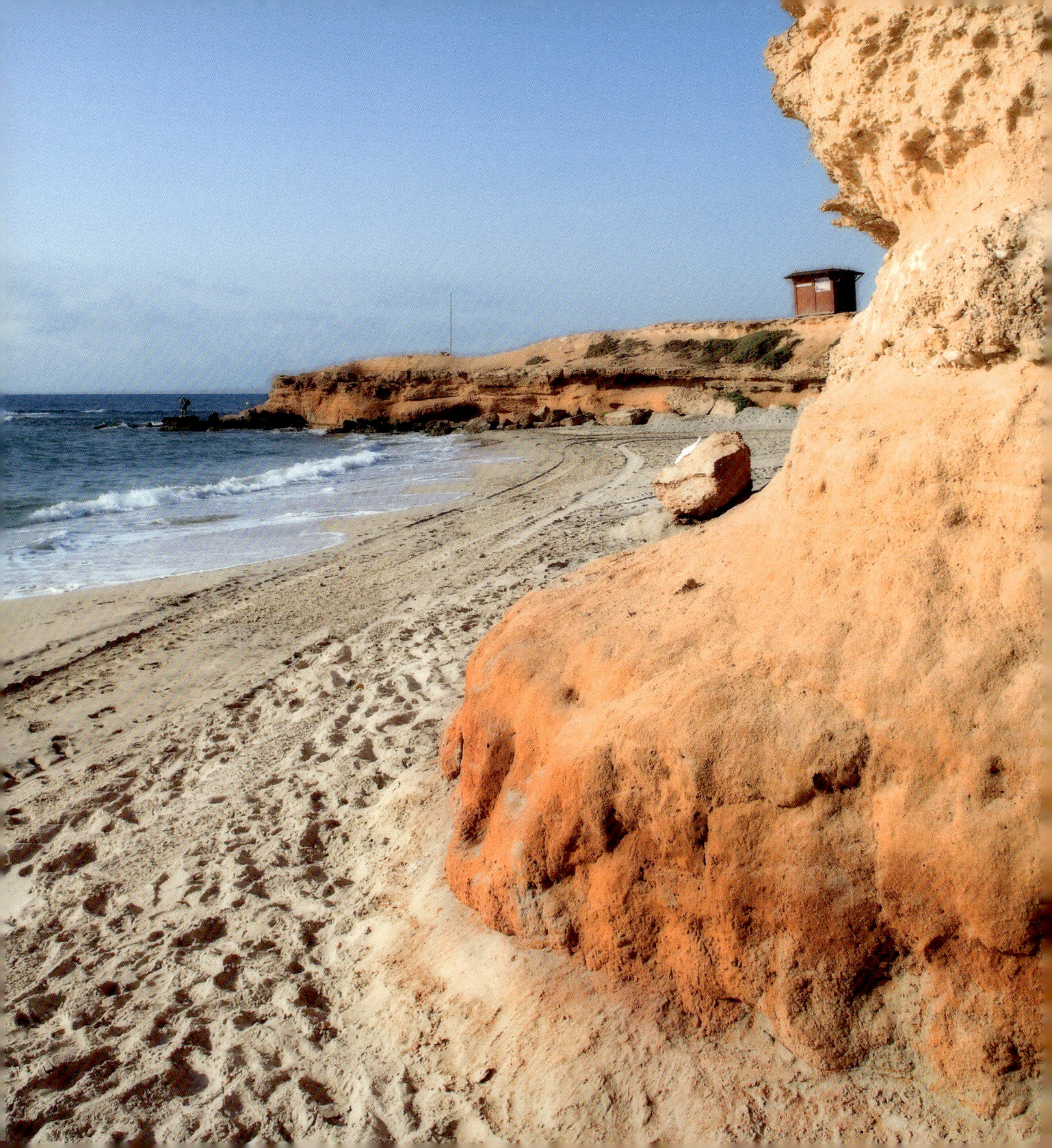

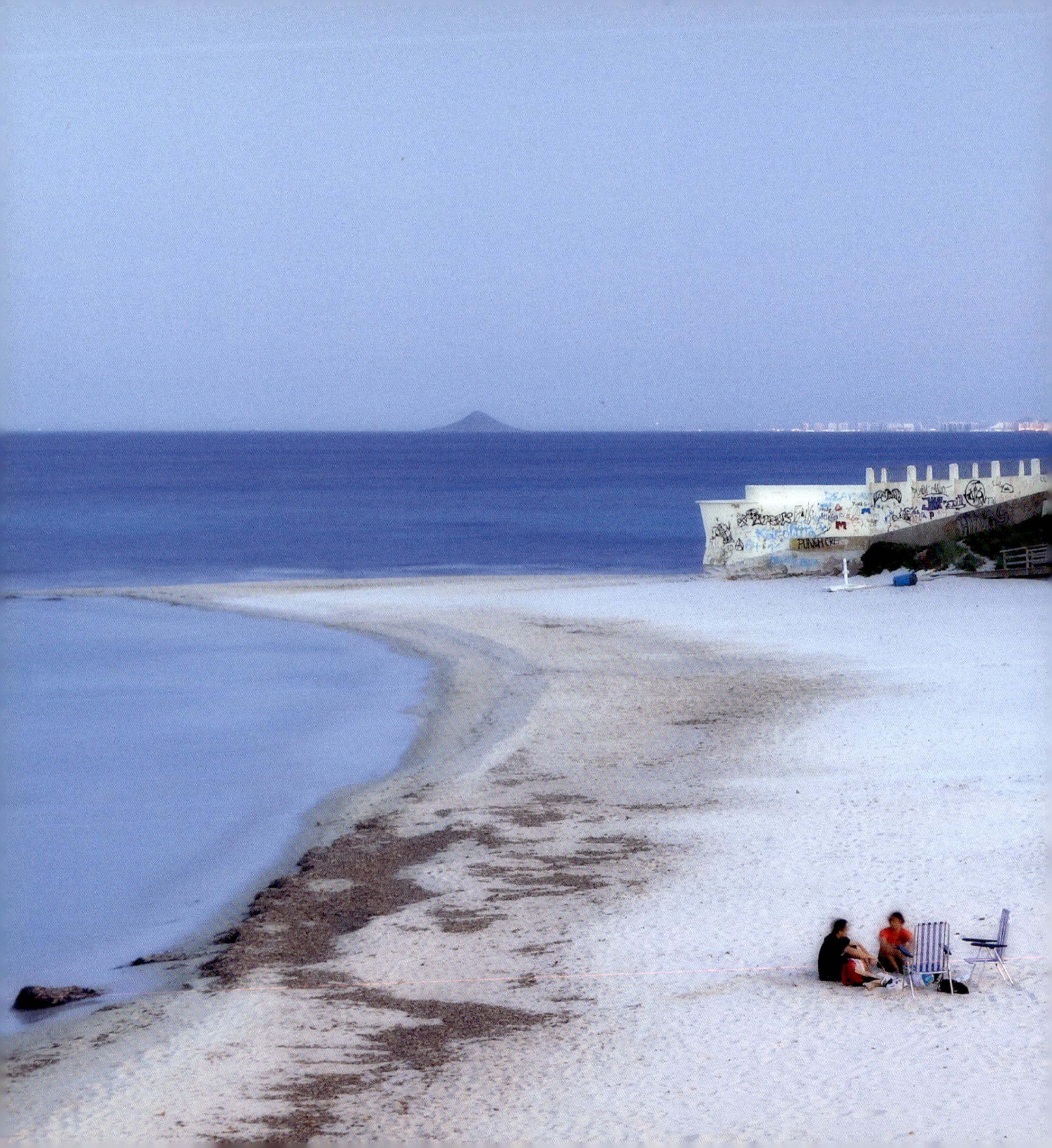

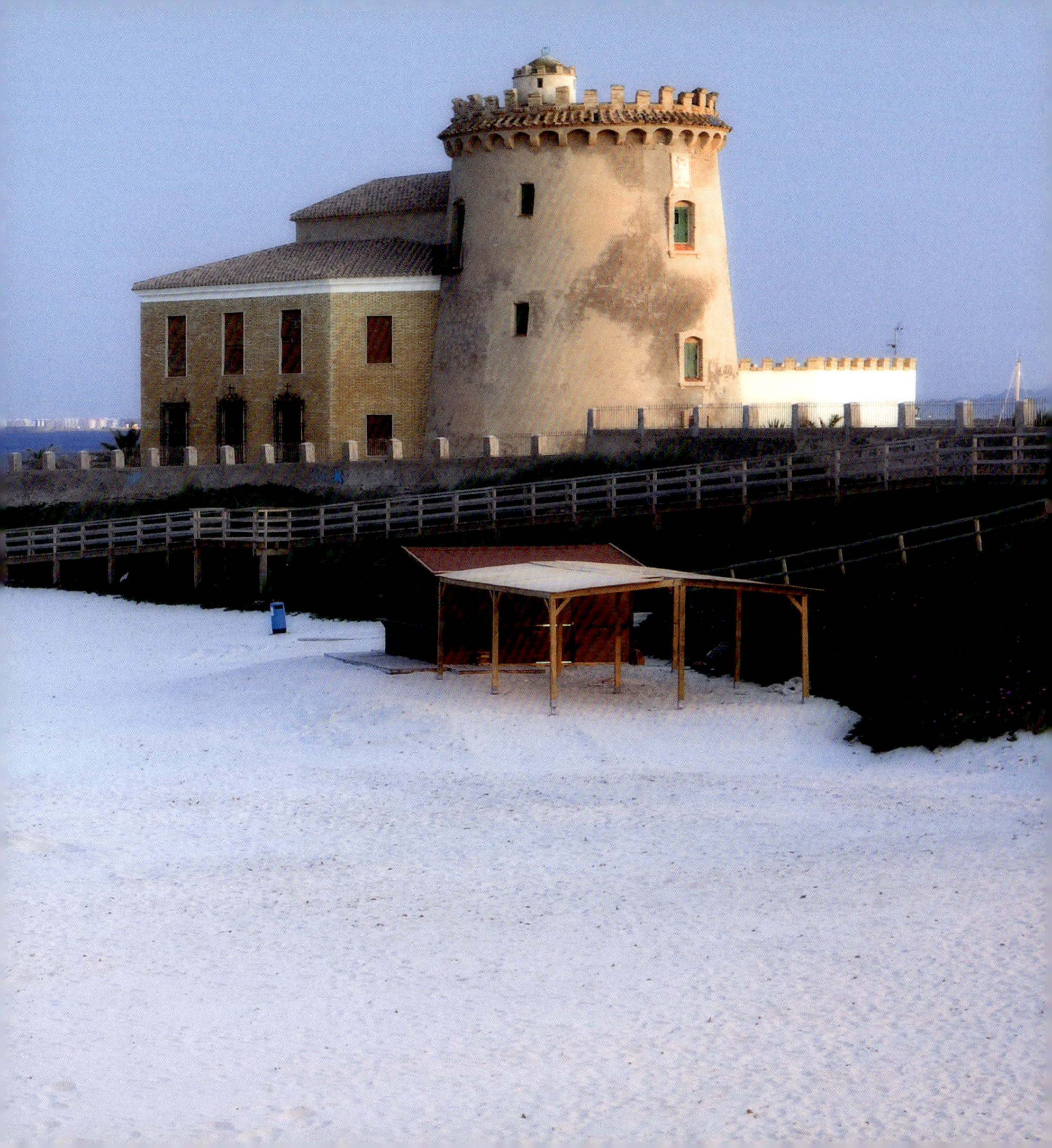

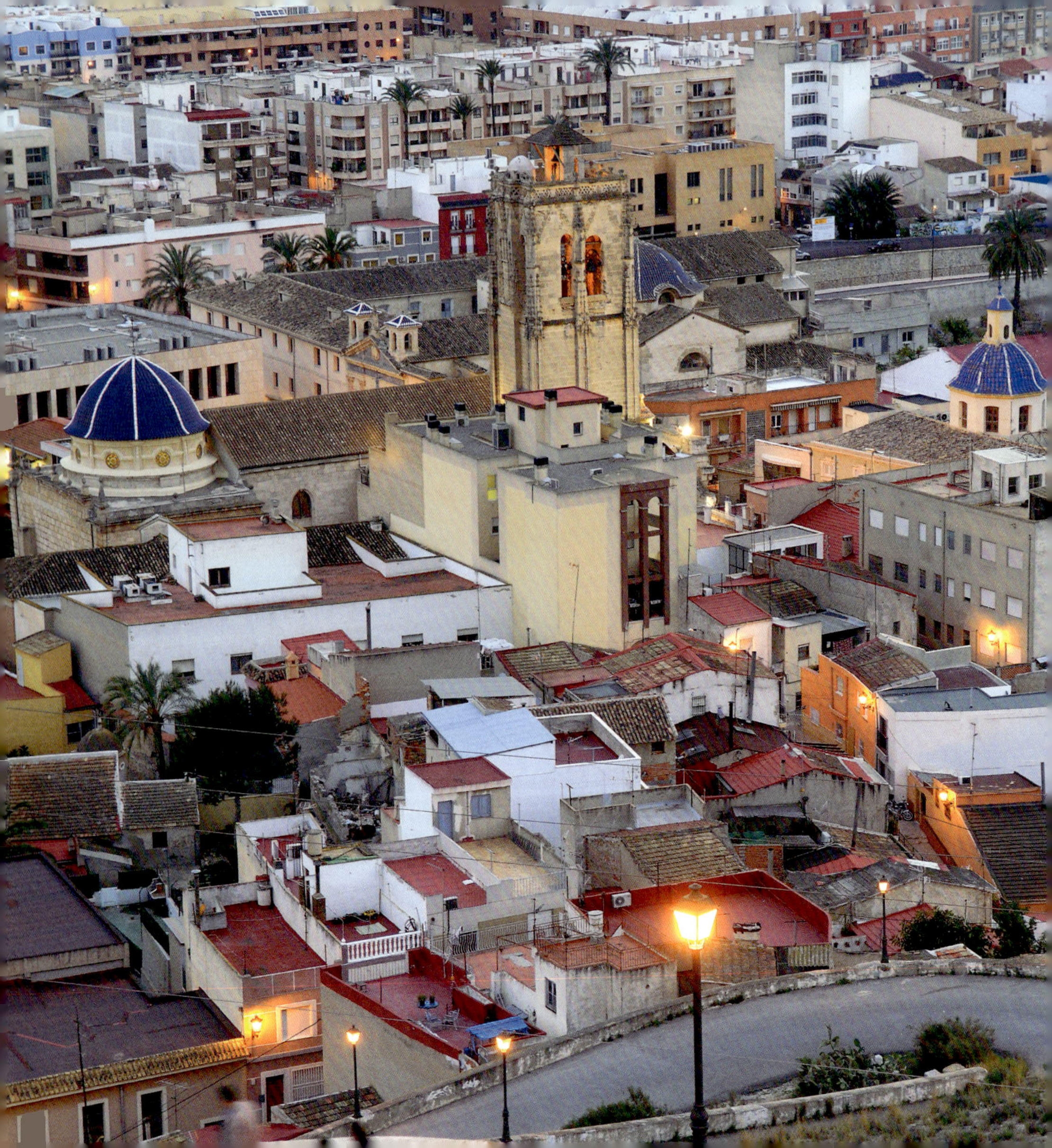

Orihuela

Going through the orchard area of the county capital, there is no way of knowing of the rich civil and ecclesiastical architectural heritage that awaits us in its streets. To find the cause we must go back to the creation of the bishopric of Orihuela in 1564. From the seminary of San Miguel, with the city at its feet, the main buildings stand out. Making a superficial tour, though every corner deserves attention, we come across the cathedral of the Salvador, the college of Santo Domingo and the church of Santiago in religious references, and the Palacio de Rubalcava or Palacio de Tudemir, today a hotel, in terms of civil architecture. As would be expected, the Easter processions are just as important as its churches.

The city was the birthplace of Miguel Hernández, the poet of the Generation of 36, who always had Orihuela present in his verses: "If you want the joy of such a pleasant sight / that the stubborn mind resists to believe; / if you want in a flowing waterfall / of colour and lights to overwhelm the sight; / if you want in such marvellous settings / like those which in dreams the high mind misses / fly around, in these miraculous verses, / contemplate my town, contemplate my land".

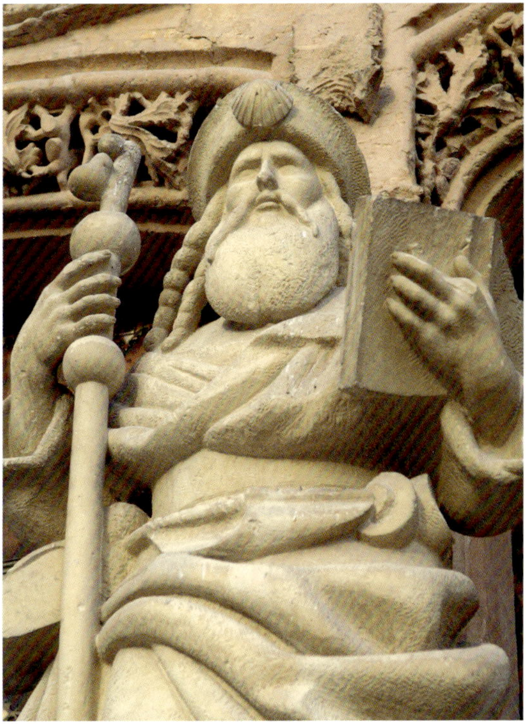

Church of Santiago. Detail of the façade.

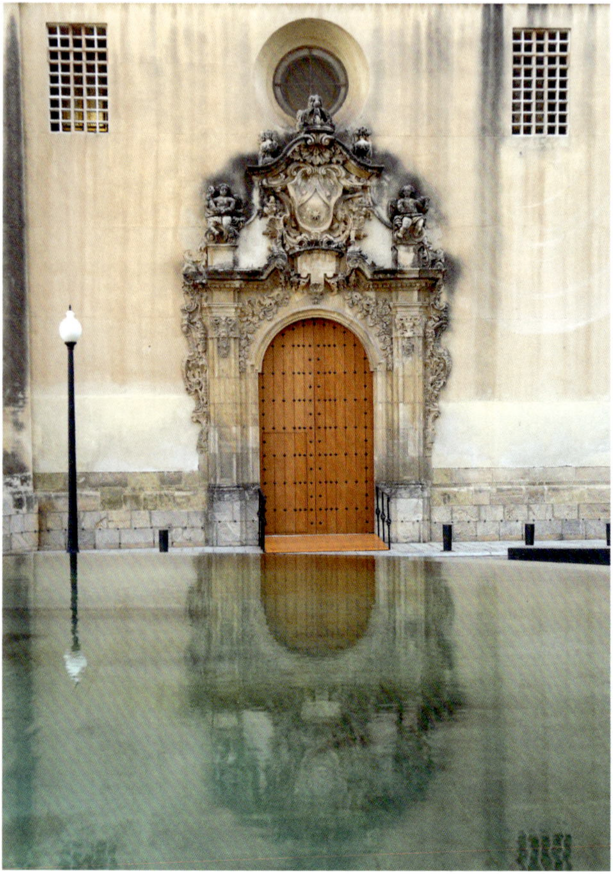

Doorway of the convent of Carmen

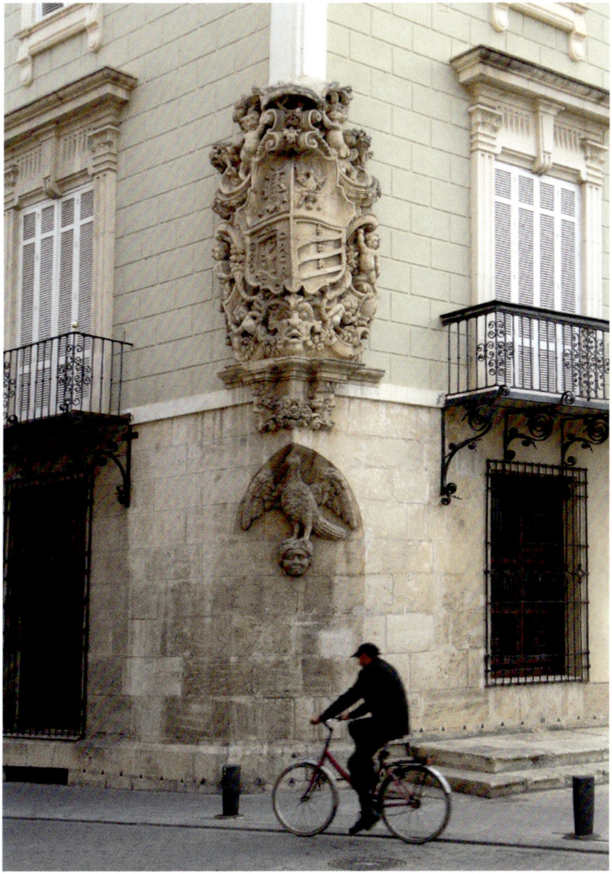

"El Pavo" corner

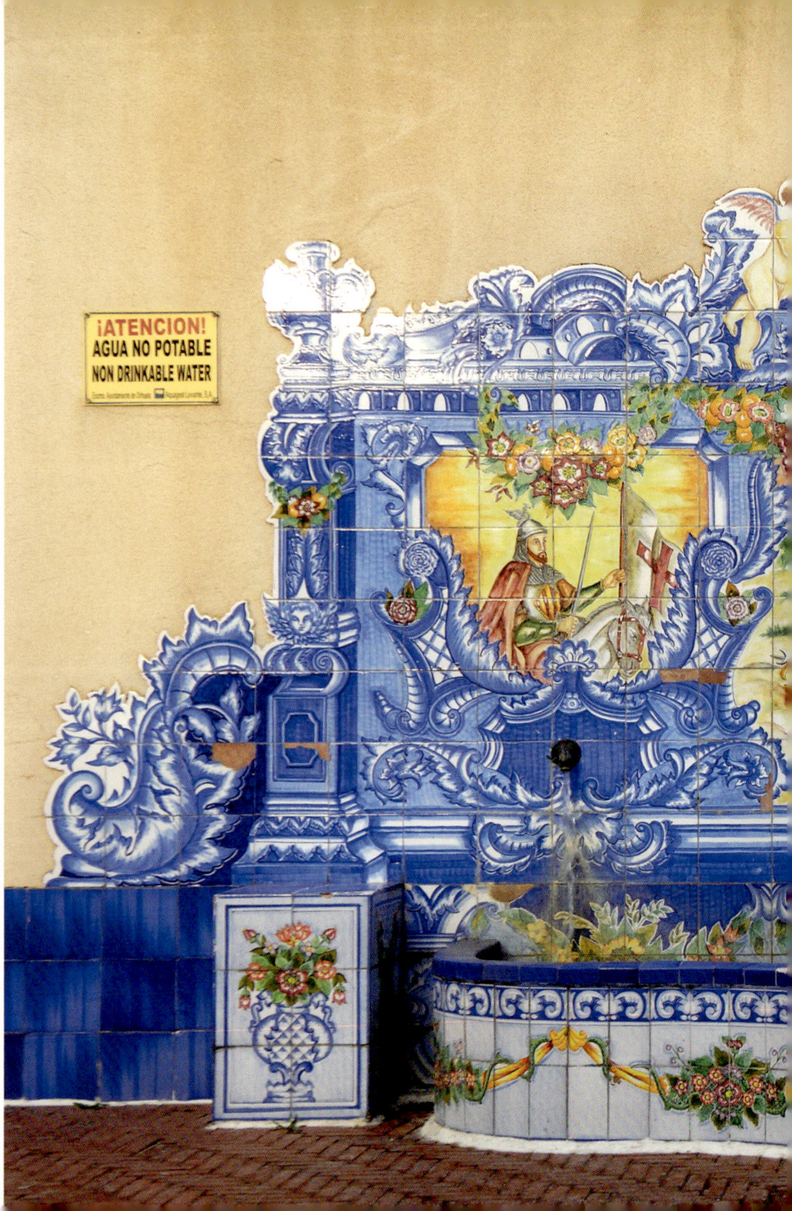

Fountain with traditional ceramic decoration →

Vaulting of the church of the College of Santo Domingo →→

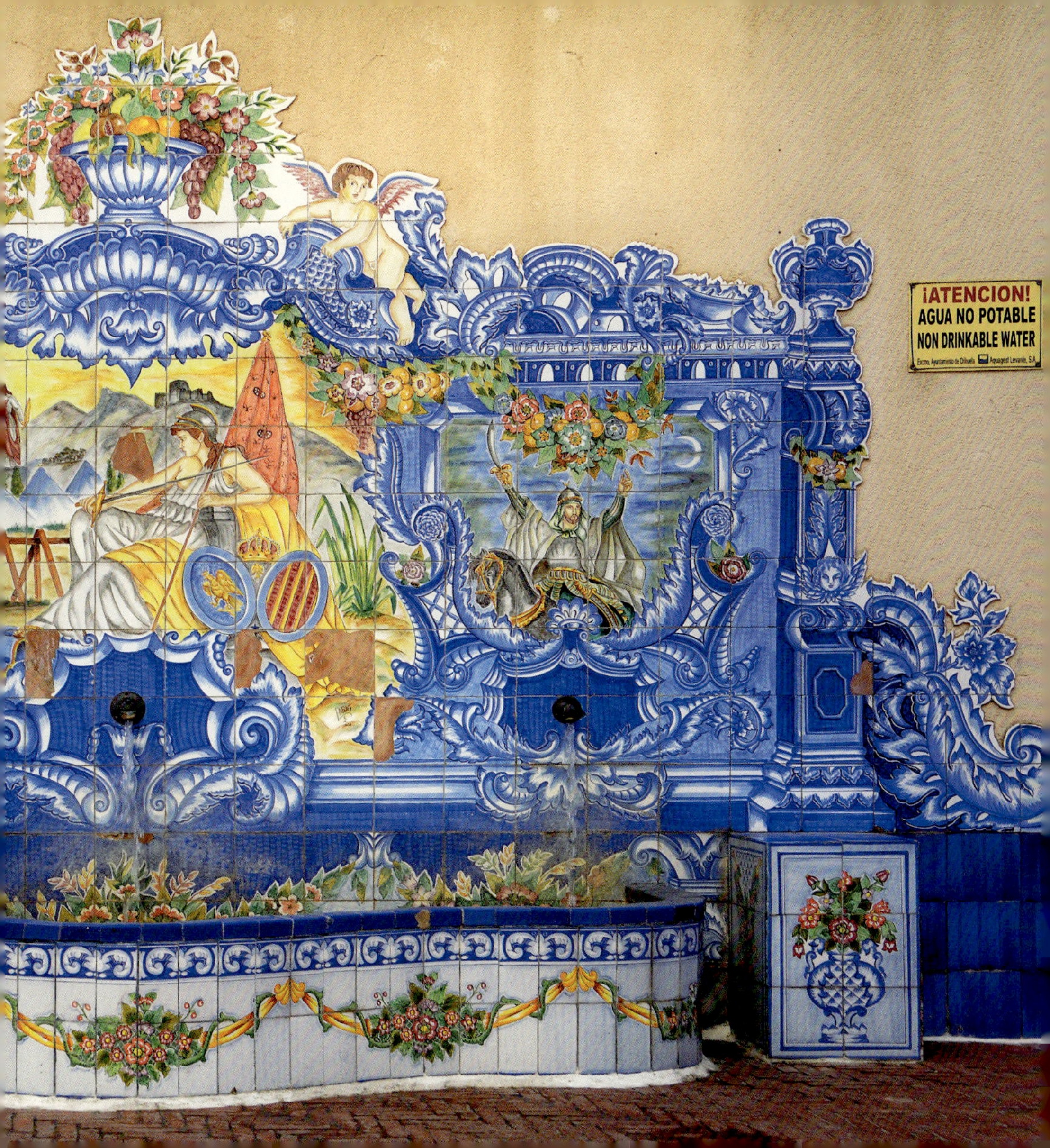
¡ATENCION!
AGUA NO POTABLE
NON DRINKABLE WATER

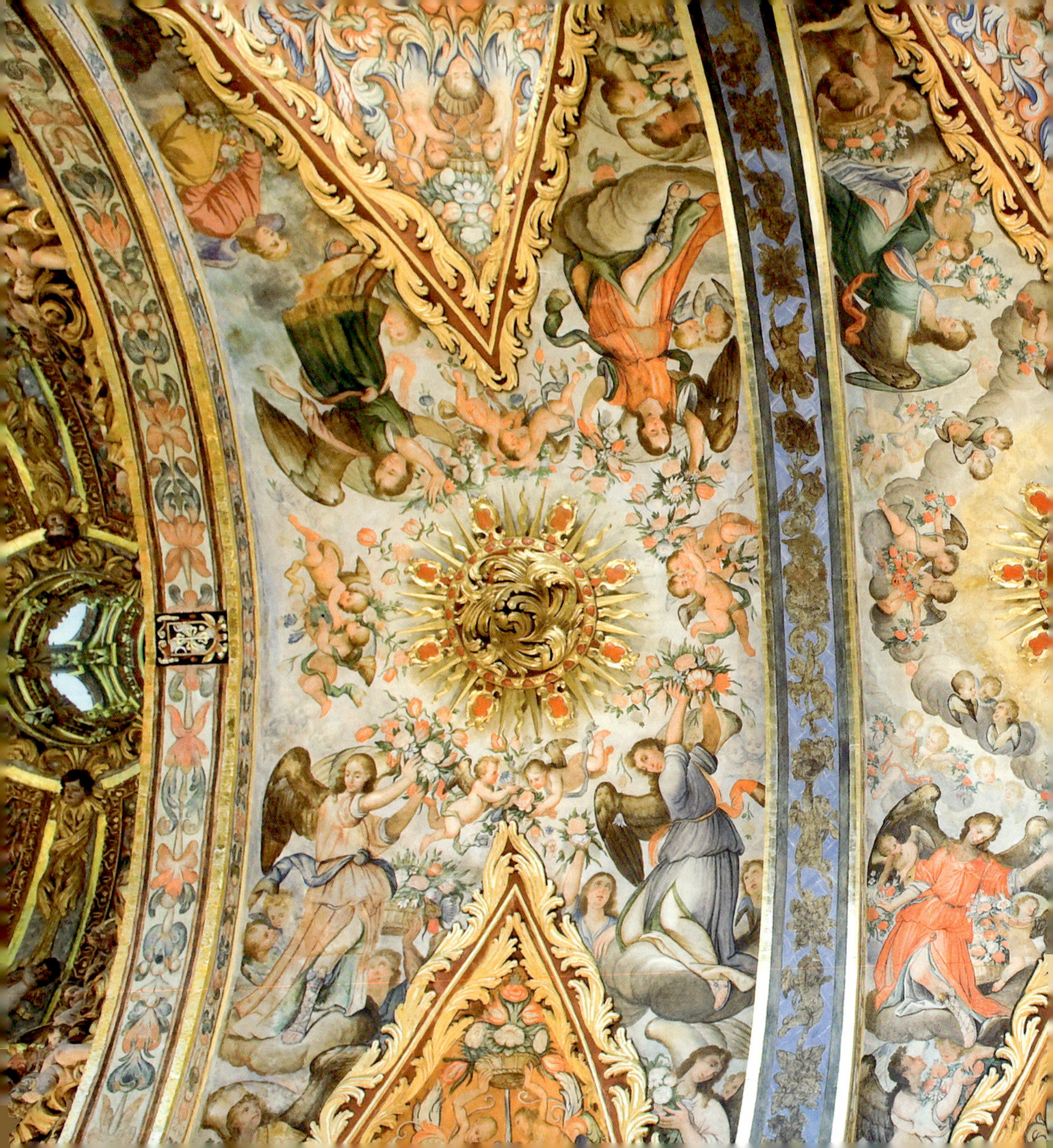

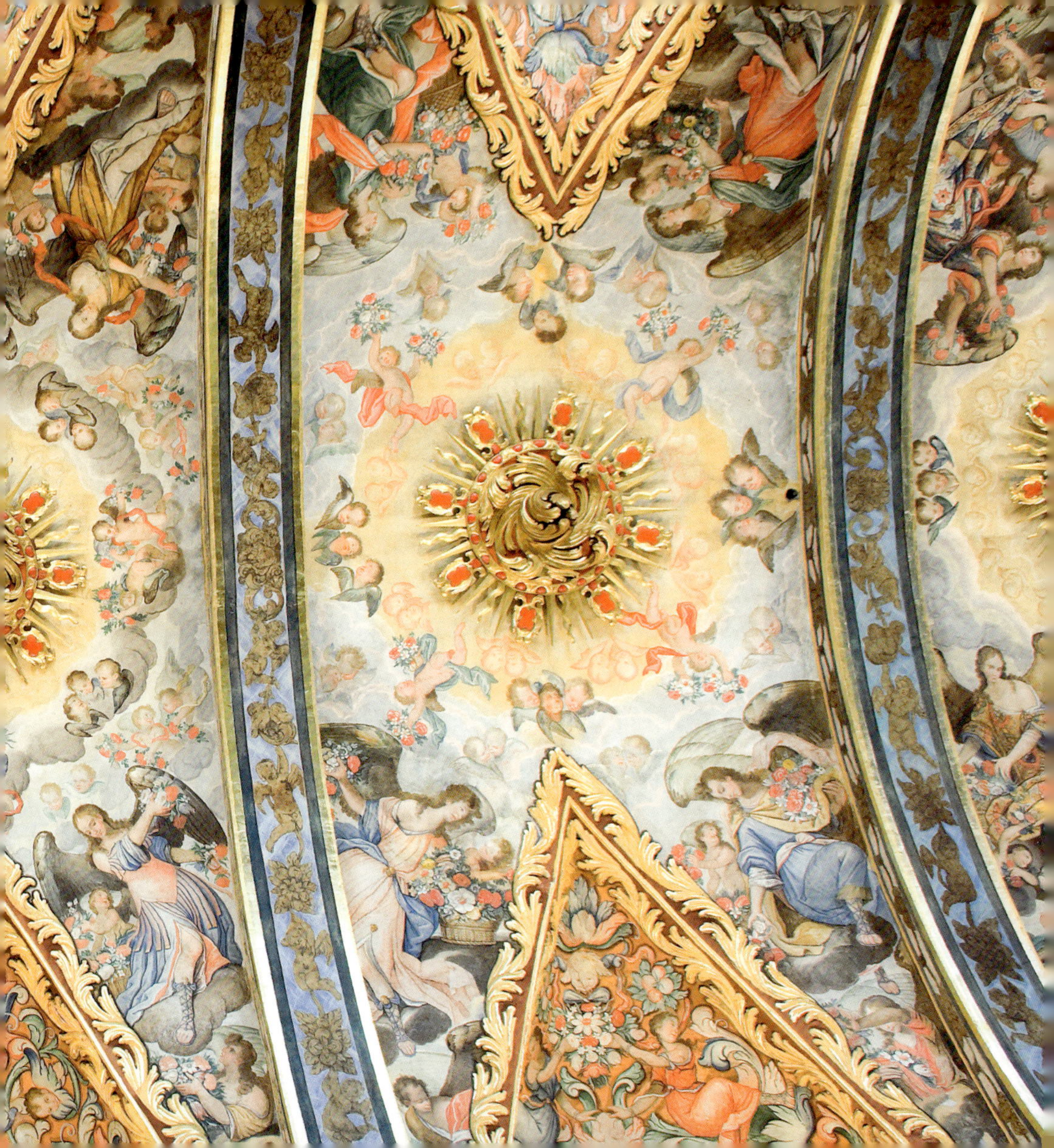

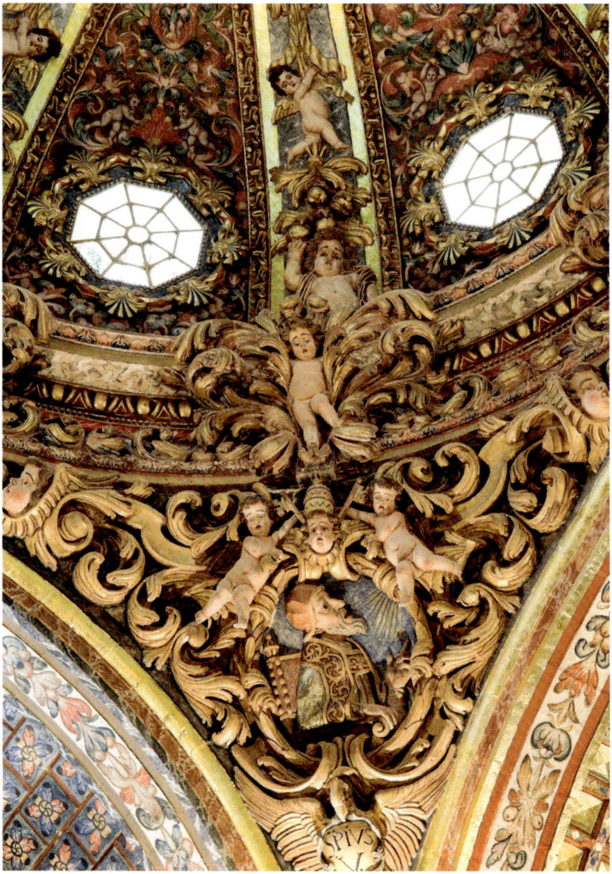

Detail of the cupola of the church of the College of Santo Domingo

Circus Theatre →

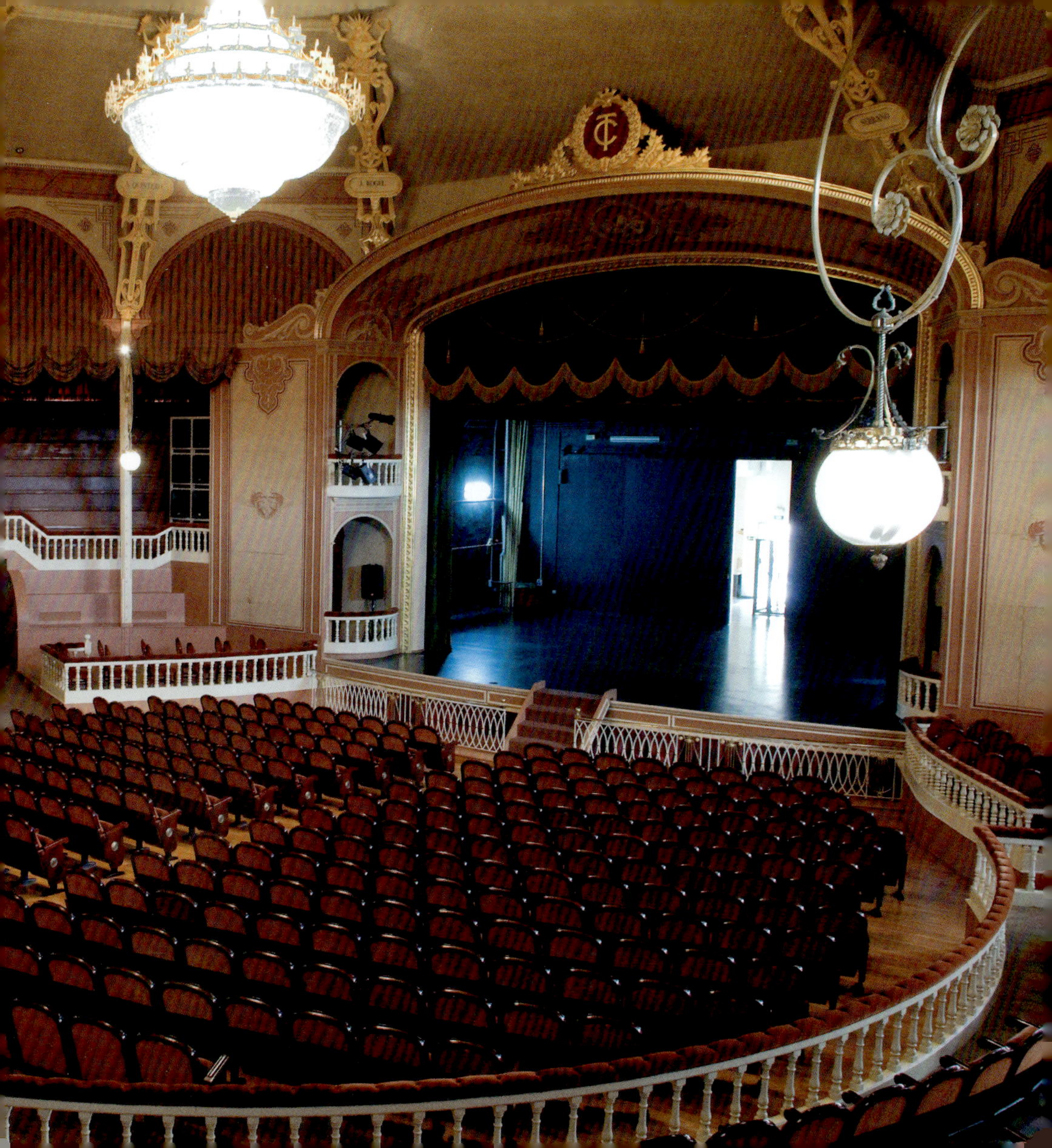

Guardamar del Segura

The coastline of the town is marked by the presence of dunes on both sides of the mouth of the River Segura. The dunes are formed by the sediments that the Levant wind drags from the river and the sea. At the beginning of the 20th century, the advance in these formations represented a danger for the town by burying crops and streets at a rate of eight metres per year. To put a stop to this the pine grove was planted, which has resulted in a landscape that today is so pleasant to wander through. Next to the mouth of the Segura are the remains of the ancient Phoenician port city of La Fonteta.

Dunes alongside Playa Campo

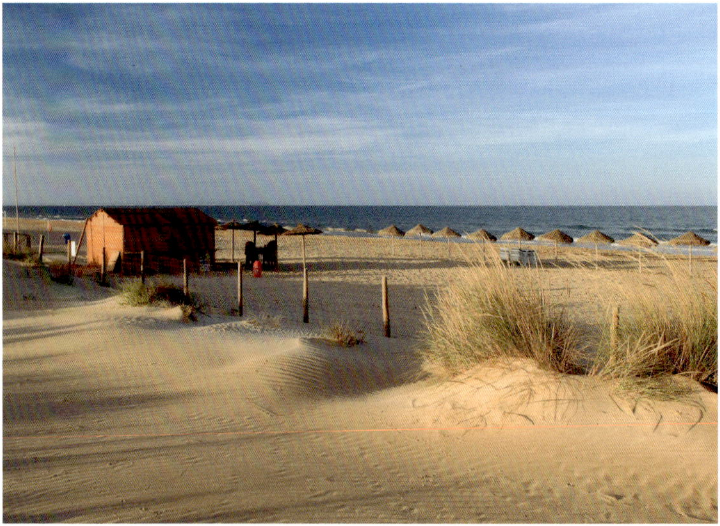

Playa Campo

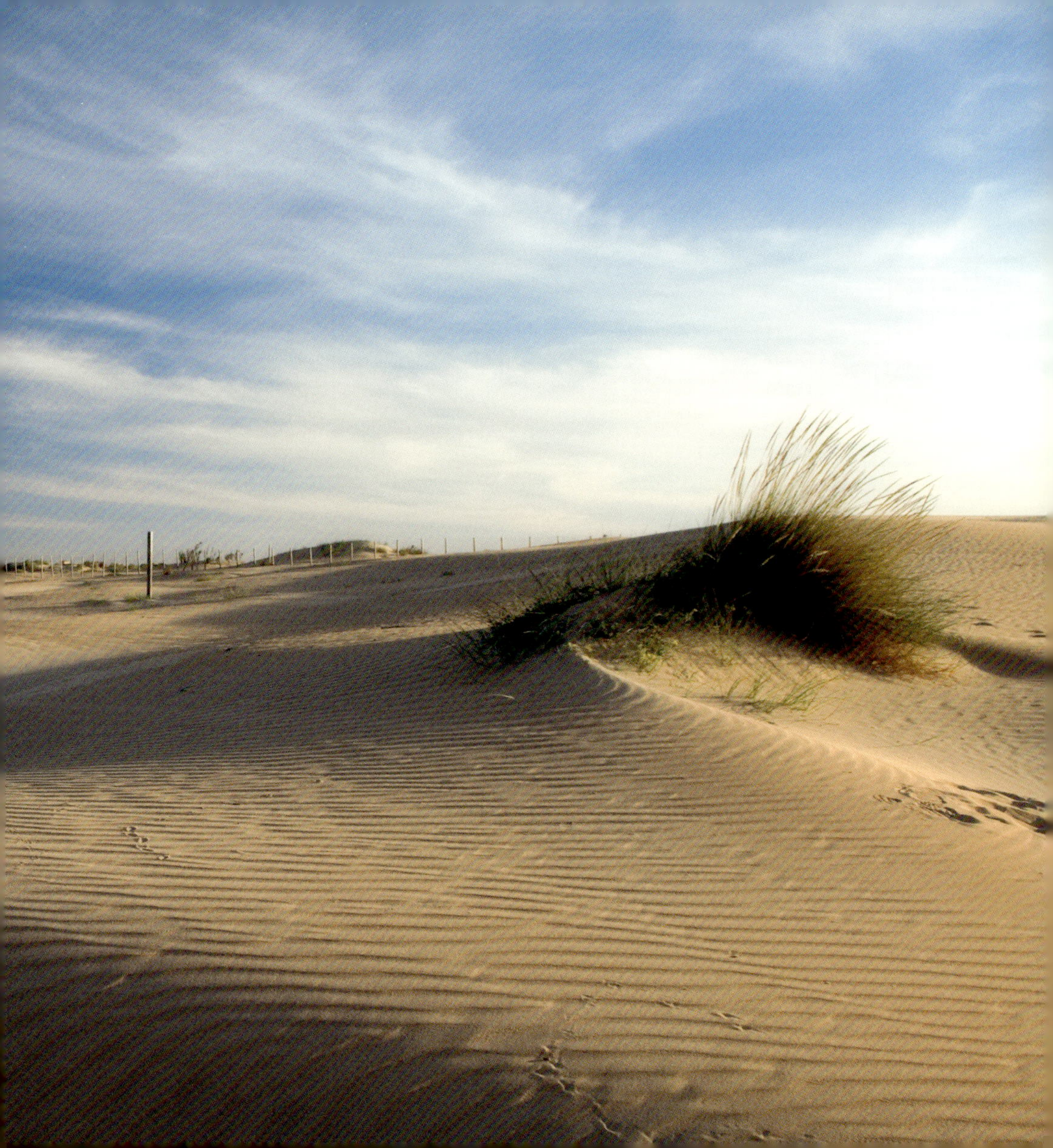

Alt Vinalopó

Route of the castles

Vinalopó Mitjà

Monforte del Cid

Novelda

Baix Vinalopó

Elx / Elche

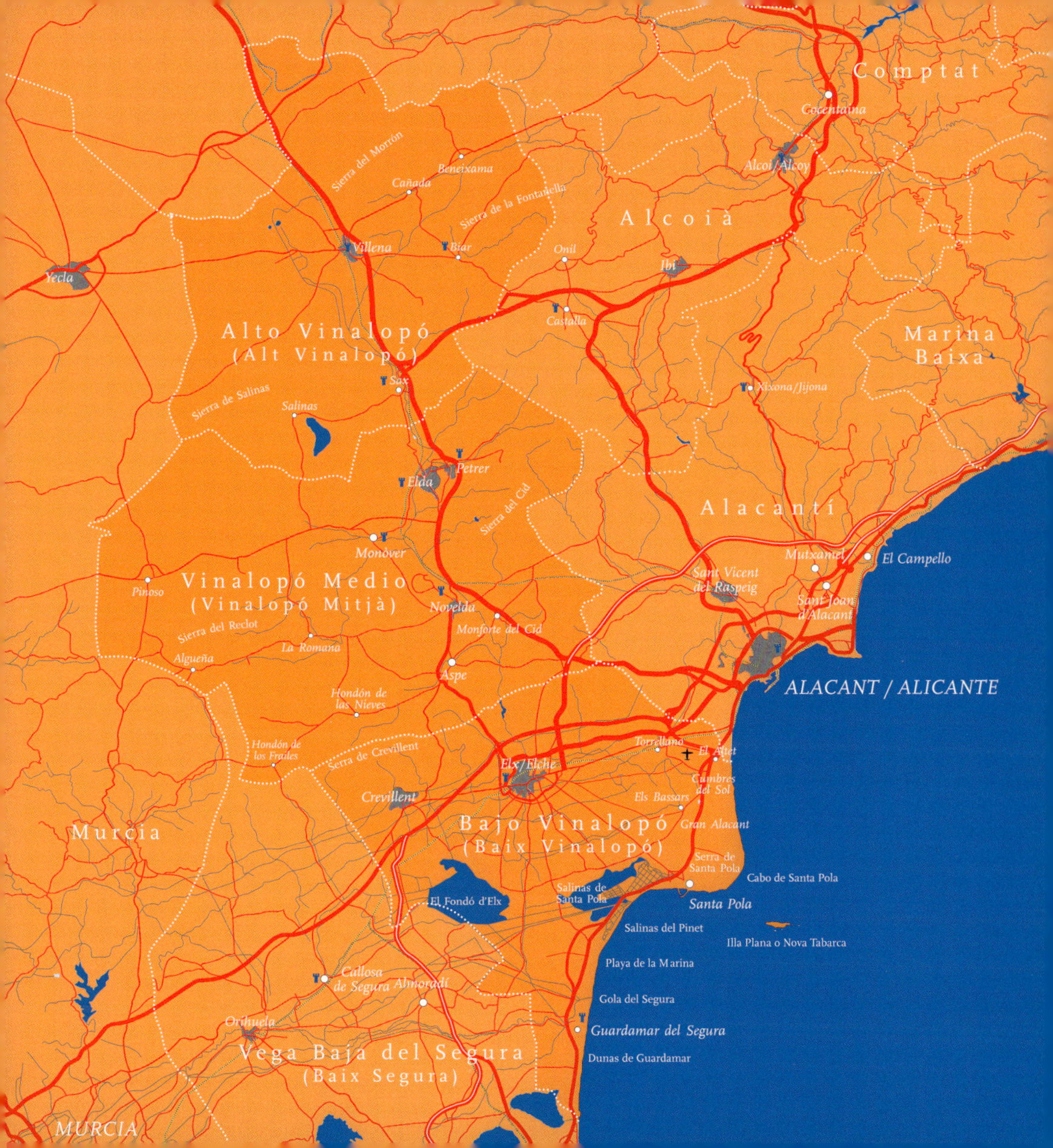
Comptat
Cocentaina
Alcoi/Alcoy
Sierra del Morrón
Beneixama
Cañada
Sierra de la Fontanella
Alcoià
Villena
Biar
Onil
Ibi
Yecla
Castalla
Alto Vinalopó
(Alt Vinalopó)
Marina
Baixa
Sax
Xixona/Jijona
Sierra de Salinas
Salinas
Petrer
Elda
Sierra del Cid
Alacantí
Monòver
Mutxamel
El Campello
Sant Vicent
del Raspeig
Pinoso
Vinalopó Medio
(Vinalopó Mitjà)
Sant Joan
d'Alacant
Novelda
Monforte del Cid
Sierra del Reclot
La Romana
Algueña
Aspe
ALACANT / ALICANTE
Hondón de
las Nieves
Hondón de
los Frailes
Serra de Crevillent
Torrellano
El Altet
Elx/Elche
Cumbres
del Sol
Crevillent
Els Bassars
Murcia
Bajo Vinalopó
(Baix Vinalopó)
Gran Alacant
Serra de
Santa Pola
Cabo de Santa Pola
Salinas de
Santa Pola
El Fondó d'Elx
Santa Pola
Salinas del Pinet
Illa Plana o Nova Tabarca
Playa de la Marina
Callosa
de Segura
Almoradí
Gola del Segura
Orihuela
Guardamar del Segura
Vega Baja del Segura
(Baix Segura)
Dunas de Guardamar
MURCIA

The castles route

The province of Alicante has more than one hundred castles, fortresses and towers.

In the arid counties of Vinalopó the best examples of that architecture can be found of which the Arab variety little remains except its origin. The continuous reforms after the expulsion of the Moors from Al-Andalus has given them a much more Castilian aspect. The course of the River Vinalopó will serve as a guide; a river that, after trying to provide water to the whole valley that connects the plateau with the coastline, it loses strength and withers away in the orchard of Elche without having reached the sea.

With the aim of defending territories and marking frontiers, the castles were built on hills from where they were able to control a large territory. At their feet grew villages concentrically around them on steep narrow streets.

From north to south, the route begins in the towns of Banyeres de Mariola and Castalla, which although belonging to the neighbouring county, their castles deserve to be included in the itinerary. In Biar, as well as the castle, the Plateresque bell tower of the church of the Asunción stands out. At the foot of the castle of the Atalaya, in Villena, the network of alleyways of Arab origin lead to the church of Santiago, of Gothic style. The Municipal Palace houses one of the best collections of Bronze Age jewellery in Europe. At the foot of the Argueña range appears Sax and, a little further south, Petrer, both with examples of well-conserved castles.

Castle of Castalla →
Aerial view of Biar →→

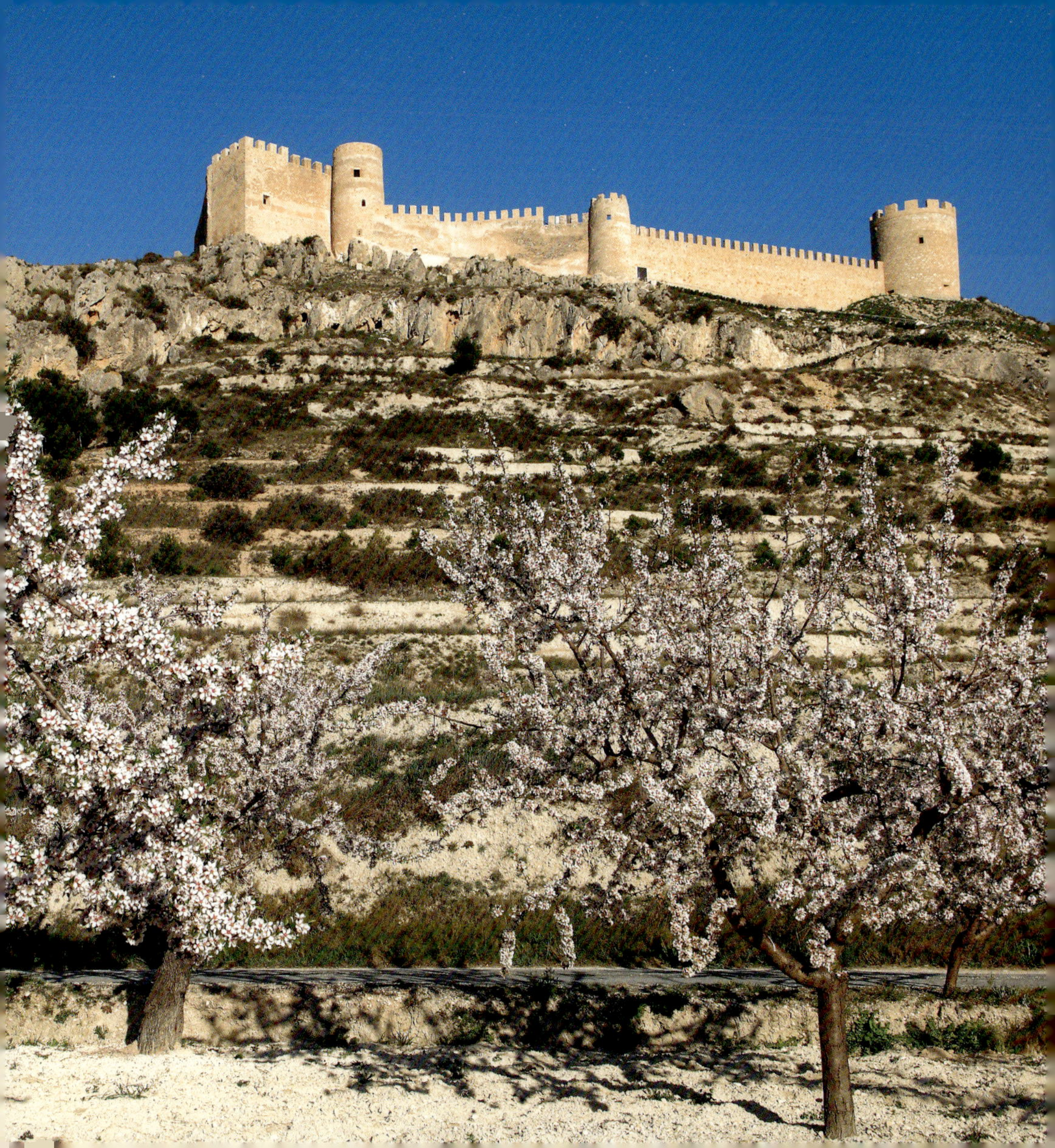

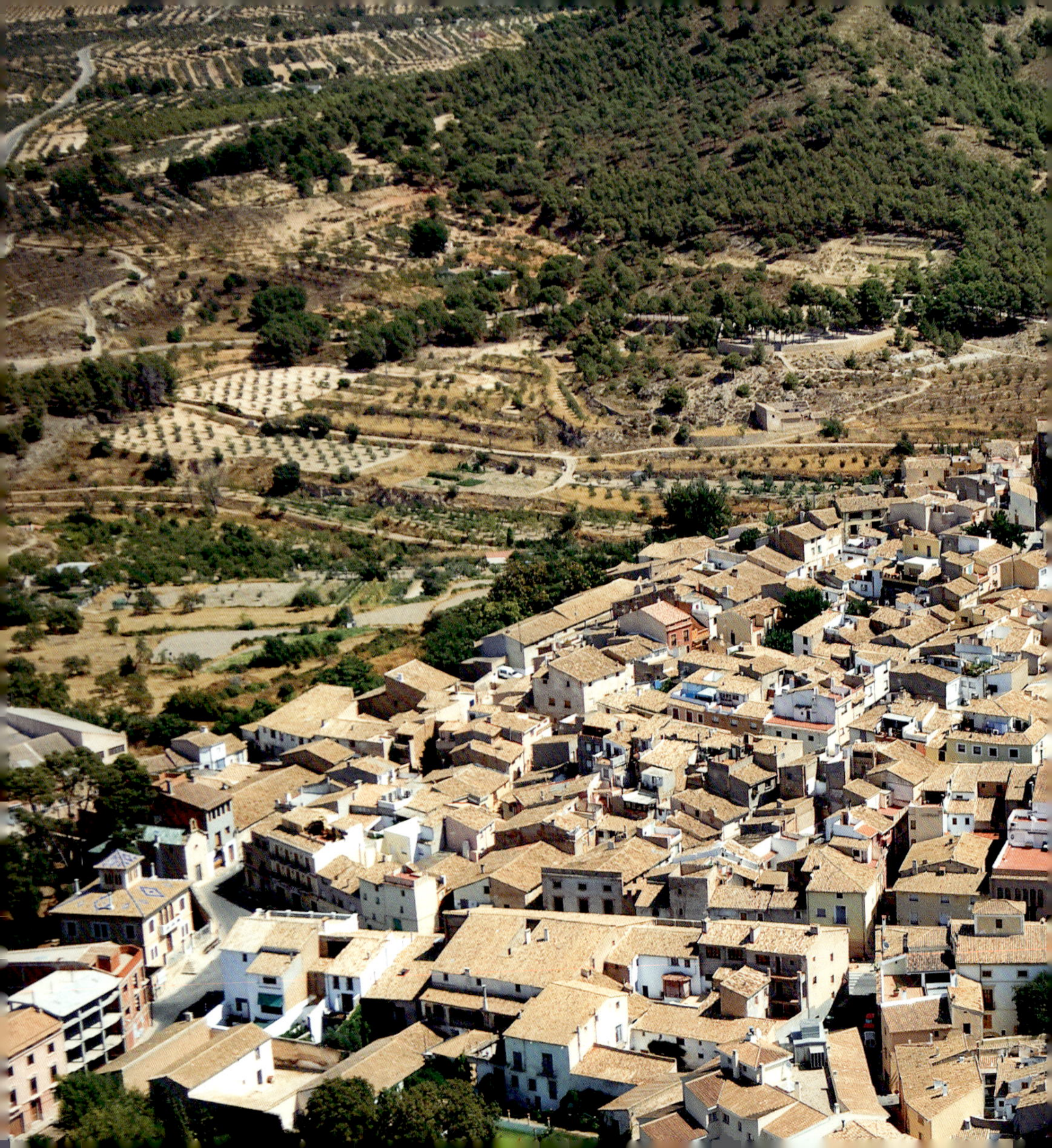

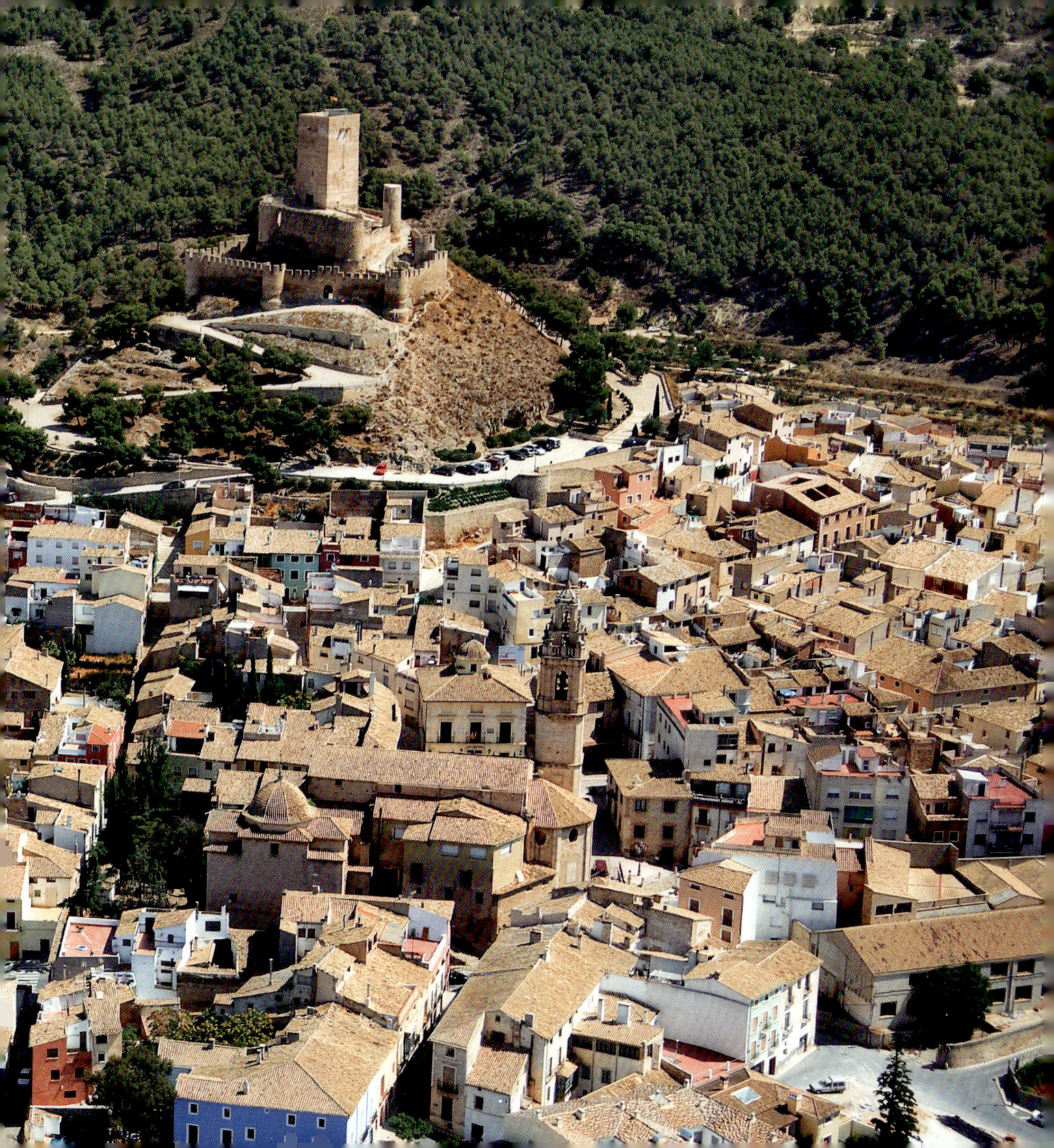

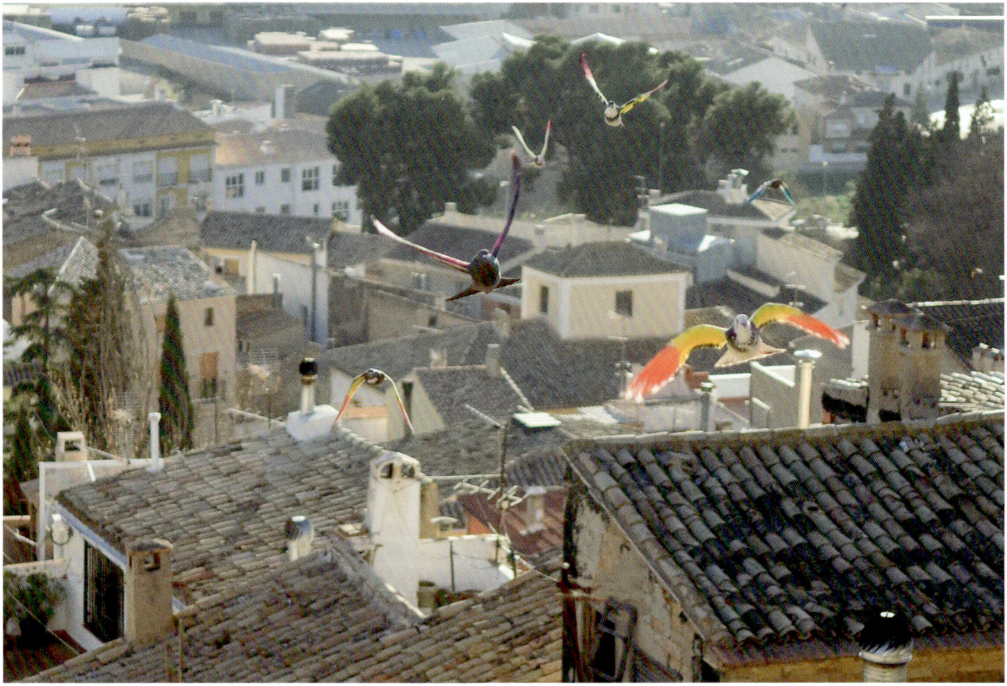

Biar, pigeon fancying

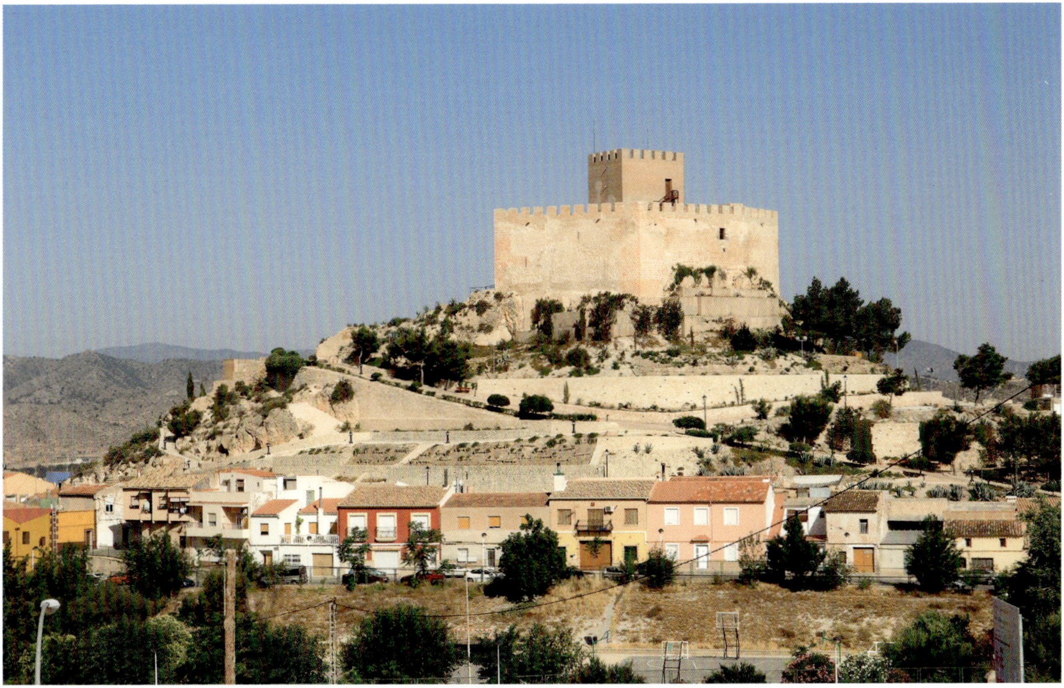

Castle of Petrer

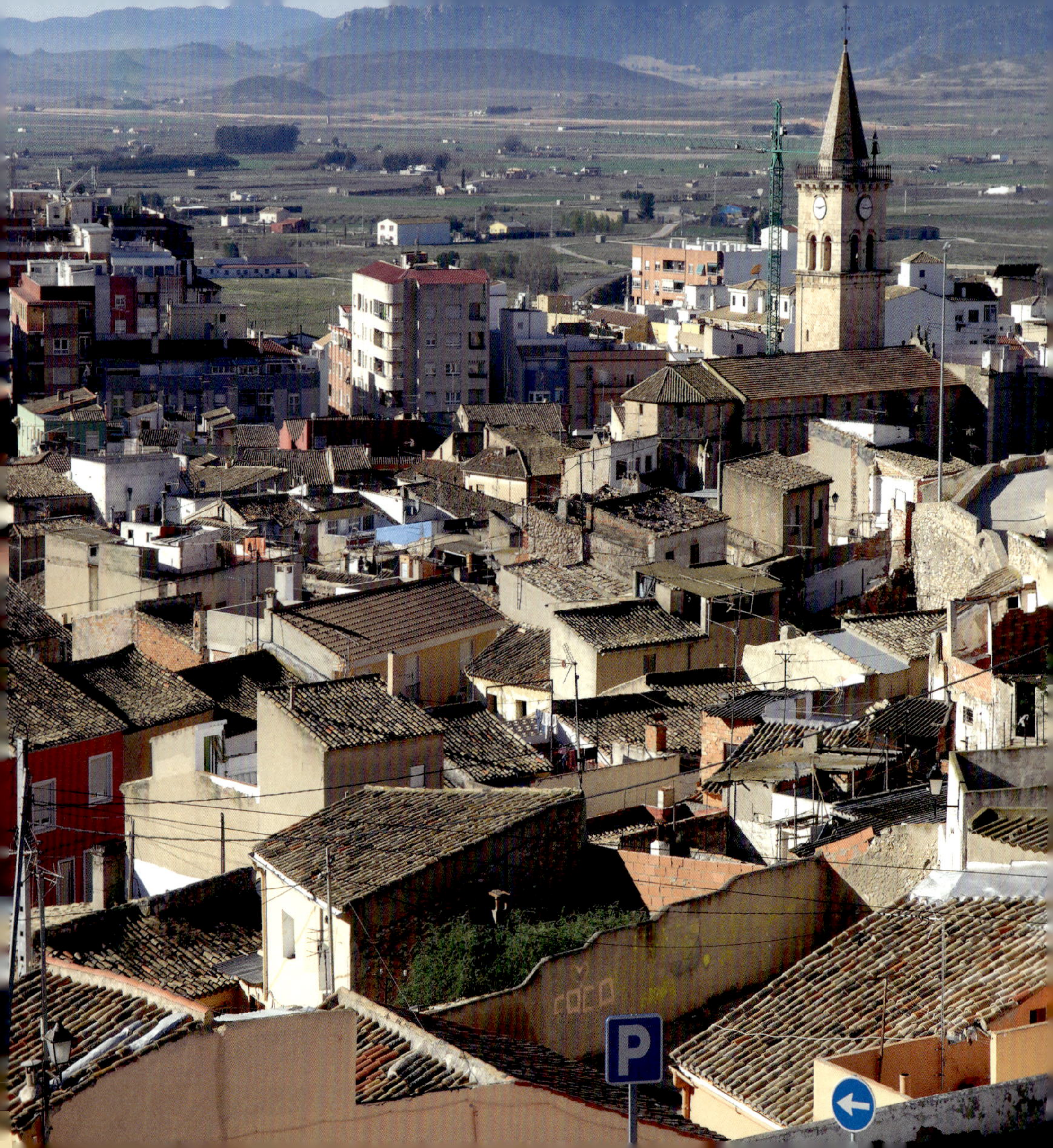
P

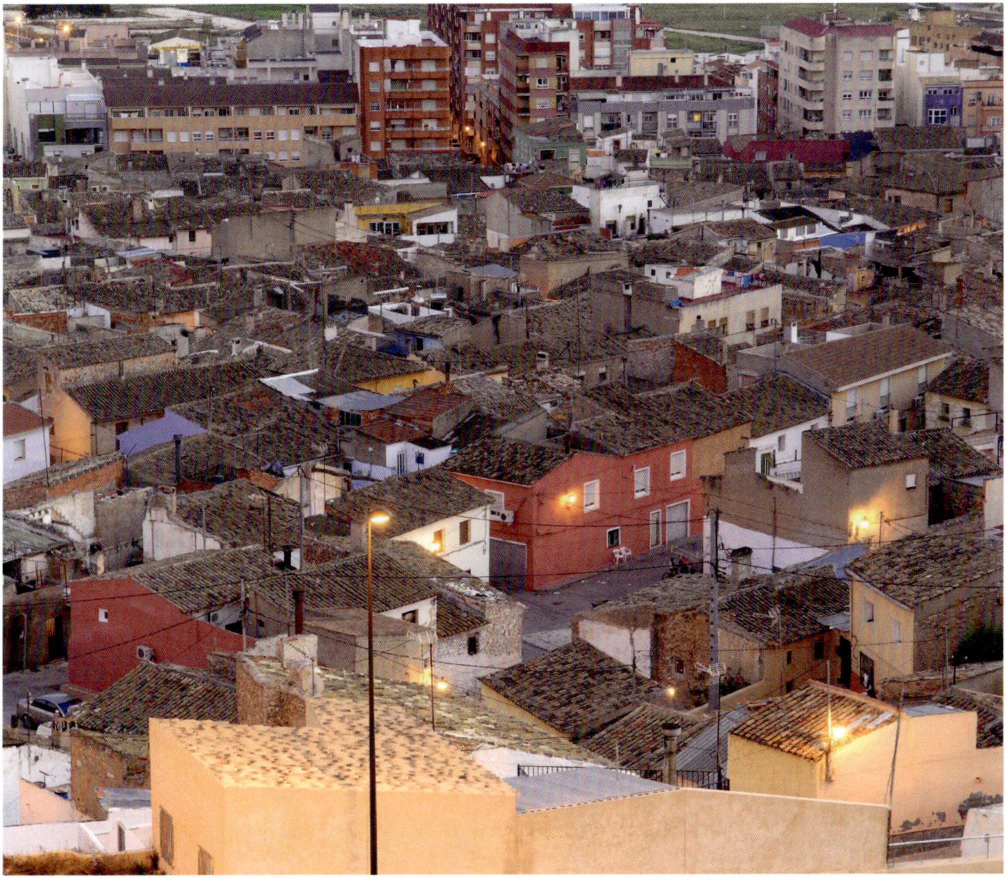

Villena
Castle of Villena →

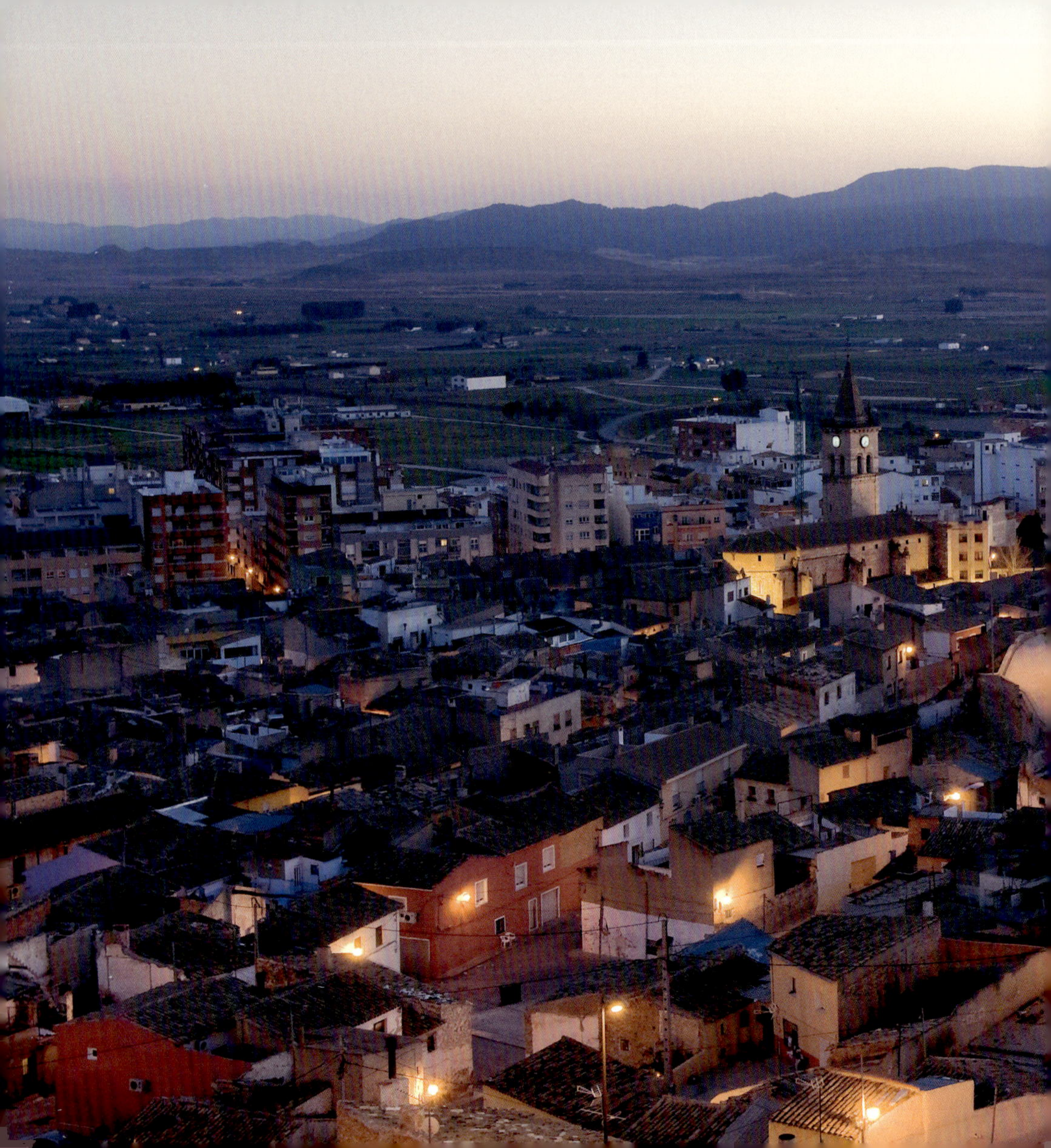

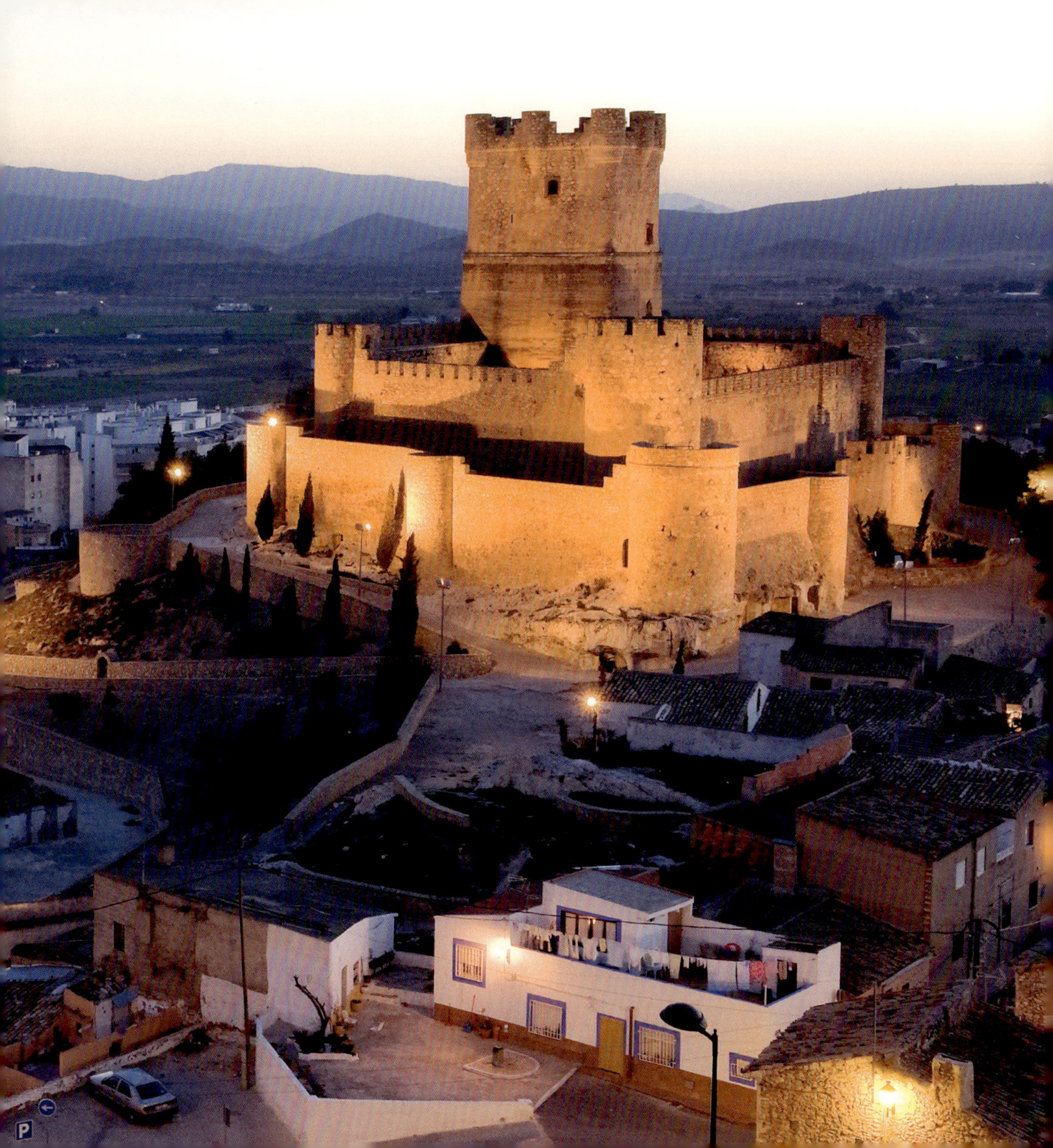

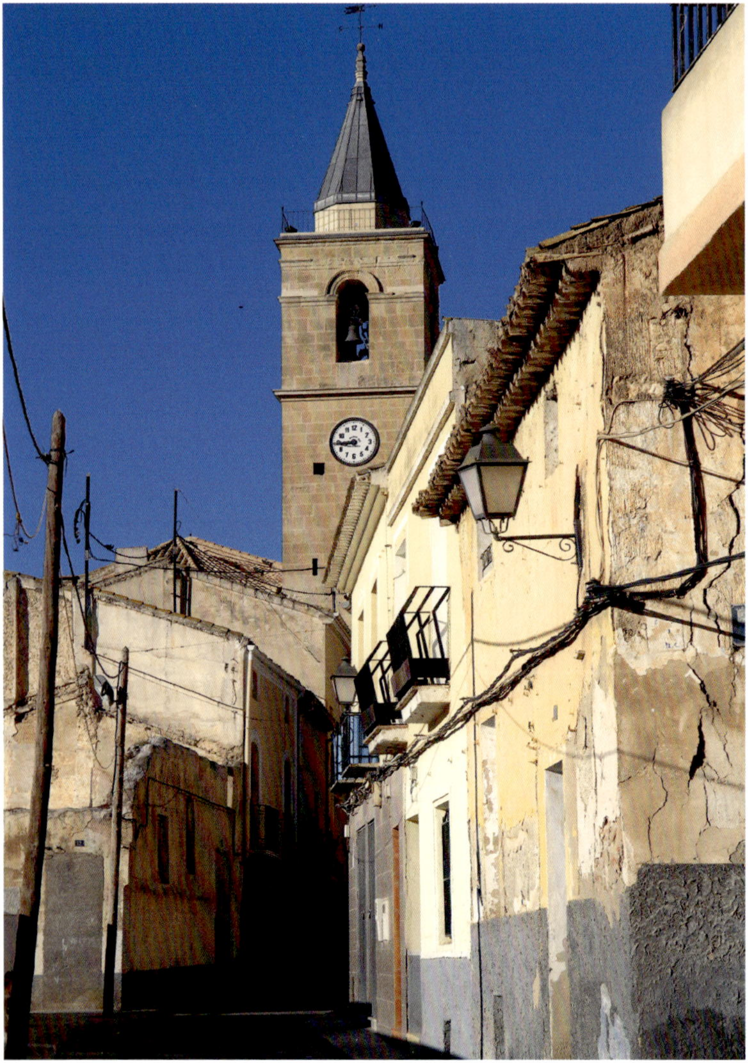

Castle of Sax

Church of Sax

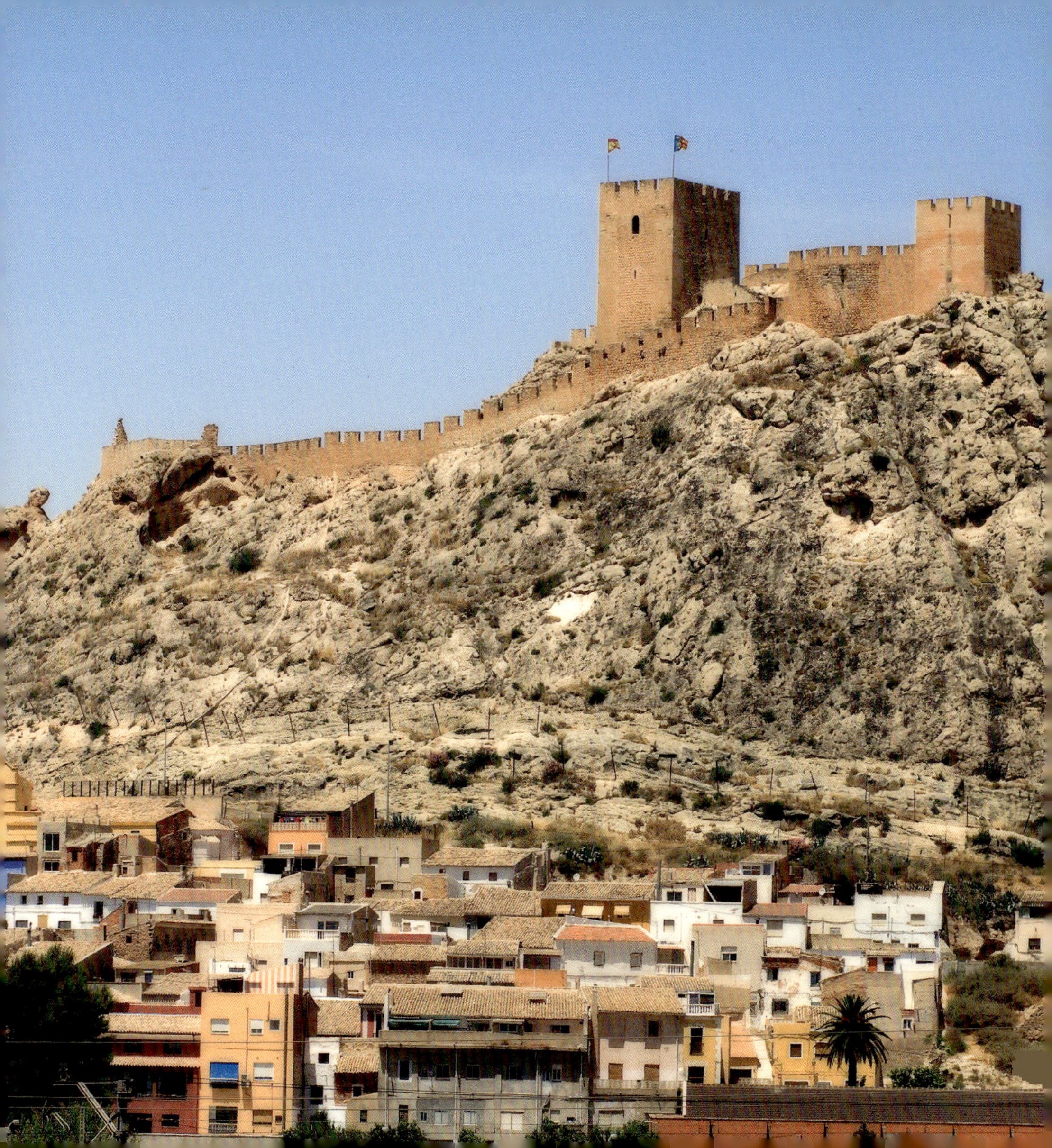

Monforte del Cid

The town of Monforte del Cid is one of the stops on the El Cid Route in the province of Alicante, which enters in the north of Vinalopó to drop towards Elche and then in direction of Orihuela, in the neighbouring county.

The archaeological remains found are reliable proof of the Iberian past of Monforte del Cid, which conserves one of the best examples of the Iberian bull of the art of this period. Another icon of the locality are the grapes which, under the DO Uva Embolsada del Vinalopó, accompany the arrival of the New Year in a deeply-rooted tradition in Spain which, according to one of its versions, arose from a surplus harvest in 1909.

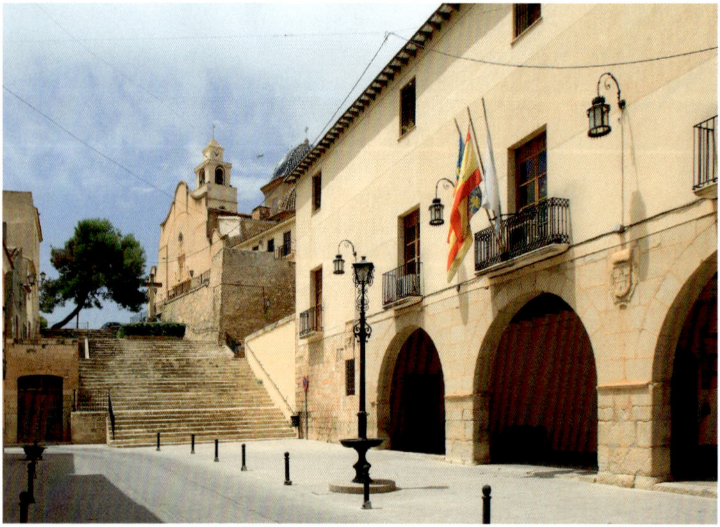

Town Hall of Monforte del Cid

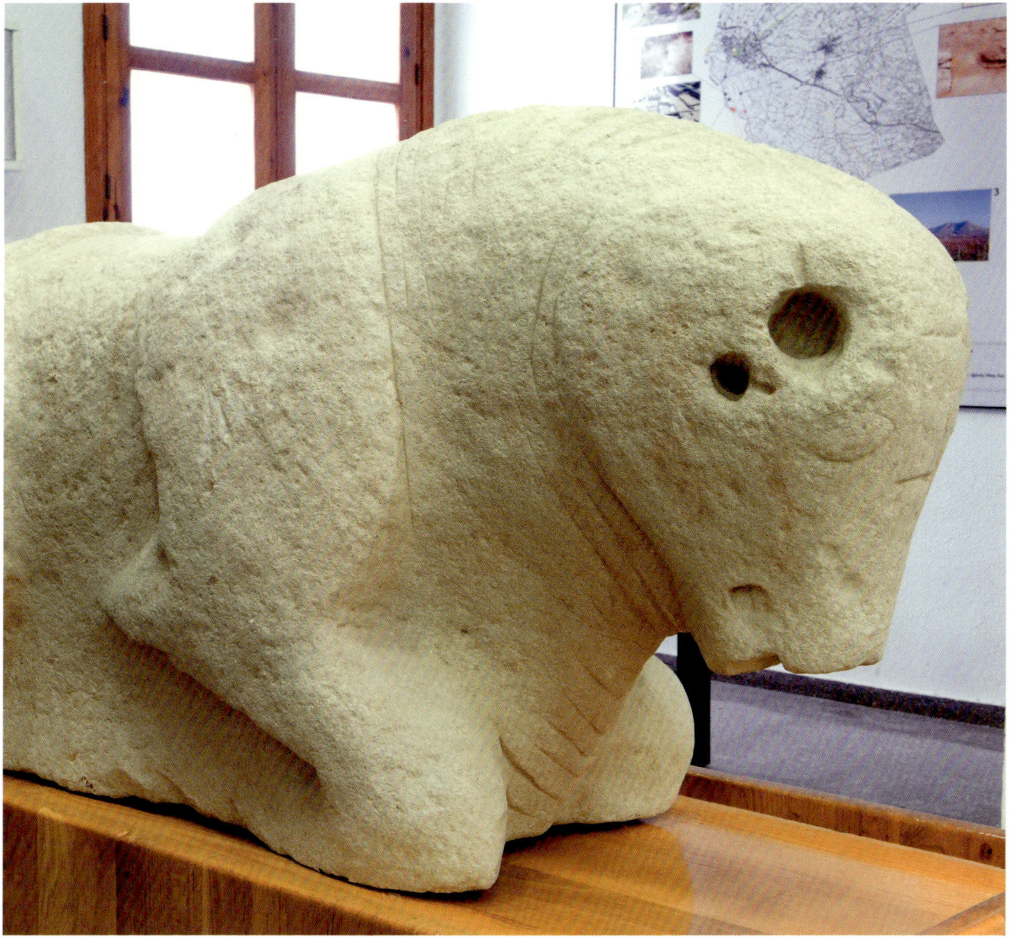

Iberian bull. Monforte del Cid

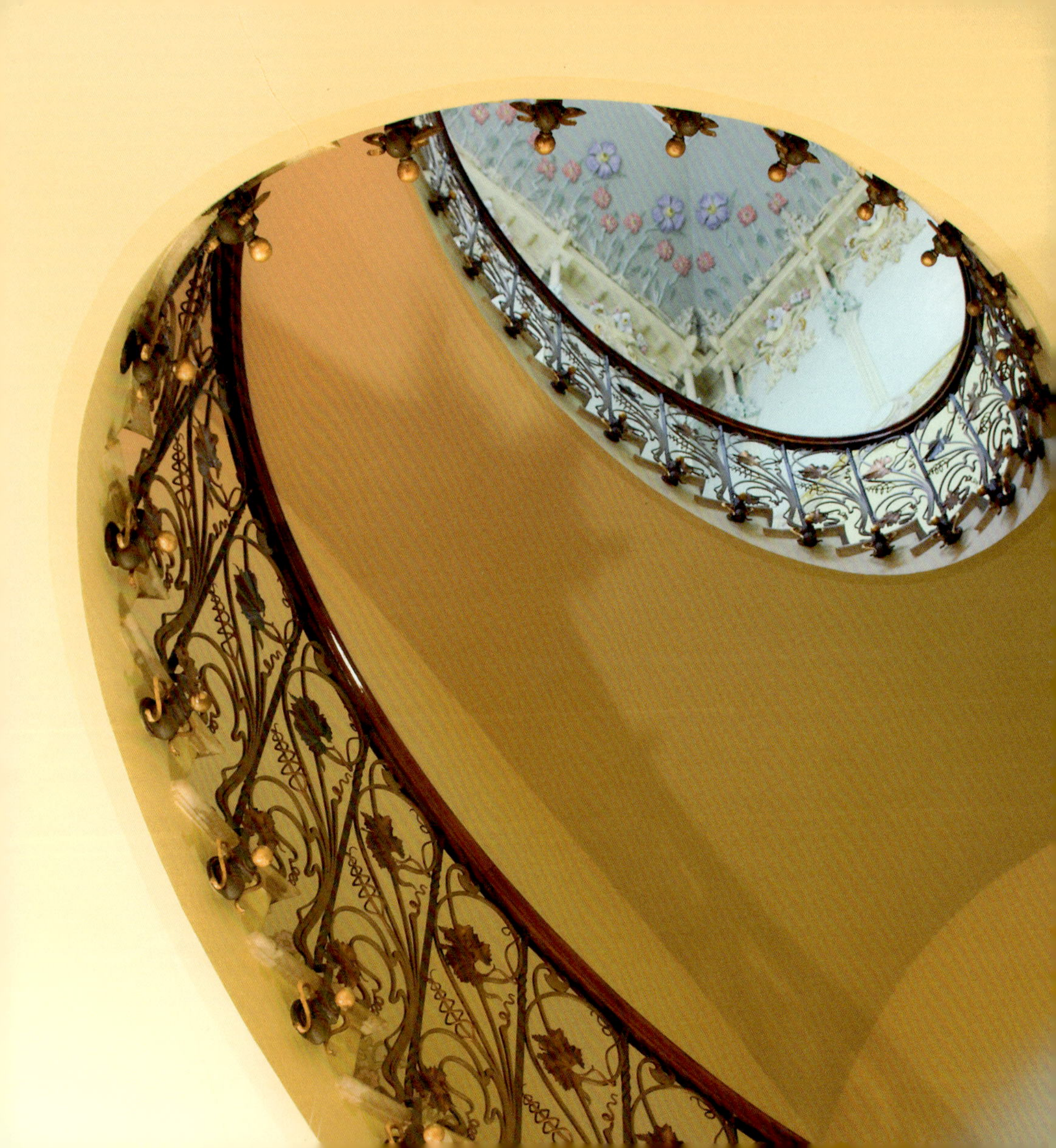

Novelda

It is the city of Modernism in the province of Alicante. Novelda has some of the best examples of this architecture in the Valencia Community. Modernism began at the end of the 19th century, with its later development and expansion in the early 20th. In a period in which the industrial revolution grew strongly all over Europe, the bourgeois families adopted Modernism as a symbol of their desire for progress and to be surrounded by aesthetic forms that placed them in the vanguard and, naturally, that distinguished them socially. We can see the delicate and sensual curves in this art in the Modernist House-Museum, in the Gómez-Tortosa cultural centre and in the sanctuary of Santa María Magdalena, of Gaudian pretensions, located in the outskirts of the city.

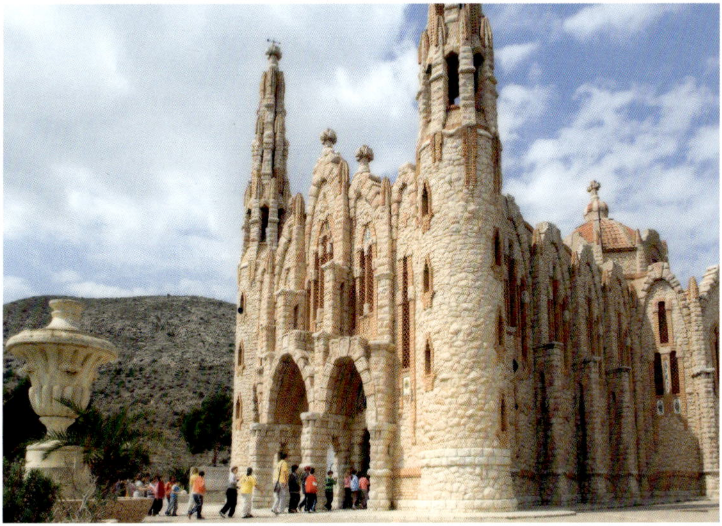

← Modernist House-Museum

Sanctuary of Santa María Magdalena

Elx / Elche

The palm grove of Elche has some very special examples such as the Imperial Palm from the Huerto del Cura. The people of Elche have made the most of the idiosyncrasy of this plant and transform the leaves of the white palm into delicate creations that can be seen all over the city on Palm Sunday. The palm grove has a place in the list of World Heritage sites with the Mystery of Elche, a sacred-lyrical drama that represents the Death, Assumption and Coronation of the Virgin Mary. The work, in two acts, takes place on the 14th and 15th of August in the Basilica of Santa María and is preceded by the Night of the Albà, where other palm trees, these ones made of fire, light up the sky of the city.

The interior of the Palace of Altamira is the home of the MAHE, the archaeological museum that exhibits pieces from the nearby excavation of La Alcudia, the place where they found the Lady of Elche. The visit to the Arab baths, in the Convent of the Merced, is another unmissable spot in Elche. Outside the city, but still in the municipality, we come to the Natural Park of Hondo and a coastline of beaches made up of pine groves and dunes.

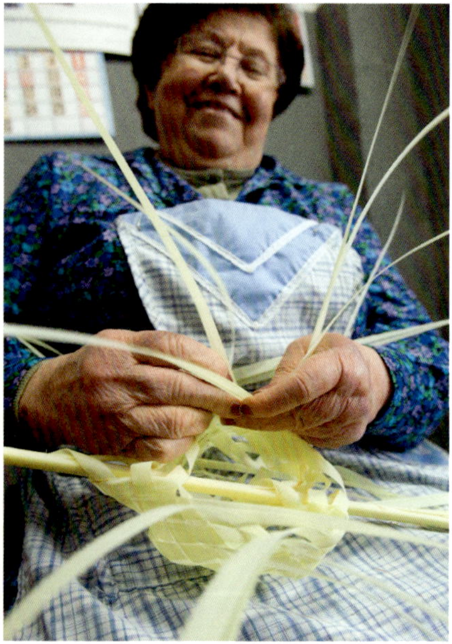

Plaiting of the white palm

Susi Díaz, chef of the La Finca restaurant →

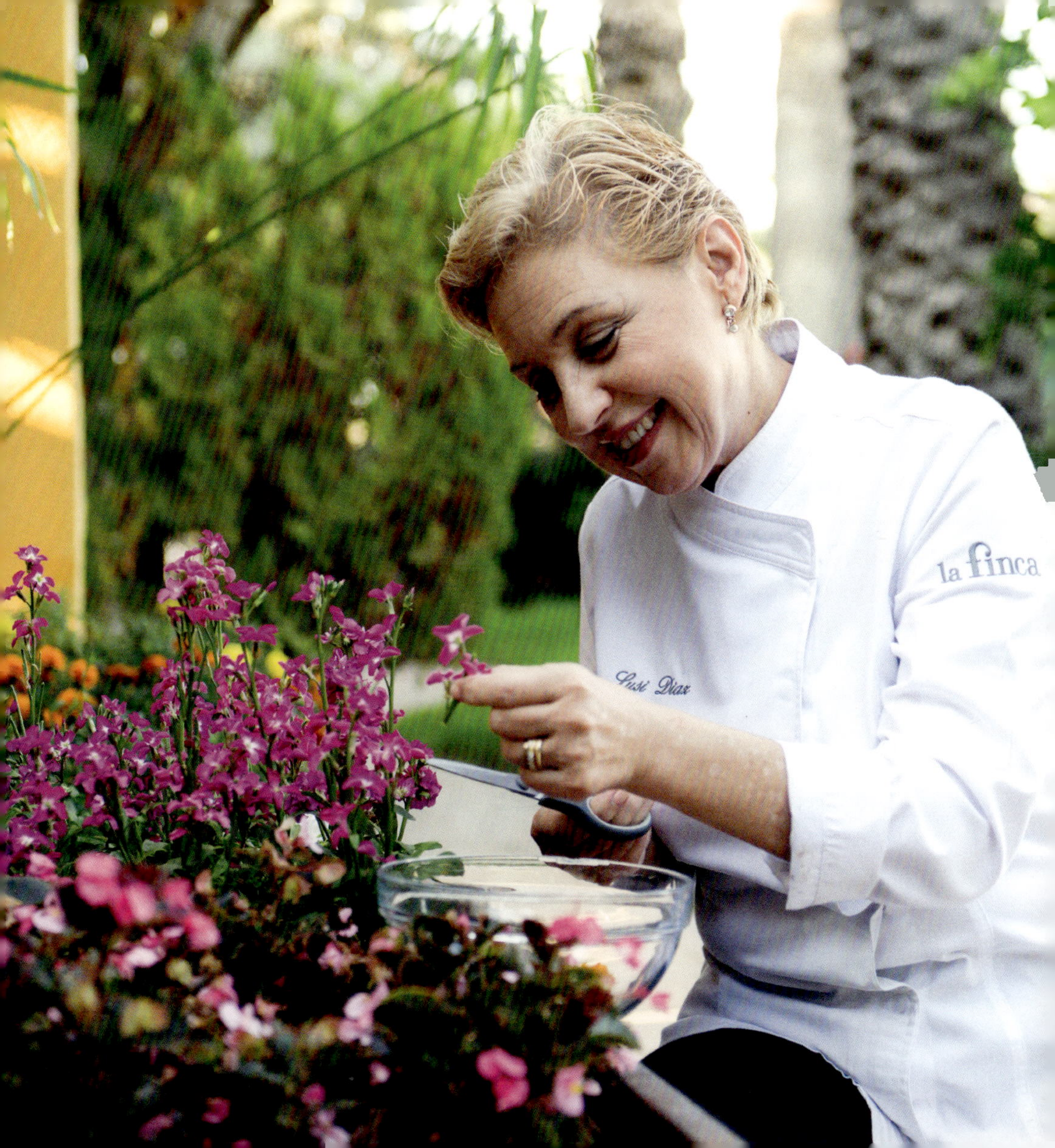
la finca
Susi Diaz

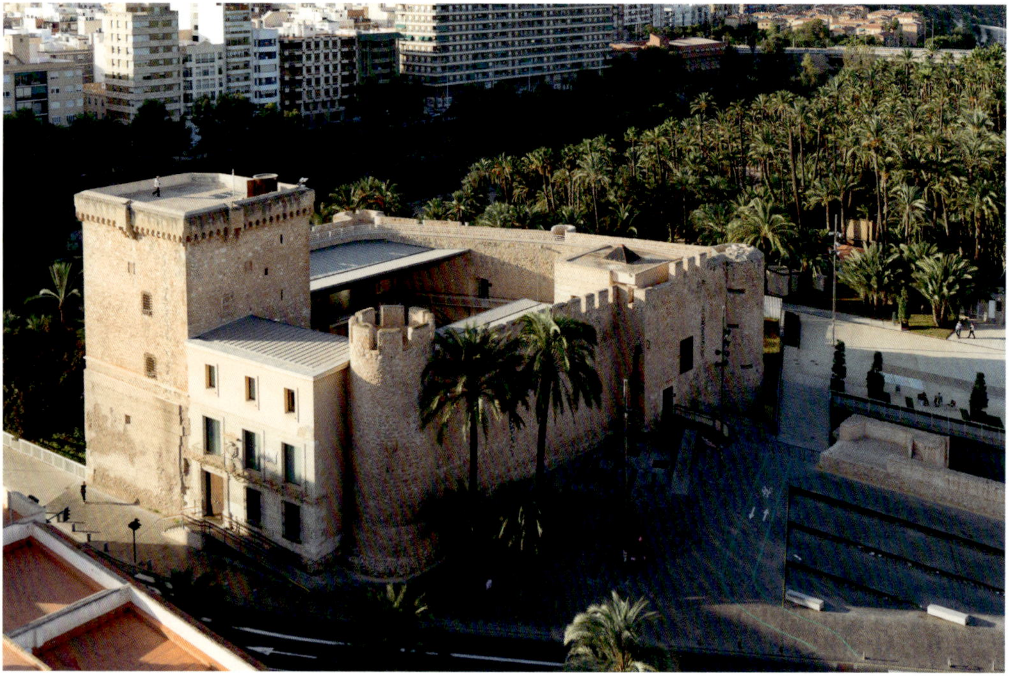

Altamira Palace

Pruning in the palm grove →

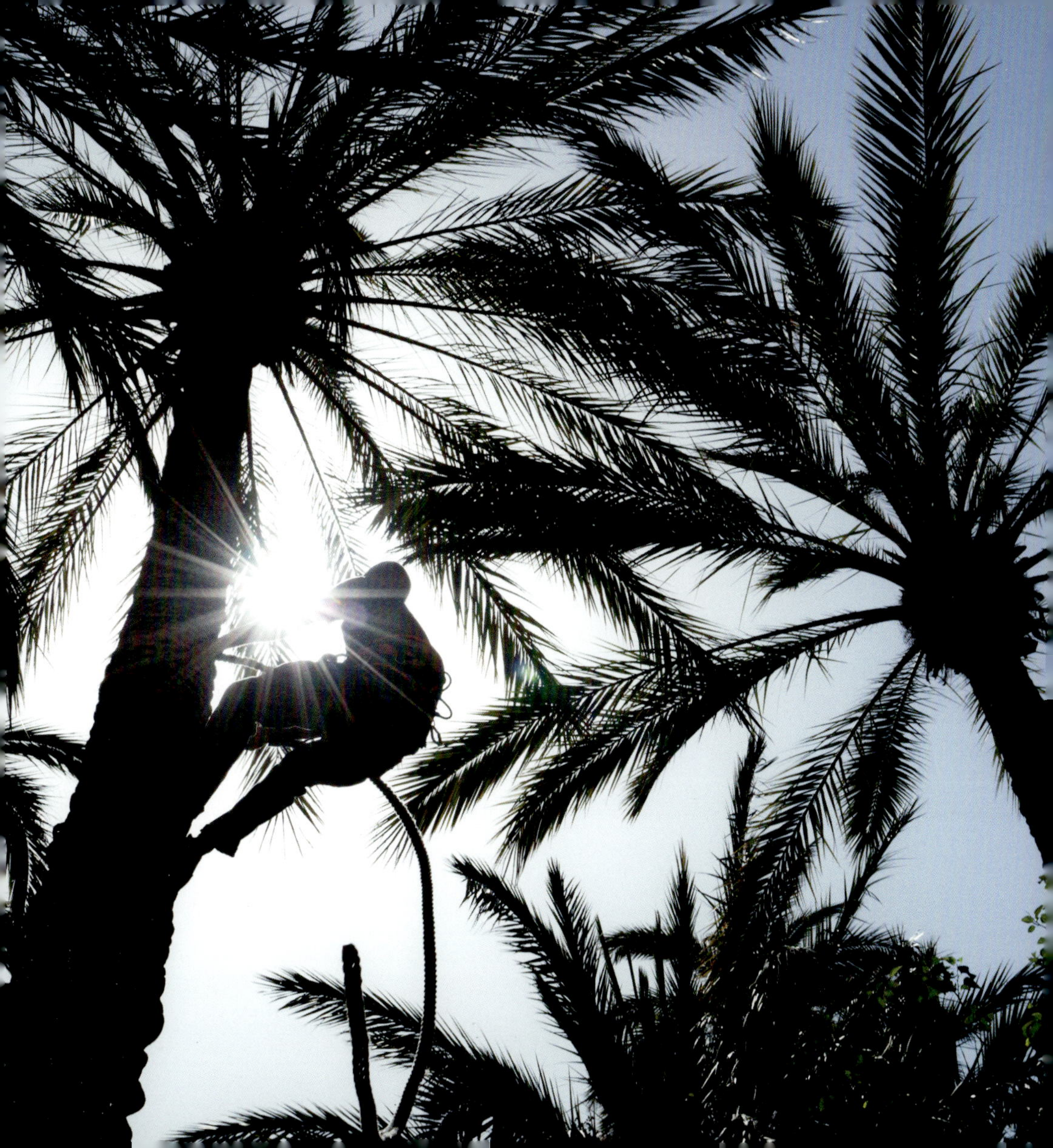

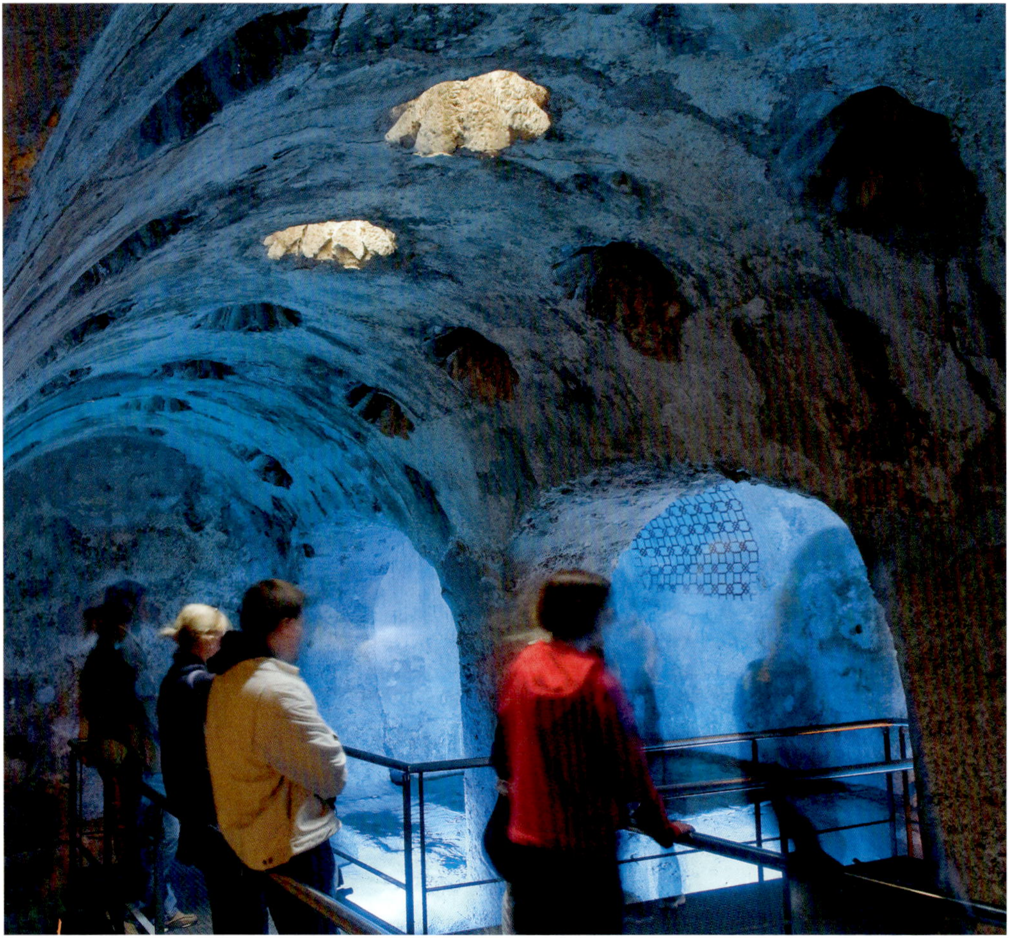

Arab baths

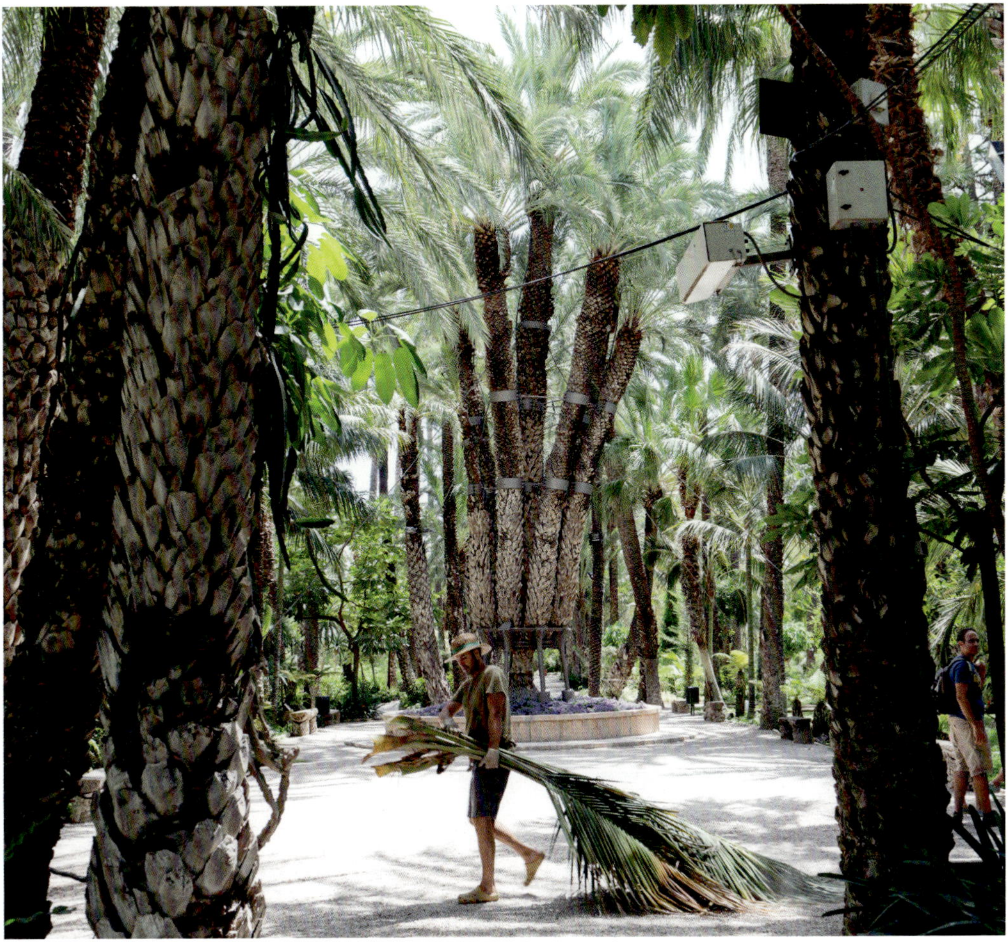

Palm grove, Huerto del cura

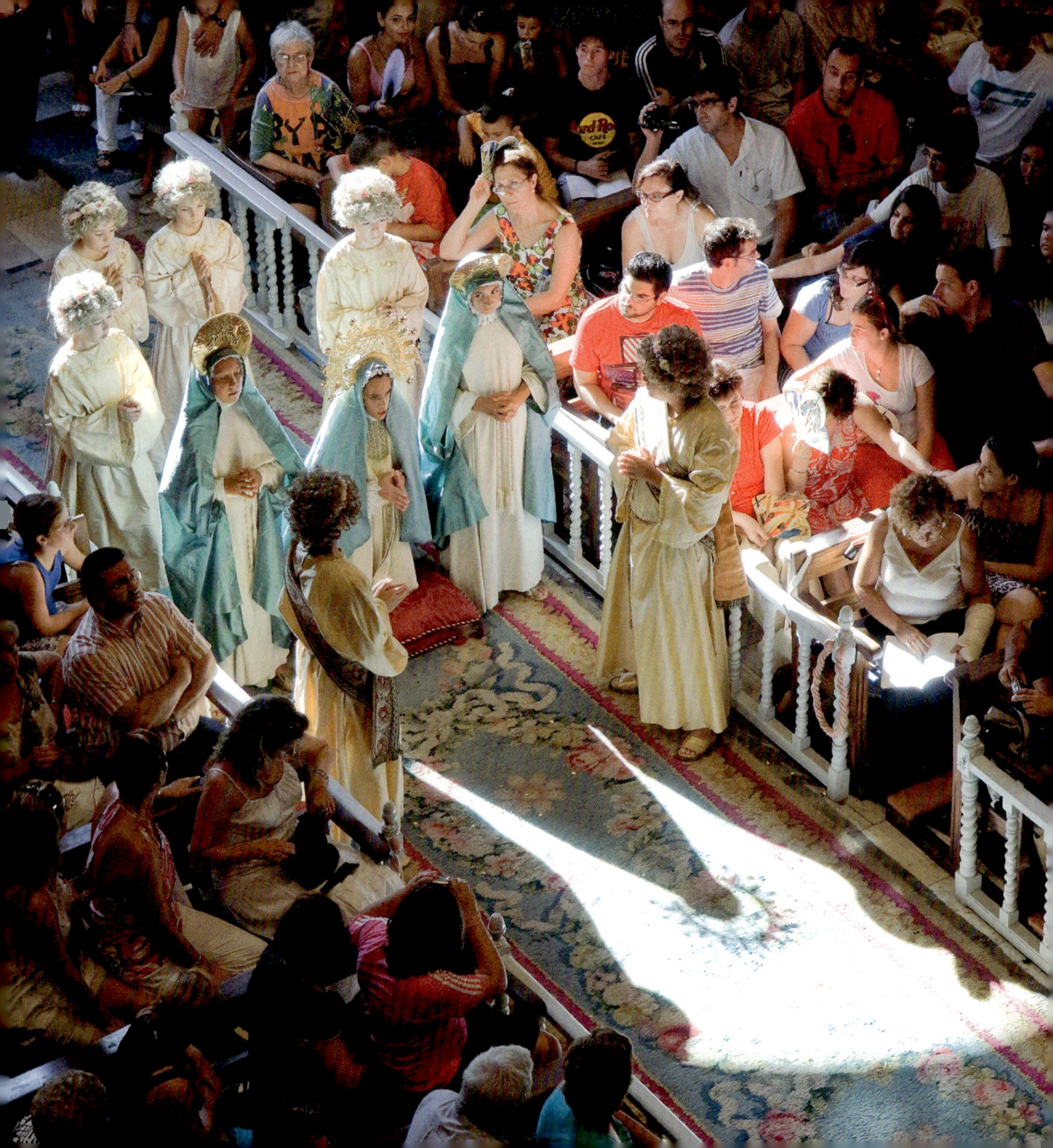

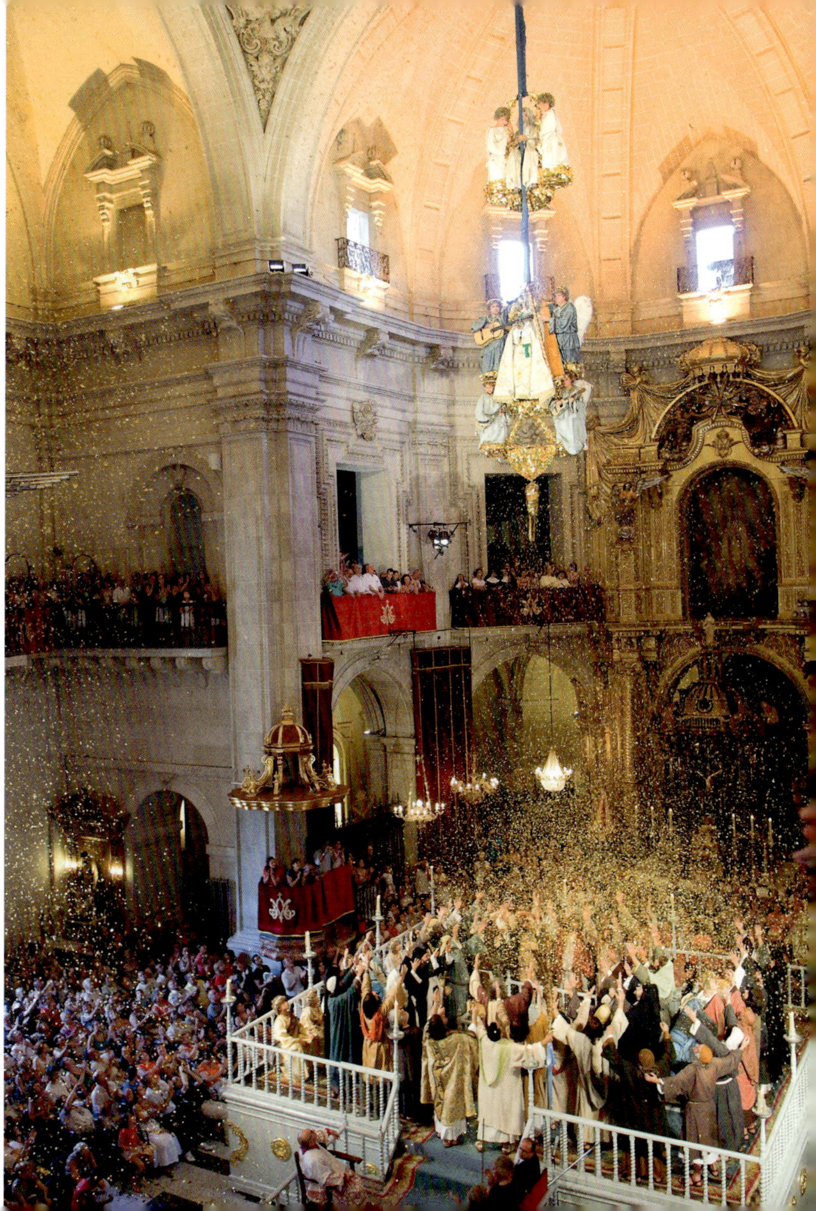

Mystery of Elche. World Heritage

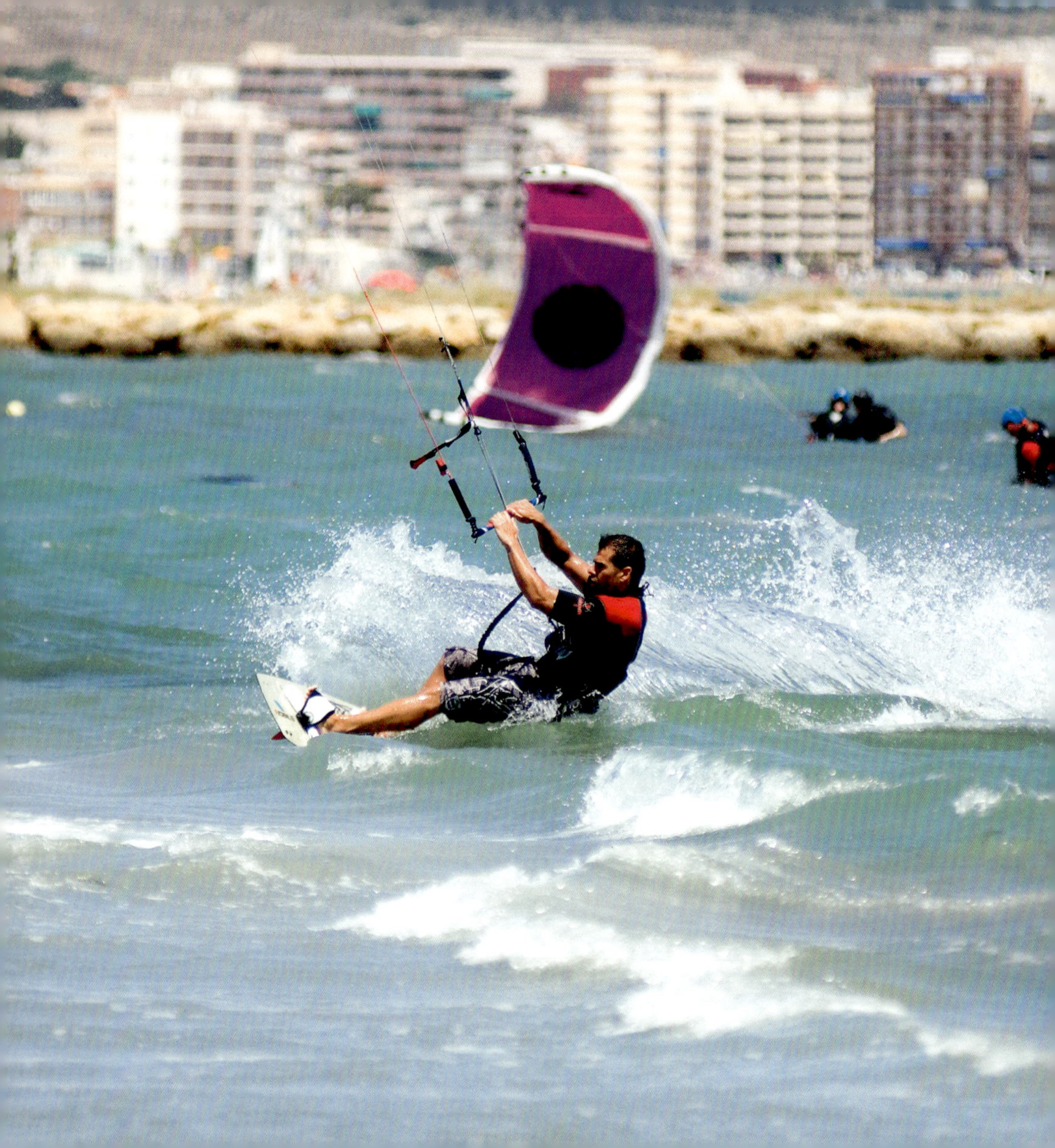

Santa Pola

Fishing activity has been linked to Santa Pola for time immemorial. Its port is among the largest on the Spanish Mediterranean. From the lighthouse of the cape of Santa Pola there are great views of the coastline, with a smattering of several beaches, some of them fitted out for kitesurfing. The beaches of Tamarit, Gola, Varadero or the coves of El Este are among the best. Santa Pola has 70% of protected space around it, in which features the Natural Park of Las Salinas, where at some times during the year it is possible to see 8,000 flamencos. The city is the closest point to Tabarca and boats leave from its port to the island.

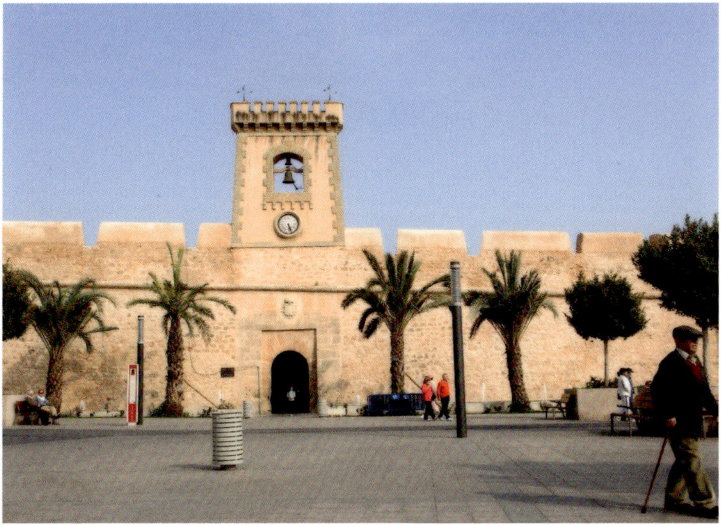

← Kitesurf
Castle of Santa Pola

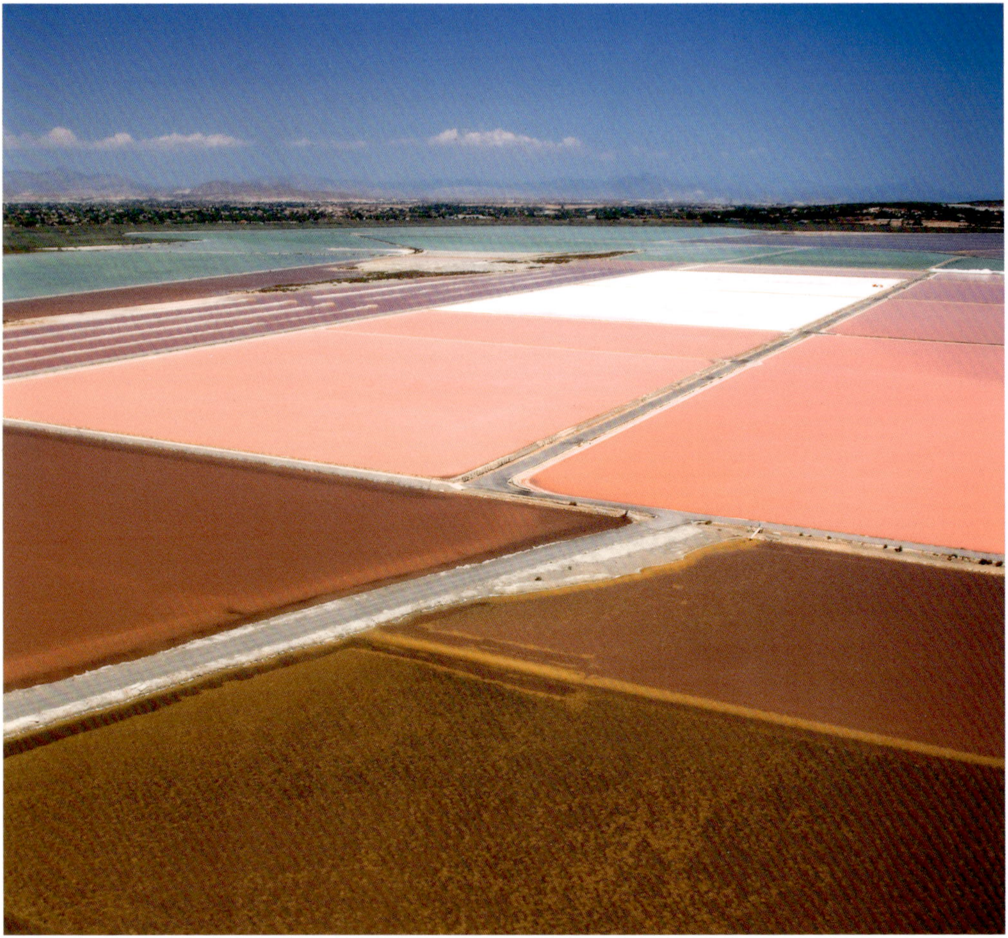

Saltworks of Santa Pola

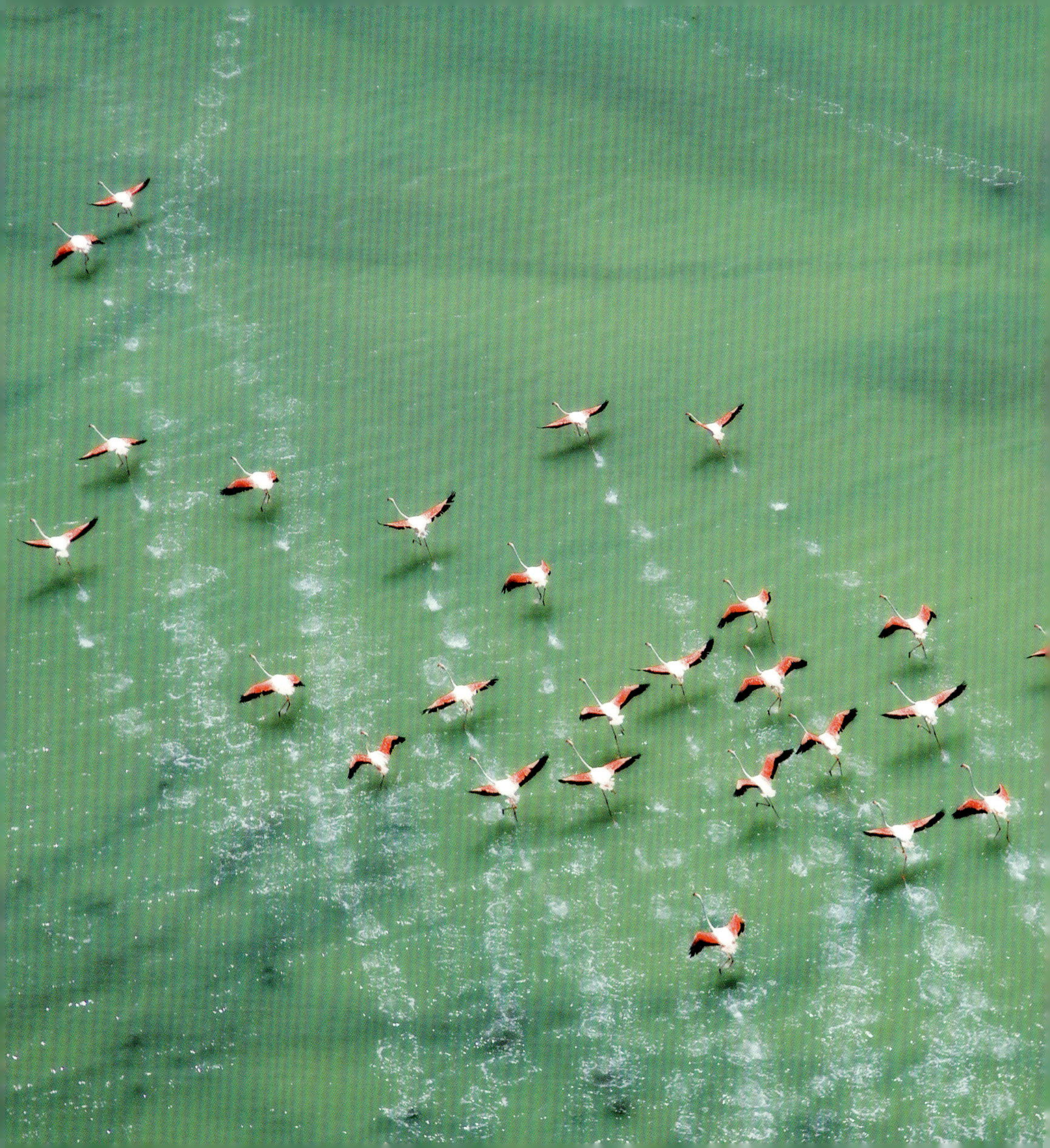

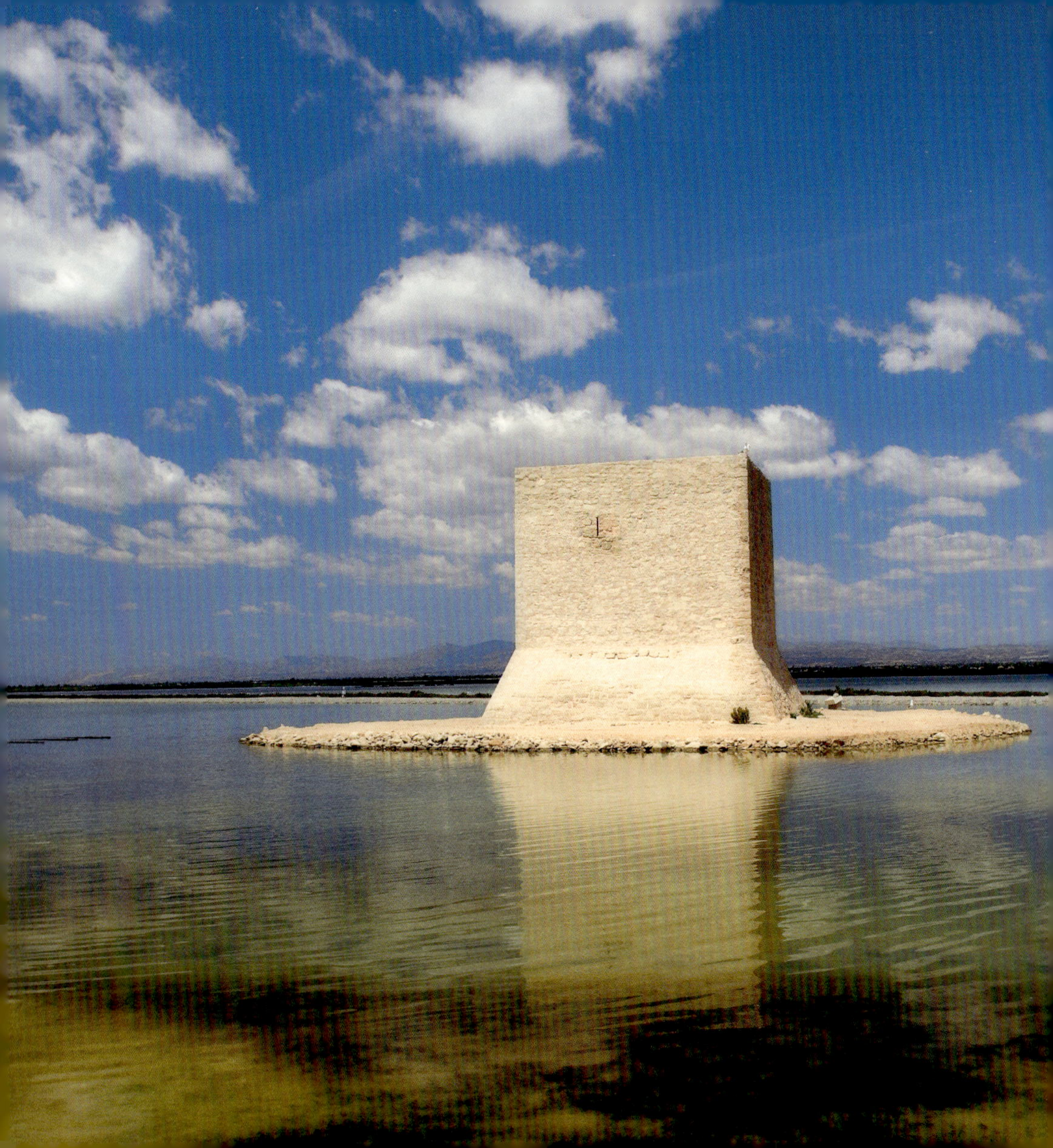

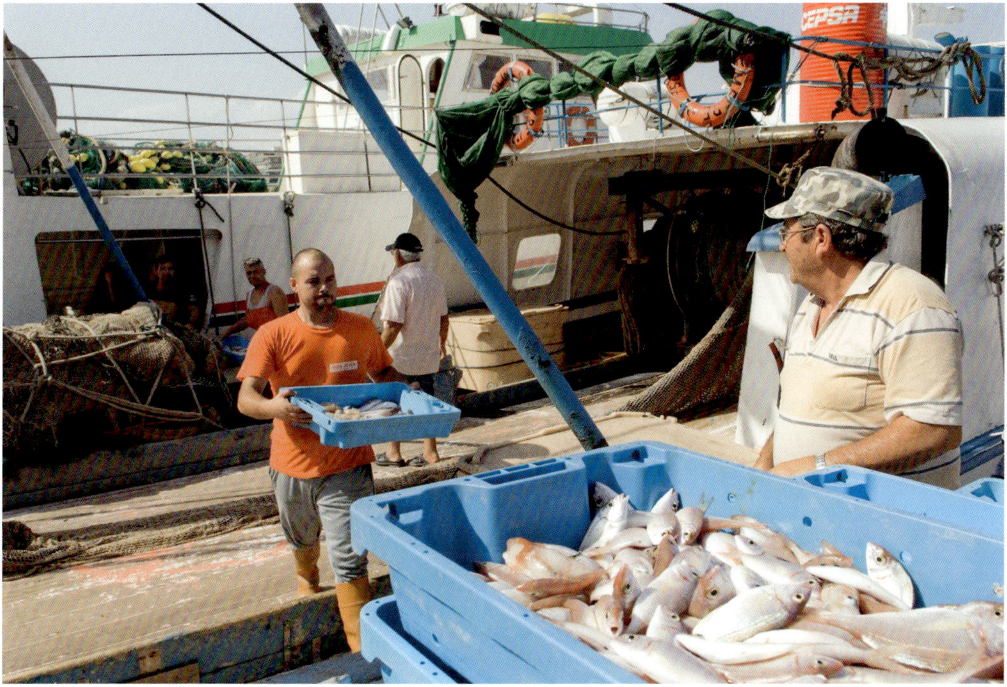

Fishing port
← *Watchtower in the saltworks of Santa Pola*

L'Alcoià

Towns between mountains

Alcoi / Alcoy

El Comtat

Cocentaina

Planes

Agres

Almond trees in flower

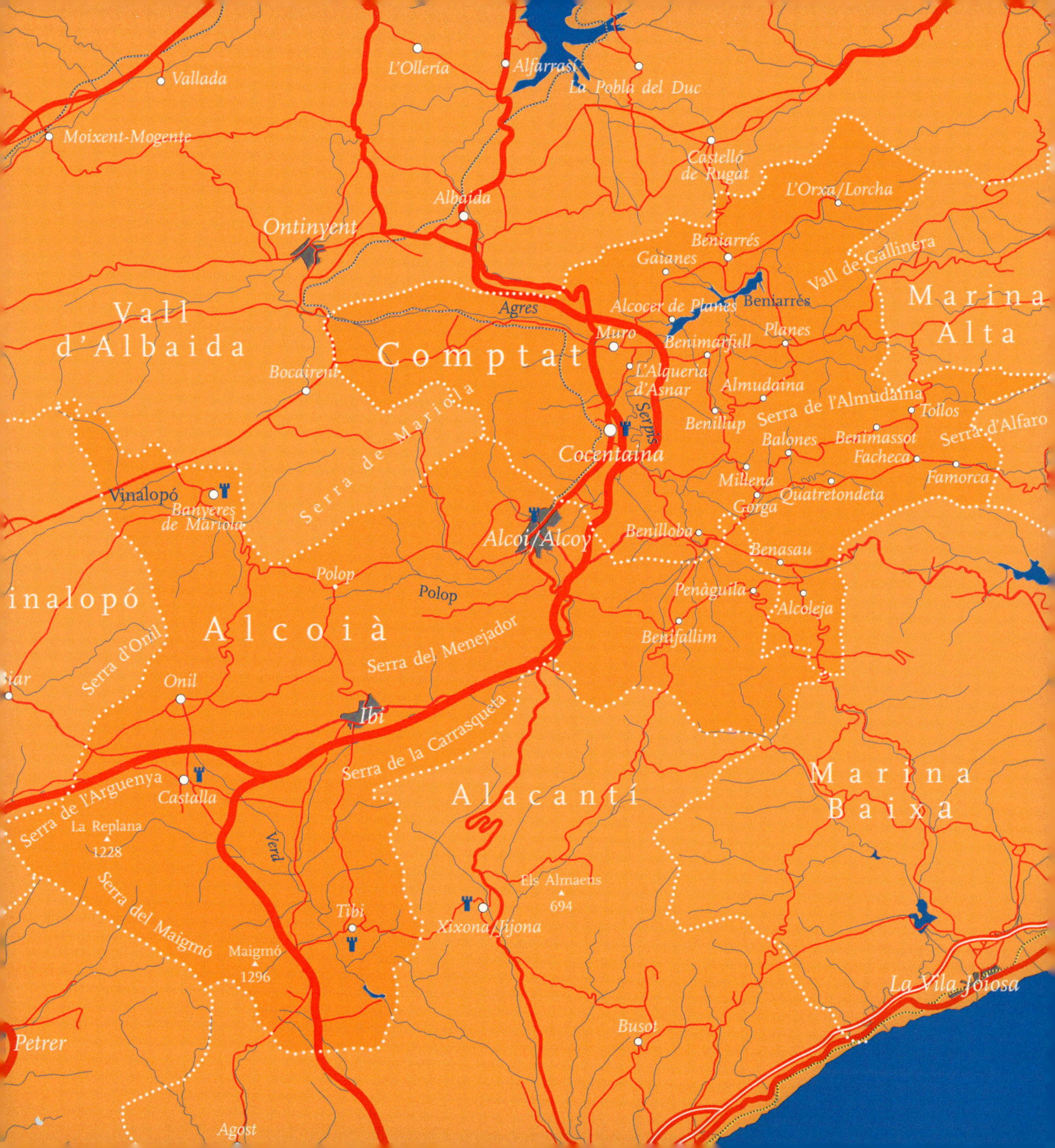

Vallada
Moixent-Mogente
L'Olleria
Alfarrasí
La Pobla del Duc
Castelló de Rugat
Albaida
L'Orxa/Lorcha
Ontinyent
Beniarrés
Gaianes
Vall de Gallinera
Marina Alta
Vall d'Albaida
Agres
Alcocer de Planes
Beniarrés
Muro
Benimarfull
Planes
Comptat
Bocairent
L'Alqueria d'Asnar
Almudaina
Serpis
Benillup
Serra de l'Almudaina
Tollos
Serra de Mariola
Cocentaina
Balones
Benimassot
Facheca
Serra d'Alfaro
Millena
Famorca
Vinalopó
Banyeres de Mariola
Gorga
Quatretondeta
Alcoi/Alcoy
Benilloba
Benasau
Polop
Polop
Penàguila
Alcoleja
inalopó
Alcoià
Benifallim
Serra d'Onil
Serra del Menejador
iar
Onil
Ibi
Serra de la Carrasqueta
Marina Baixa
Serra de l'Arguenya
Castalla
Alacantí
La Replana
1228
Verd
Els Almaeus
694
Serra del Maigmó
Tibi
Xixona/Jijona
Maigmó
1296
La Vila Joiosa
Busot
Petrer
Agost

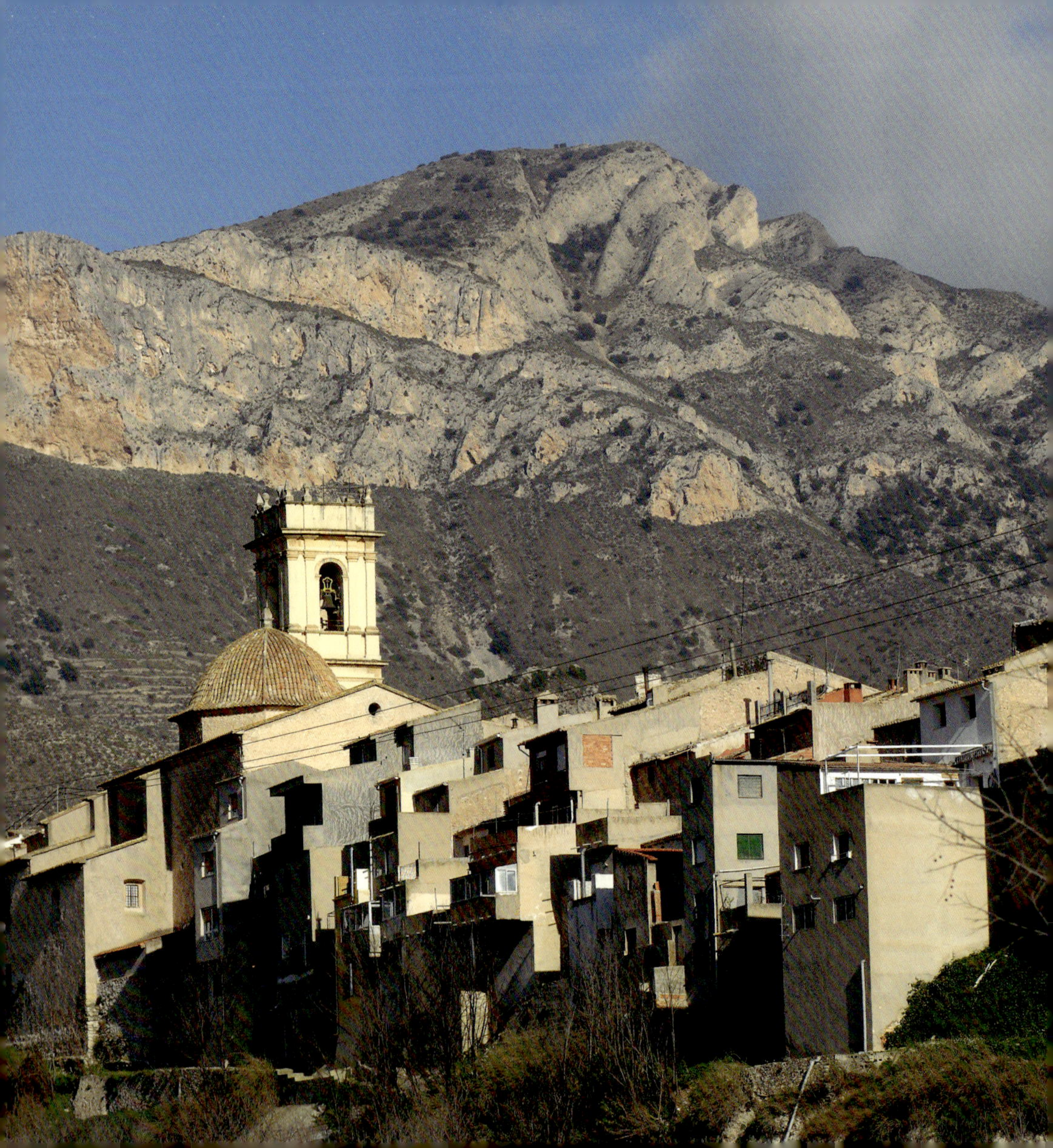

Towns between mountain ranges

The county of Alcoià is surrounded by mountain ranges and between them appear a series of small towns that are well worth a stop. In Banyeres de Mariola, a place included in the route of the Castles of Vinalopó, the tall Keep stands out. In Onil, you should visit the palace of the Marquis of Dos Aguas, of Renaissance Gothic style, currently the Town Hall. The history of the town is linked the manufacture of dolls. In the nearby village of Ibi there is an interesting Toy Museum, which explains the history of this industry, so much linked to the area.

The trip to the reservoir of Tibi, the oldest in Europe still functioning, is an interesting option for lovers of walking. On the border with the county of El Comtat, next to one of the slopes of the Aitana range, we come to the town of Penáguila.

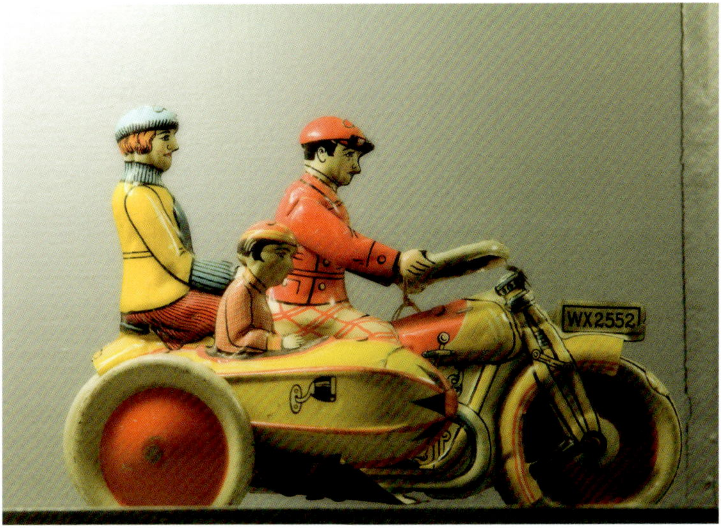

← Tibi
Toy Museum of Ibi

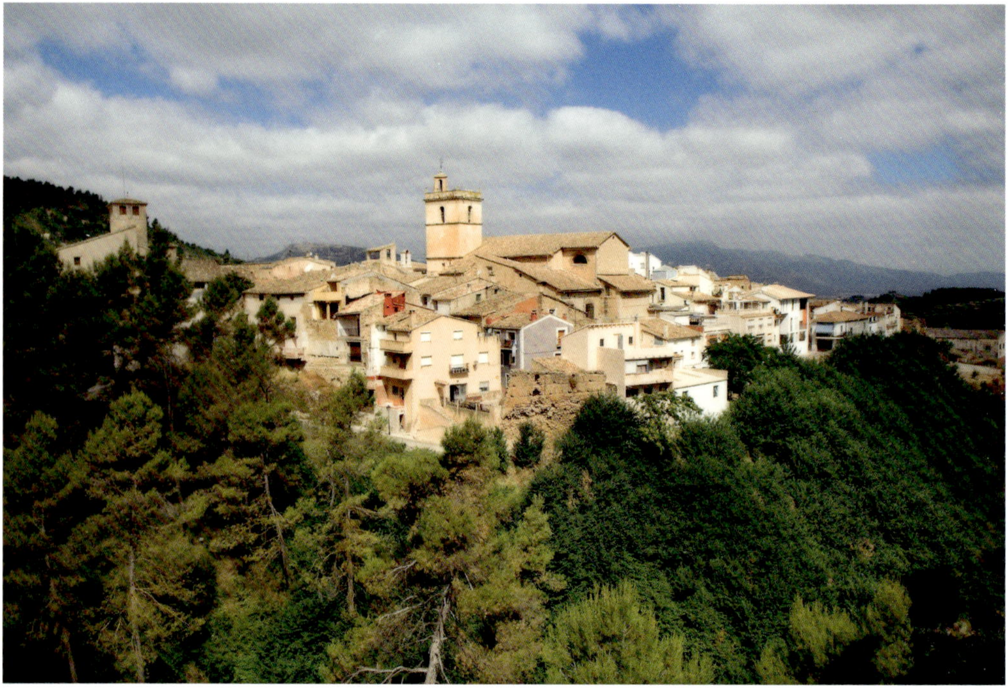

Penáguila

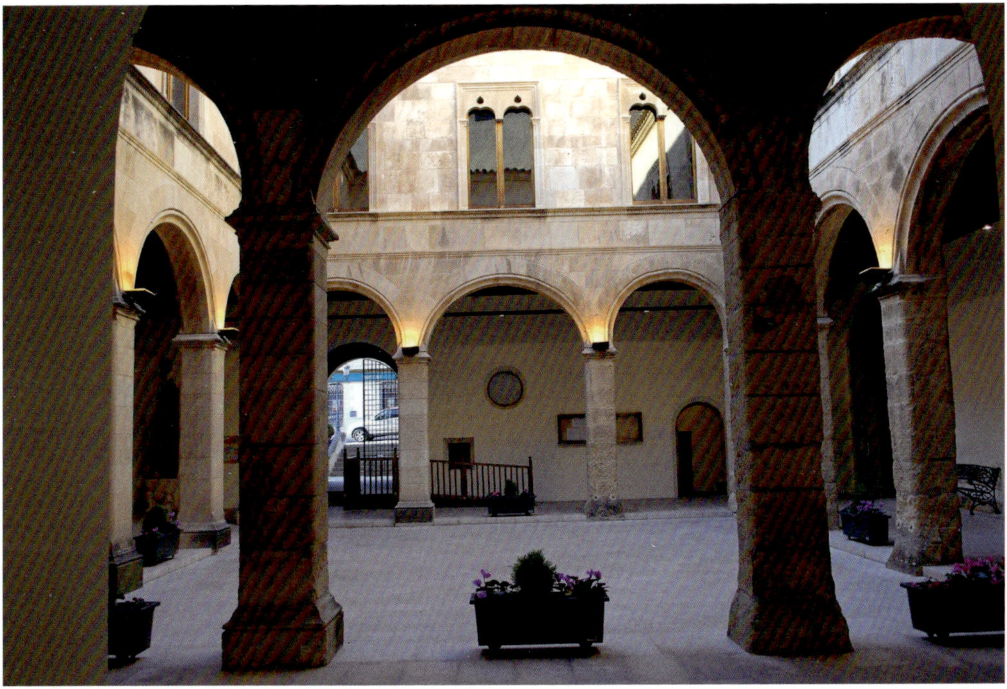

Palace of the Marquis of Dos Aguas in Onil

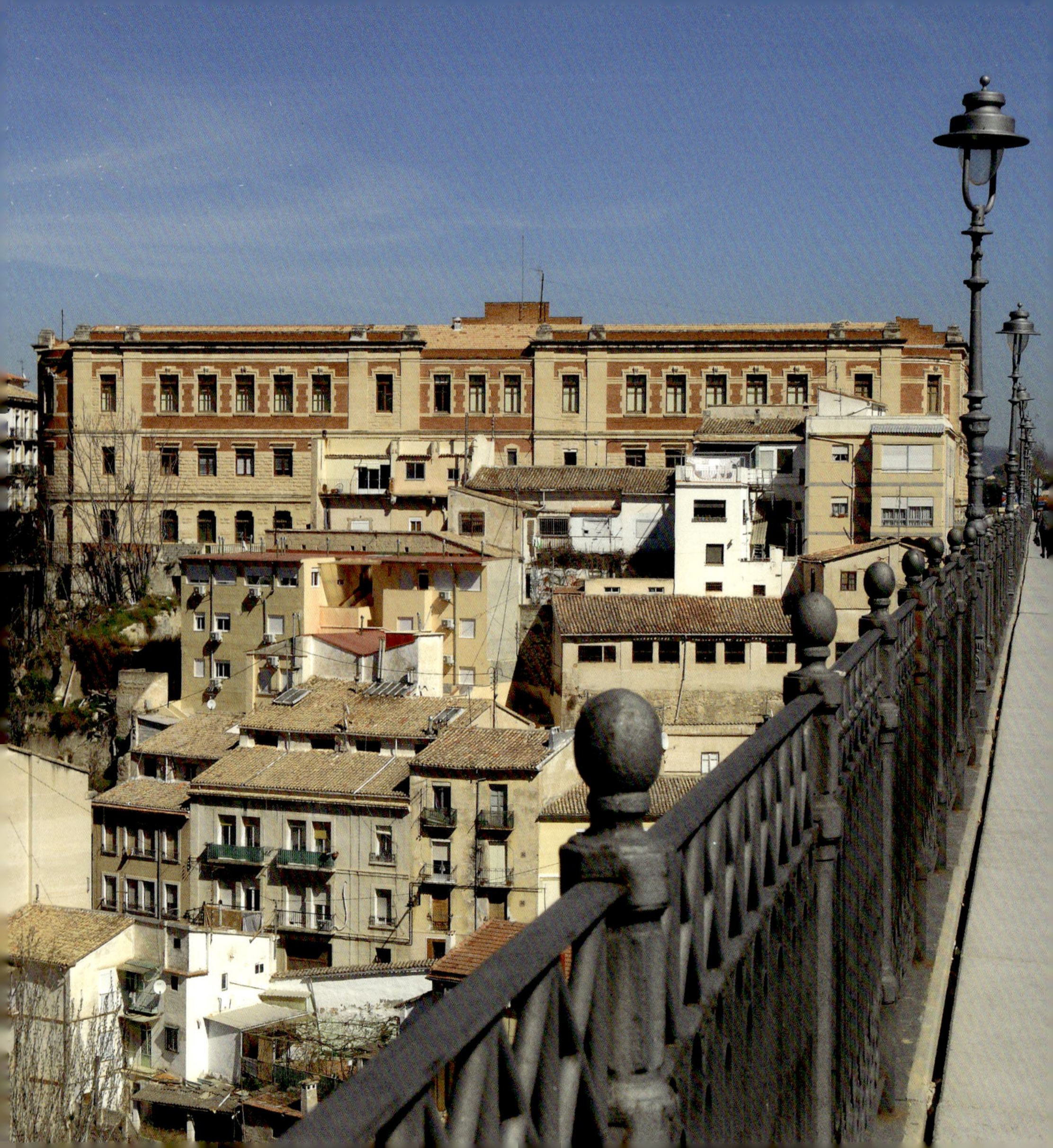

Alcoi / Alcoy

The capital of the county is the gateway to two natural parks: that of the Sierra de Mariola, where the herbs grow from which a well-known spirit is made, and the holm-oak groves of Font-Roja. A part of the architecture of Alcoy is heir to the Industrial Revolution, highlighted by Modernism. The most important examples of this architecture are the Casa del Pavo, the old Fire Station and the Círculo Industrial. Among the more modern architecture features the intervention made on the exchange of San Jorge, work of Santiago Calatrava. The complicated relief of the land over which Alcoy is seated made it necessary to build bridges that connected the different parts of the city: Siete Lunas, María Cristina or Canalejas are some of them. Celebrations have a leading place in the Alcoy calendar. Its Parade of the Three Wise Men is the oldest in Spain and the Moors and Christians held in April, in honour of St George, rivals that of Villajoyosa in terms of sumptuousness. At Christmas, the puppets of the Nativity of Tirisiti delight the younger members of the family.

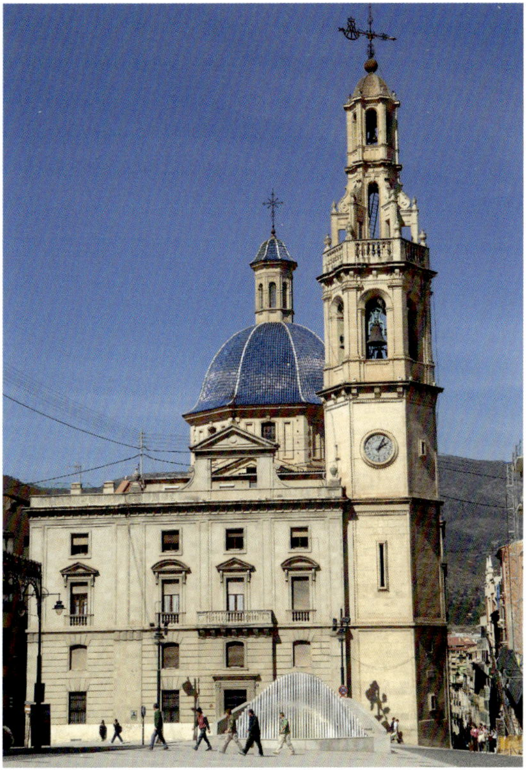

← Canalejas Bridge
Church of Santa María

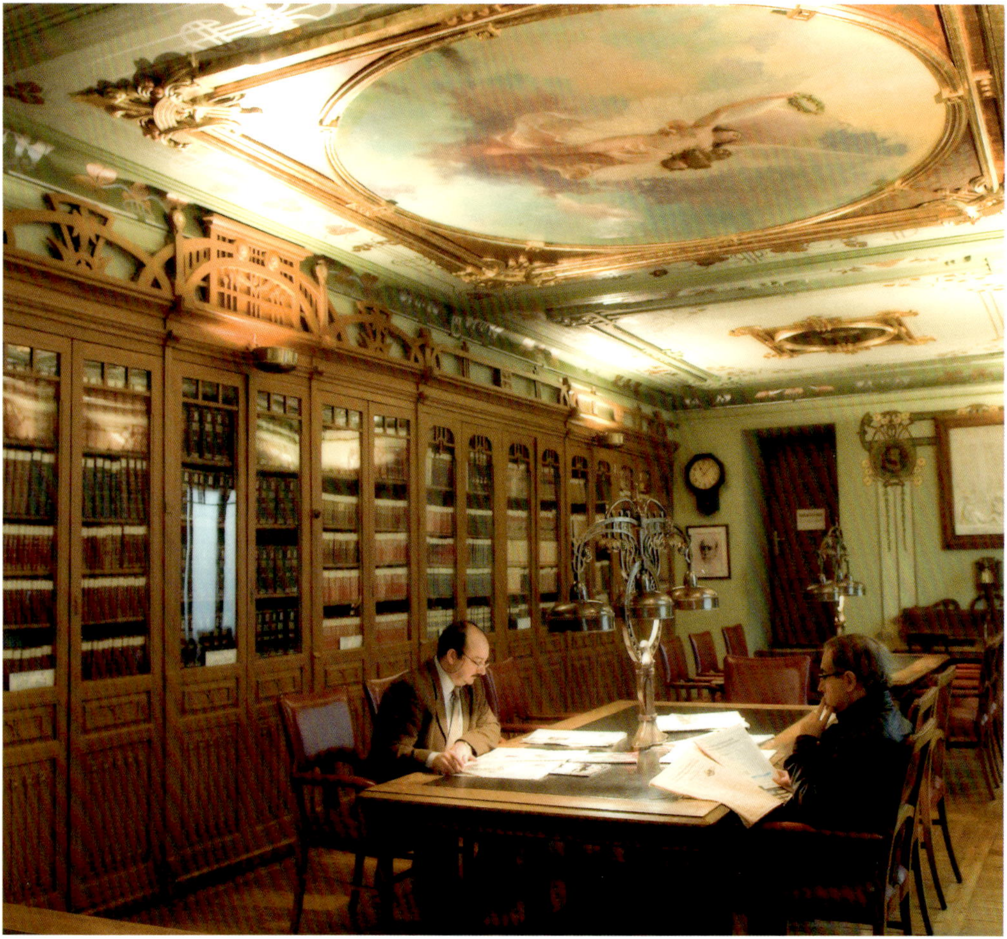

Industrial Circle

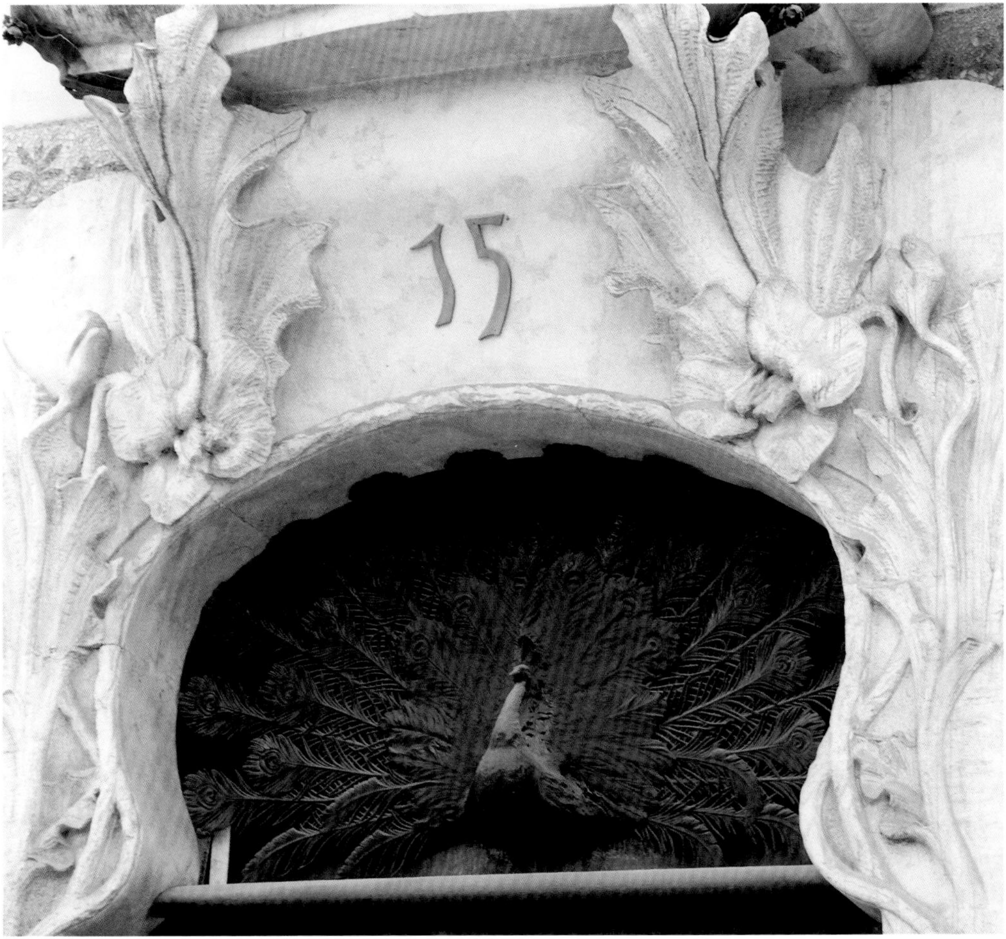

Casa del Pavo (1908-1909). Modernist building by Vicente Pascual Pastor.
Festivals of Moors and Christians →

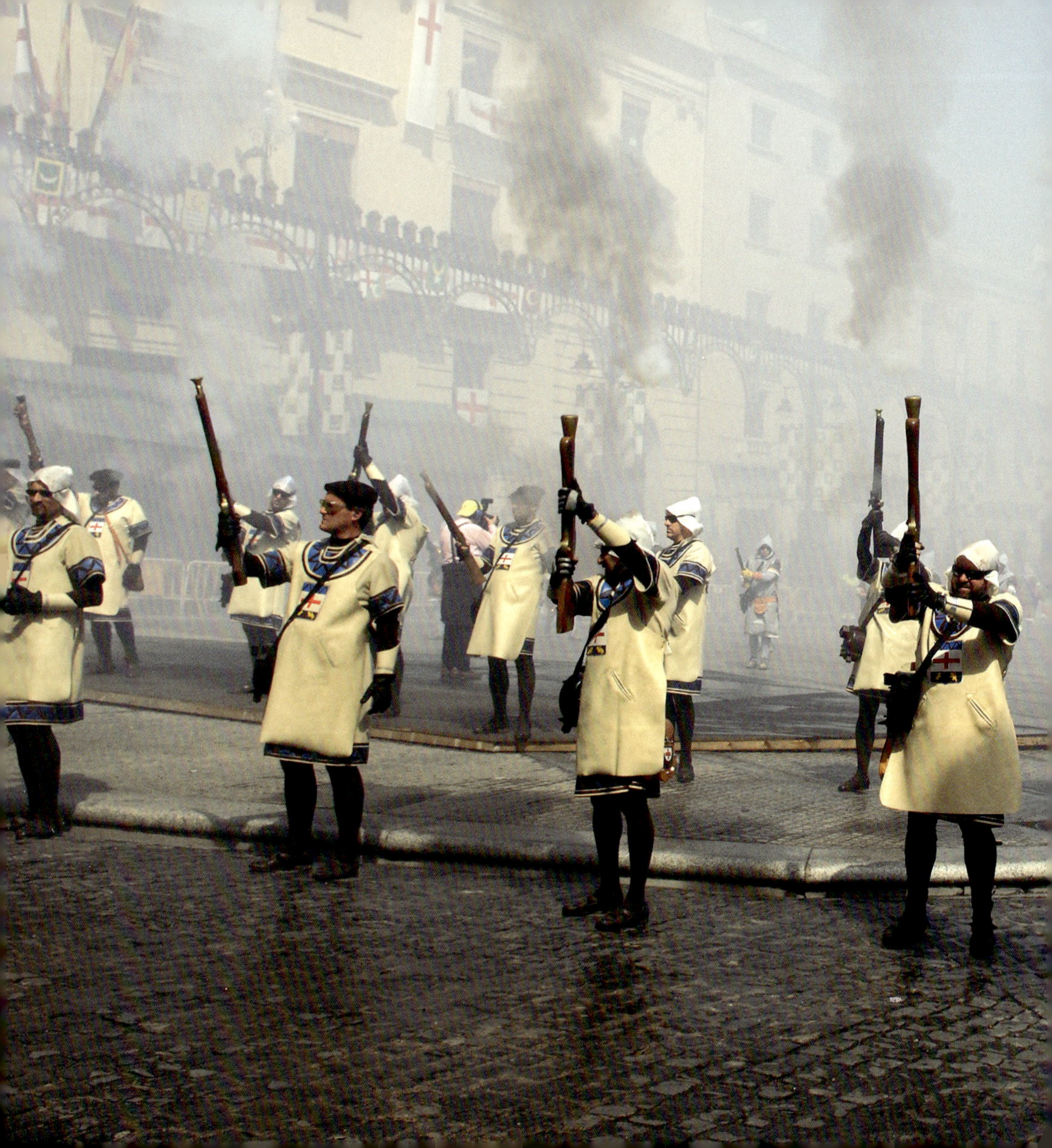

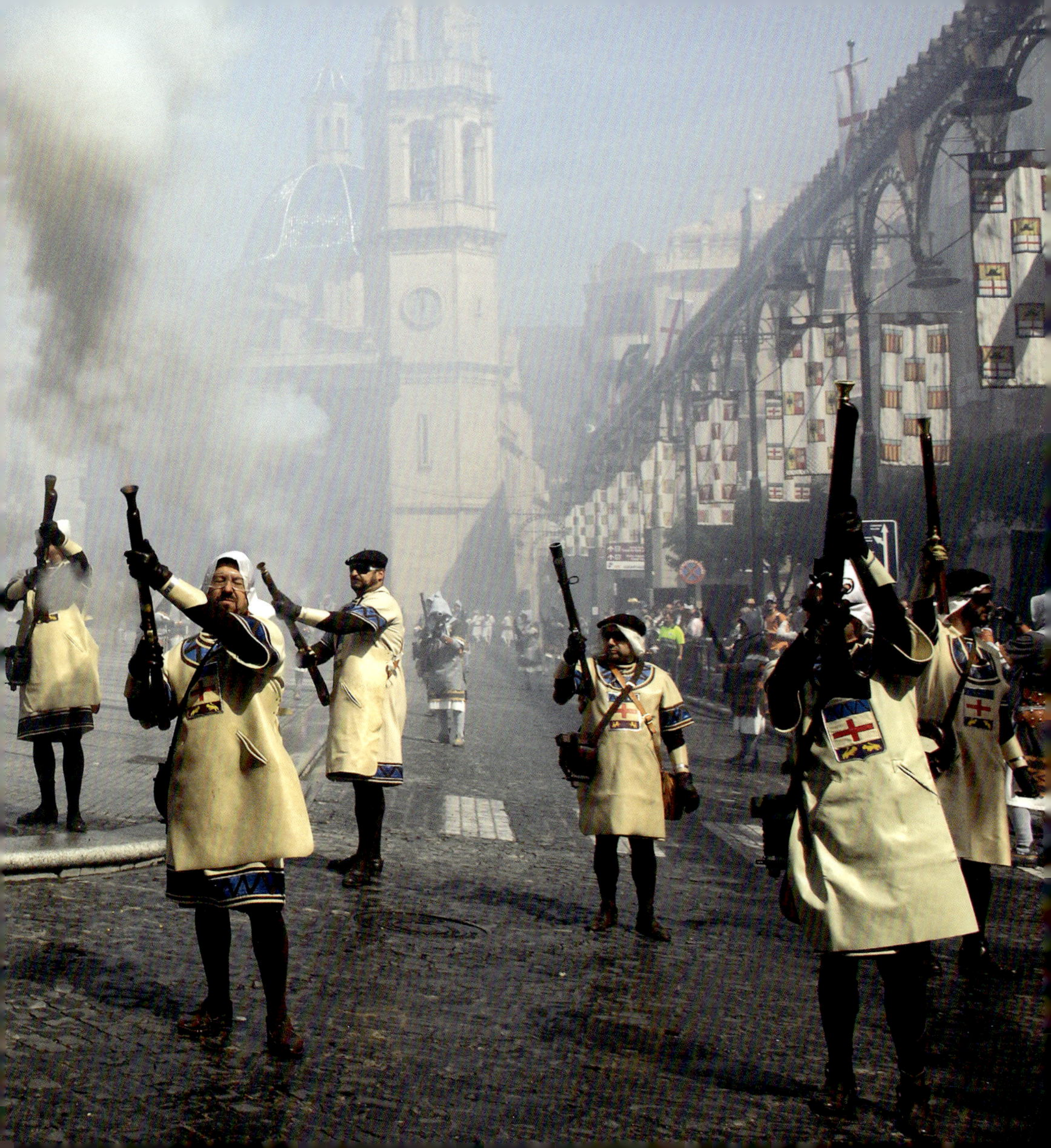

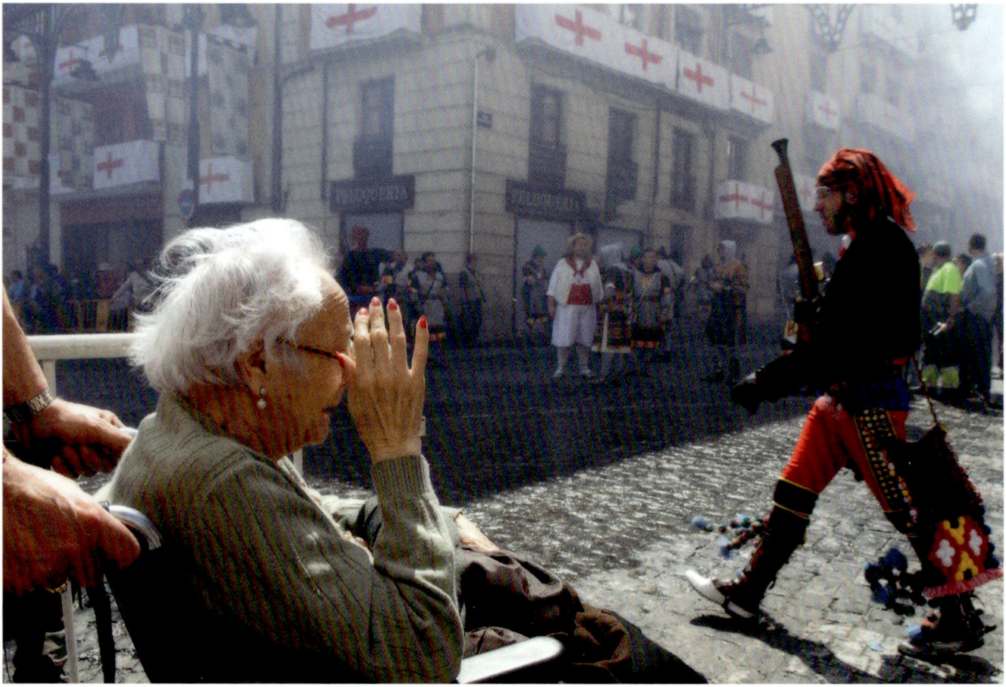

Festivals of Moors and Christians

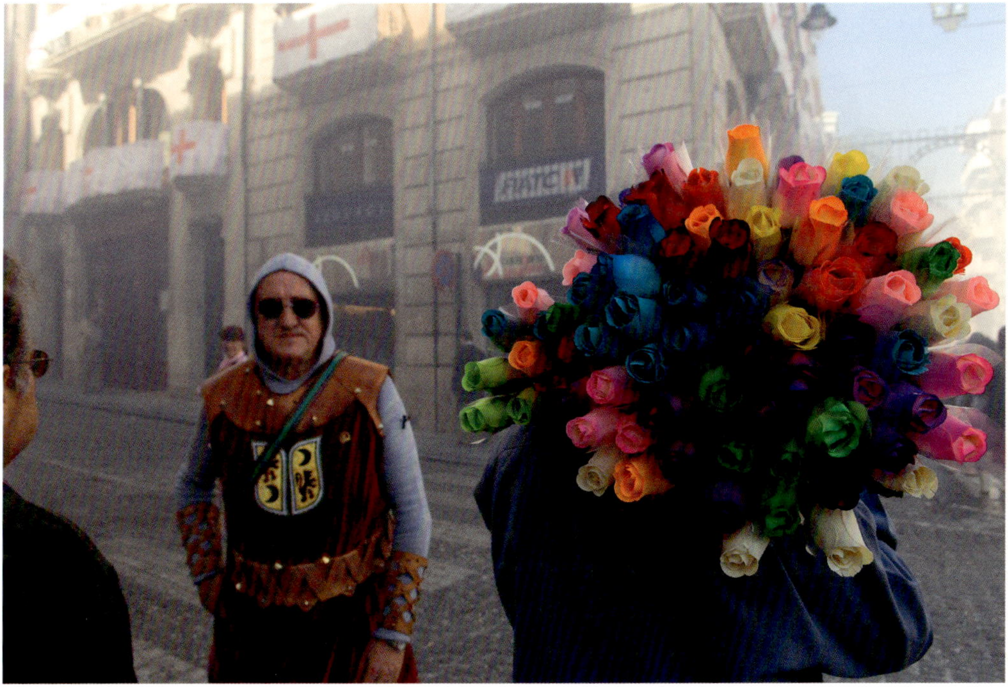

Festivals of Moors and Christians

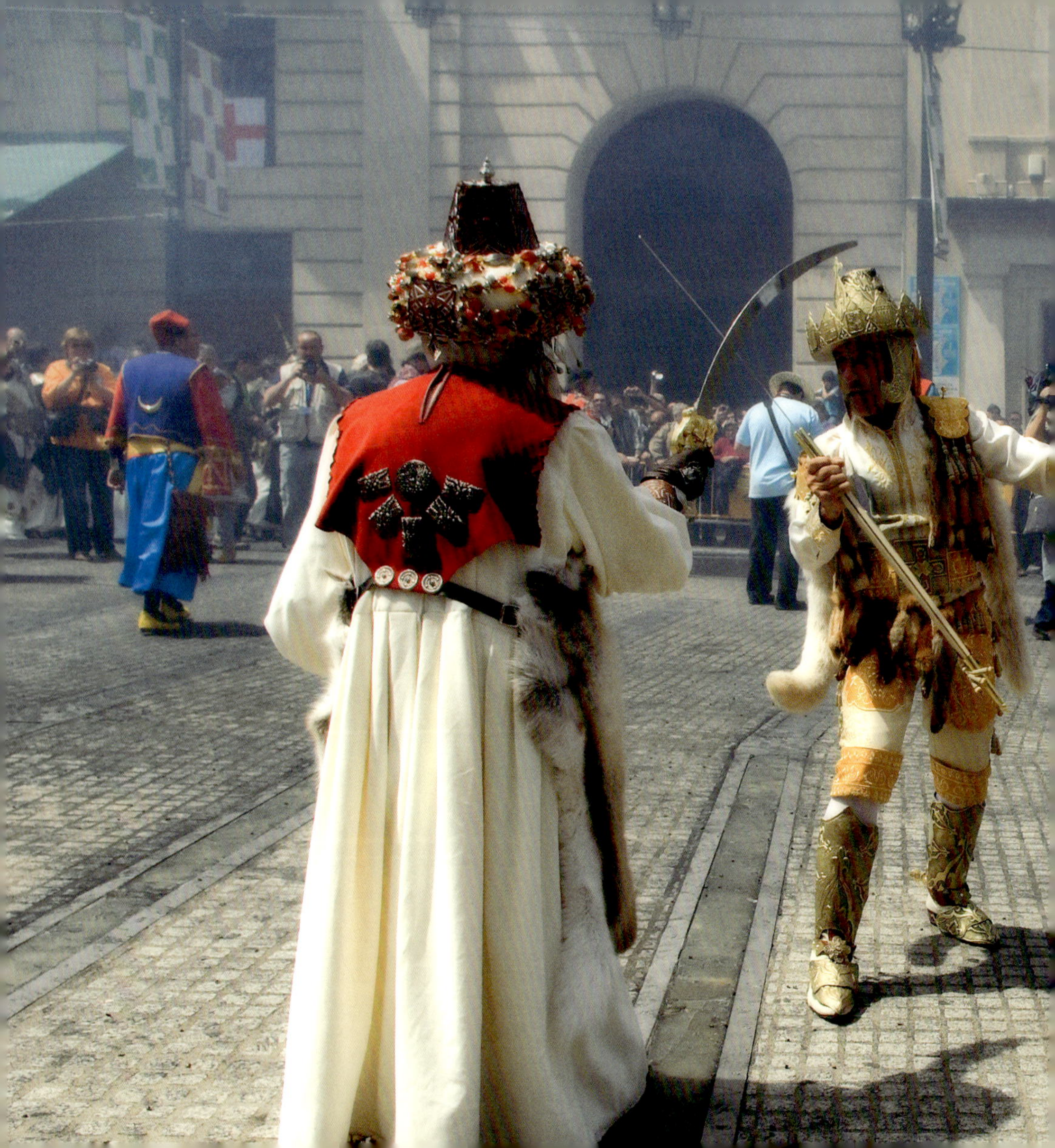

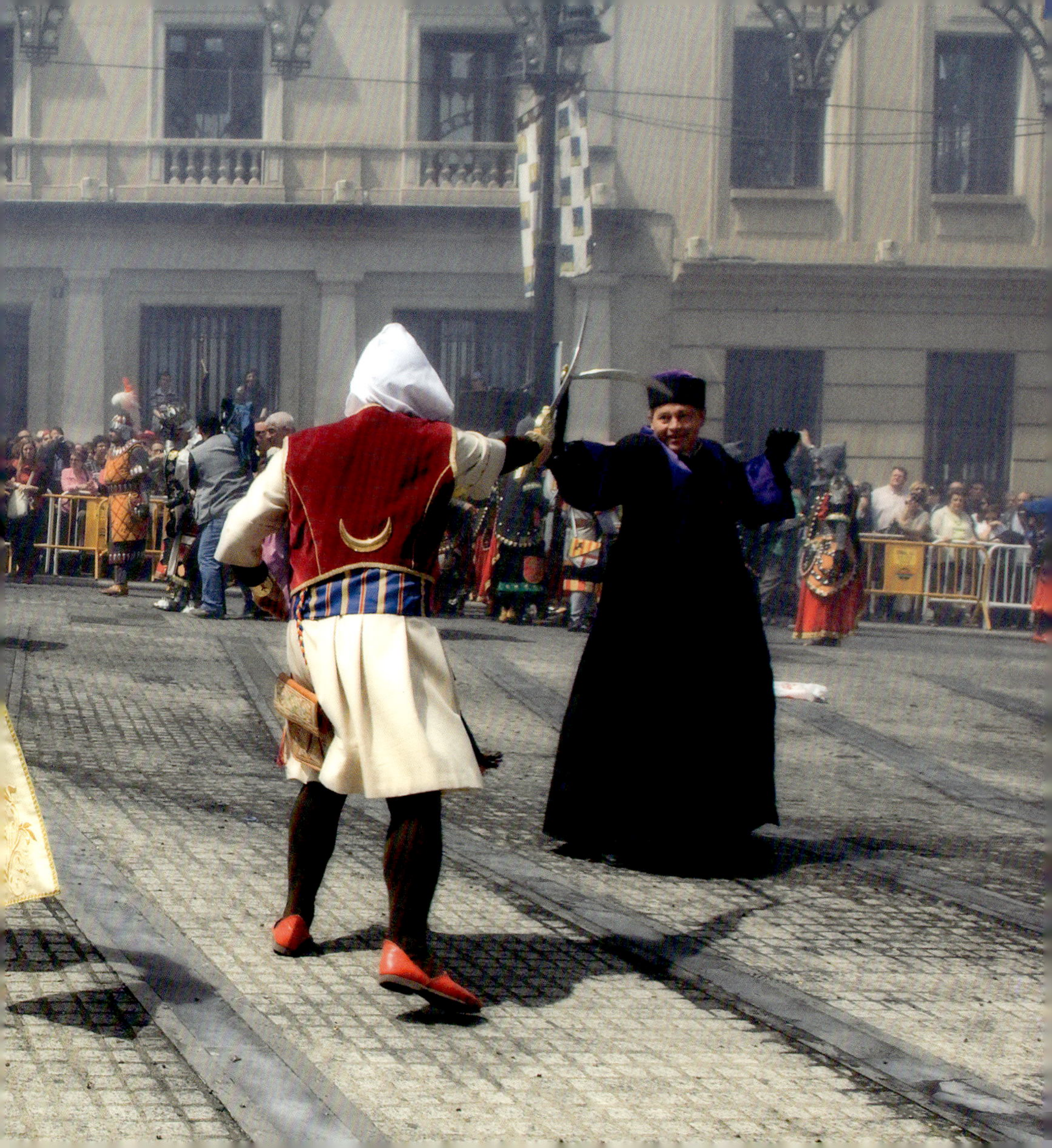

Cocentaina

The county of El Comtat, whose capital is Cocentaina, conserves its name from the period in which these lands were awarded to Roger de Llúria for services rendered. It was in 1291 and the admiral of the Almogavars became the first feudal lord of the County of Cocentaina. Just over a decade later, the burning of the place by Moorish troops from Granada gave the nickname for which it is known by the inhabitants: Socarrats (scorched). The most outstanding building of Cocentaina is the Palacio Condal, ordered to be built by Roger de Llúria.

In November a well-attended All Saints fair is held.

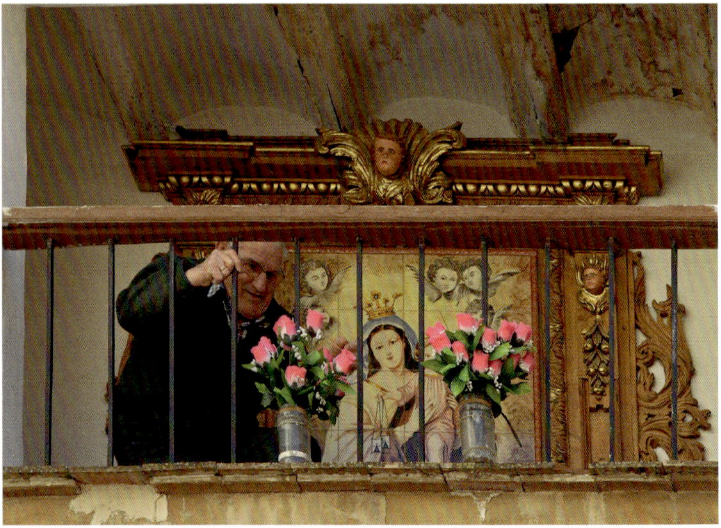

Balcony with religious image

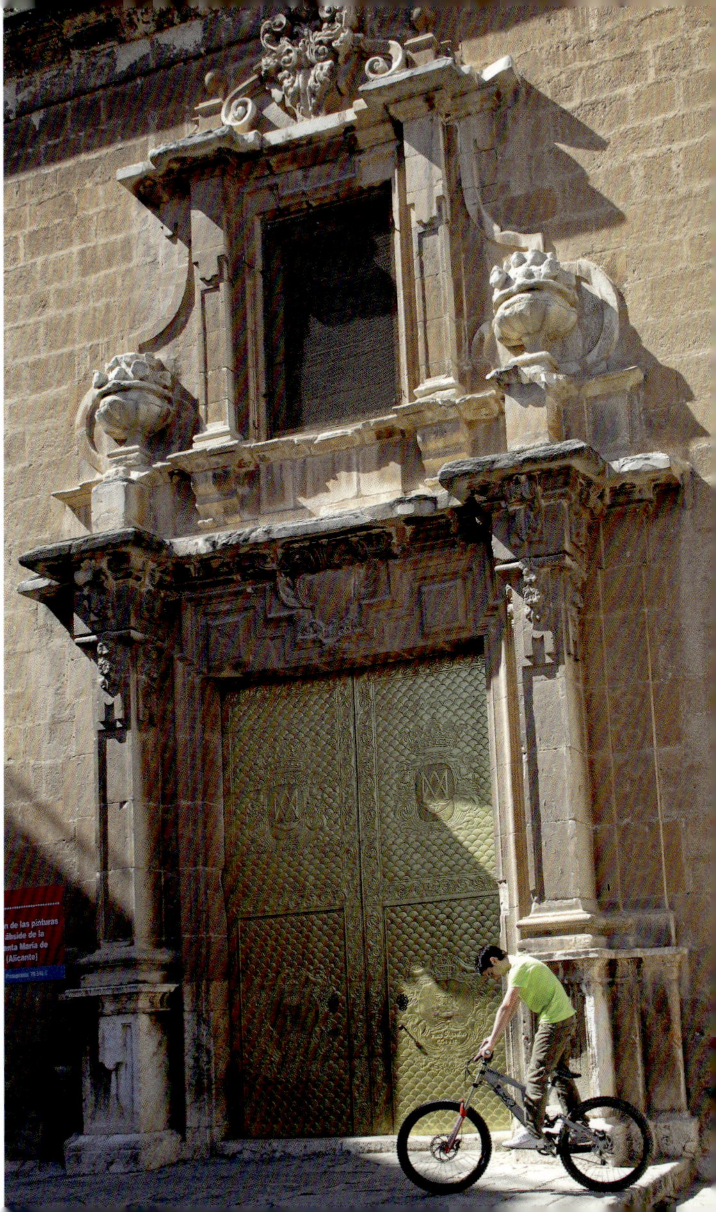

Church of Santa María

Planes

In the valley formed at the foot of the Almudaina range is Planes. On the hill that stands above the town is the castle that played an important role in the time of Al-Azraq as a gateway to the nearby valley of Alcalá. Planes was a sort of Christian island amid an ocean of Muslim domination of the area. Conserved from this part are the remains of some hydraulic constructions, such as the aqueduct.

Popular legend tells that a maiden appeared before a labourer in a cave in the nearby ravine of Encantada, where the Moors had kept a treasure. The labourer, who had to choose between a necklace and the maiden, preferred the gem, and was condemned to be unhappy for having rejected the maiden, who disappeared with the dawn. The natural spot is today a popular recreational and walking area.

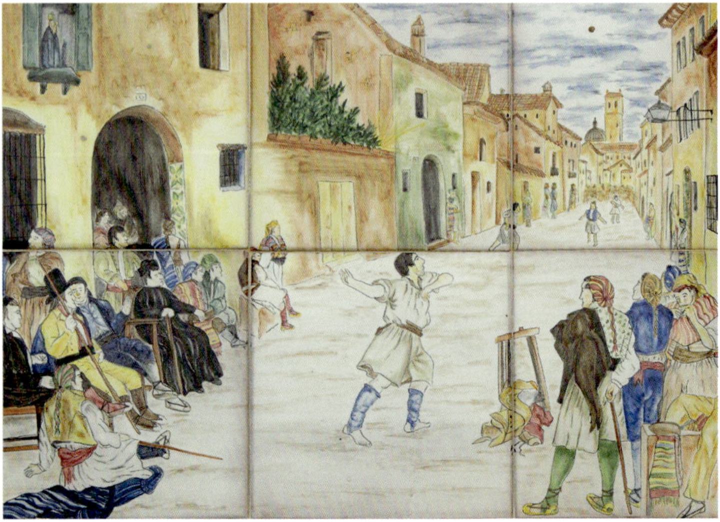

Mosaic of the game of pelota valenciana

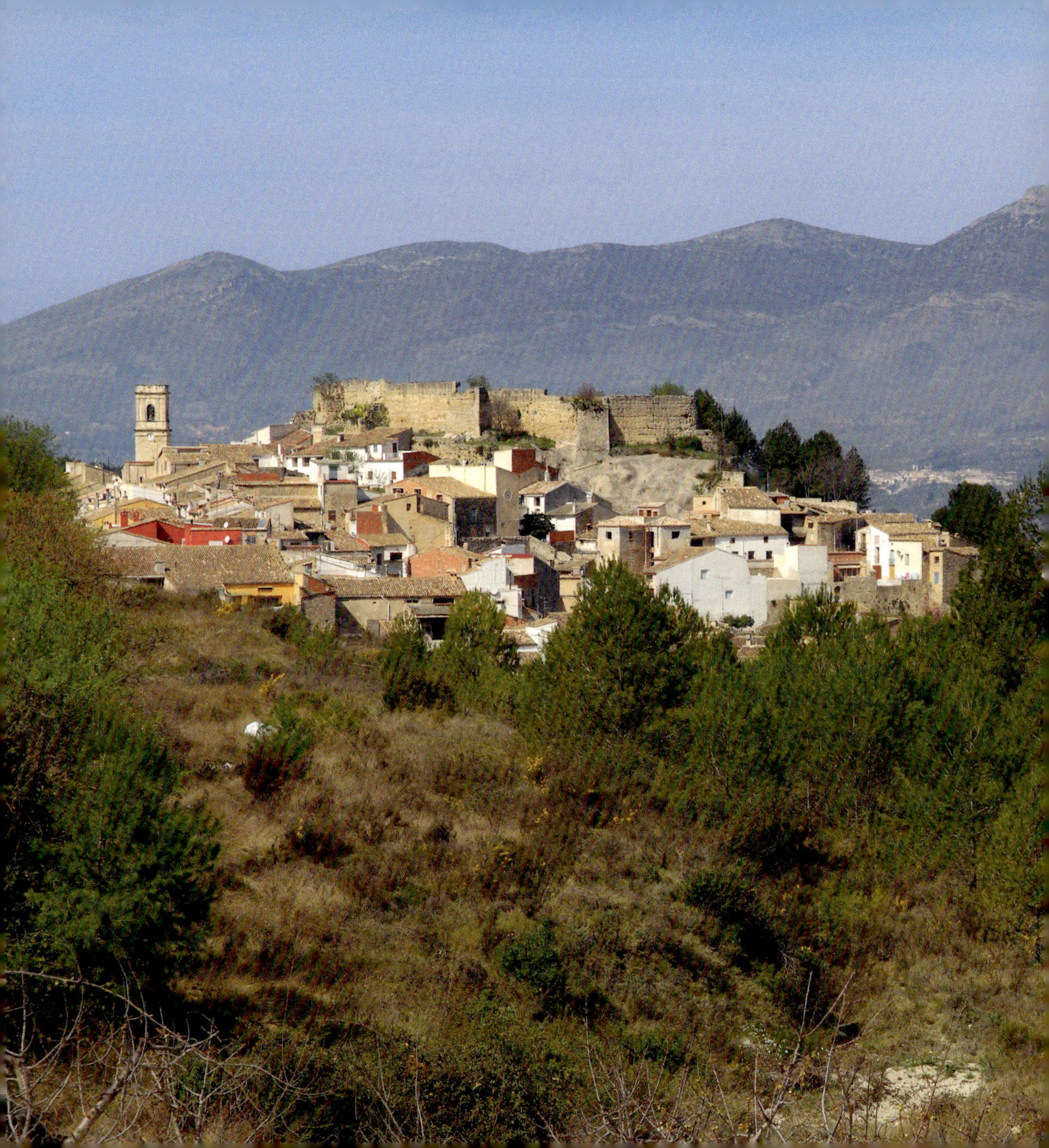

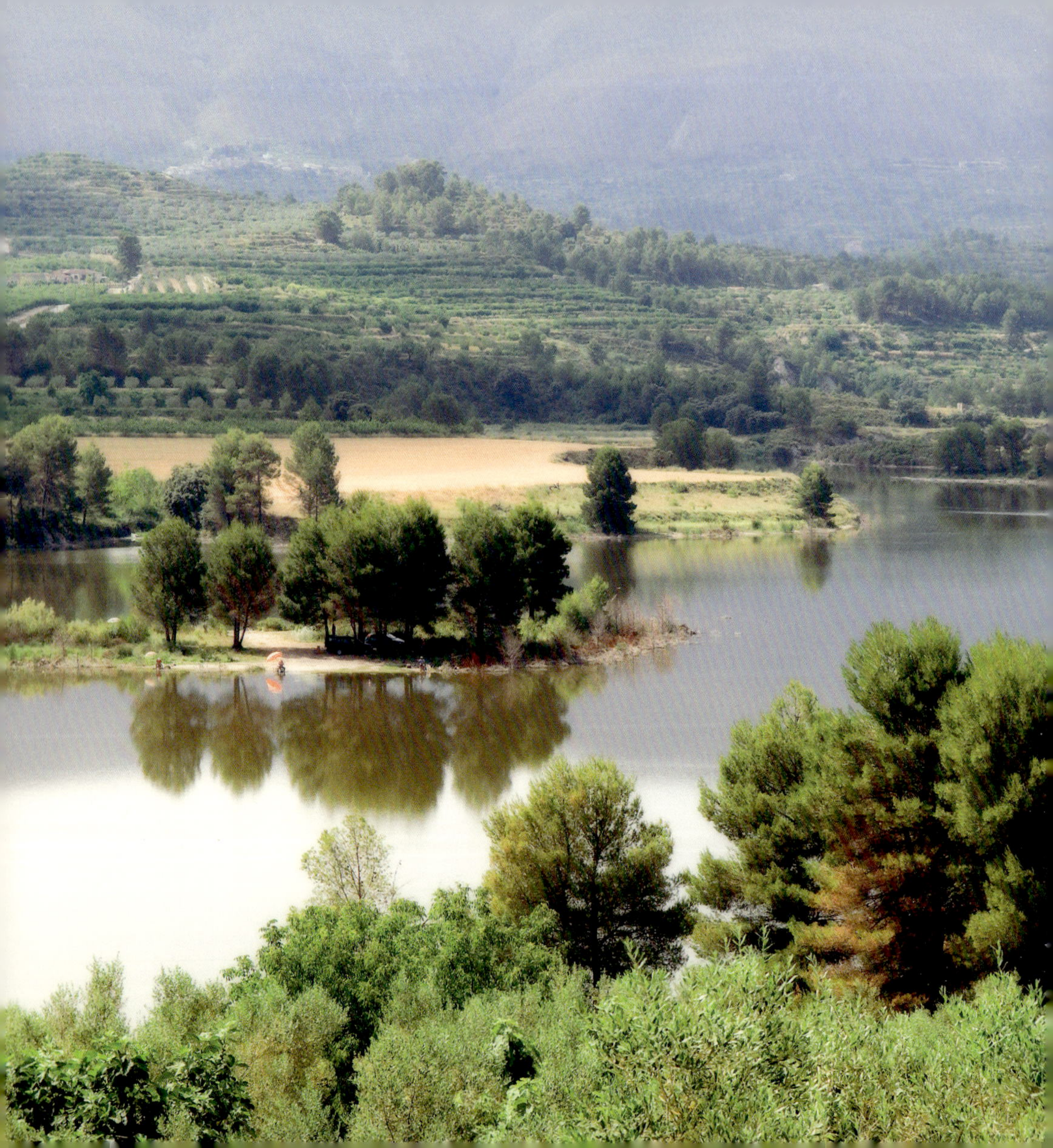

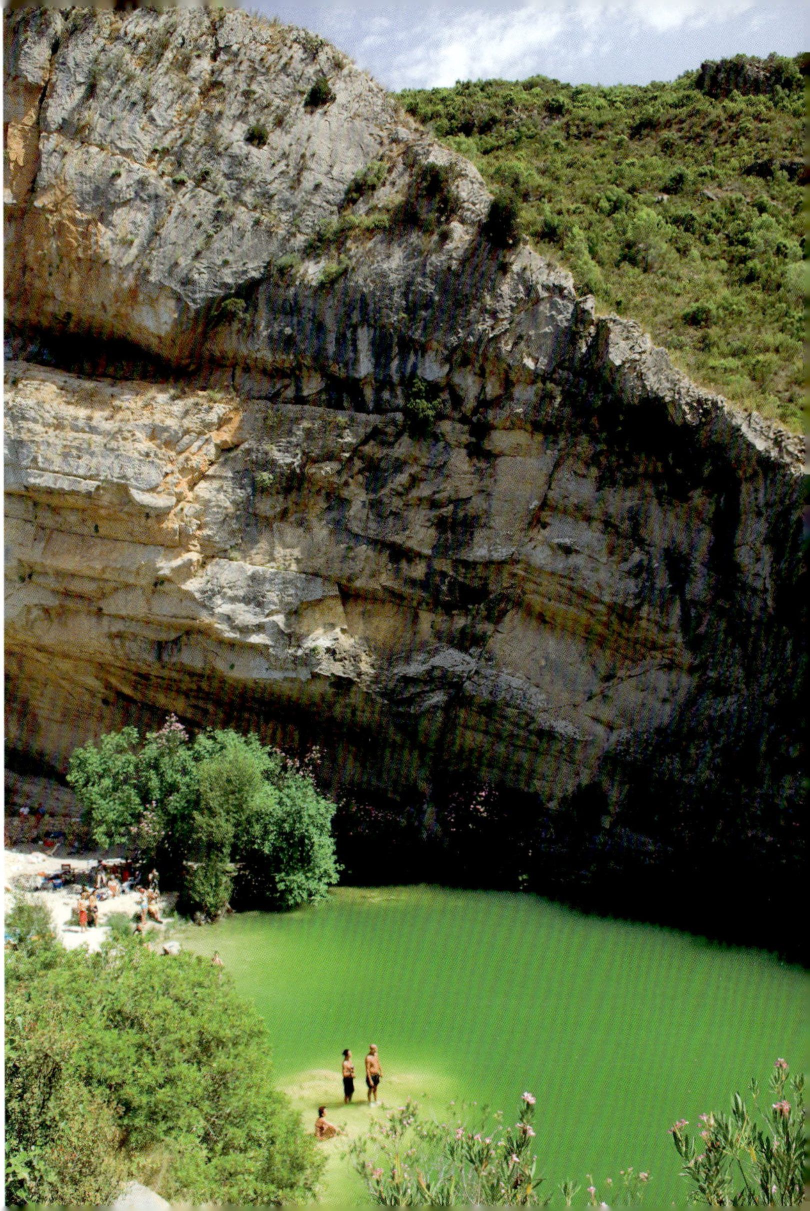

← *Beniarrés reservoir*
Barranc de L'Encantà

Agres

The water descends fresh and crystalline along the Mariola range until reaching the fountains of Agres. The village's houses, perfectly adapted to the complicated orography, still preserve the character of a mountain village, with agriculture the main activity. Routes start from the sanctuary of the Virgen del Castillo, known as the Convent, that cover the Mariola range, particularly recommendable when spring inundates the countryside with flowers. The route that climbs to Montcabrer passes alongside the Cava Arquejada, one of the old stone deposits, called snow wells, which were used to store snow in the times when there were no fridges. Once transformed into ice, it was distributed to the nearby villages.

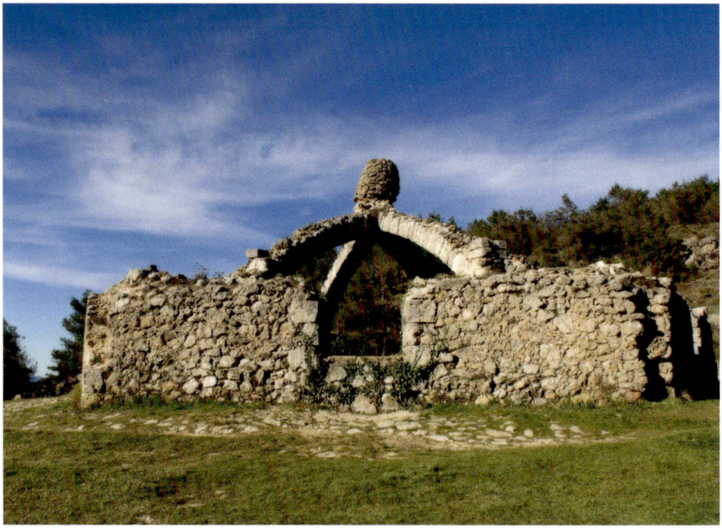

Snow cabin

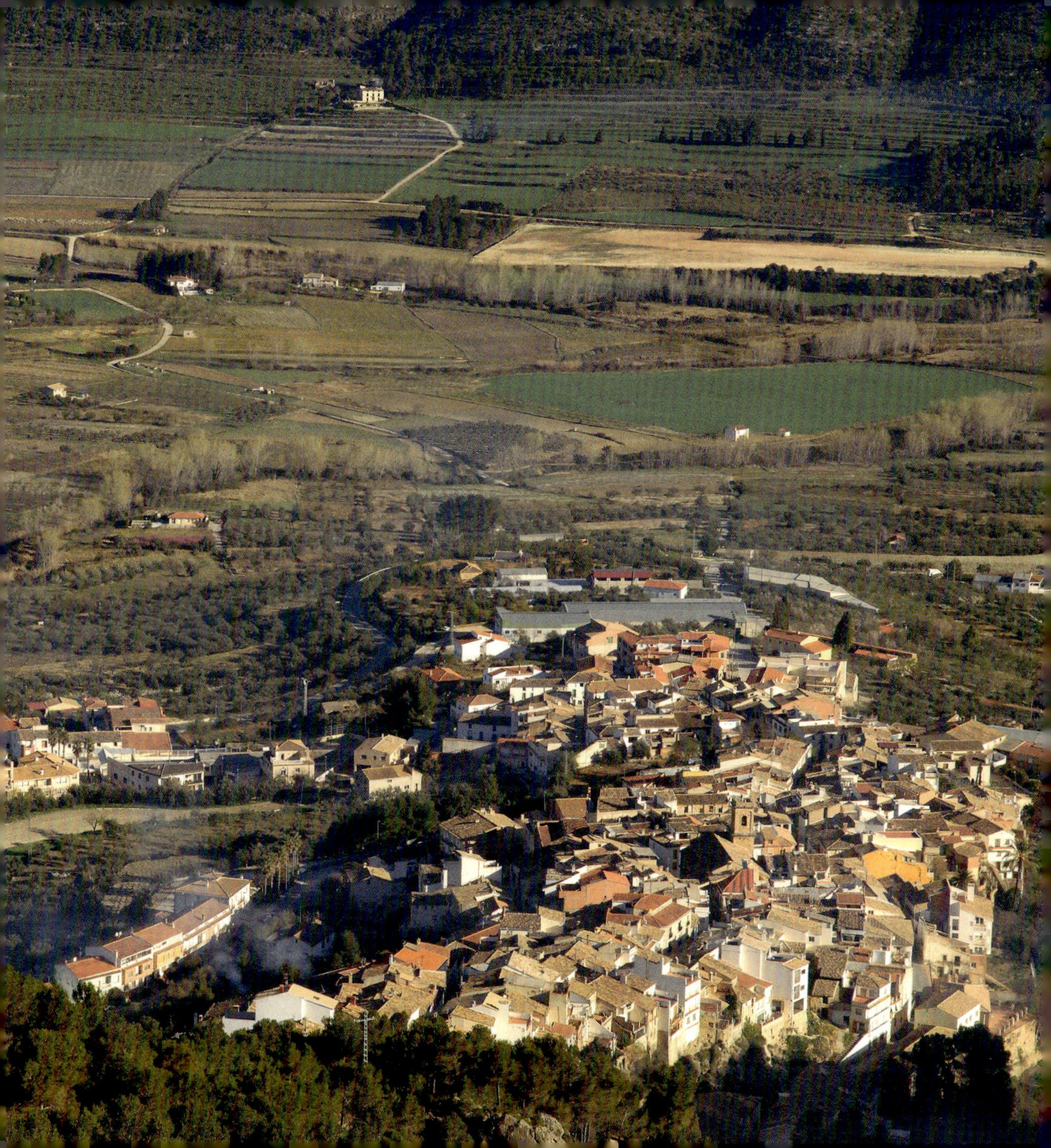

Blossoming almonds

The county of El Comtat is a production area of almonds. Every year, the explosion of colour and scent of the almond blossom tinge the fields of the area white, forming one of the loveliest visual spectacles in the province. Around the fields are a series of beautiful villages, mainly dedicated to agriculture. Some are villages with an Arab etymological origin, such as Benillup, Benilloba or Alcoleja, at the foot of the Sierra de Aitana. And there are others of more Valencian origin, such as Facheca, Famorca or the district of Ares del Comtat.

Alcoleja with Sierra Aitana in the background

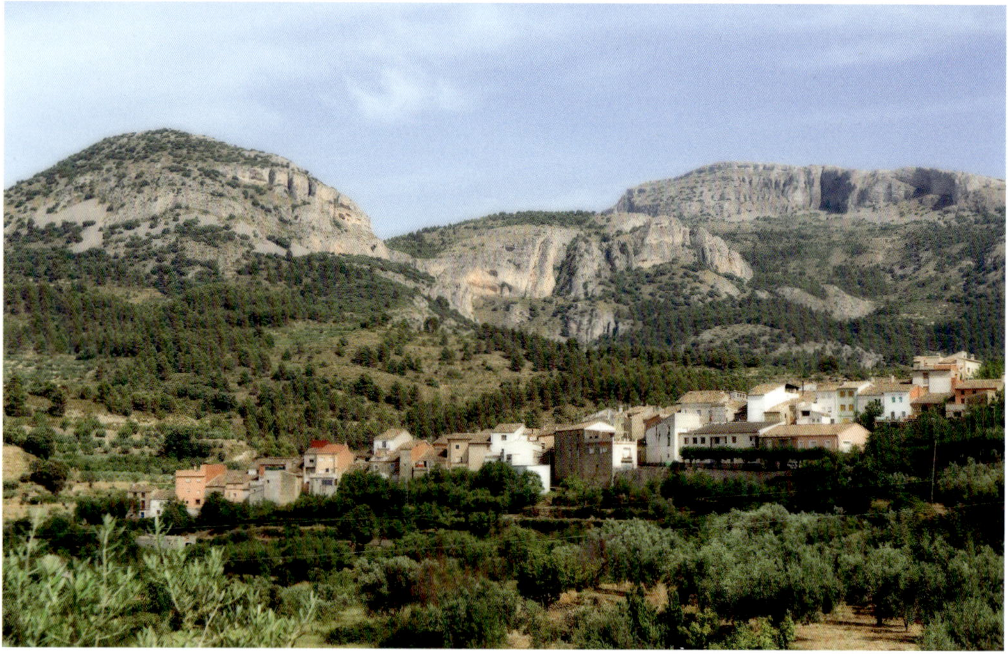

Ares del Comtat

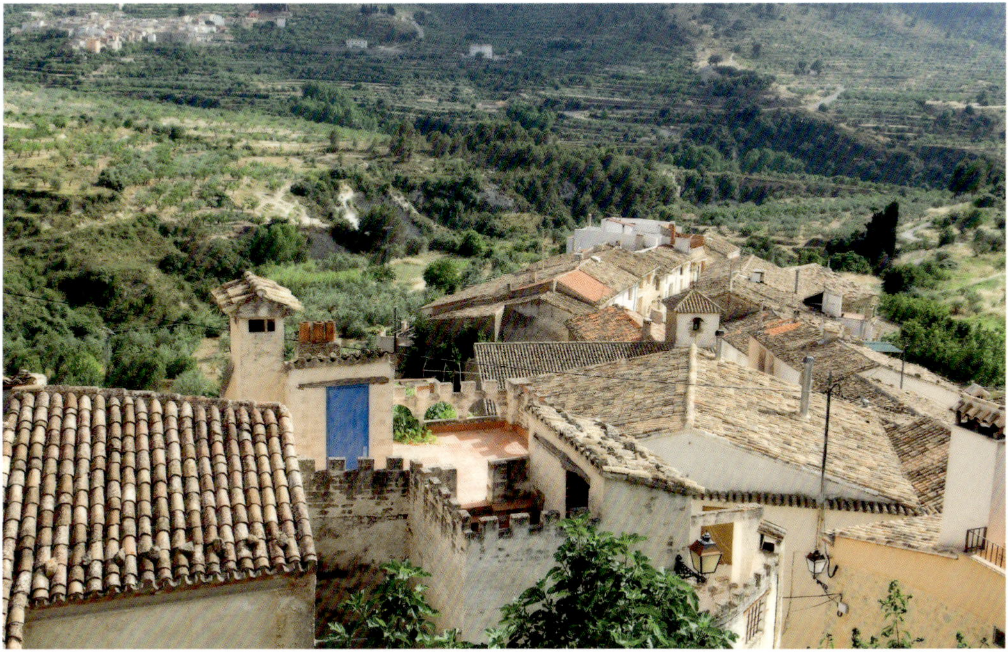

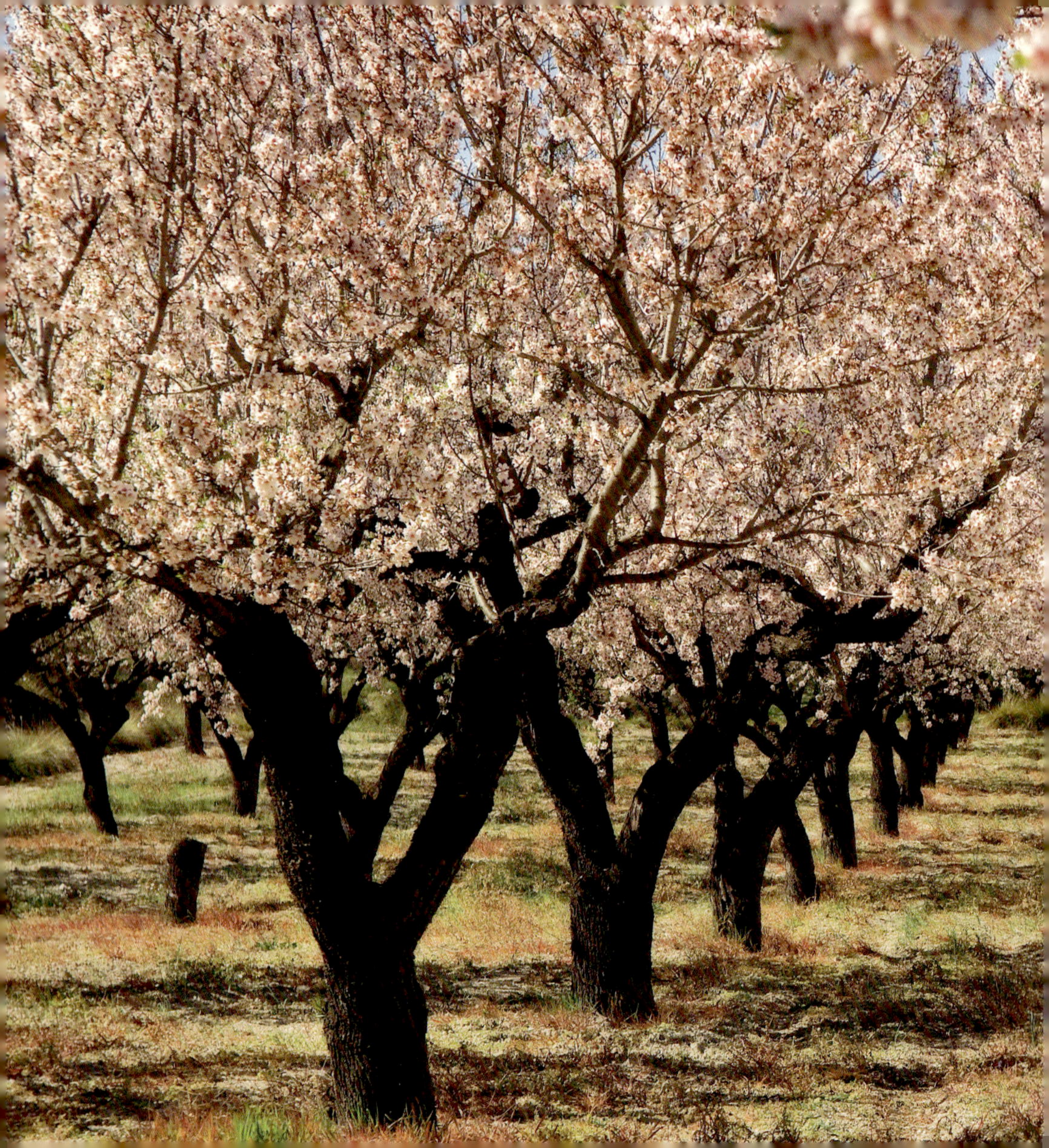

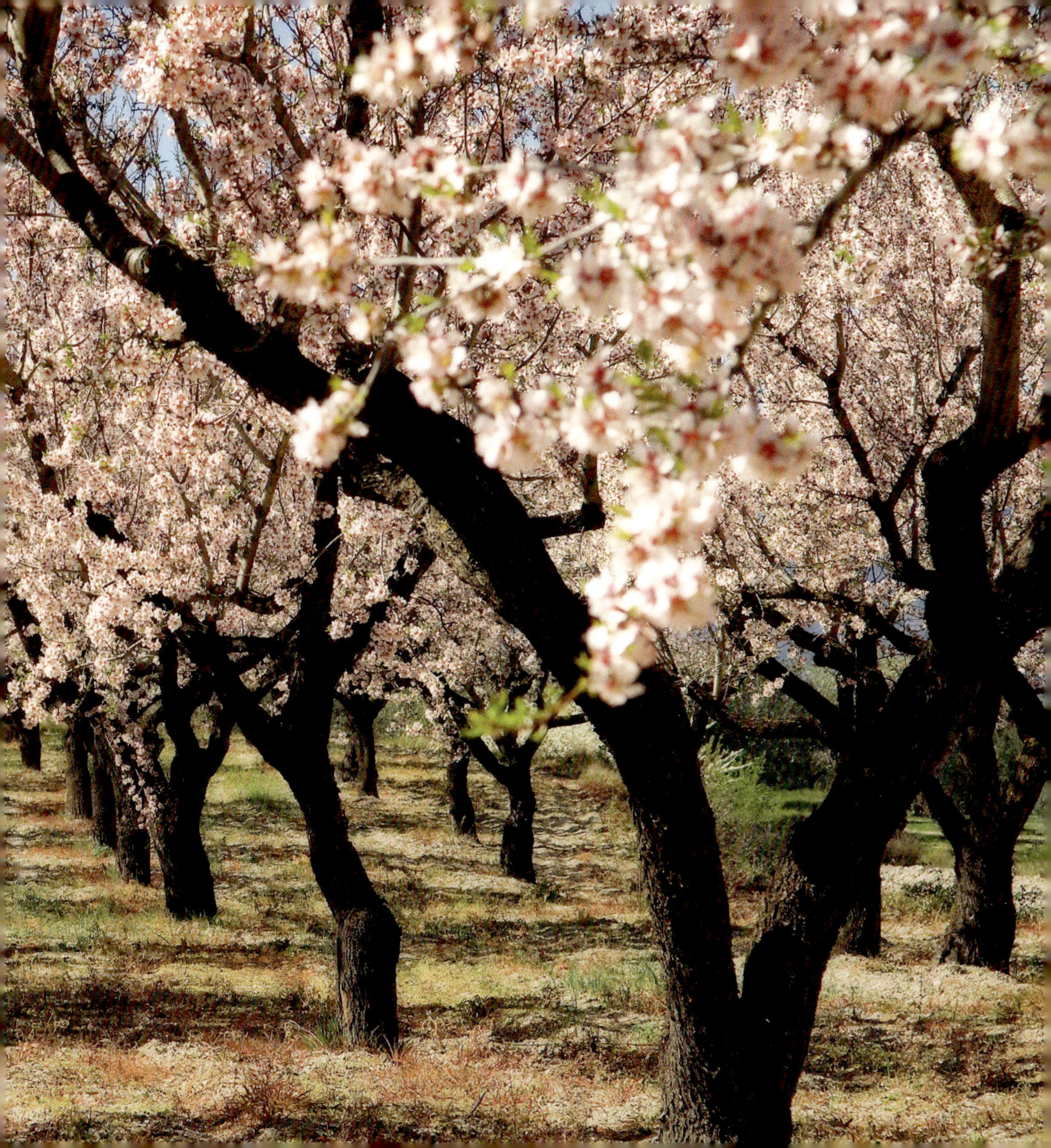

To my daughter –Rafa Pérez–

Published by
© Triangle Postals SL

Text
© Rafa Pérez

Photographs
© Rafa Pérez

Graphic edition
Aina Pla, Genís Puig

Production
Imma Planas

Translation
Steve Cedar

Printed by
Litografia Rosés
5 - 2018

Registration number
B.19547-2010

ISBN
978-84-8478-437-1

Triangle Postals SL
Pere Tudurí, 8
07710 Sant Lluís, Menorca
Tel. 34 971 15 04 51
Fax 34 971 15 18 36
www.triangle.cat
triangle@triangle.cat